AF788922

North-South Regional Trade Agreements as Legal Regimes

For Ayana

North-South Regional Trade Agreements as Legal Regimes

A Critical Assessment of the EU-SADC Economic Partnership Agreement

Clair Gammage

Lecturer in Law, University of Bristol, UK

Edward Elgar
PUBLISHING

Cheltenham, UK • Northampton, MA, USA

© Clair Gammage 2017

All rights reserved. No part of this publication may be reproduced, stored in a retrieval system or transmitted in any form or by any means, electronic, mechanical or photocopying, recording, or otherwise without the prior permission of the publisher.

Published by
Edward Elgar Publishing Limited
The Lypiatts
15 Lansdown Road
Cheltenham
Glos GL50 2JA
UK

Edward Elgar Publishing, Inc.
William Pratt House
9 Dewey Court
Northampton
Massachusetts 01060
USA

A catalogue record for this book
is available from the British Library

Library of Congress Control Number: 2016959923

This book is available electronically in the **Elgar**online
Law subject collection
DOI 10.4337/9781784719623

MIX
Paper from
responsible sources
FSC® C013604
FSC
www.fsc.org

ISBN 978 1 78471 961 6 (cased)
ISBN 978 1 78471 962 3 (eBook)

Typeset by Columns Design XML Ltd, Reading
Printed and bound by CPI Group (UK) Ltd, Croydon, CR0 4YY

Contents

Preface

My engagement with ACP-EU cooperation started as a narrow study on the legal scope of Article XXIV GATT in North-South regional trade agreements and has developed into a philosophical inquiry of the normative nature of ACP-EU relations, with law at the centre of its analysis. The transformative shift from preferential trade to reciprocity has been examined extensively in the literature of political science, international political economy and economics. While this body of scholarship is rich and diverse, ranging from the materialist focus of the rationalist theories to the normative approach of constructivism, I found the literature to be lacking in a critical perspective that conceives of regions as constituted *through* law. Analysing the regional agreements through a critical legal lens, and drawing insights from both the rationalist and constructivist schools of international political economy, this book offers a fresh perspective on the ACP-EU relationship.

When this project was in its most embryonic form, I was fortunate to secure generous funding from the Economic Social Research Council and the Worldwide University Network to carry out research on two separate field visits to South Africa. Not only am I grateful for the funding granted by the ESRC and WUN, but I am indebted to the Law Faculties at the University of Stellenbosch and the University of Cape Town for hosting me throughout my time in South Africa. In particular, I am eternally indebted to the kindness extended to me by Yolandi and her family. On these visits I was able to access texts that otherwise would have been difficult to obtain and meet with stakeholders in the Southern African region. I am particularly grateful to the Trade and Law Centre (tralac) in South Africa for their support to my research in 2010.

I have presented some of the ideas contained in this book in a variety of settings over the years. I would particularly like to extend my gratitude to my colleagues and friends in the GIFTA network. Through their constructive yet critical engagement with my work, I have been able to identify the conceptual gaps in the legal analysis and form better connections between the disciplines of law and political economy. I am especially thankful to Sangeeta Khorana, Maria Garcia and Jan Orbie for their support.

I am indebted to my academic mentor and very dear friend, Tonia Novitz, who has supported me from the very start of my academic career. Through our critical discussions, you have broadened my understanding on the contested nature of the trade:development interface. As this monograph has evolved over the past five years, I have benefited from the support of many colleagues including Adrian Flint, Steven Greer, Achilles Skordas, Patrick Capps, Julian Rivers, Eleanor Staples, Sofia Galani, Lisa Mardikian, Albert Sanchez-Graells, Philip Syrpis, and Urfan Khaliq. I am particularly grateful to Foluke Ipinyomi and Shaima Bakhsh for kindly reviewing parts of this book. All errors and oversights are mine alone.

There are no words that can express my gratitude to my loved ones, without whom this book would never have been written. To Chris, thank you for your patience, love, and support. Your commitment to us has been a great source of inspiration. To my Mam and Dad, two very special persons who have always believed in me and encouraged me to pursue my dreams in the face of many challenges. Thank you for your unwavering support over the years. Slowly, I am building your house.

Abbreviations and acronyms

AAMS	Associated African and Malagasy States
AAS	African Associated States
AB	Appellate Body
ACP	African, Caribbean, and Pacific States
AEC	African Economic Community
AFD	Agence Française de Développement
AfDB	African Development Bank
AfT	Aid for Trade
AGOA	African Growth and Opportunity Act
ANC	African National Congress
ANSA	Angola, Namibia, and South Africa
APRM	African Peer Review Mechanism
ASEAN	Association of Southeast Asian Nations
AU	African Union
BLMNS	Botswana, Lesotho, Mozambique, Namibia, Swaziland
BLNS	Botswana, Lesotho, Namibia, Swaziland
BLS	Botswana, Lesotho, Swaziland
BSO	business support office
CAFEIN	CARIFORUM EPA Implementation Network
CAFTA	Central America Free Trade Agreement
CAP	Common Agricultural Policy
CARICOM	Caribbean Community
CARIFORUM	Caribbean Forum
CCP	common commercial policy
CEAO	Economic Community of West Africa
CEB	Council of Europe Development Bank
C-EPA	CARIFORUM EPA

CET	common external tariff
CETA	EU-Canada Comprehensive Economic and Trade Agreement
CFSP	Common Foreign and Security Policy (EU)
CJEU	Court of Justice of the European Union
CMA	Common Monetary Area
COMESA	Common Market for Eastern and Southern Africa
CONSAS	Constellation of Southern African States
CONSEA	Constellation of Southern African Economies
COSATU	Congress of Southern African Trade Unions
CPA	Cotonou Partnership Agreement
CRIP	Caribbean Regional Indicative Programme
CRNM	Caribbean Regional Negotiating Machinery
CRP	Common Revenue Pool
CRTA	Committee on Regional Trade Agreements
CSME	Caribbean Single Market and Economy
CTD	Committee for Trade and Development
CTG	Committee for Trade in Goods
CTPSDP	Caribbean Trade and Private Sector Development Programme
CU	customs union
DFID	Department for International Development
DFQF	duty free quota free
DG DEVCO	Directorate-General for International Cooperation and Development
DR-CAFTA	Dominican Republic-Central America Free Trade Agreement
DSB	Dispute Settlement Body
DSU	Dispute Settlement Understanding
EAC	East African Community
EBA	Everything But Arms
EBRD	European Bank for Reconstruction and Development European Community
EC	European Community

ECCAS	Economic Community of Central African States
ECOWAS	Economic Community of West African States
ECSC	European Coal and Steel Community
EDF	European Development Fund
EEC	European Economic Community
EFSI	European Fund for Strategic Investments
EFTA	European Free Trade Area
EIB	European Investment Bank
EPA	Economic Partnership Agreement
ESA	Eastern and Southern Africa
EU	European Union
FCORs	French Caribbean Outermost Regions
FDI	foreign direct investment
FLS	Frontline States
FTA	Free Trade Agreement
FTAA	Free Trade Area of the Americas
FYR	Former Yugoslav Republic
GATS	General Agreement on Trade in Services
GATT	General Agreement on Tariffs and Trade
GBLF	Grant and Loan Blending Facility
GDP	gross domestic product
GNI	Gross National Income
GSP	Generalised System of Preferences
HCTs	High Commission Territories
HIPCs	Heavily Indebted Poor Countries
ICJ	International Court of Justice
IDC	Independent Development Corporation
IEPA	interim economic partnership agreement
ILO	International Labour Organisation
IMF	International Monetary Fund
IPE	international political economy
ISI	Import Substitution Industrialisation
ITO	International Trade Organisation

LDC	Least Developed Country
LLDC	Landlocked Least Developed Country
LPA	Lagos Plan of Action
MDC	Maputo Development Corridor
MDGs	Millennium Development Goals
MERCOSUR	Mercado Común del Sur
MFN	most favoured nation
MIF	Multilateral Investment Fund
MRAs	Mutual Recognition Agreements
NAFTA	North American Free Trade Agreement
NEPAD	New Partnership for Africa's Development
NGO	non-governmental organisation
NIP	National Indicative Programme
NRT	New Regionalism Theory
NSA	non-state actors
OAU	Organisation of African Unity
OCTs	Overseas Countries and Territories
OECD	Organisation for Economic Co-operation and Development
OECS	Organisation of Eastern Caribbean States
OHCHR	Office of the High Commissioner on Human Rights
PRSP	Poverty Reduction Strategy Papers
PTA	preferential trade agreement
QR	quantitative restriction
REC	Regional Economic Community
RIFF	Regional Integration Facilitation Forum
RIP	Regional Indicative Programme
RISDP	Regional Indicative Strategic Development Plan
RMA	Rand Monetary Area
ROO	rules of origin
RTA	Regional Trade Agreement
SACU	Southern African Customs Union
SADC	Southern African Development Community

SADCC	Southern African Development Coordination Conference
SAPP	Southern African Power Pool
SAPs	structural adjustment programmes
SDGs	Sustainable Development Goals
SDI	Spatial Development Initiative
SDT	Special and Differential Treatment
SEA	Single European Act
SIA	Sustainability Impact Assessment
SMEs	small and medium-sized enterprises
SPS	sanitary and phytosanitary
TBT	technical barriers to trade
TDCA	Trade, Development and Cooperation Agreement
TED	turtle excluder device
TEU	Treaty on European Union
TFEU	Treaty on the Functioning of the European Union
TISA	Trade in Services Agreement
TPP	Trans-Pacific Partnership
TRIPs	Trade Related Aspects of Intellectual Property Rights
TTIP	Transatlantic Trade and Investment Partnership
UN	United Nations
UNECA	United Nations Economic Commission for Africa
UNICE	Confederation of European Business
WTO	World Trade Organization

Table of cases

INTERNATIONAL COURT OF JUSTICE

WORLD TRADE ORGANIZATION APPELLATE BODY REPORTS

WORLD TRADE ORGANISATION PANEL REPORTS

GATT REPORTS

COURT OF JUSTICE OF THE EUROPEAN UNION

Opinions

'It is the present where we get lost, if we forget the past and have no vision for the future.'

African Proverb

Introduction

Since 2004, the EU has been redefining its relationship with the African, Caribbean, and Pacific (ACP) States following the end of the long-running banana litigation at the multilateral level. Preserving this special relationship has required the shift from preferences toward asymmetric reciprocity through the Economic Partnership Agreements (EPAs). The EPAs were originally conceived of as North-South Regional Trade Agreements (RTAs) through which the comprehensive liberalisation of trade in goods, services, investment, procurement, competition, and intellectual property would be negotiated. However, to date, only one comprehensive EPA has been concluded between the EU and the Caribbean States (CARIFORUM).

Defined as partnerships for trade *and* development, the EPAs have been projected as regimes for the promotion of sustainable development *through* trade. It is the purpose of this book to analyse the extent to which development ideals will be promoted through these North-South RTAs. The focal point of this theoretical inquiry is the EPA between the EU and the Southern African region (SADC EPA States). Signed on 10 June 2016, the SADC EPA negotiations that have lasted for over ten years have finally come to an end. Marking the first trade agreement of its kind between the EU and a regional economic community in Africa, the SADC EPA sends a signal to the rest of the world that EU-Africa cooperation is as strong as it has ever been. However, the journey toward the conclusion of this agreement has been laborious, and at various stages throughout the negotiations it was feared the conclusion of the EPA would not be realised. In part, this book seeks to understand why the outcome of the EPA negotiations has fallen short of original expectations.

Regionalism presents both opportunities and challenges to the multilateral trading system and the broader international order. While RTAs offer 'speed and flexibility' in trade liberalisation,[1] they operate in a

[1] R.V. Fiorentino, J. Crawford and C. Toqueboeuf, 'The Landscape of Regional Trade Agreements and WTO Surveillance' in R. Baldwin and P. Low (eds), *Multilateralizing Regionalism: Challenges for the Global Trading System* (Cambridge: Cambridge University Press, 2009), 29.

global order that has become increasingly differentiated. The international economic order is now characterised by both 'integration and fragmentation'[2] as non-state actors such as institutions, private organisations and civil society have penetrated the activities and functions which were traditionally assumed by the State. The function of the State has shifted from being the dominant political structure to being one of many polities operating in the global system. As a result, the structure of the global order now consists of many layers and can be described as a 'complex, multilevel political structure, in which the State assumes different functions'.[3] As the world globalises in accordance with neoliberal principles, the concern that liberal democracy has become subordinate to economic globalisation leads to a sense that the significance of the nation-state has diminished. The rise of RTAs, which are legal regimes and make governance beyond the state possible, mark an interesting shift in the global economy.

This book offers a critical reconstruction of regions as social spheres of action integrated *through* law. Understanding the significance of regionalism as a trade strategy and as a form of social interconnection requires an understanding of transformations of the modern global political economy. As societies have become increasingly differentiated and pluralistic there is little doubt that the role of the nation state, traditionally understood as the main actor in the international order, is declining. Embedded within regions are the political, social, and economic qualities that were once associated only with states and it is this cosmopolitan transformation of the global order that draws into question the way in which society integrates through the legitimate institutionalisation of the market and power namely, as this book asserts, *through* law.

In placing the law at the heart of its inquiry, and drawing insights from both the rationalist and constructivist schools of international political economy (IPE), this book offers a unique and interdisciplinary contribution to the literature on regionalism. Through a critical analysis of the EPAs this book makes two claims. The first claim is that regions represent spheres of social action integrated through law. With reference to the Habermasian paradigm of *law as discourse*, this book asserts that regions are best understood as legal regimes through which the economic

---

[2] M. Farrell, B. Hettne and L. van Langenhove (eds); *Global Politics of Regionalism: Theory and Practice* (Ann Arbor, MI: Pluto Press, 2005).

[3] F. Söderbaum, 'Exploring the Links between Micro-Regionalism and Macro-Regionalism' in M. Farrell, B. Hettne, L. van Langenhove (eds), *Global Politics of Regionalism: Theory and Practice* (Ann Arbor, MI: Pluto Press, 2005).

and political systems are institutionalised. Only law that has been created through the correct democratic procedure, which requires participation and deliberation among all those who will be affected by the law, can make a normative claim to legitimacy. Law, as an expression of *ideology*, is a structural *sine qua non* of the global system and of regional integration. As an ideal type of law, the discourse theory provides a grand narrative on how legitimate law should be created. Although this paradigm of law is highly-abstracted and idealised, it does have explanatory potential particularly in the context of the EPAs which, as legal regimes, have been modelled on the Habermasian paradigm of law-making through deliberation and participation of various stakeholders.

Formally, the legal architecture of the EPAs set out in the Cotonou Partnership Agreement supports participation and deliberative democracy. Article 8 of the CPA provides that the EPA States "shall regularly engage in comprehensive, balanced, and deep political dialogue leading to commitments on both sides" which "shall contribute to peace, security, and stability and promote a stable democratic political environment." Dialogue should "focus on specific political issues of mutual concern" but may be "formal or informal" and conducted "within and outside the institutional framework." The EPAs have, therefore, been conceived of as discursive spaces to promote political dialogue and deliberation among state and non-state actors with a view to creating what I have termed a 'development-friendly' trade agreement. It follows that the construction of the EPAs in these (Habermasian) terms should result in a partnership of equals.

The second claim set out in this book relates to the shift toward *interregionalism*, or the creation of region-to-region spaces integrated through law. While interregionalism remains relatively under-researched, it is a claim of this book that where a power asymmetry exists between the two regional partners, which is often the case in North-South RTAs like the EPAs, the potential for a discursive space for deliberation and argumentation to emerge is reduced. As the discursive space diminishes, the potential for a partnership of equals to materialise seems increasingly implausible. Through a Gramscian lens, this book proposes that interregional relationships between unequal partners may facilitate the reproduction of hegemonic ideology through legal regimes. This book seeks to critique power in North-South RTAs, drawing insights from Gramscian hegemonic theory, to argue that these forms of RTAs are *hegemonic* legal regimes through which the norms of the dominant partner can potentially be exported. However, it is submitted that the success of norm exportation hinges on the existence of a 'discursive fit' or 'resonance' between the ideologies of the interregional partners.[4] This book puts forth a theory of law as *ideology* and, in the context of North-South RTAs, law as hegemonic discourse that regulates material production and reinforces power asymmetry through interregional legal regimes. To this end, it will be argued that the EPAs were crafted as hegemonic legal regimes that reinforce the EU's position of dominance vis-à-vis the ACP States.

Analysing the EPAs through discourse theory provides an opportunity to reflect upon how interregional relationships affect our understanding of modern global society and an interrogation of the claim that the EPAs constitute hegemonic legal regimes reveals interesting and unexpected shifts in the political economy of the ACP-EU relationship. This book will show that the implementation of the only full agreement in place, the CARIFORUM EPA, has failed to materialise in accordance with original expectations. Arguably, the implementation deficit in the CARIFORUM group signals a normative shift, albeit an incremental one, away from traditional EU dependency. Furthermore, the conclusion of the SADC EPA as a 'goods only' agreement has fallen short of the original ambitions of the EU to conclude a comprehensive EPA with African states. From an analysis of the results of the negotiation and implementation phases of these two agreements it may be inferred that there is a lack of discursive fit or resonance between the normative ideologies of the EU and the ACP States. This book aims to show how the behavioural attitudes of the ACP countries challenge the EPAs normative claim to legitimacy. While the EPAs are framed as hegemonic North-South legal regimes, their practical application suggests that the political economy of ACP-EU cooperation is changing.

The EPAs have been designed as 'drivers of development' albeit 'development' has been defined in accordance with the EU's neoliberal conception of that term. This book contests the instrumentalist view that promotes a vision of development focused on production, efficiency, and wealth maximisation, and draws insight from the capabilities approach of Amartya Sen. Bridging the schools of ethics and economics, Sen proposes a theory of development where freedom is both the principal means and the principal end of development.[5] Moving against the orthodox instrumentalist assumption that economic growth presupposes other substantive freedoms, Sen argues that these values should be seen as primary goals which will in turn stimulate growth. Development is,

---

[4] T. Hopf, 'Common-Sense Constructivism and Hegemony in World Politics' (2013) 67 *International Organisation* 317–54.

[5] A. Sen, *Development as Freedom* (Oxford: Oxford University Press, 2001).

therefore, conceptualised as 'a process of expanding the real freedoms that people enjoy'[6] economic growth perceived as a 'means' towards the realisation of those substantive freedoms. With poverty eradication as one of the stated primary objectives, the EPAs seek to translate the normative framework of the Cotonou Partnership Agreement into development-friendly regional trade agreements. Incorporating provisions on labour standards, good governance, the promotion of human rights, and the protection of the environment into the trade agreement marks a new step in the ACP-EU relationship. Rhetorically, at least, the EPAs appear to promote development as freedom. However, while ethical norms and the principle of political dialogue scaffold the commercial provisions of the EPAs, on closer inspection these appear to be nothing more than vacuous commitments devoid of meaningful substance. The ambiguous nature of the sustainable development provisions draws into question the extent to which the EPAs will promote development *through* trade. Overall, it is argued that the neoliberal economic paradigm, which is supported by a formalist legal framework, is seemingly at odds with the discourse of development as freedom.

Chapter 1 presents the main epistemological framework and ontological claims of the book and asserts that regions should be understood primarily as legal regimes. Through the marriage of material power, ideational forces, and institutions this book aims to promote an understanding of regions as fundamentally legal regimes. The law generates an assumption of the 'right' and 'just' way to live, guiding behaviour of institutions and of people through legal codification of norms. Legal philosophers are concerned with the validity of legal norms, their claim to correctness, and to understanding the reasoning and logic of the legal system while sociologically informed analyses of law seek to reveal the practical or empirically valid nature of legal norms in relation to other spheres of action, such as politics and the economy. Using the discourse theory of law, this book proposes that legitimate law is that which is normatively perceived to provide 'good' reasons for action. This book aims to demonstrate how legitimate law can emerge from a discursive and participative process of deliberation. It will be argued that the EPAs have created discursive spaces for deliberation albeit the inclusion of non-state actors in that process across the regional groupings has been limited. As such, the extent to which the EPAs constitute legitimate legal regimes in a Habermasian sense is questionable.

[6] *Ibid*, 3.

Chapter 2 provides a critical assessment of the legal bases for regionalism enshrined in the multilateral rules. Article XXIV of the GATT 1994 provides the legal basis for creating regional agreements, where at least one member of the regional group is a developing country. It permits derogation from the principles of MFN and non-discrimination on the assumption that trade will be increased by promoting the regional interdependence of countries, through customs unions and free trade areas. Regionalism has, therefore, been conceptualised as a means towards *economic* freedom, through closer integration between Members. Although the jurisprudence relating to Article XXIV is limited, it does offer some insight into the interpretive dimension of this provision and suggests a gradual 'legalisation' and rationalisation of Article XXIV.[7] It will be argued that this process of rationalisation seals off the potential for alternative forms of integration schemes to emerge and, in doing so, promotes the neoliberal paradigm of regionalism thus restricting the space for deliberation and participation in the construction of new regional spaces.

In Chapter 3, the normative role of the EU as a regional actor will be discussed in detail. It will be shown that the EU's strength as an international trade partner, or 'market power',[8] has enabled it to become a 'normative actor', which aims to export universal values through trade.[9] It will be argued that the EU's normative power in external relations hinges on its market power. As such, an analysis of the common commercial policy set out in Article 209 of the Treaty on the Functioning of the European Union (TFEU) will be presented highlighting its parallelism with the EU's internal trade strategy. Defining the EPAs as trade *and* development cooperation agreements, this chapter will also explore the relationship between the common commercial policy and the development cooperation policy under Article 209 TFEU. If the EPAs have been built on the principles of 'partnership' and 'equality', it follows that the agreements should foster trade in a 'development-friendly' way. However, the remaining chapters of this book will demonstrate that the language of the legal texts suggests the primacy of

[7] J. Mathis, 'The "Legalization" of GATT Article XXIV – Can Foes Become Friends?' in K. Bagwell and P. Mavroidis (eds), *Preferential Trade Agreements: A Law and Economics Analysis* (Cambridge: Cambridge University Press, 2011).

[8] C. Damro, 'Market Power Europe: Exploring a Dynamic Conceptual Framework' (2015) 22 *Journal of European Public Policy* 1336–54.

[9] I. Manners, 'The Normative Ethics of the European Union' (2008) 84 *International Affairs* 45–60.

economic rules over the promotion of ethical norms reinforcing the EU's neoliberal conception of development.

Chapter 4 examines the normative character of the principle of sustainable development and assesses the extent to which it constitutes a justiciable norm. Through the analysis of the jurisprudence from the WTO's Dispute Settlement Body and the UN International Court of Justice, the normative content of the principle of sustainable development will be revealed. Building on the work of Virginie Barral,[10] it will be argued that the principle of sustainable development has served as an important hermeneutic tool in both judicial settings, giving *colour, texture* and *shading* to legal rights and obligations. Given the development focus of the EPAs this finding is particularly significant because it suggests that the sustainable development provisions of the agreements lack justiciability. Simply put, it implies that the sustainable development provisions in the agreement may not be enforceable through the dispute settlement mechanisms established under the EPAs. Nevertheless, in scaffolding the commercial aspects of the agreement around the principle of sustainable development it is herein submitted that the parties must apply the EPA in a development-friendly way.

Chapter 5 marks the beginning of the analysis of the EPAs, providing a rich and historically sensitive account to the transformative nature of ACP-EU cooperation. In this chapter, the various shifts in the ACP-EU relationship will be explored which will enable a better understanding of *why* this relationship has endured for so long. For many decades, the ACP countries enjoyed non-reciprocal preferential access to the EU market under the Yaoundé and Lomé agreements. Following changes at the multilateral level, and in accordance with the recommendations of the Appellate Body in the *EC-Bananas III* dispute, the ACP countries are no longer eligible to receive non-reciprocal market access for their exports to the EU market.[11] Nevertheless, the EU has been keen to preserve its long-standing relationship with former colonies in the ACP and has done so by offering reciprocal, but asymmetric, preferential market access under the Cotonou Agreement and through the EPA framework. Although the primary purpose of the EPAs is to eradicate poverty and facilitate the

---

[10] V. Barral, 'Sustainable Development in International Law: Nature and Operation of an Evolutive Legal Norm' (2012) 23 *European Journal of International Law* 380.

[11] The only exception to this rule is where the country concerned qualifies for special and differential treatment.

gradual integration of ACP countries into the global economy,[12] these agreements mark a significant transformative shift in ACP-EU cooperation as trade facilitation and reciprocal market access now form key parts of the agreements for the first time.

Chapter 6 critically reflects upon the emergence of African regional regimes. Providing an overview of African regionalism is important for the contextualisation of the analysis of the SADC EPA. Drawing insight from the work of James Gathii, this book asserts that African regionalisms represent 'flexible' legal regimes[13] that pursue multifaceted policy objectives. As such, African regionalisms do not fit neatly into the straitjacket of Article XXIV legal regimes discussed in Chapter 2. Nevertheless, it will be argued that these regions constitute regimes integrated *through* law and have offered a space in which 'norms of solidarity'[14] or expressions of collective political will have been contested, shaped and reproduced.

Chapter 7 explores the dynamism of regionalism in Southern Africa, with a focus on the Southern African Customs Union (SACU) and the Southern African Development Community (SADC). While trading patterns long-preceded the colonial and post-colonial periods, this chapter focuses on the manner in which these regional arrangements have been historically constituted as a part of the region's development strategy through colonial rule, Apartheid, and democratisation. It will be shown that the influence of South Africa, alongside the hegemonic force of normative power Europe, has formalised the construction of the region and has restricted space for the creation of more 'flexible' legal regimes to emerge effectively.

Chapter 8 provides a critical and factual presentation of the full EPA signed between the EU and the SADC EPA States in June 2016. From the outset, it was clear that the success of the EPA negotiations would depend on the convergence between institutionalised legal norms at the

---

[12] Article 1 Partnership Agreement between the members of the African, Caribbean, and Pacific Group of States of the one part, and the European Community of the other part, signed in Cotonou on 23 June 2000, [2000] OJ L317/3 as amended through Decision No. 3/2008 of the ACP-EC Council of Ministers of 15 December 2008, [2008] OJ L352/59 to adopt the revised provisions set out in [2010] OJ L287/3, hereinafter referred to as the 'Cotonou Partnership Agreement 2014'.

[13] J.T. Gathii, *African Regional Trade Agreements as Legal Regimes* (Cambridge: Cambridge University Press, 2011).

[14] L. Dirar, 'Norms of Solidarity and Regionalism: Theorising State Behaviour Among Southern African States' (2016) 24 *Michigan State International Law Review* 667–723.

WTO level (Article XXIV compatibility) and the EU's normative preferences expressed through its external trade policy in relation to trade *and* development.[15] Overall, the perceived desirability of the EPA would be elicited from a good discursive fit between the ideational preferences of the EU and the Southern African countries. Through an analysis of the negotiations, it will be shown that the rhetorical argumentation that took place in this discursive space enabled the Southern African negotiators to reinforce the importance of the development dimensions of the EPA. An interesting approach adopted by the SADC EPA countries, and other ACP States, has been a form of rhetorical action known as 'mimetic challenge'.[16] Through normative argumentation, these countries have harnessed the EU's rhetoric of the EPAs as 'drivers of development' to strategically direct the negotiations toward development objectives. The contentious issues raised in the negotiation phase will be discussed with particular reference to the MFN clause, infant industry protection, and the dispute settlement mechanism. This chapter will identify the potential interpretive difficulties that might arise on implementation and provide an overview of the implications this could have for the development potential of the SADC EPA States.

Chapter 9 presents the findings of the EU commissioned 'Five Year Report' of the EPA negotiated between the EU and the Caribbean States (CARIFORUM). As the first comprehensive EPA to be concluded and implemented since 2008, the Report offers a rare opportunity for the other EPA regions to analyse the extent to which the benefits of the agreement are being realised by Caribbean businesses. A critical deconstruction of the Report identifies an information deficit, an implementation deficit, a financial deficit, and a development deficit. There appear to be inadequate monitoring mechanisms in place to measure the effect of trade liberalisation on the promotion of sustainable development, suggesting that the commercial aspects of the EPA have been prioritised over the social aspects of the agreement. Unsurprisingly, the Report tells a cautionary tale for the other EPA groups and one to which they should listen very closely, especially in relation to non-tariff barriers to trade and financial support for the implementation of the agreements. However, in the context of CARIFORUM, it also sends a signal to the EU that the Caribbean states are seeking out other markets and this may suggest a

---

[15] T. Heron, 'Trading in Development: Norms and Institutions in the Making/Unmaking of European-African, Caribbean, Pacific Trade and Development Cooperation' (2014) 20 *Contemporary Politics* 11.

[16] S. Hurt, D. Lee and U. Lorenz-Carl, 'The Argumentative Dimension to the EU-Africa EPAs' (2013) 18 *International Negotiation* 67–87.

shift away from post-colonial dependency on the EU market. Where the CARIFORUM States seek to negotiate new regional arrangements with other countries and regions, the inclusion of the MFN clause in the EPA may become particularly significant for the EU in retaining its dominant position in the global economy.

1. Integration through law

This chapter offers a critical reflection on the conceptualisation of regions expressed in the dominant rationalist tradition and aims to reconstruct an understanding of regions as social spheres of action integrated *through* law. Understanding the significance of regionalism as a trade strategy and as a form of social interconnection requires an understanding of transformations of the modern global political economy. As societies have become increasingly differentiated and pluralistic there is little doubt that the significance of the nation state, which has been traditionally understood as the main actor in the international order, has diminished. Where the rationalist and hegemonic stability theories of state action once dominated the discourse on legitimate authority, global governance has increasingly become a focal point of theoretical inquiry. Embedded within regions are the political, social and economic qualities that were once associated only with states and it is this cosmopolitan transformation of the global order that draws into question the way in which society integrates through the legitimate institutionalisation of the market and power, namely, as this book asserts, *through* law.

The dominant modern Western world view, reflected in the state-centric theories of (neo)realism and (neo)liberalism, is rationalistic and conceptualises social action as a form of ends-oriented materialist rationality. From this perspective, regions have emerged from neofunctional beginnings as constructs guided by economic imperatives. Rationalist theories subscribe to the idea that 'behaviour can be adjudged objectively to be optimally adapted to the situation',[1] looking at the world as it *is*, rather than how it *ought* to be and in this regard it is not seeking to make normative claims about behaviour. Presenting a statist vision of the world, and one which emphasises the 'constraints on politics imposed by human nature and the absence of international government',[2] they abstract social action away from the normative

[1] H.A. Simon, 'Human Nature in Politics: The Dialogue of Psychology with Political Science' (1985) 79(2) *American Political Science Review* 293–304, 294.

[2] J. Donnelly, *Realism and International Relations* (Cambridge: Cambridge University Press, 2000), 9.

content of practical reason, or 'good' reasons for action, and instead conceive of action as inherently materialist. In other words, the historical motivation for coming together as a regional order of states is conceived of as driven by strategic and short-termist capitalist goals. Rationalist theories nevertheless provide a useful framework to understand the materialist orientations of state behaviour at the multilateral and regional levels but they do not go far enough in explaining the *ideas* that shape the pursuit of strategic capitalist action.

With the end of the Cold War and the rise of neoliberal political and economic ideology, the global order has become increasingly differentiated. The international economic order is now characterised by both 'integration and fragmentation'[3] as non-state actors such as institutions, private organisations, and civil society have penetrated the activities and functions which were traditionally assumed by the state. The function of the state has shifted from being the dominant political structure to being one of many polities operating in the global system. As a result, the structure of the global order now consists of many layers and can be described as a 'complex, multilevel political structure, in which the state assumes different functions'.[4] Constructivism is concerned with revealing not only material interests but ideational or ideological interests that shape the spheres of social activity between these different actors. In placing the emphasis on the different state and non-state actors involved in the construction of regions, the material and non-material ideational forces that shape trade policy in trade negotiations can be revealed. From this perspective, it is submitted that the negotiation process represents a discursive space of argumentation through which values, norms, and interests are shaped, contested, and reproduced.

In placing the law at the heart of its inquiry, and drawing insights from both the rationalist and constructivist schools of international political economy (IPE), this book offers a unique and interdisciplinary contribution to the literature on regionalism. Through a critical analysis of the Economic Partnership Agreements (EPAs) negotiated between the African, Caribbean, and Pacific (ACP) countries and the European Union (EU), this book makes two claims. The first claim is that regions represent spheres of social action integrated through law. With reference

[3] M. Farrell, B. Hettne and L. van Langenhove (eds), *Global Politics of Regionalism: Theory and Practice* (Pluto Press, 2005).

[4] F. Söderbaum, 'Exploring the Links between Micro-Regionalism and Macro-Regionalism' in M. Farrell, B. Hettne and L. van Langenhove (eds), *Global Politics of Regionalism: Theory and Practice* (Ann Arbor, MI: Pluto Press, 2005).

to the Habermasian paradigm of *law as discourse*, this book asserts that regions are best understood as legal regimes through which the economic and political systems are institutionalised. According to this theoretical perspective, only law that has been created through the correct democratic procedure, which requires participation and deliberation among all those who will be affected by the law, can make a normative claim to legitimacy. Law, as an expression of *ideology*, is a structural *sine qua non* of the global system and of regional integration. As an ideal type of law, the discourse theory provides a grand narrative on how legitimate law should be created. Although this paradigm of law is highly abstracted and idealised, it does have explanatory potential, particularly in the context of the EPAs which, as legal regimes, have been cast as spaces which should promote political dialogue and deliberation among state and non-state actors. An important caveat to the epistemological claims of this book is that it would be absurd to assume that each and every free and equal legal person who may be affected by the EPA can or should engage in the performative argumentation of trade policy formulation. Rather, it proposes that trade policy should be shaped by the participative deliberation of State and non-state actors in a meaningful way in order that a partnership of equals can emerge.

Seeking to govern the social space in which they operate, Regional Trade Agreements (RTAs) are historically situated, temporal and transformative concepts. Regions are constructed realities that are steeped in historicity but not fixed in space or time. Understanding the role that law plays in shaping these social spaces and stabilising behavioural expectations within these spaces is the central theoretical focus of this book. Challenging the assumptions implicit in the dominant neoliberal rational theories, this chapter aims to demonstrate the law's function as a medium of integration. Through a reconstruction of law, this book aims to situate material and non-material ideational forces that have influenced social changes in the EU's relationship with the ACP countries and, in particular, with the Southern African region in the SADC-EPA negotiations.

The second claim set out in this book relates to the shift toward *interregionalism*, or the creation of region-to-region spaces integrated through law. While interregionalism remains relatively under-researched, it is the claim of this book that where a power asymmetry exists between the two regional partners, and this is typically the case in North-South RTAs like the EPAs, the potential for a discursive space for deliberation and argumentation to emerge may be reduced. Through a Gramscian lens, this book proposes that interregional relationships between unequal partners facilitates the reproduction of hegemonic ideology through legal regimes. The claim that the EPAs are hegemonic legal regimes that serve to reinforce the EU's position in the global economy will be the subject of interrogation throughout this book.

Adopting an interdisciplinary approach to the analysis of region formation serves to fill some of the conceptual gaps left by the rationalist schools of thought. In the first section of this chapter, the rationalist conception of regions will be presented with a view to explaining the different waves of regionalism that have emerged over time. In the second section, the constitution of regions through ideology will be examined identifying the material and non-material interests that underpin the (re)construction of regional spaces. The third section shifts the focus of this inquiry toward law as a medium of regional integration and through discourse theory highlights the interconnections between law, politics and economics. The final section presents the claim that North-South RTAs are *hegemonic* legal regimes. Extending the constructivist approach to an analysis of regions as legal regimes through discourse theory enables a better understanding of the ways in which the law institutionalises political ideology and economic imperatives in social spheres.

THE POLITICAL ECONOMY OF REGIONALISM

A useful starting point for the theoretical inquiry of this book is to examine the rationalist understanding of regionalism, how regions are formed, and for what purpose. Jagdish Bhagwati has written extensively on regionalism, and he has identified three 'waves' of regionalism which neatly set out distinct phases or bursts of regional activity that correspond to economic and political shifts in the global polity and enables a better understanding of the next phase of the regional project, *interregionalism*.

Waves of Regionalism

The first phase of regional activity, known as 'first regionalism' or 'old regionalism' is characterised by the post-war industrialisation and the widely adopted import substitution (IS) policies. Import substitution industrialisation (ISI) policies encourage high tariffs on imported products in specific sectors on the assumption that this will result in economic growth in the domestic industry. Historically, this was considered to be a favourable and suitable approach for developing countries that lacked comparative advantage across the manufacturing sectors. Adopting a free trade model was considered to be inappropriate for promoting economic growth in developing countries as it was feared that adopting liberal trade policies would 'trap' them into being primary commodity producers indefinitely.[5] ISI strategies were developed and introduced to promote industrialisation through infant industry protection because capital accumulation for manufacturing was believed to be at the heart of economic development in these economies.

Although the ISI policy was intended to be a temporary measure, it became a more permanent feature in developing countries and resulted in their industrial sectors becoming increasingly inefficient.[6] Since ISI by its very nature implies protection, it is at odds with the liberalist approaches to trade which stress reliance on international market forces and free trade. Placing power in the hands of bureaucrats would mean that decision-making, in relation to which industries should be encouraged and prioritised, would no longer be subject to market forces. While Western financial institutions promoted ISI policy as their preferred economic development strategy, an alternative trade strategy was being implemented on the other side of the globe. In South East Asia, the popular ISI policy was abandoned in favour of outward-orientated export approaches to trade.[7] Taiwan, Korea, Hong Kong and Singapore – collectively known as the East Asian 'Tigers' – encouraged trade growth through higher exports coupled with measures to protect the domestic industries. Arguably, the economic gulf that exists today between the ACP countries and the East Asian Tigers is in part attributable to the different economic strategies pursued in each region.

For a number of decades, the outward-orientated export approach remained popular, but by the 1990s the project of regionalism was revived. Marking the 'second wave' of regional integration, the number of RTAs being used as trade strategy began to increase. From a rationalist approach, when considering whether or not to join a RTA, each country will consider the economic welfare benefits and the political viability of such an arrangement. In essence, the government of that country will be pursuing a well-defined objective, or strategic motivation, albeit one that

---

[5] A.O. Krueger, 'Trade Policy and Development: How We Learn' (1997) 87(1) *The American Economic Review* 1–22, 3.

[6] S. Edwards and M. Savastano, 'Latin America's Intra-Regional Trade: Evolution and Future Prospects' in D. Greenaway, T. Hyclack and R. Thornton (eds), *Economic Aspects of Regional Trading Arrangements* (London: Harvester Wheatsheaf, 1989), 190.

[7] H.J. Bruton, 'A Reconsideration of Import Substitution' (1998) *Journal of Economic Literature* 903–36.

is economic, political, social or cultural. Multilateralism, and regionalism, presupposes cooperation among states. However, states may have strong, and even conflicting, preferences where trade policy is concerned. Game theory is a useful tool for unravelling state behaviour particularly in the context of trade negotiations, as it explores cooperation and conflict between states. It is a cooperative strategy where a state takes into account the interests of other players but it assumes that those state actors are rational, conscious, goal-seeking actors.

Understanding cooperation from a realistic perspective, with reference to game theory, enables us to focus on the state as it has been historically constructed: as the sole actor in multilateral negotiations. While there are inevitably shortcomings with this approach insofar as it assumes actors to be *rational*, *self-interested*, and *goal-seeking*, it is a useful tool for analysing behaviour at the state level. A game commonly used to infer preferences from bargaining positions is the Prisoner's Dilemma.[8] Within the Prisoner's Dilemma model there are four possible outcomes: exploiting another; mutual cooperation; mutual defection; or being exploited. In international trade, strategic action is usually described in the binary form of liberalisation through a free trade model (F) or protectionism (P). Table 1.1 outlines the four scenarios that exist within the cooperative game:

Table 1.1 Scenarios in a cooperative game

Country A	Country B	Outcome
P	F	Country A – Gain Country B – Exploited
F	F	Mutual Cooperation – Both gain
P	P	Mutual Defection –No gain
F	P	Country B – Gain Country A – Exploited

Game theory is a rationalist approach that allows us to predict behaviour. However, forecasting the welfare effects of FTA is, for the most part, problematic because they create complex economic impacts for each member. Different economic actors may be affected in different ways.

[8] For an extensive discussion of the Prisoner's Dilemma and the Nash Equilibrium model see: M. Osborne, *An Introduction to Game Theory* (New York: Oxford University Press, 2004).

While a RTA may be welfare enhancing for a producer who exports to the new trading partner it may also adversely affect domestic producers who will lose out to cheaper competitors as a result of the new RTA coming into force. An interesting political economy explanation for the rise in RTAs during the 'second wave' is presented by economist Richard Baldwin in the 'domino theory'.[9] Domino theory proposes that the deepening of integration among existing RTA members will increase the incentive for non-members to join the RTA. As integration among RTA members deepens, so too does the divide between members and non-members. The widening chasm results in trade diversion and loss for non-members which, in turn, incentivises the non-members to become members of the RTA. As the membership of the RTA grows, it becomes ever more attractive to non-members. Membership and accession increases the pressure for non-members to join the RTA since it is no longer politically optimal to remain an outsider.[10]

Building on this idea, Bhagwati extended the Vinerian analysis of RTAs through his articulation of the 'dynamic' approach to the role of RTAs in the multilateral system. His theoretical framework questions whether RTAs will act as 'stepping stones' or 'stumbling blocks' to the WTO's agenda for a trading world without tariffs.[11] In essence, the dynamic time path theorem examines the extent to which RTAs accelerate or hinder multilateral liberalisation. This approach goes beyond the analysis of the immediate, or static, effects of forming a RTA and instead considers the dynamic dimension of the RTA itself. If economic integration is endogenous there is likely to be both reduced protection for members and a correlative increase in the level of external protection for non-members.[12] This exemplifies the concept of 'inclusion/exclusion' within the RTA framework where members will benefit from freer trade within the boundaries of the regional arrangement whilst maintaining external tariffs to non-members. In any situation, it is necessary to quantify the payoffs relative to maintaining the status quo. What will a

---

[9] R. Baldwin, 'Multilateralizing Regionalism: Spaghetti Bowls as Building Blocs on the Path to Global Free Trade' (2006) 29(11) *The World Economy* 1451–518, 1467.

[10] *Ibid*, 1468.

[11] J. Bhagwati, *The World Trading System at Risk* (London: Harvester Wheatsheaf, 1991), 36.

[12] R. Findlay and A. Panagariya, 'A Political-Economy Analysis of Free Trade Areas and Customs Unions' in J. Bhagwati, P. Krishna and A. Panagariya (eds), *Trading Blocs: Alternative Approaches to Analyzing Preferential Trade Agreements* (Cambridge, MA and London: MIT Press, 1999), 334.

country gain from choosing to protect its market rather than liberalise its tariffs? Maintaining the status quo will not render any improvement and has zero welfare gain. From the information available, each actor will need to establish their 'best response' in relation to the actions of other actors.[13] Agricultural trade is a good example of trading partners choosing the 'best response' policy. The EU has for many years pursued a dominant strategy of protection through its Common Agricultural Policy (CAP) which is often mimicked by the subsidised policies implemented by the USA.[14] As illustrated in Table 1.1, if Country A openly chooses to adopt a protectionist strategy in agricultural trade it will come as no surprise that Country B will also choose that approach. In short, protectionism will be met with protectionism. To do otherwise would leave Country B open to exploitation from Country A in the trade of agricultural goods. As more players enter the game, the bargaining process becomes more complex and this game becomes entirely antithetical to the liberal agenda of free trade.

If we accept that the developed countries such as the EU and the USA often choose defection (P) over cooperation (F), we must question whether the developing nations can afford to bear the costs of mutual defection. Dambisa Moyo categorises countries as either 'winning globalisers', 'non-globalisers' or 'losing globalisers'.[15] Winning globalisers, such as the developed Western countries, have embraced liberalisation and witnessed economic growth. On the other hand, losing globalisers have liberalised but have not experienced growth while non-globalisers have not sought to liberalise and consequently have not experienced growth. The ACP countries, on which this book focuses, tend to fall within the 'losing globalisers' category. Let us now consider the game theoretic example in the context of agricultural negotiations using Country A (a developed country) and Country B (a developing country). If Country A decides to protect its agricultural market by using subsidies and sourcing from regionally situated countries, can Country B afford to operate in a similar way? Or in other words, can African countries

---

[13] G. Harrison and E. Ruström, 'Trade Wars, Trade Negotiations and Applied Game Theory' (1991) 101 *The Economic Journal* 420–35, 423.

[14] The EU's CAP was established as a mechanism to ensure food security in times of crises. See G. Skogstad, 'Ideas, Paradigms and Institutions: Agricultural Exceptionalism in the European Union and the United States' (2002) 11 *Governance* 463–90 and J.S. Ingram, P. Ericksen and D. Liverman, *Food Security and Global Environmental Change* (London: Taylor & Francis, 2010).

[15] D. Moyo, *Dead Aid: Why Aid is Not Working and How There is Another Way for Africa* (London: Penguin, 2010), 114–15.

(Country B) compete with the subsidy schemes operated in the EU (Country A)? With most developing countries in crippling debt as a result of implementing policies promoted by the international financial institutions,[16] they are not in a financial position to compete with this level of investment in protecting their agricultural market. Protecting their markets in this way has enabled developed countries to become 'winning globalisers' while the ACP countries, which remain producers of primary commodities, remain 'losing globalisers'.

That said, between 2000 and 2010 the African continent achieved a real rise in GDP of 5.4 per cent. Such significant growth, in a period when the rest of the world was feeling the effects of the global recession, led to the African economies being described as 'lions on the move'.[17] While the 'economic lions' have witnessed a decline in real GDP over the past five years, the African continent nevertheless grew by 3 per cent over the past ten years. Therefore, with the appropriate infrastructure and removal of capacity constraints, the African economies have the potential to become 'winning globalisers'.

To avoid reaching a negotiating stalemate, trade concessions are made on a reciprocal basis. Reciprocity, or symmetry, is a fundamental principle of multilateralism in avoiding the Prisoner's Dilemma and a mechanism to avoid protectionism.[18] In the absence of reciprocity countries could liberalise on an *à la carte* basis, choosing to cherry-pick those sectors to liberalise on a global MFN basis and those to exclude from liberalisation altogether. Bagwell and Staiger define reciprocity in general terms as referring to 'the ideal of mutual changes in trade policy that bring about equal changes in import values across trading partners'.[19] In this respect, reciprocity builds fairness and equity into the

---

16 Liberals would contest this point, as they would argue that developing countries were already bankrupt when they came to the international financial institutions. For an example of how the international financial institutions have tried to implement policies to encourage investment in African developing countries see, J.D. Sachs and A.M. Werner 'Sources of Slow Growth in African Economies' (1997) 6 *Journal of African Economies* 335–76.

17 McKinsey Global Institute, 'Lions on the Move: The progress and potential of African Economies' (June 2010) Report of McKinsey & Company available online at http://www.mckinsey.com/global-themes/middle-east-and-africa/lions-on-the-move.

18 D. Das, *Regionalism in Global Trade* (Cheltenham, UK and Northampton, MA, USA: Edward Elgar, 2004), 101.

19 K. Bagwell and R. Staiger, 'Will Preferential Agreements Undermine the Multilateral Trading System?' in J. Bhagwati, P. Krishna and A. Panagariya (eds),

world trading system, reinforcing the idea that all members are equal. In lowering tariff levels reciprocally, members should enjoy higher welfare gains.[20]

A significant political factor was the dissolution of the former USSR and Former Yugoslav Republic (FYR) which resulted in fragmentation and uncertainty for the countries in Eastern Europe. In order to protect their industries and to promote sustainable development after many years of protracted violence, these transition economies sought regional cooperation with the EU and European Free Trade Area (EFTA) states. This has been described as a process of 'action-reaction' whereby:

> … the creation of discriminatory arrangements by one country is matched by an equal reaction (often defensive) by other countries, [and] seems to have become irreversible, almost as if RTA proliferation has reached a critical point from which there is no turning back.[21]

Other considerable geopolitical factors have also acted as a catalyst for the proliferation of RTAs.[22] In the mid-1980s there was growing concern among the contracting parties of the GATT that the Uruguay Round negotiations would collapse. RTAs were perceived as an insurance measure for trade in the event that the multilateral system failed to overcome the negotiating impasse. There is almost a sense of déja-vu in today's global economy, as the struggle to conclude the Doha Round rumbles on almost 16 years after it began. Without doubt, the perceived failure of the Doha Round has acted as stimulus toward RTA proliferation in this time period. With the conclusion of the Uruguay Round and the mass proliferation of RTAs generally, we are now in the 'third wave' of regionalism.

Trading Blocs: Alternative Approaches to Analyzing Preferential Trade Agreements (Cambridge, MA and London: MIT Press, 1999), 515.

[20] See generally Richard Baldwin's political economy 'juggernaut' model of reciprocity: Baldwin (n. 9) and R. Baldwin, '21st Century Regionalism: Filling the Gap between 21st Century Trade and 20th Century Trade Rules', WTO Staff Working Paper ERSD-2011-08 (2011).

[21] Baldwin, '21st Century Regionalism' (n. 20), 46.

[22] R. Fiorentino, J. Crawford and C. Toqueboeuf, 'The Landscape of Regional Trade Agreements and WTO Surveillance', in R. Baldwin and P. Low (eds), *Multilateralizing Regionalism: Challenges for the Global Trading System* (Cambridge: Cambridge University Press, 2009), 44.

Collectively, the second and third waves have been coined as 'new regionalism'.[23] New regionalism is characterised by overlapping membership and an increasingly complex cartography of regional organisations, from which the question of 'who governs' becomes more difficult to discern. Countries are often party to more than one RTA and the systemic problem of overlapping membership and complicated tariff negotiations has resulted in the phenomenon aptly referred to as 'spaghetti bowl' regionalism or the 'noodle bowl' effect.[24] This analogy refers to the criss-crossing tariff commitments and non-harmonised rules of origin (ROO) that results from multiple membership. Naturally, as a country joins more than one RTA particular products will be subject to varying tariff levels depending on the terms of each RTA. Not only are new regional arrangements being negotiated, but previously abandoned RTAs across the globe have been revitalised, such as the Andean Pact in Latin America and the Common Market for Eastern and Southern Africa (COMESA) on the African continent. The scope of regionalism now seems to be shifting toward a more ambitious and inclusive trade policy, liberalising trade in goods, services, competition and procurement as evidenced in the negotiations of the Trans-Pacific Partnership (TPP), the Transatlantic Trade and Investment Partnership (TTIP), the EU-Canada Comprehensive Economic and Trade Agreement (CETA), and the Trade in Services Agreement (TISA), to name but a few. A comprehensive approach to liberalisation has also been adopted in the CARIFORUM EPA, which will be examined in Chapter 9 of this book.

The significance of the rationalist accounts of regionalism should not be understated as they offer important insight into the materialist strategic orientations of states engaged in the negotiation process. However, in doing so, the normative content of action becomes further abstracted. It is the purpose of this book to present an account of the materialist and non-materialist ideational forces that come to shape strategic action.

---

[23] Bhagwati (n. 11), 58; B. Hettne, 'Beyond the 'New' Regionalism' (2005) 10 *New Political Economy* 543–71. Drawing on the work of Ernst Haas, Björn Hettne describes the 'new' wave of regionalism as being related to, and a reaction to, globalisation whereas the 'old' wave of regionalism was more concerned with the functional approach to integration. The New Regionalism Theory, on the other hand, is a critical theory that is used as a problem-based approach to the study of the ideas, beliefs and norms that have shaped regional processes within a globalising world.

[24] Introduced by President Haruhiko Kuroda, cited in Bhagwati (n. 11), 63.

CONSTRUCTING REGIONS THROUGH IDEAS

While conventional rationalist theories recognise that non-economic factors and non-state actors may influence regional processes, a critical constructivist approach perceives international trade to be a specific type of 'social interaction' through which social orders are created. For constructivist analyses, the international economic order spreads:

> ... knowledge, norms, and values through traders who often cross boundaries and settle into new communities and by the content of the products or services purchased by the members of different communities. Socio-cultural factors do not necessarily support international economic relations, and resistance to the expansion of global economic integration is often based on socio-economic concerns.[25]

It is the emphasis on different actors, and their role in shaping international trade policy, that is perhaps the most distinguishing feature of these approaches to international economic law. Economic sociology, of the type developed by Mark Granovetter, considers economic activity as 'embedded' in social life and in social action. It is an explicit response to 'over-socialised' or 'under-socialised' accounts of economic behaviour provided by other schools of thought.[26] While the neoclassical economic position outlined in the previous section envisages economic actors as individual rational utility maximisers, for economic sociologists:

> Actors do not behave or decide as atoms outside a social context, nor do they adhere slavishly to a script written for them by the particular intersection of social categories that they happen to occupy. Their attempts at purposive action are instead embedded in concrete, ongoing systems of social relations.[27]

Cooperation is also a focal point for constructivists, but the analysis goes further than game-theory by exploring what constitutes cooperative relations among states. Of particular significance to sociological accounts of international trade is the intersubjective nature of trade and the role of interpersonal trust between parties involved in economic transactions.

---

[25] M. Hirsch, 'The Sociology of International Economic Law: Sociological Analysis of the Regulation of Regional Trade Agreements in the World Trading System' (2008) 19 *European Journal of International Law* 227–99, 281.

[26] M. Granovetter, 'Economic Action and Social Structure: The Problem of Embeddedness' (1985) 91(3) *American Journal of Sociology* 481–510.

[27] *Ibid,* 487.

Granovetter proposes that the trust that facilitates economic activity is found in social relations and not in institutional arrangements or generalised morality. Since social relations penetrate different sectors of economic life in different ways and to different degrees, this allows room for distrust, opportunism and disorder. Economic sociology highlights the ways in which economic activity is coordinated by groups, such as firms, rather than rational, self-interested states, as the rationalist model leads us to believe.[28]

Since 1995, the WTO has acted as the multilateral forum in which this game is played, with members striving to secure a balance between progressive trade liberalisation and protectionism. In return for market access, a member must offer trade concessions on a reciprocal basis. For this 'dance of contradictory impulses'[29] to move fluidly, there must exist rules, norms and practices at the institutional level to support the game. Governance and regulation set the boundaries in which the members can play/dance. Actors involved in trade negotiations across the different spatial levels are not mere automatons – they are active participants who develop a 'feel for the game' that guides and influences their policy choices. It is through their social interactions that government officials and trade professionals co-construct international economic law. Their interpretations of the text give meaning to its provisions.[30]

From a Habermasian perspective, trust is derived from the legal rules themselves. Kent Jones highlights a more subtle dimension of trust within the WTO system, based on 'fair bargaining'.[31] While members will seek to maximise utility during negotiations, we must remember that these negotiations are led by human beings, who will be sensitive to the nuances of the game. This is particularly the case in asymmetric partnerships, where countries will continually strive to strengthen their bargaining positions at the next round of negotiations by 'shaping the

---

[28] M. Granovetter, 'Problems of Explanation in Economic Sociology' in R. Eccles and N. Nitin (eds), *Networks and Organisations: Structure, Form and Action* (Boston: Harvard Business School Press, 1992).

[29] K. Jones, *The Doha Blues* (New York and Oxford: Oxford University Press, 2010), 6.

[30] A. Lang, *World Trade Law after Neoliberalism: Reimagining the Global Economic Order* (Oxford: Oxford University Press, 2011), 164–5.

[31] Jones (n. 29), 11–12.

negotiation agenda … exploiting particular issues and forming coalitions'.[32] This type of behaviour is evident in the WTO's dispute settlement system, which will be discussed at greater length in the next chapter.

A constructivist approach that emerged during the wave of 'new regionalism' is that of New Regionalism Theory (NRT). Developed principally by Bjorne Hettne and Fredrik Söderbaum, NRT encourages a focus on '*by whom*, *for whom* and *for what purpose*' regions are created.[33] Inherently intersubjective in character, NRT seeks to critically reconstruct the rationalist, positivistic tendencies of conventional theories of regionalism. Conceiving of rationalist theories as being both 'overly concerned' with methodology and 'under-concerned' with the 'socio-economic circumstances and historical context of regionalism', this theoretical school offers an alternative lens through which regional processes can be interrogated and understood.[34]

Transcending the traditional approaches that treat the state as if it is 'the ontological and moral equivalent to individual persons',[35] NRT focuses on the interaction of various actors across different spatial levels. Scholars of New Regionalism understand regionalism as a historically situated, multidimensional process in which regions are constructed, deconstructed and reconstructed; intentionally and/or unintentionally; for negative and/or positive purposes, by informal and formal actors. As the international order has become differentiated, so too has the space they occupy. Institutions may emerge at different levels within, alongside and across the space occupied by the state. The different actors in the global system may have overlapping, competing and even conflicting interests, goals, policies and projects. NRT does not prioritise formal or informal regionalism; rather it seeks to highlight the involvement of all actors that may influence the construction, deconstruction and reconstruction of regional space. In the context of this book, the focus is primarily on state and regional actors in the EPA negotiations. However, reference will be made to the non-state actors that have played a role in steering the negotiation process. Non-state actors shape the interests pursued at the state level through formal and informal networks and therefore the focus should be on all actors operating within the formal inter-state framework.

---

32 *Ibid*, 12.

33 F. Söderbaum, *The Political Economy of Regionalism: The Case of Southern Africa* (Basingstoke: Palgrave MacMillan, 2004), 2–3. Emphasis added.

34 *Ibid*, 193.

35 Söderbaum, 'Exploring the Links between Micro-Regionalism and Macro-Regionalism' (n. 4), 89.

A significant obstacle to a full analysis of the way in which norms are shaped by both state and non-state actors is the lack of transparency, particularly in the context of the EPA negotiations. Much like other trade negotiations, very little has been made publicly available and therefore gathering data presents notable challenges. Beyond the limited information made publicly available through the EU or ACP sub-regional groups which might indicate the motivations of the state actors to enter into these agreements, a sense of the public reaction to the new trade and development regimes can be discerned through statements from civil society organisations and media reports.

From a constructivist perspective, actors both construct and are subjects of the region. These actors are constantly engaged in processes of interaction that can construct and de/re-construct spatial boundaries. Under this theoretical framework, the region is perceived to be a social construct with regionalism being what the actors make of it:

> Individual countries … are not islands in the sea of globalism, but interact with close neighbours in ways that impact upon both their own national development and global interactions. Within each region, the character of interaction helps to define the possibilities of each national development. Regions are shaped by the world order and reciprocally, reshape that world order.[36]

In identifying the different actors involved it is important to acknowledge that they do not operate in a mutually exclusive way. A distinguishing feature of new regionalism is the emergence of global actors. The region can itself be both an arena in which actors engage in processes of regionalisation and an actor participating in regional activity. It is both an author and a subject of the region. Drawing insights from critical political economy, this book conceives of the EU as a *normative* global actor that actively seeks to export universal norms through its regional trade strategy. The idea that a region can become an actor, capable of articulating transnational interests, emphasises the cohesiveness and coherence required to become an actor. Agency is given a broad interpretation with a regional actor being defined as that which 'takes part – consciously or unconsciously – in activities on a regionally defined area'.[37] Agency of regional actors, with the exception of the EU, is

[36] C.B. Thompson, 'Regional Challenges to Globalisation: Perspectives from Southern Africa' (2000) 5 *New Political Economy* 43.

[37] B. Hettne, 'EU Foreign Policy: The Interregional Model' in F. Söderbaum and P. Stålgren (eds), *The European Union and the Global South* (Boulder, CO: Lynne Reinner, 2010), 20–8.

relatively under-researched, but it will be shown in Chapter 3 that the EU has used its regional presence to effect an external policy that parallels its internal policies.

LAW AS A MEDIUM OF INTEGRATION

The rationalist and constructivist schools provide rich and interesting theoretical views of regionalism although the significance of law as a medium of integration is obscured. The following section aims to fill the conceptual gaps of these theoretical perspectives and asserts that regions represent spheres of social action that are integrated through law. In order to ground this claim it is first necessary to explore the concept of social action, which has long been the subject of sociological inquiry.

Reclaiming Rationality

The first, and arguably one of the most significant theories of social action, was articulated by German sociologist, Max Weber. In his paradigm of action theory, Weber identified four types of social action, or rationality, and three forms of legitimacy, which are inherently intersubjective and 'oriented to the past, present or expected future behaviour of others'.[38] Weber conceptualised action as oriented toward four types of rationality: *instrumentally rational*, *value-rational*, *affectual* and *traditional.*[39] Instrumentally-rational social action is oriented towards achieving a particular end, with the actor knowingly choosing a behaviour regardless of the costs to those and to others. It is determined by 'expectations as to the behaviour of objects in the environment and of other human beings; these expectations are used as 'conditions' or 'means' for the attainment of the actor's own 'rationally pursued or calculated ends'.[40] By contrast, value-rational action is determined in accordance with the 'conscious belief in the value for its own sake of

---

[38] M. Weber, *Economy and Society: An Outline of Interpretive Sociology* Vol. 1, G. Roth and C. Wittich (eds) (Berkeley, CA: University of California Press, 1978), 22.

[39] Social action oriented of the *affectual* kind is determined by the actor's "feeling states" while the *traditional* orientation is determined by "ingrained habituation". See Weber (n. 38), 25.

[40] Weber (n. 38), 24.

some ethical, aesthetic, religious or other form of behaviour, independently of its prospect of success'.[41] One of the earliest articulations of a *strategic* form of rationality is found in the Aristotelian concept of teleological action – that is, the way in which an actor chooses a particular action in order to attain a particular end 'guided by maxims and based on interpretation of the situation'.[42] Teleological action can be extended to a strategic or instrumental form of rationality, in which actors choose a particular path among alternatives in pursuit of a particular goal or desired state and are guided by utilitarian principles. Both teleological and strategic action share a common framework which presupposes the relationship between the actor and the 'objective world', or in other words, between an individual and their understanding of the state of affairs in the external world.

It is submitted that social orders go beyond the individual rationalist strategic action of state actors:

> the content of a social relationship [will] be called an order if the conduct is, approximately or on the average, oriented toward determinable 'maxims'. Only then will an order be called 'valid' if the orientation toward these maxims occurs, among other reasons … because it is in some appreciable way regarded by the actor as in some way obligatory or exemplary for him.[43]

These determinable maxims, or norms, provide reasons for action which individuals feel compelled, or obligated, to accept. In general, the word 'norm' refers to 'a standard of appropriate behaviour for actors with a given identity.'[44] This definition can be expanded to the legal system to define *legal* norms as providing a *legal* standard of appropriate behaviour for actors with a given identity or, simply put, norms that constitute 'legal reasons for action'.[45] It is generally accepted among legal scholars that valid legal norms prescribe reasons for action backed by some form of coercive measure. Legal norms are limited by historical time and social space, applying only to the legal actors in the particular territory defined by law, and are valid until such a date that they are repealed. Of course,

---

41 *Ibid.*

42 J. Habermas, *The Theory of Communicative Action: Reason and the Rationalisation of Society*, Vol. 1, T. McCarthy (trans.) (London: Beacon Press, 1984), 85.

43 Weber (n. 38), 31.

44 M. Finnemore and K. Sikkink, 'International Norm Dynamics and Political Change' (1998) 52 *International Organisation* 887–917, 891.

45 T. Spaak, 'Legal Positivism, Law's Normativity, and the Normative Force of Legal Justification' (2003) 16 *Ratio Juris* 469–85.

not all norms within a social space are legal norms. Within any given social order there may be a multiplicity of norms that are cultural, traditional, ethical, political or economic in character. Theories of social action aim to discover the normative bases of social orders to explain *why* individuals conform to certain patterns of behaviour. From a social theory perspective, the function of the law is that of social integration. Understanding *why*, *for whom*, and *for what purpose* regional and interregional spaces are constructed through law is a central theme of this book.

Sociological theories of law have long sought to explain the integrative function of the law through social contract, utilitarianism and individualistic theories. One of the earliest integrative theories is found in the writings of Emile Durkheim, who presented a sociological theory of law conceived of as an expression of the conscience collective from which the individual is born.[46] In identifying two forms of social solidarity, mechanical and organic, Durkheim sought to construct an understanding of the law's integrative function. Mechanical solidarity is exhibited in homogenous societies where law is repressive in terms of its punishment for non-compliance. As the division of labour is not pronounced in this type of society, there are strong societal bonds based on a common belief system and the expression of a conscience collective is strong since there is little room for individualism. As societies modernise and the division of labour becomes increasingly differentiated, social bonds begin to disintegrate, leading to a weakened sense of 'common' identity. Organic solidarity is associated with modern societies in which there is a clear division of labour and individuals take on specialised roles within the economy. However, individualism comes at the cost of losing the sense of belonging to a more homogenous or common group. While the law in this type of society is less repressive in terms of punishment it nevertheless serves an integrative function to prevent a state of *anomie*, wherein common values, norms and morals are no longer understood or accepted.[47] *Anomie* represents a state of *normlessness* where common bonds have weakened without new norms having emerged to guide societal expectations. It is the function of the law to prevent the state of normlessness by sealing off, or closing, society through a process of (re)integration.

Admittedly, there are a number of shortcomings with Durkheim's rather simplistic theory but it does offer an interesting platform from

---

[46] E. Durkheim, *The Division of Labour in Society*, W.D. Halls (trans.) (New York: The Free Press, 1984).

[47] E. Durkheim, *Suicide: A Study in Sociology* (Abingdon: Routledge, 2002).

which other notable sociological theories of law have emerged. These theories aim to capture the complexity of modernity and problematise social action through a critical lens, highlighting the shift from pre-modern to modern societies. In pre-modern societies, social behaviour was influenced predominantly through religious ideology with the clergy representing the 'most colossal utopia'.[48] Over time, the dominating ideology in the West has shifted toward a rationalist bureaucracy in secular societies with the logics of economics, law and politics as structural pillars of the system. Replacing the role of religion, the law operates as a 'unity-creating ideological institution', especially in capitalist societies.[49] Both Weber and contemporary German philosopher Jürgen Habermas conceive of the law as a sphere of social action that is open to formal rationalisation; and with an increasingly complex institutional framework of society, the law 'becomes more and more indispensable as the moral sources that supply the necessary motives to the occupational system dry up'.[50] Weber's writings in the *Protestant Ethic* and *Law and Economy*, demonstrate how the anchoring of modern law has marked a shift from metajuristic to juristic principles, which have nothing more than a hypothetical status. Anchoring the law in juristic principles reinforces the autonomy of the law but nevertheless retains the relationship between law and extra-legal contexts. As society has become increasingly bureaucratised, the law has become ever more rational. Weber explored different archetypes, or 'ideal types', of law which would support and facilitate economic production and noted that the *rationalisation* of law created a more predictable and stable environment. By contrast, a lack of rationality implies a state of chaos under which capitalism would collapse resulting in a state of *anomie*. Central to Weber's thesis is the concept of authority, and in the legal-rational typology of law authority is found in the impartiality of legal rationality where officials act with 'formalistic impersonality'. Deconstructing the concept of authority provides an explanation of why we feel obligated to respect the law, even in the absence of coercive forces. Although Weber provided one of the most influential contributions on the rationality of modern law he expressed ambivalence toward the dominant discourse of rationality as 'it threatens to dehumanise our existence and confine us to

---

[48] A. Gramsci, *Prison Notebooks*, J. Buttigieg (ed.) (New York: Columbia University Press, 1992), Q4 §45.

[49] S. Buckel and A. Fischer-Lescano, 'Gramsci Reconsidered: Hegemony in Global Law' (2009) 22 *Leiden Journal of International Law* 437–51, 441.

[50] Habermas (n. 42), 251.

an *iron cage of rationality*'.[51] Habermas sought to reclaim rationality as a standpoint from which we can understand the differentiation between the *system,* a term used to broadly refer to the complex institutional framework governing society at the national, regional and international levels, and the *lifeworld,* a term which refers to society in general. While he was critical of the dominant discourse, he nevertheless (critically) supported the project of rationalisation on the basis that the realisation of the projects of rationality and modernity could be achieved through an alternative epistemological approach.

Habermas offers a theory that is both sociological and historical, with a focus on how law operates in modern society, providing a normative account of legitimate law as a medium that integrates society. Recognising that modernity has broken down long-established traditions, such as religion, he asserts that we are now living in an increasingly *functionally differentiated* world. Conceiving of society as a system of interconnected spheres of social action, Habermas places rationality at the heart of the discursive process showing that modern law reintegrates societies that have become increasingly individualistic and normless. In order to coordinate our actions in a world that lacks common understandings we must engage in deliberative processes to reach consensus on particular issues. Law fosters integration in an increasingly fractious world because it sets default rules for interaction and therefore creates reliable expectations. Drawing insights from John Rawls' political philosophy, Habermas proposes that positive (enacted) law must be concerned with redistributive justice in society to ensure that all free and equal legal persons are entitled to the same rights. These expectations are not only underpinned by threats of punishments sanctioned by the law but through the mutual agreement between free and equal legal persons, engaged in a performative process of argumentation, to be bound by legal rules. Through his discourse theory and deliberative democracy model, Habermas conceives of law as an indispensable condition of society through which political ideology and economic imperatives are institutionalised. It will be recalled that this is an *ideal* type of law but it nevertheless has explanatory value particularly in the context of the EPAs, as these trade agreements are anchored in a deliberative democracy model.

---

[51] E.O. Eriksen and J. Weigård, *Understanding Habermas: Communicative Action and Deliberative Democracy* (London: Continuum, 2003), 2.

A Discourse Theory of Law

To contextualise the discourse theory of law it is worthwhile briefly considering Habermas' earlier writings. In *A Theory of Communicative Action*, Habermas grounds his theory in a participant-centred discourse of intersubjective communicative capabilities and proposes an alternative form of rationality[52] that is constituted through subject-to-subject interaction between individual actors. Through this process of intersubjectivity, individuals can make claims to correctness based on the procedure through which we reach certain decisions and conclusions. Communicative action presupposes a background knowledge which is intersubjectively shared by the participants of a particular community.[53] Much like the Gramscian concept of 'common-sense', background knowledge represents an uncritical philosophy that is generally accepted by society. Interpretation, which involves the negotiation of definitions of terms and reaching consensus, is central to the concept of communicative action. Habermas conceives of the *lifeworld* (society) as constituting the interconnecting complexity of cultural traditions, social orders, and the individual identities of actors. Inherent to the theory of communicative action is the supposition that the actors possess the requisite ability to understand the linguistic and interpretive medium in which the deliberation should take place. However, the conclusions drawn from these deliberations must be open to interrogation: they are not infallible.

The significance of law as a medium of integration in modern societies is unmistakable when contrasted with social action in pre-modern societies wherein the individual was socialised through familial, religious and cultural networks of reciprocal social relations. As a result, the individual was not conceived purely as an autonomous entity but rather their identity was intertwined with relationships of mutual recognition and

---

[52] While Habermas identifies four modes of action that are either *strategic*, *normatively regulated*, *dramaturgical*, or *communicative* in orientation, this book is predominantly focused on the manner in which strategic and normatively regulated actions interfere with the spheres in which communicative action *should* take place. Normatively regulated action refers to the compliance of a community with norms in order to fulfil a generalised expectation of behaviour. Habermas extended Weber's analysis to show that different rationalities can affect the ability to achieve communicative action through the process of procedural rationality. Of most importance to this book is the notion of purposive or instrumental rationality which is strategic and ends-focused and the way in which this form of rationality can inhibit communicative rationality. See Habermas (n. 42), 87.

[53] Habermas (n. 42), 11.

reciprocity. This sense of common identity grounds the law in a real way and it is the 'symbolic construction' of 'a people' that transforms the modern state into a nation-state.[54] As societies modernise, the relationships that were once defined by personal bonds become abstracted relationships between strangers who agree to be bound together by legal rules that both guarantee their freedom and inhibit their liberty:

> Growing pluralism loosens ascriptive ties to family, locality, social background, and tradition, and initiates a formal transformation of social integration. With each new impulse toward modernisation, intersubjectively shared life worlds open, so that they can reorganise, and close once more.[55]

As society becomes increasingly differentiated and pluralistic the law plays a normative regulatory role in reintegrating society. In doing so, the law acts as a hinge between the system and the lifeworld to fill the gaps where the integrative capacities of social orders have become 'overtaxed'. Habermas asserts that law is the only medium in which moral obligated relationships of mutual respect between strangers can be achieved.[56]

In *Between Facts and Norms*, Habermas seeks to provide an account of modern societies through which the enforcement of positive law (facticity or empirical efficacy) is intertwined with the law's claim to legitimacy (validity). Modern law, Habermas submits, is 'Janus faced' and enables actors to choose between two distinct paths toward the law: facticity and validity.[57] Individuals can conceive of the law as factual constraints on social action and adopt a strategic rational approach in their behaviour. Legitimate law is that which satisfies the *discourse principle* which requires the assent of all participants in rational discourses that might be affected by the legal norm. Conceiving of legal subjects as both authors and addressees of law, Habermas asserts:

> *As* legal subjects, they must anchor this practice of self-legislation in the medium of law itself; they must legally institutionalise those communicative presuppositions and procedures of a political opinion- and will-formation in which the discourse principle is applied. Thus the establishment of the legal code, which is undertaken with the help of the universal right to equal

[54] J. Habermas, *The Postnational Constellation: Political Essays*, M. Pensky (trans.) (Cambridge: Polity Press, 2007), 64.

[55] *Ibid*, 83.

[56] J. Habermas, 'Postscript' in *Between Facts & Norms*, W. Rehg (trans.) (Cambridge: Polity Press, 1996), 460.

[57] *Ibid*, 448.

> individual liberties, must be *completed* through communicative and participatory rights that guarantee equal liberties for the public use of communicative liberties. In this way, the discourse principle acquires the legal shape of a democratic principle.[58]

Legal norms must be seen as having a dual character, both to protect our freedom and to prevent interference with our freedom. This is particularly true of capitalist societies, wherein modern law has been constructed around a liberal conception of freedom which places emphasis on individual and property rights. By way of example, my individual right to liberty free from the interference of others is a freedom which is guaranteed by the law and this serves to protect my individual liberty while simultaneously constraining the liberty of others. Coercion, in a legal sense, is justified as protecting each individual's right to liberty from the encroachment on that liberty by other actors. Habermas identifies an internal connection between coercion and freedom as law's claim to legitimacy derives from its guarantee to liberty. This leads Habermas to conclude that 'legal norms are at the same time but in different respects enforceable laws based on coercion and the laws of freedom'.[59] Drawing insights from Kant's idealism, Habermas identifies the dual character of law's validity from the perspective of social action theory. If the law's validity is both coercive and liberating in nature then this gives the individual actor a choice of action orientation – either to respect the normative constraint on action to ensure that the liberty of others is preserved, or to encroach on another person's liberty and face the penalty for non-compliance with that particular legal norm. Alternatively, individuals can adopt a *performative* attitude to the law in which they view legal norms as conditions for behaviour and obey these norms out of sheer respect for the law. The law's claim to legitimacy is achieved through the acceptance of the population by a discursive democratic process that the law is normatively 'good' and 'just'.

Modern society is characterised by social integration of institutions at the macro-level through power (democracy) and economics (the market). Using counterfactuals, Habermas strives to illustrate how the legitimacy of law is derived from the 'self-imposed' will of individuals. In other words, Habermas seeks to explain why individuals obey the law beyond reasons of bare coercion. Law serves as the binding structural force between the two competing social interests of power and money. His

---

58 *Ibid*, 458.

59 J. Habermas, *Between Facts & Norms*, W. Rehg (trans.) (Cambridge: Polity Press, 1996), 29.

analysis of the *system* is expressed in his discourse theory, an idealised and multi-dimensional paradigm that bridges Habermas' interest in political theory and rationality. It rests on the assumption that actors possess the capacity to recognise the intersubjective quality of normative claims and can reach a mutual understanding on what is *good* for the whole of that social order. Cooperation is therefore rooted in validity claims, the content of which Habermas recognises to be rational and cognitive in character. From a Habermasian perspective, the *philosophy of consciousness* tells a tale of rationality in the Cartesian sense, in which the actor seeks to interpret facts and events through a predominantly cognitive form of reason. In doing so, the actor attempts to rationally understand these facts and events against an ever changing environment to achieve his/her goals or subjective preferences. Rationality, through this process of consciousness, becomes instrumental.

Participation in this process is not merely an empirical practice, it is *performative* in character. As a discursive process it entails the presentation of counterfactual 'pragmatic presuppositions' through which each individual has an equal opportunity to present arguments and the best argument is that which is most persuasive in line with rational argumentation. Legitimate norms, or *good reasons for action*, are those which have been achieved through a mutual understanding of the participants. In other words, all actors accept that their behaviour should be guided by a particular norm, and agree to be bound to that norm, because it is rationally the most persuasive. This leads to the neo-Kantian conception of obligation that actors agree to a form of social coordination as a matter of their 'free will'.

As an abstracted, highly idealised and multi-dimension paradigm Habermas strives to demonstrate how discourse theory can be used to critically reflect upon the real-life institutional choices taken in complex, modern societies. He does so through the *discourse principle* wherein the validity of a norm is derived from the consent of all actors to whom the norm affects, provided that the consensus is achieved through reasonable discourse that is free from coercive forces. However, far from seeing the law as an autonomous sphere of social action detached from other spheres of social action like systems-theorists, Habermas conceives of law as a medium of social *integration*. The social spheres of economics and politics are institutionalised through legal procedures and regulations, which in turn is socially integrated through communicative action in the lifeworld. Anchoring the economic and political systems *in* law, Habermas argues that law bears the task of holding society together. It is through the creation of the administrative state, a subsystem of society which is constituted through binding positive law, that collectively binding norms are created. As a specialist subsystem, the administrative state is separate from society and this serves to institutionalise the market through private property rights.[60] One effect of this differentiation between system and society is that markets appear to be self-regulated, impersonal and abstracted from society.

In a globalising world order, the validity of republican autonomy loses its critical strength as the significance of nation states begins to diminish. Faced with a complex social order comprised of global and regional institutions, nation states and regional arrangements, the idea that societies are able to democratically self-direct becomes the focal point of critical inquiry. In seeking an alternative theory through which the democratic self-legislation of individuals in society can be credibly realised, Habermas does not propose a 'self-dismantling' of neoliberalism but rather a way to transpose the existing democratic process beyond a nation-state analysis.[61] The only legitimate democratic process is one which allocates rights fairly and equally. Although his theory is anti-majoritarian, in the context of law Habermas proposes that bargains may be reached among the participating actors who the law might affect. The struggle of reaching consensus among large groups is certainly evident in the WTO. Having been originally created as the GATT in 1947 by just 23 Contracting Parties, the WTO is now an organisation of 164 members. Since 1947, the legal text of the GATT has constituted the legal rules governing the reduction of tariffs in trade and goods and has remained unchanged to this day. As demonstrated through the protracted Doha Round negotiations, it is difficult to achieve consensus among the existing 164 members and it is unlikely that they would all share the vision of the original 23 members.

Social action in modern Western society is inexplicably driven by a capitalist logic which can be harmful to private autonomy and, therefore, it is of paramount importance that the democratic constitutional state provides safeguards and social conditions that mitigate against the infringement of private autonomy. Redistributive justice becomes a key concern for the state, and social welfare emerges from the dialectic between legal equality and factual inequality, or between formal equality and substantive equality. To guarantee liberty and the law's claim to legitimacy, human rights must be available to all legal persons in order to prevent disadvantages for minority groups. It is the social intervention of the state that 'expands the self-legislation of the citizens of a nation-state

[60] Habermas (n. 54), 61.
[61] *Ibid.*

into the democratic self-steering of a nation-state society'.[62] Applying the discourse principle to the international level results in a cosmopolitan theory wherein the state guarantees individual freedoms in the form of human rights, which Habermas defines as 'legal norms with an exclusively moral content'.[63] Human rights circumscribe the strategic orientations of political orders, namely democracies, within which political and economic institutions operate often in a materialist and strategic manner.

Recognising that there is an internal relation, and not merely a historical association, between law and democracy, the reconstructive paradigm of law is rooted in democratic proceduralism, providing an account of how free and equal legal individuals associate in a society constructed through positive law. Where an actor acts in a purposively rational manner toward others, it is primarily with a view to achieving a self-serving goal. Much like Weber, the Habermasian critique perceives rationality as inherently 'one-sided' with the focus on material production and coercion over other interests. However, it is important to note that the expansion of rationality reflected in the increasing complexity of action systems does not necessarily result in an increasing rationalisation of the actor's orientations in the lifeworld.[64] If we observe the ongoing complexities of modernity characterised by the rise of bureaucratic institutions and their separation from political control, the fissure between societal expectations and bureaucratic goals becomes pronounced. It is this division between the bureaucratic institutions and the social sphere, the *system* and the *lifeworld*, which becomes a discursive space for challenge and contestation.

To prevent the law becoming a tool of domination by the bourgeois, Habermas conceives of the public sphere of the mass media as a potential space for discursive deliberation. The mass media has the potential to play a critical role for enabling the deliberative potential of democracy to be realised.[65] Today's world is increasingly interconnected through technology, and a symptom of the technological age is the creation of a 'commodified homogenous culture'.[66] Rationality is lost as mass culture comes to dominate the 'common sense' of society, leading to an

---

62 *Ibid*, 65.

63 *Ibid*, 108.

64 Habermas (n. 42), 145.

65 J. Habermas, 'The Crisis of the European Union in Light of a Constitutionalization of International Law' (2012) 23 *European Journal of International Law* 335–48, 347.

66 Habermas (n. 54), 75.

increased expression of apathy and disengagement among the people. Popular sovereignty is institutionalised through civil society, wherein free and equal legal persons voluntarily associate in civil society organisations and non-governmental organisations. As distinct institutions from the state and the economic institutional order, they play an important role in challenging the decisions taken by political elites. Reclaiming the discursive space requires the media to be responsive to participatory processes, and if it does so, the role of the media in presenting counter-arguments and opposition to the rationally motivated actions of political elites could prove to be powerful. However, if structural social inequalities exist within a legally defined space, be it a nation-state, region, or interregional arrangement, then the discursive potential is undermined.[67]

ECONOMIC PARTNERSHIP AGREEMENTS: TOWARD INTERREGIONALISM

Conceiving of regions as legal regimes, and using the discourse theory of law to interrogate the EPAs, provides an alternative conceptualisation of regionalism. The rise of RTAs, which are legal regimes and make governance beyond the state possible, mark an interesting shift in the global economy. It is the constitutionalisation of international law,[68] the willingness to be bound as nation-states by a supranational legal order, that enables a common political ideology and economic imperatives to become institutionalised at a regional level. As the EU continues to exhibit strength as a *normative* regional actor, an analysis of *regional governance* becomes increasingly important. The discourse theory can be expanded to analyse regional agency and examine the extent to which such action is legitimate.

If we accept that social relationships are mediated through law, then development is both normatively *constrained* by law but nevertheless realised *through* law. The Habermasian concept of social justice relies on the application of a deliberative democratic process from which the law derives its normativity. However, when the political and economic asymmetry of the EU and ACP is taken into account, our frame of analysis must be reconstructed to accommodate for a discourse that conceives of law as an integrative function that facilitates the diffusion of hegemonic doctrine. Although the study of interregionalism is relatively

67 Habermas (n. 65), 348.
68 *Ibid*, 348.

under-researched, region-to-region interaction appears to be the next logical step in the neoliberal turn of modern society. This is expressed through the transformation of ACP-EU relations, as the non-reciprocal preferences of Lomé have been abandoned in favour of an inclusive trade and development cooperation framework. ACP-EU cooperation under the EPAs is now 'underpinned by a legally binding system' characterised by 'equality', 'ownership of the development strategies', and 'participation'.[69]

Executed at an interregional level, the EPAs are modelled on the Habermasian paradigm of law and democracy that acknowledges 'a political environment guaranteeing peace, security and stability, respect for human rights, democratic principles and the rule of law, and good governance is part and parcel of long-term development.'[70] Collectively, the EPA countries commit to a programme of interregionalism *through* law that gives 'the process of globalisation a stronger social dimension'.[71] Social integration in the new interregional space is encouraged through wider participation beyond state actors:

> apart from central government as the main partner, the partnership shall be open to ACP parliaments, and local authorities in ACP states and different kinds of other actors in order to encourage the integration of all sections of society, including the private sector and civil society organisations, into the mainstream of political, economic, and social life.[72]

Analysing the EPAs through discourse theory provides an opportunity to reflect upon how interregional relationships affect our understanding of modern global society. Moving away from state-centric analyses of rational action, wherein regions are conceived of as functional cooperative frameworks motivated by predominantly materialist interests, this book understands interregional spaces as historically situated and intersubjective transnational societies that are created not only to promote economic liberalisation but with a view to creating a transnational social

---

[69] Article 2 of the 'Partnership Agreement between the members of the African, Caribbean, and Pacific Group of States of the one part, and the European Community of the other part, signed in Cotonou on 23 June 2000', [2000] OJ L317/3 as amended through Decision No. 3/2008 of the ACP-EC Council of Ministers of 15 December 2008, [2008] OJ L352/59 to adopt the revised provisions set out in [2010] OJ L287/3, hereinafter referred to as the 'Cotonou Partnership Agreement 2014' or 'CPA'.

[70] Recital in the Preamble to the Cotonou Partnership Agreement 2014.

[71] *Ibid.*

[72] Article 2 Cotonou Partnership Agreement 2014.

order. Bringing together social orders through the medium of law creates a space that *should* be constituted through the discursive and performative argumentation of all free and equal legal persons within that space.

Formally, the legal architecture of the EPAs set out in the Cotonou Partnership Agreement supports participation and deliberative democracy. Article 8 of the CPA provides that the EPA states 'shall regularly engage in comprehensive, balanced, and deep political dialogue leading to commitments on both sides' which 'shall contribute to peace, security, and stability and promote a stable democratic political environment.' Dialogue should 'focus on specific political issues of mutual concern' but may be 'formal or informal' and conducted 'within and outside the institutional framework.'[73]

Habermas asserts that the codification of rights serve as an example of the moral principles in which the law is grounded. This is particularly evident in the EPAs which are framed around the promotion and protection of human rights within the interregional space. So important is human rights protection that the Cotonou Agreement provides for suspension of concessions under Article 96 where a party to the Agreement fails to comply with the standards of human rights, democracy and good governance underpinning the trade and development framework. To date, this power has been exercised once by the EU against Burundi. As such, the catalogue of rights outlined in the EPAs provide an expression of the justification of the legality of these trade agreements and represent the embodiment of consciousness in these interregional spaces.

Discourse theory requires that the law's normativity derives from the democratic deliberation among free and equal legal individuals. Implicit to this theory are the principles of equality and fairness. At an interregional level, the failure to enable intersubjective deliberation and the substantive inequality between the regional partners exacerbates the deliberative potential of society and weakens the legitimacy of the EPA framework. That the EU is on equal footing with the ACP sub-regions, or any individual state within those regions, is a gross misrepresentation of social reality, leading some to argue that the new trade regime has an 'imperial flavour'.

Analysing the EPAs as a partnership of *unequals* requires an analysis of power in the construction of interregional spaces. This book adopts the Gramscian concept of hegemony which entails the advancement of the interests of the dominant class but through a medium of language that appeals to the interests of individual actors in the general population.

[73] Article 8(4) and (6) Cotonou Partnership Agreement 2014.

Through this smokescreen, the dominant interest is universalised and accepted by society as a 'taken-for granted truth', enabling the hegemonic ideology to be maximised:

> A taken-for granted truth is one that people assume to be so without questioning its empirical or normative validity. A legitimate truth is one that people consciously regard as 'right' in a given context.[74]

Hegemonic ideas are cultivated not only by the international financial institutions, which champion the (post-)Washington Consensus, but also through the various relations between the state and its citizens through social, cultural, educative and informational sites. The role of legal practitioners, who become experts of technical knowledge through the everyday practice of law, is to be responsible for the reproduction of hegemonic argumentation, or doctrine.[75] Buckel and Lescano define *doctrine* as 'the substantive reference framework of various norms and decisions that fixes in time solutions once found and thus makes them reproducible, establishes legal figures, enables systemisation and differentiation, and stores manifold model solutions and bygone conflicts'.[76] Bureaucratic legal institutions, from courts to formal legal education in universities, create an ever-increasing rational-legal order and internal logic. It is the special effect of doctrine, combining both technical procedure and formal reasoning, that not only seals off the legal system from the lifeworld but enables hegemonic discourse to be produced and reproduced in an invisible form:

> Hegemony accordingly becomes significant precisely at the weakest point of the legal system, the fragile claim to legitimacy of its legal entities. Here is the point at which the legal intellectuals have to manage to develop a hegemonic argumentation – that is, one that formulates a 'politico-ethical',

---

[74] T. Hopf, 'Common-Sense Constructivism and Hegemony in World Politics' (2013) 67 *International Organisation* 321.

[75] From a legal perspective, doctrine serves an important purpose in sustaining and reproducing the internal logic of the legal system. Doctrine is an important infrastructure in the institution of the law, providing cohesion, predictability, and articulate principles that can guide future conduct. In one respect, doctrine can serve as points of analogous reference where similar facts arise in future cases. For example, in the common law tradition of the United Kingdom and the United States of America, scholars have argued that the doctrine of *precedent* and *stare decisis* serve the institutional adjudicative function of analogical reasoning.

[76] Buckel and Fischer-Lescano (n. 49), 446.

> albeit symmetrical consensus, a complex 'collective will' on the basis of the current relations of force.[77]

Hegemony is, therefore, not just about coercion because it refers to the 'subscription to a shared and legitimised ideology'[78] found in civil society. In Habermasian terms, the shift toward strategic and normative rationality, expressed through the dominant perspective, leads to a 'colonisation' of the forum in which deliberation should take place:

> The consequence is that relations which should be based on personal commitment, common understanding and involvement, are instead regulated on an impersonal basis, with alienation, disintegration of social responsibility and a decline of legitimacy as results.[79]

Obedience to the hegemonic order derives from an ideological proof of power's necessity or rationality in society. Gramsci posits that for the hegemon to maintain its power it must possess a *philosophy* of its own precipitating at a 'molecular' level all collective expressions of life, including the law.[80] His notion of *common sense* is 'not reducible to popular beliefs' but rather, is illuminated through the everyday lived experiences of individuals which offer a shared, or common, perspective. It follows that any attempt to revolutionise the global order cannot take place in opposition to the common sense of the population.[81] Ideological struggle represents a site of contestation between maintaining the *status quo* of the uncritical philosophy and the search for a transformative discourse that emancipates society from the yokes of hegemony. However, a successful counter-hegemonic discourse requires conditions for responsiveness.

It is herein asserted that hegemonic legal structures articulate a *common sense*, or non-critical philosophy, which is conceived by society as a taken-for granted truth. In doing so, hegemonic law regulates social relations; both the subjectivities of action and the intersubjective relations between actors. If we accept this account of the common-sense articulated through hegemonic legal regimes to be a taken-for granted truth, then legitimate truth will only emerge from a struggle for emancipation from the hegemonic regime.

---

77 *Ibid.*
78 Hopf (n. 74), 320.
79 Eriksen and Weigård (n. 51), 6.
80 Buckel and Fischer-Lescano (n. 49), 442.
81 Hopf (n. 74), 329.

Analysis of the EU-ACP negotiations and the interim and final texts of the EPAs illuminates the politico-ethical framework which renders the production of the hegemonic neoliberal capitalist discourse almost invisible. By shrouding the trade and development agreements in predominantly developmental terms, that is, with an emphasis on the concept of sustainability, the EPAs attempt to mask or conceal the neoliberal spirit in which the trade framework is couched. Rather than bringing together regional spaces through a process embedded in justice and fairness, this book argues that the EPAs represent hegemonic legal regimes oriented by the strategic action of the more powerful member: the European Union. Orienting its social action through its external trade competence, the EU has colonised the areas which should have been open to deliberation.

Deliberative democracy embraces the notion of an inclusive right to participate for all participants in the public sphere. In a contemporary society, and certainly within an interregional space, it is unlikely that all people affected will participate in a process of deliberation. For this reason alone, the limitations of deliberative models that might transcend territorial boundaries must be recognised. Seyla Benhabib overcomes this critical impasse in her assertion that there exists a 'plurality of modes of association' through which each individual person affected by a particular issue can engage in argumentation.[82] Modes of association may include social movements, local organisations, voluntary groups, political parties and trade unions, but this list is by no means exhaustive. Central to Benhabib's conception of deliberation is the notion that these modes of association are interlocking through which an 'anonymous public conversation' can take place.[83] From this perspective, and in keeping with the Habermasian ideal of popular sovereignty, grass roots organisations may play an important role in presenting the consensus achieved through a deliberative conversation in different social spheres. The mass media also assumes a pivotal role in ensuring information is disseminated so that deliberative processes can take place in civil society.

Forms of resistance and revolution are likely to arise in the general population where a discursive fit is not present, as evidenced through the 'Stop the EPAs' campaign. However, political elites may share the common sense non-critical philosophy of the general population and seek to reject the structural imposition of norms that they perceive to be incompatible with their strategic and ethical goals. Resistance from

---

[82] S. Benhabib, 'Toward a Deliberative Model of Democratic Legitimacy' in S. Benhabib (ed.), *Democracy and Difference: Contesting the Boundaries of the Political* (Princeton, NJ: Princeton University Press, 1996), 73–4.

[83] *Ibid.*

political elites, those who negotiate the agreements on behalf of their country, may manifest in a variety of forms from delaying the negotiating process to failure to implement or ratify the agreement. An interesting approach adopted by the ACP countries has been a form of rhetorical action known as 'mimetic challenge'.[84] Through normative argumentation, the ACP countries have harnessed the EU's rhetoric of the EPAs as 'drivers of development' to strategically direct the negotiations toward development objectives. Resistance of this nature has been present in almost every EPA grouping, albeit perhaps of most significance in the CARIFORUM and SADC regions. While the CARIFORUM EPA was the first agreement to be concluded and, indeed, remains the only comprehensive EPA in place, the Five Year Review shows that implementation and ratification has been poor. This, it will be argued, signals a lack of discursive fit between the ideational forces of the EU vis-à-vis the Caribbean states. For SADC, the negotiation process has been drawn-out for over 10 years with a full agreement only concluded in June 2016. It is for this reason that the EU-SADC EPA is used as a case study for this book: this EPA represents one of the most contentious groupings, with the protracted negotiations marking a site of ideological struggle.

CONCLUSION

This chapter has proposed that the law serves an integrative function in institutionalising politics and economics in a social space. It is a fundamental claim of this book that regions are regimes constituted through law. Drawing insights from the rationalist theoretical perspectives, this chapter has shown that regionalism has emerged, in part at least, as a response to the problems facing the multilateral trading system. As regionalism proliferates at an unprecedented rate it is more important now than ever before to critically reflect on the ideational forces that are shaping the new global order. Conceiving of law as a medium of social integration, this chapter has emphasised the importance of discursive spaces through which deliberative and participative processes can take place in order that the law can make a claim to normative validity. With a focus on the various actors involved in the EPA negotiation process, the remaining chapters of this book will demonstrate how these hegemonic legal regimes have presented a discursive space for the ACP countries to challenge the dominant rationality of the EU.

---

[84] S. Hurt, D. Lee and U. Lorenz-Carl, 'The Argumentative Dimension to the EU-Africa EPAs' (2013) 18 *International Negotiation* 67–87.

In the following chapter, the legally institutionalised forms of regionalism under Article XXIV and the Enabling Clause will be examined with reference to the relevant WTO jurisprudence. It will be argued that the dominant members of the WTO have interpreted the ambiguous language of Article XXIV in a legally formalistic way which has enabled them to pursue their trade interests, sometimes aggressively, in RTAs with developing countries. As a result, North-South RTAs as *hegemonic* legal regimes are an increasingly common phenomenon of the global economy. Integrating developing countries into the global economy is a fundamental goal of the WTO but given the depth and breadth of liberalisation pursued by developed countries in North-South RTAs, it is not clear whether these arrangements are an appropriate vehicle to achieve this goal.

2. Regional trade agreements as legal regimes

Described as a *partnership of equals*, and predicated on a model of participative democracy, the Economic Partnership Agreements (EPAs) have been designed as World Trade Organization (WTO) compatible arrangements that should drive sustainable development in the African, Caribbean and Pacific (ACP) countries. As an interregional space defined by the legal rules at the multilateral level, the principle of sustainable development is to be embedded in the economic and political institutional framework. Marking a shift away from purely economic liberalisation between the two regional spaces, the inclusion of development principles adds yet another layer of complexity to the legalisation of regions. Social action in interregional spaces is now strategically oriented toward the achievement of economic growth *and* sustainability. An analysis of regions as legal regimes through which societies are integrated requires a careful examination of the legal rules that govern their creation. Interregional relationships may be defined as 'North-North' wherein all members are classified as developed countries, 'North-South' which comprises an arrangement where there is at least one developed country, and 'South-South' constituting a region of countries classified as developing or Least Developed Countries (LDCs).

Drafted as a flexible provision to allow for broad interpretation, Article XXIV has been interpreted in a rational and legal formal way in the WTO jurisprudence. Legal formalism describes the interpretation of legal instruments as predictable, inflexible and self-contained. It understands the role of law not only as establishing legal doctrines which maintain the 'distribution of economic and political power' but as 'actively promot-[ing] legal redistribution of wealth against the weakest groups in society'.[1] The law can therefore be understood as regulating the behaviour of WTO members while perpetuating pre-existing structural inequalities between those members. In this respect, legal formalism can facilitate,

[1] M. Horwitz, 'The Rise of Legal Formalism' (1975) *The American Journal of Legal History* 251–264.

reinforce, and exacerbate power asymmetry between regional partners. This is antithetical to the discourse theory of law through which law serves as a medium of integration between *equal* partners. Very few would dispute that Article XXIV is a legitimate legal norm, but it is important to note that this provision was agreed upon in 1947. The GATT, now a structural centrepiece of the WTO for trade in goods and tariff liberalisation, was originally created by 23 States, or Contracting Parties as they were then known. It seems acceptable to assume that all Contracting Parties of the GATT at the time of its creation engaged in a discursive process of bargaining to reach a mutual understanding that was rationally accepted by all. However, the GATT has not been revised since 1947 while the WTO's membership has expanded to 164 members. Therefore, the extent to which this legal norm satisfies the discourse principle is questionable.

This chapter argues that the ambiguous judicial interpretation of Article XXIV's definitional boundaries enables dominant members, such as the EU, to adopt a strict interpretation of the provision which favours a 'customs union' approach to regionalism. As a result, the potential for developing countries in North-South Regional Trade Agreements (RTAs) to become marginalised becomes more real. WTO members have expressed reluctance toward the reconceptualisation of XXIV and it seems unlikely that this provision will be renegotiated unless it forms part of a broader discussion on the renegotiation of the GATT. This, too, does not seem to be forthcoming. The first section of this chapter will provide a brief overview of Article XXIV and its internal and external requirements. In the second section, it will be argued that the judicialisation of Article XXIV through the WTO's Dispute Settlement Body (DSB) has crystallised this norm as *rational* and *formal* in character. The third section provides a critical analysis of paragraph 2(c) of the Enabling Clause, the legal norm governing the creation of South-South RTAs. A reconstruction of regionalism in the context of North-South RTAs is offered in the fourth section which reveals them to be *hegemonic* in character. The final section presents a reflection on the participation of WTO Members at the DSB to identify who is shaping the norms at the multilateral level. It will be argued that Article XXIV has become a reified legal norm which serves to reinforce pre-existing structural inequalities in the multilateral system.

CREATING REGIONS: LEGAL BASES

North-North and North-South RTAs are constructed through Article XXIV GATT, a legal norm that has been constitutionalised through the WTO framework. Article XXIV GATT effectively permits derogation from the principle of most favoured nation (MFN) based on the assumption that promoting the regional interdependence of countries, through customs unions and free trade areas, will lead to economic growth. Article XXIV:4 sets out, in purposive language, the motivation for creating regional arrangements:

> [WTO] Members recognise the desirability of increasing freedom of trade by the development, through voluntary agreements, of closer integration between the economies of the countries parties to such agreements. They also recognise that the purpose of a customs union or free trade area should be to facilitate trade between the constituent territories and not to raise barriers to the trade of other Members with such territories.

It is the purpose of regional arrangements to remove internal barriers to trade, but in doing so they should not raise their external tariff to non-members as this could result in trade deflection. This forms the first dimension of the internal requirement for liberalisation, with Article XXIV:5(a) stating:

> With respect to a customs union … the duties and other regulations of commerce imposed at the institution … shall not on the whole be higher or more restrictive than the general incidence of the duties and regulations of commerce applicable in the constituent territories prior to the formation of such union …

A similar provision applies to free trade agreements, with Article XXIV:5(b) stipulating:

> … the duties and other regulations of commerce maintained in each of the constituent territories and applicable at the formation of such free-trade area … shall not be higher or more restrictive than the corresponding duties and other regulations of commerce existing in the same constituent territory prior to the formation of the free-trade area …

The second dimension of the internal requirement states that liberalisation should be implemented within a 'reasonable period of time'. Article XXIV:5(c) GATT requires that 'any interim agreement … shall include a plan and schedule for the formation of such a customs union or free-trade area within a reasonable length of time'. In the Understanding on the

Interpretation of Article XXIV of the GATT 1994 ('the Understanding'), Article 3 states that the reasonable length of time 'should exceed ten years only in exceptional circumstances'. The objective of this time constraint is to minimise the risk of introducing discriminatory preferences for an unlimited duration.[2] To date, only in rare cases has the implementation period exceeded 10 years.

Article XXIV GATT 1994 distinguishes between free trade agreements (FTAs), customs unions (CUs) and interim agreements leading to the creation of either of these. Beyond these forms of regionalism, the GATT does not legally institutionalise any other type of regional integration. This is perhaps unsurprising since, at the time of negotiation of the GATT in 1947, more complex forms of integration were not foreseen. A customs union liberalises trade among the members and maintains a common external tariff with third countries. Defined in Article XXIV:8(a), a customs union requires 'the substitution of a single customs territory for two or more customs territories', so that:

> (i) duties and other restrictive regulations of commerce … are eliminated with respect to … *substantially all the trade* (emphasis added) in products originating in such territories … and,
> (ii) … substantially the same duties and regulations of commerce are applied by each of the members of the union to the trade territories not included in the union.

Article XXIV:8 therefore has an internal and external trade element. Internally, the Members must agree to liberalise 'substantially all trade' among each other under paragraph 8(i), while externally they must apply 'substantially the same' measures to third parties under paragraph 8(ii). Paragraph 8 of Article XXIV is the source of most criticism since it provides the substantive internal requirements for creating a regional trade agreement.[3] As the language of paragraph 8 does not explicitly state

---

[2] D. Das, *Regionalism in Global Trade* (Cheltenham, UK and Northampton, MA, USA: Edward Elgar, 2004), 99. However, Article 3 of the Understanding is vague and does not elucidate what qualifies as 'exceptional' circumstances. Furthermore, there has yet to be a dispute settlement case which raises the 'exceptional circumstances' issue and as a result the interpretation of this provision remains ambiguous.

[3] K. Dam, 'Regional Economic Arrangements and the GATT: The Legacy of a Misconception' (1963) 30 *The University of Chicago Law Review* 615–665; J. Mathis, *Regional Trade Agreements in the GATT/WTO: Article XXIV and the Internal Trade Requirement* (The Hague: TMC Asser Press, 2002); J. Bhagwati, *Termites in the Trading System: How Preferential Agreements Undermine Free*

what constitutes 'substantially all trade', members have been uncertain of the legal parameters of this requirement. Historically, the EU proposed a benchmark figure of 80 per cent liberalisation as satisfying this requirement during its dialogue with the Overseas Association.[4] Today, the EU has continued to use the 80–90 per cent bracket as its interpretation of 'substantially all trade', as evidenced in the EPAs, albeit this liberalisation will be progressive and asymmetric. This means that *overall* trade between the parties will be liberalised at a rate of 80–90 per cent.[5] Australia, on the other hand, proposes that 95 per cent of tariff lines should be liberalised in order to satisfy the 'substantially all trade' requirement.[6] In the CARIFORUM EPA, the CARIFORUM States have committed, as a regional bloc, to liberalisation of 61 per cent of the value of EU imports over a 10-year period, 82.7 per cent over 15 years, and 86.9 per cent over 25 years.[7] This brings the total liberalisation of imports from the EU to an impressive 90.2 per cent. For the ECOWAS countries liberalisation of products will be at a rate of 75 per cent over 20 years, while the SADC countries will collectively liberalise approximately 80 per cent over the same time period.[8] These diverging approaches demonstrate that there is no consensus as to what the concept of 'substantially all trade' requires in practice.

If Article XXIV is interpreted in light of its Understanding, it seems to suggest that sectoral exclusion is not permitted. The Preamble of the Understanding recognises the contribution to the expansion of world trade where:

Trade (Oxford: Oxford University Press, 2008); J.T. Gathii, *African Regional Trade Agreements as Legal Regimes* (Cambridge: Cambridge University Press, 2011).

4 Mathis (n. 3), 67.

5 Traidcraft, 'Economic Partnership Agreements: Building or shattering African regional integration?' Traidcraft Report (May 2007) accessed 9 December 2016 at http://www.traidcraft.co.uk/international_development/policy_work/policy_resources/policy_reports, 29.

6 See WTO Document, Communication from Australia, Addendum, WT/REG/W/22/Add.1, 24 April 1998.

7 DG Europeaid, 'Monitoring the Implementation and Results of the CARIFORUM-EU EPA Agreement', Final Report, European Commission, EUROPEAID/129783/C/SER/multi Lot 1: Studies and Technical Assistance in All Sectors (September 2014), 71.

8 I. Ramdoo, 'ECOWAS and SADC Economic Partnership Agreements: A Comparative Analysis', ECDPM Discussion Paper No. 165 (September 2014) accessed 9 December 2016 at www.ecdpm.org/publications.

> ... the elimination between the constituent territories of duties and other restrictive measures of commerce extends to all trade, and diminished *if any major sector of trade is excluded.* (emphasis added)

However, where a regional arrangement may affect a politically sensitive sector, such as agriculture, it may be excluded from the agreement altogether. This is the case in the EU, where the Common Agricultural Policy (CAP) ensures protection of the generous subsidies offered to the EU's agricultural farmers. If sectoral exclusion is in violation of Article XXIV, this could leave the CAP in a legitimacy crisis.

The requirement under paragraph 8(ii) indicates that customs unions must adopt a common external tariff (CET). When creating a customs union, the CET may be negotiated in one of three ways: increasing all duties; increasing some duties and decreasing some duties; and, decreasing all duties.[9] Under the framework of Article XXIV, customs unions with a CET that has involved lowering all duties would qualify as a WTO compatible RTA. The situation becomes more complex when trying to ascertain whether the CET which has involved the increase and decrease of duties complies with Article XXIV.

By comparison, a FTA liberalises trade among members but each member can maintain its own external barriers to third parties. Article XXIV:8(b) defines a FTA as:

> ... a group of two or more customs territories in which the duties and other restrictive regulations of commerce ... are eliminated on substantially all the trade between the constituent territories in products originating in such territories.

Unlike a customs union there is no harmonised external policy so the defining feature of a FTA will be rules of origin (ROO). ROO are policy instruments used to identify which products should attract tariffs based on their origin, or locations of production. From a Vinerian perspective, ROO could play an important role in trade creation within an economic cooperation arrangement. ROO confer preferences by differentiating products on the basis of their origin. Determining the origin of a product is critical for members of a RTA to ensure that trade deflection is reduced. Distinguishing between the geographic and economic source of a product has become an important factor in determining the origin of a product. Geographic nationality describes the country from which the final product is exported. ROO go beyond simply determining the

[9] Dam (n. 3), 630.

geographic nationality of a product and determine the 'economic nationality' of a particular product. In determining the economic nationality, ROO describe the minimum conditions of processing and/or transformation locally for a product to be classified as originating within a particular country.[10]

ROO act as an important market access tool for defining the scope of a FTA because preferential treatment only applies to products originating in the member states of a regional arrangement.[11] Since ROO differentiate products according to whether they qualify for preferential access or MFN, they are significant mechanisms for regulating the movement of goods in the international system.[12] However, the technical rules governing ROO can take different forms and may vary across RTAs.[13] In today's global economy, it is likely that a final product will consist of inputs from various different countries as manufacturers seek out the most competitive prices. With different terms of trade and criss-crossing ROO the cartography of regional integration is become increasingly indecipherable. On the one hand, FTAs liberalise the tariffs between trading partners within a defined context. On the other hand, 'made to measure' ROO restrict the capacity for free trade by imposing onerous conditions

---

[10] E. Naumann, 'Rules of Origin under EPAs: Key Issues and New Directions' in S. Bilal and R. Grynberg (eds), *Navigating New Waters: A Reader on ACP-EU Trade Relations* (London: Commonwealth Secretariat, 2007), 305.

[11] J. Viner, *The Customs Union Issue* (Carnegie Endowment for International Peace, 1950), 19.

[12] M. Hirsch, 'Rules of Origin as Trade or Foreign Policy Instruments? The European Union Policy on Products Manufactured in the Settlements in the West Bank and the Gaza Strip' (2002) 26 *Fordham International Law Journal* 572–94, 575.

[13] Article 9(b) WTO Agreement on Rules of Origin provides that where a product is wholly produced, or 'wholly obtained' in a particular country or region then this product is considered to have originated therein. For non-preferential ROO, origin is also conferred on the country where the last 'substantial transformation' took place. Generally speaking, where a product is not wholly obtained in a particular country it should undergo a process or processes of substantial transformation in that country so as to qualify as originating therein. Substantial transformation will therefore apply to products or inputs obtained from a third country. Any product or input originating within the country or region of origin does not need to undergo processing to qualify for preferential access to the country of destination.

for product transformation. Naturally, producers often lobby their governments for restrictive ROO over products that are of most concern to them because they want to protect their industry.[14]

Article XXIV does not make provision for special and differential treatment (SDT) and consequently all negotiating members are treated as economically homogenous. The absence of SDT can be explained, in part because this framework of preferences was not introduced into the multilateral trading system until 1979, and in part because the GATT has not been revised since 1947. In addition to Article XXIV, the Enabling Clause provides another institutional exception to the GATT rule of MFN in which SDT is codified.

THE ENABLING CLAUSE: SOUTH-SOUTH COOPERATION

An alternative means through which regions can be legally constructed is found in the Enabling Clause. Under this legal framework, developing countries are granted SDT in order to assist the integration of these countries into the multilateral trading system. Paragraph 1 of the Enabling Clause stipulates:

> ... contracting parties may accord differential and more favourable treatment to developing countries, without according such treatment to other contracting parties.

A vast amount of literature is dedicated to the broader discussion of special and differential treatment (SDT)[15] for developing countries but the same cannot be said for the legal framework permitting South-South regional cooperation. The Enabling Clause establishes a different regime

---

[14] A. Krueger, 'Are Preferential Trade Agreements Trade Liberalising or Protectionist?' (1999) 13(4) *The Journal of Economic Perspectives* 105–24, 112.

[15] Some notable contributions to the field include: U. Ewelukwa, 'Special and Differential Treatment in International Trade Law: A Concept in Search of Content' (2003) 79 *North Dakota Law Review* 831–78, 831; D. Alessandrini, *Developing Countries and the Multilateral Trade Regime* (Oxford: Hart, 2010); A. Jara, 'The WTO and International Trade Law After Doha: Where Do We Go From Here?' (2007) 25 *Berkeley Journal of International Law* 384–94; A. Oyejide, 'Development Dimensions in Multilateral Trade Negotiations' in M. Moore (ed.), *Doha and Beyond: The Future of the Multicultural Trading System* (Cambridge: Cambridge University Press, 2004); C. Ochieng, 'The EU-ACP Economic Partnership Agreements and the "Development Question": Constraints

for creating preferential agreements between developing countries. Paragraph 2(c) of the Enabling Clause, the legal basis for RTAs among developing countries, states:

> The provisions of paragraph 1 apply to the ... regional or global arrangements entered into amongst less-developed contracting parties for the mutual reduction or elimination of tariffs and, in accordance with the criteria or conditions which may be prescribed by the CONTRACTING PARTIES, for the mutual reduction or elimination of non-tariff measures, on products imported from one another.

Unlike Article XXIV, there is no requirement that the parties must eliminate duties nor must they liberalise *substantially all trade* within a *reasonable period of time*. Most importantly, there is no requirement that liberalisation should be *reciprocal*. Thus, the provisions for creating South-South regional cooperation agreements are far less prescriptive than Article XXIV. The threshold for satisfying the conditions under paragraph 2(c) is clearly much lower than that under Article XXIV. However, the Enabling Clause does introduce a process of 'graduation' under Article 7, whereby developing countries through 'the progressive development of their economies and improvement in their trade situation ... would accordingly expect to participate more fully in the framework of rights and obligations under the General Agreement'. Once developing countries have reached a certain level of development they graduate from SDT and would then be subject to the conditions of Article XXIV.

The relationship between Article XXIV and the Enabling Clause is virtually absent in the case law and the literature, but it is certainly worth some attention for the purposes of this inquiry.[16] An analysis of the point at which these two legal bases meet will be presented later in this chapter in the context of the *Argentina-Footwear* and *Brazil-Retreaded Tyres* cases, which concern the compatibility of MERCOSUR, a regional

and Opportunities Posed by Article XXIV and Special and Differential Treatment Provisions of the WTO' (2007) 10 *Journal of International Economic Law* 363–95.

[16] For a thought-provoking and insightful discussion of the relationship of Article XXIV and the Enabling Clause, see S.J. Alavi, 'Regional Trade Agreements among Developing Countries: Enabling Clause Revisited' [unpublished] accessed 9 December 2016 at http://papers.ssrn.com/sol3/papers.cfm?abstract_id=1737233. The author's permission to cite work has been obtained.

arrangement notified under paragraph 2(c) of the Enabling Clause, with Article XXIV.[17]

INSTITUTIONAL FRAMEWORK FOR ASSESSING COMPATIBILITY

Institutionally, regional arrangements are subject to scrutiny by the Committee on Regional Trade Agreements (CRTA), the Committee for Trade and Development (CTD) and the Dispute Settlement Body (DSB). The assessment of whether a particular RTA is compatible with Article XXIV falls to the CRTA, while those arrangements notified under the Enabling Clause will be reviewed by the CTD. Where a complaint has been brought before the DSB that raises an issue relating to the interpretive dimension of these legal bases, the Panel and/or Appellate Body may provide a recommendation.

In 1996, the CRTA was established by the WTO General Council, for the purpose of assessing the compatibility of individual RTAs with Article XXIV and more broadly, to evaluate the systemic effects of regional arrangements for the multilateral trading system.[18] The Committee replaced approximately 25 working parties that were previously created to monitor RTAs.[19] Perceived to be relatively ineffective, the CRTA was subsequently reformed in 2006, following the adoption of the WTO General Council Decision for a Transparency Mechanism on RTAs.[20] Under this procedure, RTAs are notified to the Committee of Trade in Goods (CTG), which adopts the terms of reference and then transfers the agreement to the CRTA for examination.[21] As part of the improved transparency framework, members must make a factual presentation to the WTO Secretariat with relevant data, including details of the

---

17 While MERCOSUR was notified to the CRTA under the Enabling Clause, it has also been examined under Article XXIV in the *Argentina-Footwear* and *Brazil-Retreaded Tyres* cases.

18 WTO 'Work of the Committee on Regional Trade Agreements (CRTA)' (undated) accessed 9 December 2016 at http://www.wto.org/english/tratop_e/region_e/regcom_e.htm.

19 M. Mashayekhi and T. Ito (eds), 'Multilateralism and Regionalism: The New Interface', UNCTAD Report (2004) (UNCTAD/DITC/TNCD/2004/7), 43 accessed 9 December 2016 at http://unctad.org/en/Docs/ditctncd20047_en.pdf.

20 WTO General Council Decision on a Transparency Mechanism for Regional Trade Agreements of 14 December 2006 WT/L/671.

21 All RTAs relating to trade in services are notified to the Council for Trade in Services (CTS).

RTA's implementation timetable, within 10 weeks of notification for an Article XXIV arrangement and within 20 weeks for a regional arrangement notified under the Enabling Clause.[22] The purpose of the examination of RTAs is to ensure transparency and to enable members to evaluate the agreements consistency with a generally accepted understanding of Article XXIV, if indeed there is agreement on the interpretation of this provision. According to the information publicly available,[23] the lack of consensus among members regarding the process for examination through the CRTA has meant no examination report has been finalised since 1995.

The Transparency Decision operates on a provisional basis and will be reviewed at the conclusion of the Doha Round.[24] At this stage, it is expected that the Transparency Decision will become a permanent mechanism.[25] Although the CRTA was originally intended to evaluate the compatibility of an RTA with Article XXIV, the procedure has changed in light of the transparency mechanism. As a result, it seems likely that in the future this will shift 'the onus for any challenge to a regional trade agreement to dispute settlement'.[26] Concerns have been raised by WTO Members regarding the rising number of RTAs and the role of the CRTA in ensuring the compatibility of these agreements with the legal framework.[27] The CRTA has experienced difficulties adhering to its work programme as a result of 'delays in the receipt of statistical data from parties, data discrepancies in Members' submissions, and delays in the receipt of comments from parties'.[28] Several developing countries have raised concerns with the role of the CRTA and believe that it undermines the CTD, which has the exclusive mandate to focus on and coordinate

---

[22] WTO General Council Decision on a Transparency Mechanism for Regional Trade Agreements of 14 December 2006 WT/L/671 (18 December 2006), para 8.

[23] WTO, 'Work of the Committee on Regional Trade Agreements (CRTA)' (n. 18).

[24] *Ibid*, paras 22–23.

[25] WTO Press Release 'General Council Establishes Transparency Mechanism for Regional Trade Agreements' (15 December 2006) accessed 9 December 2016 at http://www.wto.org/english/news_e/news06_e/rta_15dec06_e.htm.

[26] *Ibid.*

[27] WTO Committee on Regional Trade Agreements, 'Note on the Meeting of 20 March 2012', Sixty-fourth Session of the CRTA, WT/REG/M/64 (16 April 2012).

[28] WTO Secretariat, 'Report (2012) of the Committee on Regional Trade Agreements to the General Council', 26 November 2012 WT/REG/22.

work on development in the WTO.[29] In light of this function, the CTD also has a role in considering the systemic issues of regionalism.

In addition to the CRTA and CTD, the compatibility of individual measures of RTAs have been assessed by the WTO's judicial mechanism, the DSB. Although Article XXIV:7 states that RTAs must be notified to the WTO, no RTA has to date been explicitly approved as being WTO consistent.[30] This is probably linked to the fact that the WTO operates on the basis of consensus and RTA parties will generally refuse to make any changes demanded by non-RTA members to the notified RTA.[31] As a result, the DSB has been used as a discursive space to address the compatibility of a RTA where a measure is challenged and Article XXIV. Having recourse to the DSB provides a safety-net for members, allowing them to bargain safe in the knowledge that they can challenge adverse trade provisions in the future if necessary. Institutional rules and norms are therefore an extremely important part of the system, ensuring that members respect, and comply with, the 'self-enforcing' trade provisions.

Although the international trade rules are contractual in nature, representing legal obligations between the members, they are not directly enforceable. The DSB is the only adjudication system of the WTO which issues binding decisions on the scope and nature of the trade rules. The decision of the Appellate Body *cannot* be contested. While a formal system of precedent does not exist, there appears to be a process of analogous reasoning adopted by the Panel and Appellate Body in similar cases, which in turn should not only deter countries from raising similar complaints but encourages members to adopt policies in line with previous recommendations. It is the aim of the DSB to expediently resolve disputes arising between the members. Special rules apply to developing countries where they are engaged in a dispute with a developing country member. In such a case, the developing country member may request that a panel can consist of at least one developing

---

[29] See the submission of India in WTO Committee on Regional Trade Agreements (n. 27).

[30] Ensuring conformity with the restrictive requirements of Article XXIV has not been forthcoming by WTO members and it is questionable whether many of the existing regional agreements actually comply with Article XXIV in the strict sense. See: World Bank, *Trade Blocks: A World Bank Policy Research Report* (Oxford: Oxford University Press, 2000), 109.

[31] G. Marceau and J. Wyatt, 'Dispute Settlement Regimes Intermingled: Regional Trade Agreements and the WTO' (2010) 1 *Journal of International Dispute Settlement* 67–95, 81.

country panelist.[32] It is not the purpose of this book to scrutinise the internal dynamics of the dispute settlement mechanism but it is suffice to say that the Dispute Settlement Understanding (DSU), the text which sets out the rules of procedure, aims to create a system that takes into account the special needs of developing countries and LDCs.[33]

With the modification of the dispute settlement procedures, we have seen a shift towards the legalisation of trade rules. The reconstruction of the DSB with the creation of the WTO was 'intended to strengthen the legitimacy of the substantive rights created by the WTO Agreements'.[34] In a sense, the DSB represents an equilibrium institution in the cooperative game since it governs what happens when a member violates the terms of trade. The dispute settlement system basically implies that a member may breach WTO rules, compensate the affected members and remain in the multilateral community. In some cases, it may be cheaper in the long-run to protect the domestic industry by deliberately breaching the rules and offer compensation instead. Compensation is only paid to the extent that it restores the balance to the position prior to the harm. It therefore operates as a 'proportionality principle' and by limiting the costs of compensation, increases the stability of the system.[35]

That is not to say that the dispute settlement system is not open to abuse. While this quasi-judicial mechanism should clarify 'grey' areas and circumscribe opportunistic behaviour,[36] the final section of this chapter will illustrate how the discursive space of the DSB is being used more frequently by some members than others. It is a key contention of this book that the use of the DSB by dominant members leads to a legalisation of legal rules which have been shaped by, and reflect, the interests of those dominant members. This is particularly evident in relation to the interpretation, and formalisation, of Article XXIV as a legal norm.

---

32 Article 8.10 WTO Dispute Settlement Understanding.

33 Article 24 WTO Dispute Settlement Understanding provides that LDCs will receive special treatment by the DSB and that Members should 'restrain' from raising a complaint against a LDC unless absolutely necessary.

34 M. Clough, 'The WTO Dispute Settlement System – A Practitioner Perspective' (2000) 24 *Fordham International Law Journal* 252–74, 252.

35 B.P. Rosendorff, 'Stability and Rigidity: Politics and Design of the WTO's Dispute Settlement Procedure' (2005) 99(3) *American Political Science Review* 389–400, 391.

36 *Ibid*, 389.

ARTICLE XXIV AS A FORMAL LEGAL NORM

From the jurisprudence three main issues relating to Article XXIV and the position of developing countries in North-South RTAs can be identified. First, under certain conditions Article XXIV may be invoked as a *defence* when members forming a RTA adopt otherwise WTO-inconsistent external measures with third parties. Second, the internal requirement to liberalise 'substantially all trade' has been interpreted in a neutral way rendering the provision ambiguous and uncertain. Finally, the treatment of developing countries in North-South RTAs and the potential for dual notification (under Article XXIV and the Enabling Clause) has been explored.

Turkey – Textiles

The legal scope of Article XXIV was first examined in the 1999 *Turkey – Textiles* dispute[37] in relation to external measures. This was the first opportunity for the DSB to interpret Article XXIV and its internal dimension.[38] As a preliminary issue, Turkey raised concerns that the panel lacked jurisdiction to undertake a compatibility assessment of individual or several measures with Article XXIV. In response, the panel asserted that the legal basis for invoking the dispute settlement system in order to challenge measures implemented during the creation of a customs union which is found in Article XXIV:12 GATT:

> The provisions of Articles XXII and XXIII of GATT 1994 as elaborated and applied by the Dispute Settlement Understanding may be invoked with respect to *any matters arising from the application* of those provisions of Article XXIV relating to customs unions, free-trade areas or interim agreement leading to the formation of a customs union or free trade area.

On the basis of this paragraph the panel determined that it had the jurisdiction to examine 'the WTO compatibility of one of several measures' arising under Article XXIV.[39] The panel noted that while members can certainly form regional arrangements in line with WTO

---

[37] *Turkey – Textiles*, Panel Report, *Turkey – Restrictions on Imports of Textile and Clothing Products* WT/DS34/R, adopted 19 November 1999.

[38] The GATT Panels had considered the scope of Article XXIV to a limited extent in *EEC – Bananas II*, GATT Panel Report, *EEC – Import Regime for Bananas*, 11 February 1994, unadopted, DS38/R/446.

[39] *Turkey – Resrictions on Imports of Textile and Clothing Products* WT/DS34/R Panel Report (19 November 1999), para. 9.5.

rules, measures under those agreements may nevertheless be scrutinised by the DSB where appropriate. The Panel set out its interpretive framework for analysing Article XXIV in accordance with Article 3.2 of the DSU. This requires that the Panel and Appellate Body interpret Article XXIV in line with Articles 31 and 32 of the Vienna Convention on the Law of Treaties. On the interpretation of treaty provisions, Article 31 of the Vienna Convention on the Law of Treaties provides that 'a treaty shall be interpreted in good faith in accordance with the ordinary meaning to be given to the terms of the treaty in their context and in the light of its object and purpose'. The Panel and Appellate Body are committed to interpreting all WTO provisions, including Article XXIV, in light of their historical context, object and purpose. Given the nature of WTO agreements as 'self-enforcing', it is all the more important that the DSB gives the legal provisions their 'full meaning' so as to ensure that members can effectively apply these rules in the future. However, the extent of investigation is limited to 'measures' under a regional arrangement and not the compatibility of the entire agreement with Article XXIV, which should remain the task of the CRTA.

Article XXIV: external measures

The panel started its assessment of the compatibility of external measures (quantitative restrictions) through a deconstructive analysis of Article XXIV:4. This paragraph was considered to be the most important within Article XXIV, as the 'conditional right to form a regional trade agreement has to be understood and interpreted within the parameters set out in paragraph 4'.[40] Noting the spread of regional arrangements and taking into account its historical origins, the panel submitted that 'the wording of Article XXIV is of *sub-optimal clarity* and has been the object of various, sometimes opposing, views among individual contracting parties and Members'.[41]

The panel interpreted paragraph 5 to mean that parties may introduce new measures ('other regulations of commerce') provided that the overall incidence of such measures is not higher after the creation of a RTA. In its argument to the panel, Turkey proposed that paragraph 5 was effectively the 'derogation clause' for members of regional arrangements to implement measures that were otherwise inconsistent with the GATT in order to permit the formation of that regional arrangement. Reading the paragraph in light of the Understanding on Article XXIV, the panel

40 *Ibid*, para. 9.105.
41 *Ibid*, para. 9.97. Emphasis added.

interpreted paragraph 5 as providing an 'economic test' for assessing the compatibility of a customs union with Article XXIV.[42] In doing so, all duties and regulations existing in one or more of the members must be taken into account. Although the panel did not provide an exhaustive list of what measures are to be considered 'other regulations of commerce' for the purposes of paragraph 4, it noted:

> ... the ordinary meaning of the terms 'other regulations of commerce' could be understood to include any regulation having an impact on trade (such as measures in the fields covered by WTO rules e.g. sanitary and phytosanitary, customs valuation, anti-dumping, technical barriers to trade; as well as any other trade-related domestic regulation, e.g. environmental standards, export credit schemes). Given the dynamic nature of regional trade agreements, we consider that this is an evolving concept.[43]

In relation to the scope of paragraph 5, the panel stressed that the provision neither permits nor prohibits the adoption of individual measures that may be more restrictive on the formation of a customs union. Rather, the language of Article XXIV:5(a) is 'general and not prescriptive' which means that 'the effects of the resulting trade measures and policies of the new regional arrangement shall not be more trade restrictive, *overall*, than were the constituent countries previous trade policies'.[44] The panel found that paragraph 5 does not act as the legal basis for implementing external measures such as quantitative restriction (QR), which are otherwise inconsistent with WTO provisions. Rather, it falls within the mandate of the CRTA to consider the overall incidence of duties and regulations when conducting a compatibility assessment.

Defining substantially all trade

Finally, the panel considered the legal scope of Article XXIV:8 and the 'substantially all trade' requirement. Turkey submitted that paragraph 8(a)(i) required it to extend to third countries the same regulations of commerce as those applied by the EU to the same third countries.[45] India, on the other hand, argued that paragraph 8 merely sets out the requirements that must be fulfilled in order to become a customs union and when read with paragraph 4, shows that the purpose of a customs

---

[42] *Ibid*, para. 9.120. Here, the Panel identifies the role of the CRTA as being responsible for the task of conducting an overall assessment of the compatibility of whole agreements with Article XXIV.

[43] *Ibid*, para. 9.120.

[44] *Ibid*, para. 9.121. Emphasis added.

[45] *Ibid*, para. 9.135.

union is not to raise barriers to third countries.[46] Having considered each parties' argument, the Panel concluded that Article XXIV:8 has an inherent 'flexibility' that allows for harmonious interpretation where the provision may conflict with another WTO provision. Furthermore, the panel recognised that the 'substantially all trade' requirement includes both qualitative and quantitative components.[47]

The panel found that each constituent member of a regional arrangement may apply or adopt different policies to regulate trade vis-à-vis third countries and that this does not contradict Article XXIV:8. In conclusion, neither paragraph 5 nor paragraph 8 permits the introduction of WTO inconsistent measures.[48] In the panel's interpretation of Article XXIV, the only WTO principle that may be derogated from is MFN. Following on from the panel's interpretation of Article XXIV, the Appellate Body examined the relationship between the paragraphs of Article XXIV and in particular paragraphs 4, 5 and 8. In *Turkey – Textiles*, the Appellate Body analysed the chapeau of paragraph 5 and noted that under certain conditions Article XXIV may permit the use of otherwise WTO inconsistent measures on the formation of a regional arrangement.[49] As such, the Appellate Body introduced a two-tier 'necessity test' that must be fulfilled in order to demonstrate the necessity of violating WTO provisions. First the measure must be introduced upon the formation of a customs union. Second, the Appellate Body found that a measure that is inconsistent with other GATT principles will be justified under Article XXIV where it is introduced upon the formation of a customs union and 'only to the extent that the formation of the customs union would be prevented if the introduction of the measure were not allowed'.[50] This means that Article XXIV can be invoked as a *defence* to justify a measure that is otherwise inconsistent with GATT provisions providing that it satisfies the above criteria.

The potential impact of the 'necessity test' for developing countries in North-South RTAs is of particular interest to this book. Victor Mosoti argues that the Appellate Body's restrictive linguistic interpretation of Article XXIV:5, in limiting the extent to which concessions granted as part of RTA formation can be defended, 'imperils the whole regional

---

46 *Ibid*, para. 9.136.

47 *Ibid*, para. 9.148.

48 *Ibid*, para. 9.208.

49 *Turkey – Restrictions on Imports of Textile and Clothing Products*, Report of the Appellate Body, WT/DS34/AB/R (22 October 1999), para. 58.

50 *Ibid*, para. 46.

enterprise'.[51] Regionalism, as promoted through the EPAs, is articulated as a development strategy for ACP countries. However, the WTO 'review' of these RTAs may find them to be inconsistent with Article XXIV. If that is the case, then the argument in support of regionalism as a development strategy will become obsolete. While there are certainly merits in Mosoti's concerns, this logic could apply to any existing regional arrangement, including the EU. In short, the problem relates to the ambiguous definition of Article XXIV elucidated through the jurisprudence, which therefore opens up the provision to abuse by more dominant trade members, like the EU which excludes agriculture from its RTAs. Excluding agriculture was symbolic of the GATT, which was essentially a 'rich countries' club' that served the interests of powerful members at the expense of weaker members.[52] In a similar vein, the EPAs provide that 'sensitive' products may be excluded from the agreement. This is common practice for RTAs and, provided that overall 90 per cent of trade is liberalised, does not seem to go against a literal interpretation of Article XXIV. It does, however, seem to go against the spirit of the provision as it does not explicitly provide for this type of behaviour.

Although the substantially all trade requirement was not directly at issue in the case, the Appellate Body nevertheless made some notable comments on the provision. It explained that 'substantially all trade' is 'not the same as *all* the trade, and … is something considerably more than *some* of the trade'.[53] The substantive internal requirement to liberalise 'substantially all trade' within a 'reasonable period' of time is particularly problematic given the fact that Article XXIV does not explicate a definitive meaning of the internal requirement. However, the Appellate Body cautions that:

> … the degree of 'flexibility' that sub-paragraph 8(a)(i) allows is limited by the requirement that 'duties and other restrictive regulations of commerce' be 'eliminated with respect to substantially all' internal trade.[54]

---

[51] V. Mosoti, 'Africa in the First Decade of WTO Dispute Settlement' (2006) 9 *Journal of International Economic Law* 427–53, 449.

[52] K. Jones, *The Doha Blues* (New York and Oxford: Oxford University Press, 2010), 25. Admittedly, the WTO framework goes some way in trying to redress the weaknesses of the GATT particularly with regards to the dispute settlement system.

[53] Appellate Body Report, *Turkey-Textiles* (n. 49), para. 48.

[54] *Ibid.*

Historically, there has been little interpretation of the core criteria set out in Article XXIV and members have entered regional arrangements with no clear criteria by which to ascertain whether their RTA is, *strictly speaking*, WTO compliant. James Mathis, who has written extensively on Article XXIV, submits that the *Turkey – Textiles* case has significant institutional implications since the task of establishing what constitutes a WTO compliant regional arrangement will now fall to either a panel or the Appellate Body.[55] This is one of the unforeseen side-effects of the failure of multilateralism for the drafters of the GATT would not have expected such a task to fall to the DSB. Arguably, this task should fall exclusively to the CRTA.

Argentina – Footwear

Article XXIV was again drawn into question in the *Argentina – Footwear* case.[56] This case concerns the relationship between Article XXIV and other WTO Agreements, in particular the Safeguards Agreement.[57] In this case, the EC brought a complaint against Argentina's application of provisional and definitive safeguard measures on imports of footwear. Although dealing primarily with safeguards, this case drew into question the use of Article XXIV as a defence since the footnote to Article 2.1 of the Safeguards Agreement permits countries to exclude its fellow customs union members from the application of the safeguard.[58]

Footnote to Article 2.1 states:

> A customs union may apply a safeguard measure as a single unit or on behalf of a Member State. When a customs union applies a safeguard measure as a single unit, all the requirements for the determination of serious injury or threat thereof under this Agreement shall be based on the conditions existing

---

[55] J. Mathis, 'The "Legalisation" of GATT Article XXIV – Can Foes Become Friends?' in K. Bagwell and P. Mavroidis (eds), *Preferential Trade Agreements: A Law and Economics Analysis* (Cambridge: Cambridge University Press, 2011), 36.

[56] *Argentina – Safeguard Measures on Imports of Footwear*, Report of the Appellate Body, WT/DS121/AB/R (14 December 1999).

[57] The relationship between Article XXIV and the Agreement on Safeguards was also considered in the *US-Line Pipe* case. See generally: *United States – Definitive Safeguard Measures on Imports from Circular Wielded Carbon Quality Line Pipe from Korea*, Report of the Appellate Body, WT/DS202/AB/R (15 February 2002).

[58] Argentina applied 'minimum specific import duties' (known as 'derechos de exportaci6n especificos mínimos' or 'DIEMS') on footwear, textiles and apparels originating in third countries.

> in the customs union as a whole. When a safeguard measure is applied on behalf of a Member State, all the requirements for the determination of serious injury or threat thereof shall be based on the conditions existing in that Member State and the measure shall be limited to that Member State. Nothing in this Agreement prejudges the interpretation of the relationship between Article XIX and paragraph 8 of Article XXIV of GATT 1994.

Imports from MERCOSUR countries were not subject to the safeguard measure. In April 1998, the EU requested consultations with Argentina on its use of safeguards under Article XIX GATT 1994. The EU argued that Argentina's investigation into the use of safeguards on the imports of footwear did not prove any increase in imports, injury or causality and therefore the use of these measures violated the GATT. When challenged on this, Argentina sought to invoke Article XXIV as a defence. In the Panel report, Argentina argued that there has been no definitive interpretation of the relationship between Article XIX and Article XXIV GATT, and it is not the role of the panel to 'impose a single "methodology" as proposed by the [EU]'.[59] Furthermore, Argentina criticised the EU's formalistic approach to the text asserting that the EU's argument was based 'not a criterion of *legality* but on a criterion of logic'.[60]

Ultimately, the Appellate Body found that Article XXIV was not relevant to the material facts of the case since Argentina had not sought to explicitly invoke the Article XXIV defence to justify the use of the safeguard. In this case, Argentina was critical of the dispute settlement mechanism. Argentina argued:

> … one cannot read into the text of a treaty anything that the treaty itself does not spell out, still less in cases where a treaty explicitly states that there is no common interpretation or that the scope of the relationship between two provisions cannot be prejudged.[61]

This dialogue is informative and shows how members have used the DSB as a discursive space to challenge the normative behaviour of the more powerful States. It illustrates the problems associated with the neutrality of Article XXIV and how the lack of a common interpretation, or social consensus among WTO members, can foster further uncertainty and unpredictability. Another interesting angle to this dispute was that the status of MERCOSUR as a customs union was challenged by the EU,

---

[59] *Argentina – Safeguard Measures on Imports of Footwear* Panel Report WT/DS121/R (25 June 1999), para. 5.80.

[60] *Ibid*, para. 5.84.

[61] *Ibid*, para. 5.86.

and Indonesia as a third party, before the panel. Indonesia argued the Article XXIV did not apply to MERCOSUR, since the Members of this customs union had not notified it under GATT 1947 or GATT 1994.[62] As MERCOSUR is notified under the Enabling Clause, it seems improbable that a defence under Article XXIV would be successful.

Brazil – Retreaded Tyres

In *Brazil – Retreaded Tyres*,[63] the EU brought a claim against Brazil in relation to certain measures imposed by Brazil on the importation and marketing of retreaded (used) tyres. The measures included an import prohibition and associated fines on imported retreaded tyres. Brazil provided an exception to this rule for retreaded tyres originating in MERCOSUR states and invoked Article XXIV as a defence for the exemption. The EU sought to challenge the legality of this defence. The EU claimed that Brazil had failed to show that MERCOSUR satisfied the 'substantially all trade' requirement.[64] The EU criticised the panel for failing to verify whether MERCOSUR satisfied the requirements set out in paragraphs 8(a) and 5 of Article XXIV.[65] Furthermore, the EU claimed that MERCOSUR had not proven that the exemption was 'necessary' for the creation of MERCOSUR.[66]

This case is particularly significant in terms of the EU's actions in challenging the integrity of MERCOSUR. The message here, it seems, is that the EU is both ready to challenge other RTAs and defend its own arrangement under Article XXIV.[67] Interestingly, the US argued that where a country fails to notify the WTO of a regional arrangement under Article XXIV, it should not be able to invoke the provision as a defence.[68] Quite why MERCOSUR was being treated as an Article XXIV agreement is not entirely clear but nevertheless, the case raises important points relating to the legal construction of regions.

---

[62] Report of the Appellate Body, *Argentina-Footwear* (n. 56), para 53.

[63] *Brazil – Measures Affecting Imports of Retreaded Tyres* Report of the Panel WT/DS332/R (12 June 2007) and the Report of the Appellate Body WT/DS332/AB/R (3 December 2007).

[64] Report of the Appellate Body, *Brazil – Retreaded Tyres* (n. 63), para. 47.

[65] *Ibid*, para. 32.

[66] *Ibid*, para. 49.

[67] Mathis (n. 55).

[68] Report of the Appellate Body, *Brazil-Retreaded Tyres*, para. 116.

In *Turkey – Textiles*, the Panel highlighted that the issue of assessing the compatibility of regional arrangements with the rules of the GATT should rest with the CRTA:

> … regional trade agreements may contain numerous measures, all of which could potentially be examined by panels, before, during or after the CRTA examination, if the requirements laid down in the DSU are met. However, it is arguable that a customs union (or a free-trade area) as a whole would logically not be a 'measure' as such, subject to challenge under the DSU.[69]

This aspect is particularly interesting in light of the more recent *Brazil – Retreaded Tyres* case, where the EU seeks to do exactly what the Panel in *Turkey – Textiles* said was beyond its jurisdiction: challenge the compatibility of a RTA, in this case MERCOSUR, with Article XXIV.

This case reinforces the judgment of *Turkey – Textiles* and confirms that the question of whether the requirements of Article XXIV have been met will be decided by a panel, or Appellate Body. In *Brazil – Tyres*, the Appellate Body recognised that there is 'some flexibility' to paragraph 8 but did not further define the scope of the provision.[70] Collectively, these cases do little to clarify the internal parameters of the legal definition of regionalism. What they do demonstrate, however, is a judicialisation of regionalism through the legal formalist interpretation of Article XXIV; an interpretation that has been heavily influenced through the argumentation of actors representing EU interests.

DIFFERENTIATION: A LEGAL PRINCIPLE

In examining the granting of preferences to developing countries the Appellate Body in *EC – Drug Arrangements*[71] interpreted the Enabling Clause as meaning that 'any preference-granting countries must make available identical tariff preferences to *all similarly-situated beneficiaries*'.[72] This essentially allows for differentiation of treatment amongst developing countries based on their 'development, financial and trade needs'.[73] This finding departed from the panel report in which it was argued:

---

[69] Panel Report, *Turkey – Textiles* (n. 39), para. 9.53.

[70] Report of the Appellate Body, *Brazil – Retreaded Tyres* (n. 63), para. 81.

[71] *EC – Conditions for the Granting of Tariff Preferences to Developing Countries* Report of the Appellate Body WT/DS246/AB/R (7 April 2004).

[72] *Ibid*, para. 154 (emphasis added).

[73] *Ibid*, para. 163 (emphasis added).

> … the only appropriate way of responding to the differing development needs of developing countries is for preference-giving countries to ensure that their schemes have sufficient breadth of product coverage and depth of tariff cuts to respond positively to those differing needs.[74]

Establishing that *differentiation* of developing countries is acceptable for the purposes of granting tariff preferences could broaden the scope for systemic abuse by developed countries. In this case, the Panel and Appellate Body found the practice of the EU to be in violation of the principles of the Enabling Clause because similarly situated countries were treated differently. However, establishing differing levels of preferences among developing countries creates a further layer of complexity to the trading system. A distinction between LDCs and developing countries already exists. The Appellate Body therefore appears to be creating a new distinction among developing countries, which it could be argued is against the spirit of the Enabling Clause. The panel's suggestion that all developing countries should be considered as similarly situated and granted the same preferences seems more equitable.

However, the Appellate Body further clarified its position by stating that the criteria for distinguishing between developing countries must be *clear* and *fair.* Developing countries may be differentiated according to their 'development, financial and trade needs' according to paragraph (c) Enabling Clause. In accordance with this process of differentiation, developed countries must 'respond positively' to the needs of developing countries and ensure that identical tariff preferences are available to similarly situated countries. It was expected that by imposing these constraints the likelihood of discriminatory preferential tariff schemes arising in the future would be reduced. However, with the (re)introduction of differentiation in the EU's development cooperation policy which will be discussed in Chapter 3, this hope may have been diminished.

INSTITUTIONALISING PARTICIPATION: THE DISPUTE SETTLEMENT BODY

The preceding analysis has demonstrated that the DSB is a sophisticated site of socialisation and argumentation within the WTO and a discursive space in which members can challenge the legality of measures that they perceive to be harmful to their economy. It offers a platform for

---

[74] *EC – Conditions for the Granting of Tariff Preferences to Developing Countries* Panel Report WT/DS246/R (1 December 2003), para 7.149.

interpretive argumentation of the legal norms that have come to shape the multilateral trading system to this day. Demonstrating a high level of legalisation, the DSB represents a highly-organised and relatively transparent arbitral setting within the WTO framework. However, participation in the DSB is polarised with the system predominantly used by developed countries and a coalition of middle-income developing countries. To date, no African country has filed a complaint with the DSB.[75]

Inquiring into which countries use the dispute settlement procedure reveals interesting behavioural trends. A common myth is that developing countries fail to participate altogether but this is not strictly true. It certainly is the case that the EU and USA are the most prolific in terms of filing at the DSB, while developing countries participate less actively.[76] Emerging economies such as China, Brazil and India, are increasingly participating in the DSB both as a complainant and a respondent. Recent data shows that the USA has filed 110 complaints while the EU has filed 97 complaints.[77] Over 500 disputes have been filed since the creation of the WTO, and just over 200 of the disputes are complaints brought by developing countries. Complaints have been initiated by 28 individual developing countries, although the majority of developing countries using the dispute settlement mechanism are based in Latin America with Argentina and Brazil initiating a large proportion of these cases. Countries in this region have sought to utilise the dispute settlement system irrespective of their size or strength. While the more powerful countries, such as Brazil, are regular participators so too are smaller economies like Costa Rica, which has initiated five disputes. Even Bangladesh, a least-developed country, has used the DSB to initiate proceedings against India.[78]

In terms of ACP countries, their participation at the DSB is poor. To date, only one member has initiated a dispute: Antigua and Barbuda.[79] This particular case has proven costly and devastating for the industry

---

[75] Data on all disputes is available on the WTO's website: https://www.wto.org/english/tratop_e/dispu_e/dispu_by_country_e.htm (accessed 9 December 2016).

[76] C. Davis and S. Bermeo, 'Who Files? Developing Country Participation in GATT/WTO Adjudication' (2009) 71 *The Journal of Politics* 1033–49.

[77] WTO data (n. 75).

[78] Of the 28 developing countries that have filed, 13 are members of the Cairns group. This may suggest that the Latin American countries are in a better position to file complaints as they have the support and perhaps financial and/or technical assistance from the wealthier members of the CAIRNS group.

[79] *United States – Measures Affecting the Cross-Border Supply of Gambling and Betting Services* AB/R/DS285 (7 April 2005).

concerned. The Dominican Republic and Trinidad and Tobago have both had complaints raised against them, while African and Caribbean countries have participated as third parties in disputes. Only two African countries, Egypt and South Africa, have had claims brought against them. Africa's notable absence from the DSB is arguably the result of various intersecting factors. African countries tend to have a low margin of exports,[80] they lack the legal expertise to initiate the increasingly technical claims and use the DSB,[81] the dispute process is complicated and expensive, and they may be less willing to pursue litigation where a major trading partner or donor partner is involved.[82] This last point is particularly relevant to the African context, given that the EU is both major trading partner and a significant donor. It would seem unlikely that African countries would be willing to risk 'upsetting the apple cart' for what may result in little gain in terms of market access. In every case, a country must consider the balance between competing interests, assessing whether the legal costs associated with pursuing recommendations from the DSB will be worth the removal of a WTO inconsistent measure. Procedurally, it can take many years to implement a ruling and this is problematic given that industries may have suffered irreparable damage.[83]

A country may implement retaliatory measures where the offending government fails to comply with a ruling. One such instance occurred following the *EC – Bananas* dispute, the longest running dispute in WTO history, discussed in the final section of this chapter. In this dispute, the EU had failed to withdraw its WTO inconsistent measure and Ecuador sought to retaliate against this by targeting the EU's wine and spirits industry.[84] These represent a sensitive export sector for the EU. By retaliating against these industries, rather than pursuing action against banana exporters, Ecuador was effectively encouraging the wine and spirits producers to apply pressure to the EU and bring its banana regime

---

[80] M. Busch and E. Reinhardt, 'Developing Countries and General Agreement on Tariffs and Trade/World Trade Organisation Dispute Settlement' (2003) 37 *Journal of World Trade* 719–35.

[81] C.P. Bown and B.M. Hoekman, 'WTO Dispute Settlement and the Missing Developing Country Cases: Engaging the Private Sector' (2005) 8(4) *Journal of International Economic Law* 861–90.

[82] Mosoti (n. 51).

[83] Under Article 340 TFEU some private industries have challenged the EU's liability for failure to comply with the recommendations of the WTO. See: Case C-94/02, *Établissements Biret et Cie SA v Council* [2003] E.C.R. I-10565 and Joined Cases C-120/06P & C-121/06P, *Fabbrica Italiana Accumulatori Motocarri Montecchio SpA v Council* [2008] E.C.R. I-6513.

[84] Clough (n. 34), 263–4.

into line with WTO rules. This was a rather bold step for such a small developing country but it certainly shows that the system can benefit smaller countries too, if they know how to use it.

Who is Shaping the Rationalisation of Article XXIV?

Generally speaking, behind every complaining country is either a large corporation or a group of companies seeking to protect their own economic interests. This implies that the interpretation of Article XXIV has been influenced by materialist ideational forces of private actors. Disputes have covered products from batteries[85] to groundnuts,[86] buses[87] to tobacco,[88] showing that the disputes coming before the DSB are diverse and addressing a broad range of business sectors. Both the US and EU have made legal provision for the private sector to raise industry concerns in order to petition action from the State at the WTO level under Section 301 (USA) and the Article 133 Process and the Trade Barrier Regulation (EU). The DSB has therefore become a forum in which powerful multinational corporations can both assert and protect their interests, albeit through the guise of member representation. Through a process of interpretive argumentation at the DSB, norms become increasingly formalist and rationalist in nature. For example, behind the *Argentina – Footwear* dispute were large international sports footwear firms who were aggrieved by the implementation of safeguards and lobbied the USA and EU to challenge the measures at the DSB:

> The political economy of this case can be explained by the globalisation process of the industry, particularly the sports footwear segment, which is characterised by the existence of multinational firms that manufacture in low-wage countries, with designs and technology usually developed in their developed countries. This characteristic illustrates how an instrument like safeguards that regulates the trade between domestic and foreign producers decided on a case where local production confronted the interests associated

---

[85] *India – Anti-Dumping Measures on Batteries from Bangladesh* DS306 of 28 January 2004.

[86] *US – Tariff Rate Quota for Imports of Groundnuts* DS111 of 19 December 2007.

[87] *Peru – Countervailing Duty Investigation against Imports of Buses from Brazil* DS112 of 23 December 1997.

[88] *Australia – Certain Measures Concerning Trademarks, Geographical Indications and Other Plain Packaging Requirements Applicable to Tobacco Products and Packaging* DS441 of 18 July 2012.

with the ownership of intellectual property like designs and brands in this case, European companies.[89]

Similarly, in the *EC – Bananas* dispute, it was the interests of two major multinational bananas producers (Chiquita and Dole Foods) that were being adversely affected by the preferential EU-ACP banana scheme.[90]

Developing countries, especially in Africa, often lack a coordinated network of export industries that are willing to act collectively in order to exert pressure on their governments to challenge the behaviour of dominant States. This is compounded by the fact that most developing countries are monocultural, primary commodity producers and as such have a low margin of exports. In simple terms, this hampers their ability to secure a place within the economic hierarchy. Another issue facing developing countries is the lack of a competent private sector to commit to public-private partnerships.[91] We will see in Chapter 7 that there are public-private partnerships emerging in southern Africa, particularly in relation to the micro-regional Spatial Development Initiatives (SDIs), but these are in their infancy. For the time being, it certainly does not seem as though public-private partnerships will be established with the view of challenging any breach of WTO rules at the DSB. Not since the infamous riots at Seattle has the world witnessed such social opposition to the multilateral trading system.

This analysis leads to the question of whether the DSB is an appropriate, or legitimate, forum for developing country litigation. Given that developing countries in the ACP, and particularly in Africa, are predominantly monocultural agricultural producers it is arguable that this is not the correct forum for dealing with countries exporting and importing relatively small volumes of trade. However, to endorse this argument would imply that these sectors are symbolically less significant than others. Removing developing country litigation from the process altogether would merely serve to deepen existing structural inequalities and further marginalise them in the global economy. That said, in the African context, the lack of participation may also be regarded as

---

89 E. Baracat and J. Nogués, 'WTO Safeguards and Trade Liberalisation: Lessons from the Argentine Footwear Case' World Bank Policy Research Paper (Doc. WPS3614, May 2005), 15.

90 Subsequently in 2009, it was reported that both Chiquita and Dole Foods were subject to an EU competition probe for possible violations of its competition policy. Perhaps this was a retaliatory act for successfully challenging its lucrative banana regime with the ACP.

91 Bown and Hoekman (n. 81), 870.

symptomatic of Africa's perceived economic weakness. It is not simply a by-product of the systemic issues of the DSB. African countries collectively represent a large membership base of the WTO and their failure to participate in, or engage with, the DSB could merely reinforce the system's formalist and predictable nature, leaving them in a more precarious position in the future.

RECONSTRUCTING NORTH-SOUTH COOPERATION THROUGH NORTH-SOUTH RTAS

Having considered the judicial interpretation of Article XXIV, and having noted the special position of developing countries within the multilateral system, the question remains as to whether developing countries in North-South arrangements can expect any special treatment with respect to the 'substantially all trade' requirement. In this section, the shift from non-reciprocal preferences to reciprocal, but asymmetric, preferences for *all* members, will be presented.

The *EC – Bananas III* dispute[92] brought by non-ACP developing countries, challenged the EC's preferential and non-reciprocal market access for bananas originating in ACP countries. This policy was not extended to other non-ACP countries and as a result some Latin American producers, supported by the USA, sought to challenge the regime at the WTO. This was the third case relating to the EU's banana import scheme but because the panel recommendations of the GATT DSB were not binding, the EU refused to implement the findings of the panel.

The trade cooperation pillar of the Lomé IV framework provided non-reciprocal preferences to ACP countries exporting goods to the EC. As part of this arrangement, there were additional special protocols for goods including beef, sugar, rice, rum and bananas.[93] For example, Article 1 of the Banana Protocol (Protocol 5) provided that no ACP banana producer 'shall be placed, as regards access to its traditional markets and its advantages on those markets, in a less favourable situation than in the past or present'. The principle of non-discrimination was therefore incorporated into the Lomé framework, with the EU

---

[92] *European Communities – Regime for the Importation, Sale and Distribution of Bananas* Report of the Appellate Body WT/DS27/AB/R, adopted 25 September 1997.

[93] Article 368 Lomé IV confirms that the four protocols 'form an integral part' of the trade and cooperation framework.

committed to treating all ACP countries alike. Article XXIV only allows preferences where 'substantially all trade' has been liberalised between the parties. In 1993, the compatibility of the Lomé framework with Article XXIV was analysed by a GATT working party in the *EC – Bananas I* case.[94] Other Contracting Parties argued that the EC and ACP should have sought a waiver for the Lomé framework under Article XXV exempting them from the obligations in Article 1:1 (MFN), and various other GATT provisions, on the basis that this regime was compliant with Article XXIV. Although the working party did not come to a unanimous conclusion, the EC and ACP eventually sought a waiver under Article XXV(5).[95]

A waiver was subsequently issued, waiving only the provisions of Article 1. Although the preferential nature of the Lomé framework was not contested during the dispute, the EU maintained that the Banana Framework was compatible with Article XXIV when read in conjunction with Part IV GATT on Special and Differential Treatment.[96] Article XXXVI states:

> The developed contracting countries do not expect reciprocity for commitments made to them in trade negotiations to reduce or remove tariffs and other barriers to the trade of less-developed contracting countries.

It was therefore claimed that the trade provision of the Lomé framework satisfied the requirements for free trade areas (Article XXIV) in that 'substantially all trade' was liberalised but on a non-reciprocal basis, with non-reciprocity justified under Article XXXVI:8 of Part IV GATT. The EU argued that the relationship had to be non-reciprocal otherwise 'this would mean that it would be nearly impossible to create a free-trade area between developed and developing countries'.[97]

However, other developing countries contested this point as the principle of SDT is one based on equality and non-discrimination: *like* countries should be treated *alike*. Adopting a policy of differentiation between developing countries and only extending preferences for banana exports to its former colonies in the ACP constituted discriminatory

---

[94] *EEC – Member States' Import Regimes for Bananas DS32/R (1993) (EEC – Bananas I)* GATT Panel Report (1993).

[95] J. Huber, 'The Past, Present and Future ACP-EC Trade Regime and the WTO' (2000) 11 *European Journal of International Law* 427–38.

[96] Report of the Appellate Body, *EC-Bananas III* (n. 92), para. 25.

[97] GATT Panel Report, *EEC-Bananas I* (n. 94), para. 221.

practice. In the second *EC – Bananas* case, the panel sought to clarify the use of Article XXIV:

> Had non-reciprocal agreements between developed and developing parties been considered justifiable under Article XXIV and Part IV, the decisions of the CP (contracting parties) on the GSP [Generalised System for Preferences] and the Enabling Clause would have been largely unnecessary. Developed countries could simply have formed a 'free-trade area' with selected developing countries by reducing barriers unilaterally on imports from those countries.[98]

In their Report, the Appellate Body upheld the complaint and found the import and licence regimes of the Banana Framework to be inconsistent with WTO principles. Following the recommendations of the Appellate Body in the WTO's DSB, the EU was required to bring its trade cooperation framework within the parameters of the multilateral legal framework, creating 'WTO compatible' agreements with the ACP countries. On the 8 December 2012, the Geneva Agreement on Trade in Bananas was signed by the EU and Latin American countries, marking the end of the bananas dispute.[99]

Regionalism may be an important development tool as they are designed to increase investment flows and promote economic growth but the issue of WTO compatibility has raised concerns for developing countries. How have developed countries interpreted this concept, and what effect will it have for developing countries? Given that the EPAs are North-South trade and cooperation agreements negotiated on a reciprocal basis, and remembering that developed countries can only be recipients of preferences under an Article XXIV sanctioned regional arrangement, it follows that Article XXIV implies reciprocity. What effect will reciprocity have for developing countries?

Although SDT is an unqualified structural condition of the WTO architecture, Article XXIV is couched in ambiguous terms, and does not explicitly incorporate a development dimension. As part of their strategy to overcome the development deficit at the multilateral level, the ACP issued a communiqué to the WTO members requesting that Article XXIV be redrafted to incorporate a development dimension.[100] Identifying

---

98 *EEC – Member States' Import Regime for Bananas* GATT Report DS38/R (1994) (*EEC – Bananas II*), para. 162.

99 'Geneva Agreement on Trade in Bananas', [2010] OJ L141/3.

100 ACP Communiqué, 'Communication by the Mission of Botswana on behalf of the ACP Group of States' TN/RL/W/155 accessed 9 December 2016 at http://www.jmcti.org/2000round/com/doha/tn/tn_rl_w_155.pdf.

regionalism as a 'core development strategy', the ACP proposed that Article XXIV should include SDT for North-South regional arrangements. The underlying rationale for this proposal is that regionalism is important for development but that the legal framework does not take into account the developmental aspects of North-South Agreements. They argued:

> … while there exists some de facto flexibility under GATT Article XXIV arising from the ambiguity in terminology used therein, and in the permissive practices evolved over the years … there are no explicit provisions on de jure S&D treatment for developing countries in meeting the requirements set out in Article XXIV … such de facto flexibility cannot constitute nor substitute for legally binding, operational and effective S&D provisions.[101]

Unfortunately, the proposal has fallen on deaf ears and there are no forthcoming plans to renegotiate the terms of Article XXIV. Nevertheless, the EPAs have been constructed as Article XXIV compliant trade agreements and the implications of this requirement will be examined in relation to the SADC EPA and CARIFORUM EPA in the final chapters of this book.

CONCLUDING REMARKS

Situating the legal framework in its historical setting has enabled an interrogation of the ideational forces that have shaped the rationalisation of Article XXIV. It has been argued that the formal rationalisation of Article XXIV through the discursive space of the DSB prioritises a dominant perspective and limits the realisation of SDT within the legal framework of North-South RTAs. As a discursive space, the DSB embodies a participatory process that is formally open to members, and often informally used by multinational corporations. This analysis lends itself to the claim set out in this book that North-South RTAs are hegemonic legal regimes, defined by a formal legal rationality that limits the transformative potential of alternative perspectives. In the next chapter, the role of the EU as a normative actor in the global economy will be explored.

---

101 *Ibid.*

3. The EU as a global actor

This chapter argues that the EU exercises normative influence through its trade relations with third countries and claims that this normative power derives in part from its market power. Through a detailed analysis of the EU's evolving external market power expressed through its implied and exclusive competence in the common commercial policy (CCP), it is argued that the EU has institutionalised its normative power *through* law. Over time, the priorities of the EU have shifted from a focus on internal economic integration to outward external cooperation with other countries. To be a subject of international law and conduct international relations with other countries is an essential aspect of sovereignty. It is undisputed that the EU has legal personality[1] and has the competence to enter into many aspects of international relations. While the EU may lack the status of the sovereign state it is nevertheless considered to be 'a new legal order' with 'its own constitutional framework and founding principles, a particularly sophisticated institutional structure and a full set of legal rules to ensure its operation'.[2] Although precluded from being considered a state[3] the EU nevertheless symbolises a *sui generis* legal system.[4]

Reflecting on the nature of the EU's competence to conclude international agreements is important as more new generation agreements emerge which seek to deepen liberalisation beyond trade in goods and promote broader notions of development. With a focus on formal competences, including both primary and secondary law, this chapter will

[1] Article 47 TFEU. The EU has legal personality but, in accordance with Declaration 24 annexed to the Lisbon Treaty, this does not 'in any way authorise the Union to legislate or to act beyond the competences conferred upon it by the Member States in the Treaties'.

[2] Opinion 2/13 of the Court of 18 December 2014: Accession by the Union to the European Convention for the Protection of Human Rights and Fundamental Freedoms ECLI:EU:C:2014:2454, para. 158.

[3] *Ibid,* para. 156.

[4] Article 6(2) TFEU provides that the 'EU shall accede to the [ECHR]. Such accession shall not affect the Union's competences as defined in the Treaties'.

demonstrate the ways in which the EU's strategic orientations have shifted over time through law. Tracing the changing nature of exclusivity through the various Treaty amendments, this chapter questions the extent to which the marriage of economic and non-economic objectives within the legal framework enables the EU to use its trade policy as an effective vehicle for foreign policy. It will be shown that the EU's trade strategy has developed through the courts as much as through the Treaties, with the jurisprudence of the Court of Justice of the European Union (CJEU) playing a pivotal role in shaping the direction of EU external action, particularly where the Treaties fall silent. Through a critical assessment of the formal competence of the EU in international relations, this chapter submits that the CCP now presents a 'unique tool' for externalising policies and norms that extend beyond purely economic objectives.[5] To this end, the CCP enables the EU to assert its normative power in regional trade agreements (RTAs).

As an international actor, the EU has become a leader in international trade. Its significance within the global economy has been the subject of debate for decades, with scholars from various disciplines exploring the normative nature of the EU's economic power. As the EU has undergone various phases of enlargement, so too has its trade policy evolved. This chapter aims to demonstrate two interrelating claims of the EU as a global actor. The first claim submits that the EU has become a significant trade actor in the global economy. Its strength as a 'market power' derives from the coherence, or *parallelism*, between its internal and external commercial policies.[6] The second claim, which is presupposed by the first claim, asserts that the EU is not just a regional trade actor, but a normative actor.[7] As a regional polity, the EU has translated its market power into normative power and through its external trade policy seeks to export universal values and this is particularly evident in its neoliberal conception of development. In its external relations with the world, the EU projects its 'civilian power' employed through its own regional process as the preferred model of regionalism to be pursued.[8] This has

---

[5] A. Dimopoulos, 'The Effects of the Lisbon Treaty on the Principles and Objectives of the Common Commercial Policy' (2010) 15 *European Foreign Affairs Review* 153.

[6] C. Damro, 'Market Power Europe: Exploring a Dynamic Conceptual Framework' (2015) 22 *Journal of European Public Policy* 1336–54.

[7] I. Manners, 'The Normative Ethics of the European Union' (2008) 84 *International Affairs* 45–60.

[8] M. Telò, *Europe: A Civilian Power?* (Basingstoke: Palgrave Macmillan, 2006).

led to the conceptualisation of the EU as exhibiting a 'soft imperialism'[9] in its regional negotiations with the ACP, reinforcing the conceptualisation of the Economic Partnership Agreements (EPAs) as hegemonic legal regimes.

The first section of this chapter will provide an overview of the current internal and external trade strategies of the EU. Through a detailed analysis of the formal and implied competences in trade, this section will demonstrate how the current strategic orientation of the EU's market power has been realised through law. In the second section, the normative ethical values underpinning the creation of the EU will be explored. It will be argued that the strength of the EU to project a normative image to the rest of the world hinges on its market power. The third section provides a legal analysis of the EU's competence in development cooperation. As the EPAs are trade *and* development cooperation agreements, it is important to understand the legal (inter)relationship between the commercial and development dimensions of the EU's external action. In the fourth section, a brief overview of the main financing instrument, the European Development Fund (EDF), will be presented. It will be shown in Chapters 8 and 9 of this book that the financial element of the EPAs is arguably perceived to be one of the most significant for the realisation of 'development-friendly' trade in the SADC EPA and CARIFORUM regions.

MARKET POWER EUROPE

The EU exhibits strategic neoliberal orientations in its trade strategies, although more recently the Commission has sought to disseminate a 'more *responsible* trade and investment policy'.[10] External trade with developing countries is primarily driven by the Commission's Directorate-General for International Cooperation and Development (DG DEVCO), which is responsible for designing trade policies that are 'development-friendly'. An interesting departure from this institutional framework is evident in the EPA negotiations, agreements expressed as comprising both trade *and* development aspects, which have been led by DG Trade, rather than DG DEVCO. This implies that the commercial focus of the EPAs has been prioritised over the development aspects and

---

[9] B. Hettne and F. Söderbaum, 'Theorising the Rise of Regionness' (2000) 5 *New Political Economy* 457–73.

[10] European Commission, *Trade for All: Towards a More Responsible Trade and Investment Policy*, Trade Policy Strategy Report (15 October 2015).

may explain why the articulation of the development provisions in the EPA remain vague and ambiguous.

On 1 December 2009, the Lisbon Treaty[11] entered into force extending and clarifying the orientation of the EU's common commercial policy (CCP). In addition to the introduction of the new competence in relation to foreign direct investment (FDI), the EU now enjoys exclusive competence in matters of trade in goods, services, and commercial aspects of intellectual property. Historically, the exclusive competence of the EU to conclude negotiations on trade was narrow in its focus and limited to trade in goods. The evolving nature of the EU's exclusive and implied external power to act in the field of international relations has been reflected in both the EU's internal and trade strategies.

Internally, the EU's *2020 Strategy*[12] is built upon three mutually reinforcing objectives: smart growth,[13] sustainable growth[14] and inclusive growth.[15] A comprehensive analysis of the EU's internal growth strategy is beyond the scope of this chapter but it is worthwhile noting that it is underpinned by national (Member State), EU and international action. Both the internal and external trade policies are mutually reinforcing, seeking to improve the business environment, particularly for small and medium-sized enterprises (SMEs), in order to sustain a competitive economy. Over the next 10–15 years it is estimated that 90 per cent of global economic growth will take place outside of the EU. Therefore, the need to forge 'stronger links with the new centres of global growth'[16] is of paramount importance to the EU's relevance and longevity as an international actor. In its *2020 Strategy* the Commission notes that 'every threat is an opportunity' and 'as these countries develop, new markets will open up for many European companies'.[17] However, the EU will

[11] EU, Treaty of Lisbon amending the Treaty on European Union and the Treaty establishing the European Community [2007] OJ C306/1. The Treaty of Lisbon now comprises the Treaty on European Union (TEU) and the Treaty on the Functioning of the European Union (TFEU).

[12] European Commission, *Europe 2020: A European Strategy for Smart, Sustainable and Inclusive Growth* (3.3.2010) COM (2010) 2020.

[13] Smart growth is defined as 'developing an economy based on knowledge and innovation'.

[14] Sustainable growth is defined as 'promoting a more resource efficient, greener and more competitive economy'.

[15] Inclusive growth is defined as 'fostering a high-employment economy delivering social and territorial cohesion'.

[16] European Commission (n. 10), 8.

[17] European Commission (n 12), 6.

only be in a position to influence global policy decisions if its external representation goes hand-in-hand with its internal policies.[18]

Externally, the concept of 'responsible' trade is the overarching theme of the most recent iteration of the EU's trade policy with third countries. To ensure that EU external trade policy is 'not just about interests but also about values'[19] *Trade for All* is uncompromising on core principles such as sustainable development, good governance and human rights protection. The new external trade strategy has transformed incrementally in response to an ever changing geopolitical landscape in which the nexus between trade and development becomes more evident. Extending the CCP to incorporate trade *and* development principles, the EU envisages a central role for regional trade agreements as 'levers' to promote these universal values.[20] It is clear from the EU's trade agenda that it attaches great importance to the negotiation of bilateral and regional trade agreements as a means to secure access to those markets which it perceives to be valuable.

Exclusivity: An Evolutionary Concept

In order to critically assess the most recent trade strategy of the EU, understanding the historical context from which the current common commercial policy operates is of paramount importance. Through various Treaty amendments, the common trade policy has become the 'nucleus of the Union's external action'.[21] Formal competences, exclusive and shared, are set out in the Treaty of Lisbon. Article 3 TFEU provides that the EU has *exclusive* competence in relation to its common trading policy, while Article 4 TFEU outlines the *shared* competences between the EU and its Member States. Where the EU has exclusive competence to act, the Treaty confers power on the EU to legislate on the matter in question alone. However, in accordance with the *principle of conferral*, the Union 'shall only act within the limits of the competences conferred'

[18] *Ibid.*

[19] Foreword by Cecilia Malmström, European Commission (n. 10).

[20] The EU defines 'universal values' as those espoused in the UN Declarations. External trade with developing countries is primarily driven by the Commission's Directorate-General for International Cooperation and Development (DG DEVCO), which is responsible for designing trade policies that are 'development-friendly'.

[21] P. Koutrakos, *EU International Relations Law*, 2nd edn (Oxford: Hart Publishing, 2015).

by the Treaties.[22] The principle of conferral is circumscribed by the *principle of subsidiarity*[23] and the *principle of proportionality*,[24] which collectively prevent the EU from exercising its power beyond that prescribed by the Treaties. *Supporting competences,* or areas in which the EU has no power to legislate but merely plays a coordinating role alongside the Member States are set out in Article 6 TFEU. The focus of this chapter is on the nature of exclusive and shared competences in the CCP of the EU.

In exercising the powers conferred on them by the Treaties, the EU institutions may adopt secondary legislation in accordance with Article 288 TFEU.[25] EU trade policy is made exclusively at the EU level, meaning that the Member States are represented by the Commission, which speaks with one unified voice, to conclude international trade agreements. The only exception to this rule is where the EU lacks exclusive competence to act or where the EU and Member States have shared competence. Arguably, the restructuring of EU external policy is one of the most interesting results of the Treaty.[26] Institutionally, the Lisbon Treaty conferred greater powers on the European Parliament, which can now accept or reject a proposed trade deal. However, this power is 'all or nothing' in nature and the Parliament cannot accept or reject parts of the proposed agreement. Ratification of matters relating to the CCP now takes place by way of a simple majority vote in the

---

[22] Article 5 TFEU.

[23] Article 5(3) TFEU states that 'in areas which do not fall within its exclusive competence, the Union shall act only if and in so far as the objectives of the proposed action cannot be sufficiently achieved by the Member States, either at central level or at regional and local level, but can rather, by reason of the scale or effects of the proposed action, be better achieved at the Union level'.

[24] Article 5(4) TFEU provides: 'Under the principle of proportionality, the content and form of Union action shall not exceed what is *necessary* to achieve the objectives of the Treaty' (emphasis added).

[25] Article 288 states: 'To exercise the Union's competences, the institutions shall adopt regulations, directives, decisions, recommendations and opinions. A regulation shall have general application. It shall be binding in its entirety and directly applicable in all Member States. A directive shall be binding, as to the result to be achieved, upon each Member State to which it is addressed, but shall leave to the national authorities the choice of form and methods. A decision shall be binding in its entirety. A decision which specifies those to whom it is addressed shall be binding only on them. Recommendations and opinions shall have no binding force.'

[26] M. Cremona, 'Balancing Union and Member State Interests: Opinion 1/2008, Choice of Legal Base and the Common Commercial Policy under the Treaty of Lisbon' (2010) 35 *European Law Review* 692.

Parliament, rather than requiring each individual Member State to ratify the agreement.[27] The Council votes by way of qualified majority, albeit this is subject to two limitations. First, in the field of services and commercial aspects of intellectual property rights, unanimity is required where trade agreements 'risk prejudicing the Union's cultural and linguistic diversity'.[28] Second, where agreements in the fields of trade in social, education and health services 'risk seriously disturbing the national organisation of such services and prejudicing the responsibility of Member States to deliver them', the Council is required to vote unanimously.[29]

Examining the legal bases and doctrines for the EU's external competence, be it exclusive or implicit, is integral to an understanding of the current trade strategy. Where the Treaty is silent on a particular issue, the EU may nevertheless have the *implied* competence to act exclusively. Codification into Article 207 TFEU means that uniformity in application of the common rules is now a hallmark of the CCP; however, this has not always been the case. The exclusive competence of the EU to act on behalf of the Member States has emerged over time, in what Marisa Cremona describes as an 'evolutionary' rather than 'revolutionary' process.[30]

Externally, the EU's authority to act derives from the legal bases outlined in either the primary rules of Treaties or the secondary law of the EU. Identifying the correct legal base is of constitutional significance and failure to do so will render legal acts adopted as the EU *ultra vires* and void. Not only does the legal base determine the nature of competence but it also serves to identify the correct procedural and institutional processes to be followed. The CCP finds its origins in Article 113 Treaty of Rome[31] and Article 133 EC[32] through its various Treaty

---

[27] The powers of the European Parliament are set out in Article 218(6)(a)(i)–(v).

[28] Article 207(4)(a).

[29] Article 207(4)(b).

[30] See Cremona (n. 26).

[31] Article 113 Treaty of Rome confines the CCP to trade in goods: 'the common commercial policy shall be based on uniform principles, particularly in regard to tariff amendments, the conclusion of tariff or trade agreements, the alignment of measures of liberalisation, export policy and protective commercial measures including measures to be taken in cases of dumping or subsidies.'

[32] Article 133(1) EC states: 'The common commercial policy shall be based on uniform principles, particularly in regard to changes in tariff rates, the conclusion of tariff and trade agreements, the achievement of uniformity in measures of liberalisation, export policy and measures to protect trade such as

amendments. Uniformity, harmonisation and coherence have been the guiding principles underpinning the CPP through its many manifestations, underscoring the market power of the EU. Part V of the Lisbon Treaty sets out the underlying rationale for the common trade policy in Article 206 TFEU:

> By establishing a customs union in accordance with Articles 28 to 32, the Union shall contribute, in the common interest, to the harmonious development of world trade, the progressive abolition of restrictions on international trade and on foreign direct investment, and the lowering of customs barriers.

In its most recent articulation, Article 207 extends the strategic materialist orientation of the CCP:

> The common commercial policy shall be based on uniform principles, particularly with regard to changes in tariff rates, the conclusion of tariff and trade agreements relating to trade in goods and services, and the commercial aspects of intellectual property, foreign direct investment, the achievement of uniformity in measures of liberalisation, export policy and measures to protect trade such as those to be taken in the event of dumping or subsidies. The common commercial policy shall be conducted in the context of the principles and objectives of the Union's external action.

Where an international agreement has an effect on trade in goods, services, commercial aspects of intellectual property and FDI, Article 207 TFEU provides the legal base for such an agreement.

That the Union's external trade policy mirrors the internal commercial policy is not a new phenomenon and since the Treaty of Rome the concept of *parallelism*, in which provisions relating to external competence reflect that of internal competence, has become an integral part of the Union's CCP.[33] As the original aim of the Treaty of Rome was to create an internal market it is perhaps unsurprising that, with the various

---

those to be taken in the event of dumping or subsidies.' This is extended in paragraph (5) which provides that 'negotiation and conclusion of agreements in the fields of trade in services and the commercial aspects of intellectual property' fall within the scope of Article 133(1)–(4), provided that the provisions do not go beyond the internal powers of the EU. Paragraph (6) limits the operation of Article 133(1)–(4): 'Agreements relating to trade in cultural and audiovisual services, educational services, and social and human health services, shall fall within the shared competence of the Community and its Member States'.

[33] Parallelism is limited to the Union and not to the division of powers between the EU institutions. See Case C-327/91, *France v Commission* [1996] E.C.R. I-3641 and Opinion 2/94 (*ECHR Opinion*) [1996] E.C.R. I-1759.

phases of enlargement and the creation of a single market, the external relations of the EU have stemmed from its internal values. Notable shifts in the CCP have certainly taken place, but it has nevertheless remained inextricably linked to the values of the internal market.[34]

The nature of exclusivity has developed through the jurisprudence of the CJEU gradually over time. Indeed, the notion that exclusivity was not truly an exclusive competence of the EU was central to the development of the policy, with the CJEU playing a key role in defining that which was not set out in the primary rules.[35] Two conflicting cases demonstrate the initial difficulties that had faced the Court of Justice in articulating a clear rule on the exclusive nature of the common commercial policy: Opinion 1/75 and Opinion 1/78.

In Opinion 1/75, which predates the amendments to the CCP introduced by the Treaty of Amsterdam, the Court of Justice considered whether the Community had the express power, under Article 207 TFEU (ex Article 133 EC) to conclude the OECD Understanding on the Local Cost Standard, which sought to establish common standards on aid for exports.[36] Most significantly, the Court distinguished the 'existence' of Community powers and the 'exclusive nature' of those powers. In particular, the Court of Justice expressed concern that unilateral action by Member States with regard to export policy could result in 'disparities' and market distortions, which could only be avoided by the 'uniformity' of conditions granted by all Member States.[37] Famously, the Court stated:

> To accept the contrary were true would amount to recognizing that, in relations with third countries, Member States may adopt positions which differ from those which the Community intends to adopt, and would thereby *distort the institutional framework, call into question the mutual trust within the Community and prevent the latter from fulfilling its task in the defence of the common interest.*[38]

Adopting a teleological interpretation of the Treaty, the Court found that the exclusive nature of the EU's external powers flows directly from its internal aims and objectives. Thus, the EU's competence in relation to the common commercial policy is exclusive *a priori*. This decision is

[34] Case C-41/76, *Suzanne Criel, née Donckerwolke and Henri Pchou v Procureur de la République au Tribunal de Grande Instance, Lille and Director of Customs* [1976] E.C.R. 1921.

[35] Koutrakos (n. 21), 29.

[36] Opinion 1/75 (*re OECD Local Cost Standard*) [1975] E.C.R. 1355.

[37] *Ibid*, 1364.

[38] *Ibid.*

important not only in shedding light on the nature of the EU's external competence, but also in confirming the Court's role as the 'ultimate arbiter' of disputes arising in relation to international trade relations.[39]

Following this decision, the nature of exclusive competence was once again examined by the Court of Justice in Opinion 1/78,[40] in which the Union's competence to enter into negotiations on the International Rubber Agreement was drawn into question. Arguably, this decision is distinguishable as it related to a complex international commodities agreement which also contained a financial policy instrument. If the EU was to bear the financial burden, then it had exclusive competence to negotiate the Agreement. However, if the Member States were to bear the financial burden, then the Court submitted that this Agreement would fall under the shared competence of the EU and the individual Member States. In the Council's submission to the Court, it proposed that, in order to determine if the measure falls within the scope of the common commercial policy, it is necessary to establish 'whether its object or principal object is to alter the volume or pattern of trade'.[41] Acknowledging that the 'question of external trade must be governed from a wide point of view',[42] Court sought to define the boundaries of EU autonomy to act in external relations. From the analysis of the International Rubber Agreement it was clear that annexing a separate financial instrument indicated that this was more than an agreement to regulate international trade. As this financial policy instrument would require the individual Member States to contribute, the Court found that the Member States' participation in the negotiations was justified.

Implied External Power

Unlike exclusivity *a priori* which, by its very nature exists without any action by the Union, implied competence requires an internal action of the Union from which external competence then flows.[43] The lack of harmonisation in the application of the rules had resulted in a 'significantly differentiated approach ... that reflected a highly fragmented

---

[39] Koutrakos (n. 21), 32.

[40] Opinion 1/78 (*re International Agreement on Natural Rubber*) [1979] E.C.R. 2871.

[41] *Ibid.*

[42] *Ibid*, para. 45.

[43] See Dimopoulos (n. 5); T. Hartley, *Constitutional Problems of the European Union* (Oxford, Hart Publishing, 1999); and Koutrakos (n. 21).

policy'.[44] The doctrine of implied exclusive power finds its origins in the seminal decision of the Court in the *ERTA* case,[45] which related to implementation of the common transport policy under secondary legislation, Regulation 543/69.[46] The Commission submitted that the legal provision conferred on the Community powers that were defined in wide terms and that the provision would have been exhaustive had it intended to limit the external action of the EU. On the other hand, the Council argued that Article 95 TFEU (ex Article 75 EC) related only to internal measures and, therefore, this could not be an appropriate legal basis on which the Community could conclude an international agreement. In paragraphs 15–16, the Court declared the *ERTA* principle:

> To determine in a particular case the Community's authority to enter into international agreements, regard must be had to the whole scheme of the Treaty no less than to its substantive provisions. Such authority arises not only from an express conferment of the Treaty … but may equally flow from other provisions of the Treaty and from measures adopted, within the framework of those provisions, by the Community institutions.[47]

Through a purposive interpretation of the Treaty, the Court concluded that 'the system of internal Community measures may not therefore be separated from that of external relations'.[48] The significance of the *ERTA* principle cannot be overstated for it establishes the doctrine of implied external power: the EU may still be competent to enter into international agreements even where the power is not conferred by the Treaty but can only be 'implied' from the Treaty provisions. Extending the *ERTA* principle in the *Kramer* case,[49] it was recognised that there will be implied external powers where internal measures have been adopted, even if no common rules are yet in place.[50] However, the judgment failed

---

[44] Koutrakos (n. 21), 23.

[45] Case 22/70, *Commission v Council (re European Road Transport Agreement)* [1971] E.C.R. 263 ('*ERTA*').

[46] [1969] OJ L77/49. This regulation has since been repealed by Regulation 3820/85 [1985] OJ L370/1.

[47] *ERTA*, paras 15–16.

[48] *ERTA*, para. 19.

[49] Joined Cases 3/76, 4/76 and 6/76, *Cornelius Kramer and Others* [1976] E.C.R. 1279.

[50] *Kramer* at paras 19–20: '… authority arises not only from an express conferment by the Treaty, but may equally flow implicitly from other provisions of the Treaty, from the Act of Accession and from measures adopted, within the framework of those provisions, by the Community institutions.'

to clarify whether adopting internal measures was a prerequisite for establishing the Union's implied external power.

In Opinion 1/76, the *Rhine Navigation* case,[51] the nature of the EU's implied external power was clarified further. This case concerned an agreement with Switzerland to rationalise the waterways of the Rhine and other rivers. There had been no internal measures adopted by the EU to rationalise the waterways, as it was thought to be futile without the cooperation of Switzerland. As the Treaty was silent on the matter of competence in transport, the Commission requested an opinion from the Court to ensure legal certainty regarding the doctrine of exclusivity. Building on previous decisions, the Court held:

> … the power to bind the Community vis-à-vis third countries nevertheless flows by *implication from the provisions of the Treaty creating the internal power* and in so far as the participation of the Community in the international agreement is, as here, *necessary for the attainment of one of the objectives of the Community*.[52]

While Article 91 TFEU provides the legal base for concluding agreements relating to the Common Transport Policy, adopting common rules on that basis would not 'fully attain the objective pursued' in the proposed agreement relating to the navigation of the waterways. Circumventing the absence of a legal base in the Treaty, the Court conferred power on the EU to act by virtue of its 'authority to enter into the international commitments necessary for the attainment of that objective even in the absence of an express provision in that connexion'.[53]

Further clarification of the *Rhine Navigation* principle was provided in Opinion 1/94,[54] concerning the EU's competence to conclude the WTO Agreements that had been negotiated within the framework of the Uruguay Round. Not only was this a significant decision in terms of the EU's competence in relation to the CCP, but also as a statement regarding the EU's capacity role in international relations. Requesting the CJEU to confirm the exclusive competence of the EU to conclude the WTO Agreements that had been negotiated in the framework of the Uruguay Round, the Commission argued that all sectors fell within the exclusive

---

[51] Opinion 1/76 (*re Draft Agreement establishing a European laying-up fund for inland waterway vessels*) [1977] E.C.R. 741.

[52] *Ibid.*

[53] *ERTA*, para. 3.

[54] Opinion 1/94 (*WTO Agreements*) [1994] E.C.R. I-5267.

competence of the Union.[55] The Council and a number of Member States contested the 'extravagant' assumption of the Commission that the EU had exclusive competence to conclude the WTO Agreements.[56] This case illustrates the tension between the need for harmony and unity at the EU level so that its market power can be preserved while recognising the need to ensure Member State sovereignty is not eroded at the multilateral level.

The Court exercised caution in its approach to the division of competences between the EU and its Member States. In its analysis of trade in services, the Court stated that cross-border supplies (mode 1), which is not dissimilar to trade in goods, fell within the exclusive competence of the EU, while modes 2–4 fell within the shared competence of the EU and the Member States.[57] Historically, modes 2–4 were cited separately[58] from the CCP and could not be considered to fall within the exclusive competence of the EU. Furthermore, in the Court's opinion the EU did not have exclusive competence in relation to TRIPS obligations.[59] Eventually, the inclusion of trade in services and the commercial aspects of intellectual property rights as part of the CCP was codified in Article 133(5) EC (Amsterdam). Only in the circumstances in which secondary legislation has been passed in relation to services and commercial aspects of intellectual property would the EU have exclusive implied external competence to regulate those sectors. Therefore, the Court did not find that the *Rhine Navigation* principle applied to certain modes of services or intellectual property in this case because the internal power was not 'inextricably linked' to the exercise of the implied external power in these sectors.[60]

---

[55] This case is particularly interesting as the Advisory Opinion was delivered in a very short period of time. Unusually, the hearing was not public and all Advocate Generals were invited to give an opinion on the nature of the EU's competence in relation to the conclusion of the WTO Agreements. The hearing was held on 11 October 1994 and the Opinion was handed down on 15 November 1994.

[56] For an excellent analysis of the Opinion see M. Hilf, 'The ECJ's Opinion 1/94 on the WTO – No Surprise, but Wise?' (1995) 6 *European Journal of International Law* 245–59.

[57] The modes of services that fall under the shared competence of the EU and the Member States were: consumption abroad (mode 2); commercial presence (mode 3); and, presence of natural persons (mode 4).

[58] These modes of services were set out in Articles 48, 52 and 59 EC.

[59] Opinion 1/94 (*WTO Agreements*) [1994] E.C.R. I-5267, para. 60.

[60] *Ibid*, para. 86.

In short, where the Treaty lay silent on a matter of competence, the EU would be found to have exclusive competence if exercising such power was necessary in the pursuit of a Community objective outlined elsewhere in the Treaty (*ERTA* principle), or where it had the power to enter into an international agreement that was necessary for the attainment of a particular objective (*Rhine Navigation* principle). A liberal reading of the *Rhine Navigation* necessity test suggests that the principle is unconditional and 'purely a matter of political will'.[61] Indeed, this interpretation of the *Rhine Navigation* principle is evident in two noteworthy Opinions of the CJEU. First, in Opinion 2/91 concerning safety in the use of chemicals at work as set out in Convention No. 170 of the International Labour Organisation (ILO)[62] and second in Opinion 2/94, on the EU's accession to the ECHR.[63]

On examination of the nature of ILO Convention No. 170, the Court considered that it fell within the social policy of the Union and, as such, was within the competence of the implied external power of the Union.[64] However, the Court does not explicitly rely on the necessity test laid down in the *Rhine Navigation* case and, therefore, it is not clear that this lends itself to the notion that the *Rhine Navigation* principle is unqualified in nature. However, in the *ECHR Opinion* (1994) the Court reintroduces the concept of necessity explicitly:

> Whenever Community law has created for the institutions of the Community powers within its internal system for the purpose of attaining a specific objective, the Community has authority to enter into the international commitments *necessary* for the attainment of that objective.[65]

Introducing the necessity test as a means to attain exclusive competence once again demonstrated the inextricable link between the EU's internal and external action. Reinforcing the doctrine of parallelism, *in foro interno, in foro externo,* provides that the 'system of internal Community measures may not therefore be separated from that of external relations'.[66]

---

[61] R. Holdgaard, *External Relations of the European Community: Legal Reasoning and Legal Discourses* (Aalphen aan den Rijn: Kluwer Law International, 2008), 56.

[62] Opinion 2/91 (*re Convention No 170 ILO*) [1993] E.C.R. I-1061.

[63] Opinion 2/94 (*re Accession to the ECHR*) [1996] E.C.R. I-783.

[64] Opinion 2/91 (n. 62), para. 19

[65] Opinion 2/94 (n. 63).

[66] *ERTA*, para. 9.

Competence in relation to transport was once again considered in the *Open Skies* judgment, concerning bilateral aviation agreements between eight Member States and the United States.[67] It is important to note that transport is not explicitly mentioned in Article 207(1) TFEU and, therefore, remains a sector of shared competence for the EU and its Member States.[68] Overcoming the issues stemming from the lack of interpretive coherence surrounding the external power to act, Article 216(1) TFEU now codifies the doctrine of implied external powers:

> The Union may conclude an agreement with one or more third countries or international organisations where the Treaties so provide or where the conclusion of an agreement is *necessary in order to achieve, within the framework of the Union's policies, one of the objectives referred to in the Treaties, or is provided for in a legally binding Union act or is likely to affect common rules or alter their scope.* (emphasis added)

In essence, Article 216 provides the legal base for the Union's implied competence where it is 'necessary' to achieve the objectives set out in Article 216(1). Interestingly, Article 216 does not appear to codify the judgment of any particular case of the CJEU, or if it does there is no explicit mention of the case.[69] However, it appears to incorporate the various threads of implied external power that have been articulated in the aforementioned cases.

It has been noted that Article 207 TFEU extends and clarifies the orientation of the CCP in terms of the sectors of trade in which the EU has exclusive competence to act. The exclusive competence of the EU to negotiate and conclude agreements under the CCP is subject to the limitation that in exercising such competence it 'shall not affect the delimitation of competences between the Union and the Member States, and shall not lead to harmonisation of legislative or regulatory provisions of the Member States in so far as the Treaties exclude such harmonisation'.[70] With that exception aside, Article 207 TFEU explicitly brings

---

[67] Joined cases C-466/98, C-467/98, C-468/98, C-469/98, C-471/98, C472/98, C-475/98, C-476/98, *Commission v United Kingdom, Denmark, Sweden, Finland, Belgium, Luxembourg, Austria, Germany* [2002] E.C.R. I-09855.

[68] Article 207(5) provides that agreements in the field of transport are subject to Title IV of Part III of the Treaty and Article 218.

[69] T. Konstadinides, 'EU Foreign Policy under the Doctrine of Implied Powers: Codification Drawbacks and Constitutional Limitations' (2014) *European Law Review* 511–30.

[70] Article 207(6) TFEU reinforces the competences set out in Article 4 TFEU.

the entire scope of the CCP within the exclusive competence of the EU, including the sensitive sectors that had been recognised as falling within the competence of the Member States under Article 133 EC. This section will examine the historical development of shared competence, or mixity, which may take many forms and have various guises.[71]

Shared Competence

Prior to the implementation of the Lisbon Treaty, the Court's approach to the choice of legal base in mixed agreements was elucidated in Opinion 1/2008.[72] This case concerned the competence of the EU under Article 207 TFEU (ex Article 133 EC), following the accession of Member States, to amend the Schedule of concessions under GATS, which was originally concluded in 1994. In finding that the nature of external competence in relation to trade in services is shared, the Court stated that the legal base:

> allows the interest of the Community in establishing a comprehensive, coherent and efficient external commercial policy to be pursued whilst at the same time allowing the special interests which the Member States might wish to defend in the sensitive areas identified by [Article 133(6) EC] to be taken into account.[73]

This case reiterated the nature of external competence in relation to trade in services as being shared before the introduction of the Treaty of Lisbon and, much like the many other cases in which the concept of external competence has been raised, it demonstrates that the Court has adopted a strict approach to its interpretation. However, the lack of harmonisation in the application of the rules had resulted in a 'significantly differentiated approach … that reflected a highly fragmented policy'.[74]

Investment

In 2014, the EU was the leading exporter of FDI and was the second highest recipient of FDI inflows, after the United States.[75] Even through

[71] Koutrakos (n. 21), 163.
[72] Opinion 1/2008 (*re GATS Agreement*) [2010] 2 C.M.L.R. 13.
[73] *Ibid.*
[74] Koutrakos (n. 21), 23.
[75] UNCTAD, *World Investment Report: Reforming International Investment Governance,* New York and Geneva (UNCTAD/WIR/2015), Annex 3.

the financial crises, the EU has remained a leader in investment and accounts for almost half of global investment flows. While FDI has seen a dramatic decrease across developed countries, inflows to developing countries have spiked at historically high levels in the 2014–2015 period.[76] Although the financial crisis has undoubtedly had an adverse effect on investment globally, signs of market recovery are beginning to show. In 2014, the EU announced *The Investment Plan for Europe*,[77] which aims to create a better and more transparent environment for investment with the assistance of the European Fund for Strategic Investments (EFSI) with a view to enabling the investment market to recover.

Investment has, historically, been a trade issue of mixed competence so bringing this within the exclusive competence of the CCP is perhaps one of the more significant changes introduced by the Treaty. Marking a monumental step towards coherence and harmonisation, the Treaty of Lisbon confers power on the EU to conclude investment agreements for the first time. It has been noted that Article 207 eradicates some of the interpretive difficulties associated with ex Article 133 EC and clarifies the scope of the CCP, but with that clarification has come new interpretive difficulties. FDI falls unequivocally within the exclusive competence of the EU's CCP; however, the Treaty fails to define the term. Elsewhere, FDI has been defined as 'the form of participation in an undertaking through the holding of shares which confers the possibility of participating effectively in its management and control'.[78]

It has been argued that the deliberate use of the term 'FDI', rather than 'investment', circumscribes the scope of the EU's new competence. FDI is not synonymous with the broader concept of investment, with the former implying a controlling stake in a business and the latter including portfolio investments.[79] If we are to accept this line of argumentation, then Article 207 TFEU does not confer on the EU the power to conclude

---

[76] *Ibid*, 2.

[77] Communication from the Commission to the European Parliament, the Council, the European Central Bank, the European Economic and Social Committee, the Committee of the Regions and the European Investment Bank, *An Investment Plan for Europe*, COM (2014) 903 final, 26 November 2014.

[78] The only other primary rule relating to investment is Article 64(1) TFEU relating to the free movement of capital, which provides that FDI includes real estate. Find case (see Koutrakos (n. 21), 46, fn. 109 for case).

[79] J. Chaisse, 'Promises and Pitfalls of the European Union Policy on Foreign Investment – How will the New EU Competence on FDI Affect the Emerging Global Regime?' (2012) 15(1) *Journal of International Economic Law* 8.

agreements relating to portfolio investments. The Commission has asked the CJEU for an opinion on the legal status of the EU-Singapore Free Trade Agreement and, in particular, the Court has been asked to interpret the scope of the new competence.[80] According to the Curia website, the Full Court will hear this case on 12 September 2016 following which an Opinion will be given.

In light of the interpretive difficulties, Chaisse argues that some aspects of expropriation will remain under the competence of the Member States by virtue of Article 354 TFEU and thus investment policy, broadly defined, is not within the exclusive competence of the EU.[81] On the basis of this analysis, it seems likely that FTAs, which seek to incorporate elements of trade and investment, and indeed some international investment agreements, will continue to be negotiated as mixed agreements. Mixity is, therefore, a continuing reality for the EU in the exercise of its common external trade policy. Interpretive difficulties aside, the new competence will certainly enable the EU to strengthen its negotiating power in relation to liberalising investment; it nevertheless has an impact on those agreements that were negotiated prior to the Lisbon Treaty which included an investment chapter. As the EU Member States collectively account for approximately half of the investment agreements in force globally, the new competence is likely to enable the EU to shape global policy on investment.[82]

This section has demonstrated that the boundaries of the CCP have gone through various phases of redefinition and reconstruction. It is a concept that has been actively shaped through the legislature, the executive and the judiciary, affirming a core claim of this book that the EU's market power has been constituted through law.

THE EU AS A NORMATIVE ACTOR

While the EU's external trade policy seeks to maintain high regulatory standards, achieving these 'broader objectives' remains central to the

[80] Opinion 2/15 (*Request for an opinion submitted by the European Commission pursuant to Article 218(11) TFEU*) [2015] OJ C363/22.

[81] *Ibid*, 11.

[82] UNCTAD, *World Investment Report 2011 – Non-Equity Modes of International Production and Development*, New York and Geneva (UNCTAD/WIR/2011) 26 July 2011, at 101.

overall trade philosophy.[83] A far cry from its relatively simple (neo)functional beginnings, the EU's modern trade strategy embodies a complex framework that seeks to embed neoliberal values and sustainability both internally and externally. The EU has become a site of governance with institutions, norms and values supporting its infrastructure. These values have been constitutionalised through the various treaties signed by the EU Member States. Although the Common Foreign and Security Policy (CFSP) is separately laid out in the Treaty,[84] other external policies are found to fall within the context of the EU's external action under the TFEU. Part V of the TFEU projects the aims and objectives of development cooperation,[85] economic, financial and technical cooperation,[86] humanitarian aid,[87] and restrictive measures,[88] of which may fall within the orientation of the CCP.

The conceptualisation of the EU as a *normative* actor asserts that the EU 'changes the norms, standards, and prescriptions of world politics away from the bounded experience of state-centricity'.[89] Normative ethical power is exhibited in the universalisation of ethical norms through the EU's external relations. Implicit to the EU's perceived claim to normative validity is the sociological concept of legitimacy, that is, the EU's normative power will only be sustainable if it is perceived to be 'right' and 'good' by those who experience it. The normative characteristics of the EU which have been internally constituted through law in the Lisbon Treaty, are also now actively promoted through the EU's external trade relations marking a paradigmatic shift away from market power toward an expression of normative power.

Embedding Liberal Democratic Principles

Internally, the aim of the Union is 'to promote peace, its *values*, and the well-being of its people'.[90] Article 2 of the Lisbon Treaty sets out the common values of the Union:

---

[83] C. Malmström, 'Values in EU Trade Policy – Targeting Corruption' Speech of 19 April 2016, 4th OECD Integrity Forum, Paris accessed 9 December 2016 at http://trade.ec.europa.eu/doclib/docs/2016/april/tradoc_154461.pdf.

[84] Provisions on the CSFP are set out in Chapter 2 of the TFEU.

[85] Articles 208–211 TFEU.

[86] Articles 212–213 TFEU.

[87] Article 214 TFEU.

[88] Article 215 TFEU.

[89] Manners (n. 7).

[90] Article 3 TFEU.

> The Union is founded on the values of respect for human dignity, freedom, democracy, equality, the rule of law, and respect for human rights, including the rights of the persons belonging to minorities. These values are *common* to the Member States in a society in which pluralism, non-discrimination, tolerance, justice, solidarity, and equality between women and men prevail.

Externalising the internal values of the EU in its relations with the wider world, Article 3(5) TFEU provides that the EU will 'uphold and promote its values and interests' in its relations with non-EU countries while an equivalent statement is made with regard to the EU's external relations in Article 21(1) TFEU:

> The Union's action on the international scene *shall be guided by the principles which have inspired its own creation, development and enlargement, and which it seeks to advance in the wider world*: democracy, the rule of law, the universality and indivisibility of human rights and fundamental freedoms, respect for human dignity, the principles of equality and solidarity, and respect for the principles of the United Nations Charter and international law. (emphasis added)

Constitutionalising its normative values of good governance, democracy, protection for human rights, and social solidarity through the Lisbon Treaty projects the EU conception of the 'good' to the rest of the world. Promoting these values through its external action, and conceiving of regionalism as a 'lever' to promote these values, a regional ideology of the EU as an interregional actor has emerged. This regionalist ideology 'not only justifies and enhances the EU's own existence and efficiency as an "actor" [but] the strategy also promotes the legitimacy and status of other regions'.[91]

The EU and its Member States 'coexist in international relations both as a matter of law and practice'.[92] Free trade agreements (FTAs) such as the EU-Korea FTA and the EPAs between the EU and African, Caribbean and Pacific (ACP) states are mixed agreements. In mixed agreements there may be a number of legal bases legitimising the EU's external action, or in other words, a number of legal justifications for exporting the EU's ethical normative framework. For example, the commercial aspects of these agreements have three legal bases: Article 207 governing trade in goods, services, commercial aspects of intellectual property

---

[91] F. Söderbaum and L. van Hangenhove, 'The EU as a Global Actor and the Role of Interregionalism' (2005) 27 *Journal of European Integration* 249–62, 257.

[92] Koutrakos (n. 21), 161.

rights, and FDI; Article 100(2) governing trade in transport; and, Article 167(3) governing culture. Thus, the Treaty of Lisbon recognises the delimitations of the exclusive competence of the EU in its CCP. However, there may be instances in which the ratification of these Agreements is unduly delayed because the nature of mixity entails complex legal processes.[93] For example, the EU-CARIFORUM EPA has not yet been ratified by all States, in spite of the Agreement being applied since 29 December 2008. Agreements like the EU-Korea FTA and the EPAs also incorporate development cooperation, which is covered under Articles 208–11 TFEU.[94] Strictly speaking, however, the legal basis for development cooperation is Article 4(4) TFEU which defines competence as shared between the EU and the Member States.[95]

Arguably, the use of the CCP as a unique foreign policy tool enables the EU to conduct its foreign affairs based entirely on materialist strategic interests under the guise of a 'development-friendly' approach. The extent to which this short-termist approach is sustainable remains a point of contestation, and Manners submits:

> The creative efforts and longer-term vision of the EU normative power towards the achievement of a more just, cosmopolitical world which empowers people in the actual conditions of their lives should and must be based on more universally accepted values and principles that can be explained to both Europeans and non-Europeans alike.[96]

Constructing a trade policy that dovetails with the EU's broader development goals and foreign policies, while maintaining the parallelism of the EU's internal and external objectives, is key to the success of the EU as a normative actor.[97]

---

[93] Voting procedures may need to be established under mixed agreements and the Union does not have a 'one-size-fits-all' approach to determining how the process of ratification should be established.

[94] Article 212 TFEU also enables the EU to conclude trade and cooperation agreements with non-developing third countries.

[95] Article 4(4) provides: 'In the areas of development cooperation and humanitarian aid, the Union shall have competence to carry out activities and conduct a common policy; however, the exercise of that competence shall not result in Member States being prevented from exercising theirs.'

[96] Manners (n. 7), 60.

[97] See European Commission (n. 10), 7.

THE TRADE:DEVELOPMENT INTERFACE

Development cooperation has long been a part of the Union's external action. Provisions governing development cooperation were originally set out in Article 130u EC Treaty and provided that cooperation should foster 'the sustainable economic and social development of the developing countries, and more particularly the most disadvantaged among them', facilitate the 'gradual integration of developing countries in the global economy' and finally, 'campaign against poverty in the developing countries'.

In defining the objectives of development cooperation, Article 208 TFEU states that it 'shall be conducted within the framework of principles and objectives of the Union's external action'.[98] It is clear from this element of Article 208 TFEU that aspects of development cooperation may fall within the general scope of the CCP. Furthermore, the provision provides that development cooperation 'shall have as its primary objective the reduction and, in the long term, the eradication of poverty'. Stating the 'primary objective' of development cooperation as the reduction and eradication of poverty seems to suggest that any other objective falling under Article 21 TFEU will only be 'incidental', or secondary, to that primary aim. Panos Koutrakos argues that the articulation of Article 208 in this way illustrates its dual function as both 'inclusive' and 'exclusive': in providing what appears to be a bridge between development cooperation with other aspects of the EU's external relations (such as the CCP) it simultaneously limits reliance on Articles 208–211 TFEU to those objectives that seek to reduce or eradicate poverty.[99]

External action in relation to development cooperation finds its legal base in Article 209 TFEU, which provides:

---

[98] The full text of Article 208(1) TFEU reads: 'Union policy in the field of development cooperation shall be conducted within the framework of principles and objectives of the Union's external action. The Union's development cooperation policy and that of the Member States complement and reinforce one another. The Union shall have as its primary objective the reduction and, in the long term, the eradication of poverty. The Union shall take account of the objectives of development cooperation in the policies that it implements which are likely to affect developing countries.'

[99] Koutrakos (n. 21), 523.

> The Union may conclude with third countries and competent international organisations any agreement helping to achieve the objectives referred to in Article 21 of the Treaty on the European Union and in Article 208 of this Treaty.

This provision reflects the concept of development as set out in the *The European Consensus on Development*,[100] which sought to define common principles on development cooperation. Situating the *European Consensus* in the international framework of the Millennium Development Goals (MDGs) – and now the Sustainable Development Goals (SDGs) – the overarching aim of the EU is to implement an all-encompassing programme of development which addresses the social, economic and political aspects of development. The *European Consensus* is currently in the process of being revised with publication of a new policy expected later in 2016.

While the CJEU has recognised that 'the link between trade and development has become progressively stronger in modern international relations',[101] legality of including human rights clauses within trade agreements has been challenged only once. In the case of *Portugal v Council*[102] the exclusive competence of the Union to conclude a cooperation agreement[103] with India which included human rights clauses was challenged by Portugal. It argued that concluding an agreement which provided for human rights clauses went beyond the competence of the Community and, furthermore, that the specific fields of cooperation were outside the competence of the CCP. The Court was satisfied that Article 130u EC Treaty provided the legal base for the essential elements clause set out in Article 1(1) of the Indian cooperation agreement, which provided that respect for human rights formed the basis of cooperation between the parties.

---

[100] Joint declaration by the Council and the representatives of the governments of the Member States meeting within the Council, the European Parliament and the Commission on the development policy of the European Union entitled 'The European Consensus' (2006) OJ C46.

[101] Case 45/86, *Commission v Council (re GSP)* [1987] E.C.R. 1493, para. 17.

[102] Case C-268/94, *Portugal v Council* [1996] E.C.R. I-6219.

[103] Concluding association agreements with third countries is one means through which the EU can externalise its norms and finds its legal basis in Article 217 TFEU, which states: 'The Union may conclude with one or more third countries or international organisations agreements establishing an association involving reciprocal rights and obligations, common action and special procedure.'

In this case, the Court noted that while the Community had competence to conclude cooperation agreements 'that competence is not exclusive but is complementary to the Member States'.[104] Furthermore, the Court made two notable statements about the scope of measures that fall within the development cooperation policy of the Union. First, the Court found that requiring a separate legal base for specific matters that fall within the broad understanding of development cooperation 'would in practice amount to rendering devoid of substance the competence and procedure prescribed in Article 209 (ex Article 130y)'. Second, and drawing on Opinion 1/78, the Court highlights the nature of development cooperation in paragraph 39:

> … the fact that a development cooperation agreement contains clauses concerning various specific matters cannot alter the characterization of the agreement, which must be determined having regard to its essential object and not in terms of the individual clauses, provided that those clauses do not impose such extensive obligations concerning the specific matters referred to that those obligations in fact constitute objectives distinct from those of development cooperation.

In doing so, the Court reinforces the importance of choosing the correct legal base. This case highlights the ways in which the CCP and development cooperation policy dovetail to provide the legal bases for cooperation agreements.

Adopting a prescriptive and formalistic approach to the human rights dimension of the cooperation Agreement was disappointing, particularly in light of the passionate comments made by Attorney General La Pergola. In his Opinion, La Pergola recognised that the nature of development is a 'complex vision' which is 'the product of interaction between its economic, social and political aspects'.[105] His comments in relation to human rights and development policy are particularly interesting:

> … the democracy clause must indeed be deemed *necessary* if development cooperation policy is to be lawfully pursued. I might venture to add that it would be the *failure to adopt* a clause of that type that would compromise the legality of Community action, because compliance with the specific wording of Article 130u would no longer be guaranteed.

---

[104] *Portugal v Council* (n. 102).

[105] Opinion of Advocate General La Pergola, Case C-268/94, delivered on 23 May 1996, para. 13.

In the judgment, the Court found that human rights violations 'may be, amongst other things, an important factor for the exercise of the right to have a development cooperation agreement suspended or terminated.'[106]

Recently, in the case of *Commission v Council*[107] the choice of legal base in mixed agreements was once again considered by the Court in reference to the Council's decision to sign a Partnership and Cooperation Agreement with the Philippines.[108] At the heart of this challenge was the Council's reliance on a number of legal bases: Article 207 TFEU (CCP), Article 209 TFEU (development cooperation), Article 79 TFEU (re-admission of third country nationals), Article 91 TFEU and Article 100 TFEU (Transport), and Article 191 TFEU (Environment). In this case, the Commission argued that the correct legal bases are Article 207 TFEU and Article 209 TFEU since the trade element was not merely 'incidental' to the development cooperation aspect of the Framework Agreement.[109] Furthermore, and in disagreement with the Council, the Commission submitted that the provisions relied upon in the Lisbon Treaty relating to readmission of third party nationals, transport and the environment fell within the context of Article 209 TFEU. Drawing on the Court's findings in *Portugal v Council* (1996), the Commission noted that when reading Article 207 TFEU and Article 209 TFEU in conjunction with Article 21(1) TFEU, development cooperation is a 'broad notion' that is 'conducted in the framework of a wide range of policy objectives'[110] and unless a trade element is distinct from the broad understanding of development cooperation then it does not require a separate legal base beyond Article 209 TFEU.

The question for the Court to consider in this case was whether those provisions relating to readmission of third party nationals, transport and environment fall within the scope of development cooperation policy or require their own legal base. With reference to cooperation agreements, which may be settled on a number of legal bases, the Court first references the traditional 'centre of gravity' test relating to the aim and content of the particular measure:

---

[106] *Ibid*, para. 27.

[107] Case C-377/12, *Commission v Council* ECLI:EU:C:2014:1903.

[108] Council Decision 2012/272/EU on the signing, on behalf of the Union, of the Framework Agreement on Partnership and Cooperation between the European Union and its Member States, of the one part, and the Republic of the Philippines, of the other part, [2012] OJ L134/3.

[109] *Commission v Council* (n. 107), para. 12.

[110] *Ibid,* paras 18–19.

> If examination of a European Union measure reveals that it pursues a twofold purpose or that it has a twofold component and if one of those is identifiable as the main or predominant purpose or component, whereas the other is merely incidental, the measure must be founded on a single legal basis, namely, that required by the main or predominant purpose or component. By way of exception, if it is established that the measure pursues several objectives which are inseparably linked without one being secondary and indirect in relation to the other, the measure must be founded on the various corresponding legal bases. However, no dual legal basis is possible where the procedures required by each legal basis is incompatible with each other.[111]

Noting that Article 21(1) TFEU states poverty eradication as the primary objective of development cooperation, the Court also found that those measures aimed at pursuing the objectives set out in Article 21(2)(d) TFEU of fostering sustainable economic, social and environmental development of developing countries fall within the development cooperation policy, provided they are *aimed at* eradicating poverty.

The Council sought to distinguish this case from that of *Portugal v Council* (1996) on the grounds that development cooperation has evolved significantly since the mid-1990s. While the nature of measures included in the Framework Agreement were more extensive, they nevertheless align with the EU's shared vision of development cooperation as set out in the *European Consensus on Development* in 2006,[112] reiterates the eradication of poverty as its 'primary and overarching objective' in paragraph 5. In paragraph 7, the broad notion of development co-operation is evident:

> We reaffirm that development is a central goal by itself, and that sustainable development includes good governance, human rights and political, economic, social and environmental aspects.

In addition, the adoption of Regulation 1905/2006,[113] which establishes a financing instrument for development cooperation as complemented by Regulation 234/2014,[114] which establishes a partnership instrument for cooperation with third countries, demonstrates a concrete expression of the broad notion of development cooperation by the Union. The Court

---

111 *Ibid*, para. 34.

112 European Union, *The European Consensus*, [2006] OJ C46/1.

113 [2006] OJ L378/41. Paragraph 2 states: 'The Community pursues a development cooperation policy aimed at achieving the objectives of poverty reduction, sustainable economic and social development and the smooth and gradual integration of developing countries into the world economy.'

114 [2014] OJ L77/77.

found in this case that the specific matters of readmission of third party nationals, environment and transport pursue the goals set out in the European Consensus and, therefore, 'do not contain obligations so extensive that they may be considered to constitute objectives distinct from those of development cooperation that are neither secondary nor indirect in relation to the latter objectives'.[115]

Perhaps most significantly, while the Court does not discuss Article 207 TFEU in its judgment it appears to recognise the inextricable link between Articles 207 TFEU and 209 TFEU, with neither being secondary or 'incidental' to the other. The decision of the Court is instructive for cooperation agreements as it reaffirms the broad notion of development cooperation and the measures that fall within the context of this policy. With regard to cooperation agreements, the assumption of the Court in their assertion that neither the CCP nor development cooperation are merely incidental to one another is significant for two reasons. First, this has implications for the choice of legal base. Where a cooperation agreement is negotiated that includes elements of both trade and development cooperation, it will be necessary to conclude the agreement using two legal bases: Article 207 TFEU and Article 209 TFEU. Where other objectives fall within a broad notion of development, they do not require a separate legal base even where the Treaty might provide for one. Second, and perhaps of more importance, the requirement that Article 207 TFEU is read in light of Article 209 TFEU *and* Article 21(1) TFEU would appear to suggest that the broader development principles fall explicitly within the CCP. If that is the case, then to what extent will the EU be required to ensure that its external trade relations are inherently 'development friendly'? For example, might the EU be precluded from enacting certain trade measures where such measures interfere with, or create harmful effects for, the environment? This is certainly a legal question that is worthy of interrogation.

DEVELOPMENT COOPERATION

Financial assistance has been provided to the ACP countries through the European Commission's European Development Fund (EDF)[116] since its launch in 1959. While a heading for the Fund in the European Union has been reserved since 1993 by the request of the European Parliament, the EDF does not fall within the EU's general budget. Rather, the individual

---

115 *Commission v Council* (n. 107), para. 59.

116 The EDF was created under the Treaty of Rome in 1957.

Member States contribute funds on a voluntary basis and the EDF is subject to its own financial rules and regulations.[117] It comprises two financial limbs, the Grant Facility and the Investment Facility. Since 1959, the ACP States and Overseas Countries and Territories (OCTs) have received financial support from the Commission through the EDF. To date, there have been ten previous cycles of EDF financing and it is now in the eleventh phase. Typically, each cycle of EDF correlates with a particular international and/or partnership between the EU and the ACP. It remains the world's 'largest and most advanced financial and political contractual framework for North-South cooperation'.[118]

However, in recent cycles there has been a shift toward 'blending' of loans through what the Commission defines as 'Innovative Instruments' wherein development aid is combined with other private or public sector sources of funding, such as loans, equity, capital and/or risk.[119] Given the ongoing needs for developing countries in the pursuit of achieving the SDGs, the blending mechanism offers an alternative source of funding in addition to the voluntary funds allocated by EU Member States. In a bid to improve the quality and quantity of development assistance the EU, as part of its commitments in the Paris Declaration of Aid Effectiveness (2007), the Accra Agenda for Action (2008), and the European Code of Conduct on Division of Labour in Development Policy (2007), introduced a new form of assistance known as Grant and Loan Blending Facilities (GBLFs).

Since 2007, the EU has established GBLFs which involve development aid from EU Member States and financial assistance from the following private sector actors: European Investment Bank (EIB), the Agence Française de Développement (AFD), the KwF Bankengruppe, the European Bank for Reconstruction and Development (EBRD), and the Council of Europe Development Bank (CEB).[120] In line with the World Bank's vision of country ownership, the blending of financial instruments

---

[117] European Commission, 'Summary of the European Development Fund' [undated] accessed 9 December 2016 at http://eur-lex.europa.eu/legal-content/EN/TXT/?uri=URISERV%3Ar12102.

[118] M. Gavas, 'Reviewing the Evidence: How well does the European Development Fund perform?' ODI Report of 31 January 2012 accessed at https://www.odi.org/sites/odi.org.uk/files/odi-assets/publications-opinion-files/8218.pdf, 3.

[119] S. Bilal and F. Kratke, 'Blending Loans and Grants: To blend or not to blend?' ECDPM Report 2013 accessed 9 December 2016 at ecdpm.org/wp-content/uploads/2013/11/Blending-Loans-Grants-Blend-Not-Blend.pdf.

[120] J.N. Ferrer and A. Behrens, 'Innovative Approaches to EU Blending Mechanisms for Development Finance' CEPS Special Report (18 May 2011)

'guarantee a voice and ownership on the part of the beneficiaries by drawing them into the strategic decision-making body.'[121] The partner country works with the financial institution to develop the strategic operations of the proposed project to ensure that appropriate financial forecasts are made and adequate support is provided for the realisation of the project.[122] For some, the positive effects of the blending mechanism have to date been uncontroversial.[123] However, the relative youth of this programme of financing has meant that effective monitoring of their implementation is yet to be established. Under the 11th EDF, the EU Commission has stated that €30.5 billion will be available to ACP countries for the period 2014–2020. From a development-effectiveness perspective, the desirability of the principle of differentiation has been questioned although the following section demonstrates that some of these fears appear to have been unfounded.

Agenda For Change[124]

Eradicating poverty is the primary objective of the EU's development policy and as the 2015 target for the MDGs approached, the EU found itself at a critical juncture with regard to its development policy. Recognising the interconnection between its internal EU-2020 Strategy and its external relations in which development policy is now firmly anchored, the Commission sought to redefine the framework through which development assistance is delivered. In identifying that 'the objectives of development, democracy, human rights, good governance, and security are intertwined' the Commission noted that it 'is critical for societies to offer a future to young people'.[125] While not explicitly referring to the concept of *sustainable development,* this nevertheless recognises the intergenerational nature of development policy. Noting that 'EU development policy must take into account the increased

---

accessed 9 December 2016 at https://www.ceps.eu/publications/approaches-eu-blending-mechanisms-development-finance, i.

121 *Ibid*, ii.

122 The financing facilities typically comprise a strategic board, an operational board and a financiers group in which the partner country participates at all levels.

123 *Ibid.*

124 Communication from the Commission to the European Parliament, the Council, the European Economic and Social Committee and the Committee of the Regions, 'Increasing the impact of EU Development Policy: an Agenda For Change' COM (2011) 637 Final of 13 October 2011.

125 *Ibid*, 3.

differentiation between developing countries' the proposal for the Agenda for Change marked a significant shift in the EU's provision of development assistance.[126]

In its Communication to the other EU institutions, the Commission proposed that development assistance should be focused toward human rights, democracy and other key elements of good governance, and inclusive and sustainable growth for human development. It stated that in order to 'ensure best value for money' that these objectives would be best achieved through a three-pronged approach: differentiated development partnerships; coordinated EU action; and improved coherence among EU policies.[127]

Marking a departure from the rhetoric of sustainable development, the Commission refers to 'inclusive growth' which is 'characterised by *people's ability to participate in, and benefit from, wealth and job creation*'.[128] Development is once again defined in economic terms, based on the assumption that better engagement with the economic sphere and productive base will yield correlative improvements in other social dimensions. Reinforcing the materialist concept of development, the Commission notes that the 'EU should take a more comprehensive approach to human development' which 'involves supporting a healthy and educated population, giving the workforce skills that respond to labour needs, developing social protection, and reducing inequality of opportunity'.[129] On the basis of these assertions, the commodification of human beings in developing countries so that they might contribute to the reproduction of the materialist core seems apparent. As stated throughout this book, economic development is necessarily a part of inclusive development, but in promoting economic growth we should do so in a manner that is respectful of cultural, social and religious normative frameworks.

A differentiated approach to development cooperation finds its legal base[130] in Article 3(2) of Regulation 233/2014 which provides that assistance will be 'tailor-made' based on four criterion:

---

[126] *Ibid.*

[127] *Ibid*, 4.

[128] *Ibid*, 7 emphasis added.

[129] *Ibid*, 7.

[130] Regulation (EU) No 233/2014 of the European Parliament and of the Council of 11 March 2014 establishing a financing instrument for development cooperation for the period 2014–2020, [2014] OJ L77/44.

(a) their needs, based on criteria such as population, income, per capita, the extent of poverty, income distribution and the level of human development;
(b) their capacities to generate and access financial resources and on their absorption capacities;
(c) their commitments and performance, based on criteria and indicators, such as political, economic and social progress, gender equality, progress in good governance and human rights, and the effective use of aid, in particular the way a country uses scarce resources for development, beginning with its own resources; and
(d) the potential impact of Union assistance in partner countries.

The implementation of financial assistance is divided into geographic programmes, thematic programmes (including the Public Global Goods and Challenges programme and the Civil Society and Local Authorities Programme), and the newly established Pan-African programme.[131] Phasing out of bilateral grant assistance will apply to countries that are classified as upper-middle income countries or those countries with a gross domestic product (GDP) greater than one per cent of global GDP.[132] However, an exception applies to those countries with whom the EU enjoys a 'special' or 'strategic' relationship. Article 5(2)(b)(ii) of Regulation 233/2014 provides that in some instances, the phasing out of bilateral grant assistance with upper-middle income countries may be supplemented by a separate development envelope. Of the ACP countries, only South Africa will enjoy this privilege.[133]

Differentiation is central to the 11th EDF. In its Communication to the EU institutions, the Commission set out the underlying rationale for this approach:

> Grant based aid should not feature in geographic cooperation with more advanced developing countries already on sustained growth paths and/or able to generate enough own resources. Conversely, many other countries remain heavily reliant on external support to provide basic services to their people. In between, there is a spectrum of situations requiring different policy mixes and cooperation arrangements. A differentiated EU approach to aid allocation and partnerships is therefore key to achieving maximum impact and value for money.[134]

---

[131] Article 4 Regulation (EU) No 233/2014.
[132] Article 5(2)(b)(i) Regulation 233/2014.
[133] The EU also has a Strategic Partnership with Brazil, Canada, China, Japan, India, Mexico, Russia, South Korea, and the USA.
[134] Communication 2011, 9.

In assessing which countries shall be eligible for assistance, the Commission proposed that country needs, capacities, country commitments and performance, and potential EU impact are determining factors. Differentiation enables the EU to provide more focused development assistance in response to the direct needs of individual countries. Most significantly, however, the Agenda for Change proposes the phasing out of bilateral grant assistance to those countries that are classified as middle- or high-income. Under this proposal, the EU would no longer offer bilateral grant assistance to upper middle income countries and those countries representing a share of more than one per cent of the world's GDP. The Agenda for Change was formally adopted in 2011 and is in operation.

Departing from the Lomé framework in 2000, the principle of differentiation in ACP cooperation was introduced under the Cotonou Partnership Agreement (CPA) wherein differentiated levels and methods of development cooperation were provided according to individual country and regional needs. Blending is therefore within the spirit of the CPA. Within the ACP levels of development vary from country to country. Fears that the EU would effectively cut bilateral grant assistance to upper-middle income developing countries have perhaps been overstated. Analysis of the allocation of funds under the 11th EDF to the SADC EPA States illustrates that some provision is being made for those countries classified as upper-middle income. The SADC EPA region contains four upper-middle income countries (Angola, Botswana, Namibia, and South Africa) and two lower-middle income countries (Lesotho and Swaziland).

South Africa has been allocated €241 million through the DCI for the period 2014–2020 for three main sectors: employment creation, education, and capacity building.[135] Within the region, South Africa maintains a special relationship with the EU as manifested through the 'Strategic Partnership'. Blending as a financial mechanism is already in place, with South Africa receiving approximately 70 per cent of total development assistance from the EU: 25 per cent from the EDF, 20 per cent from the EIB, and 25 per cent from individual Member States.[136] According to the World Bank, development assistance constitutes only 0.3 per cent of South Africa's Gross National Income (GNI),[137] which certainly implies that South Africa is far from being dependent on aid.

[135] European Commission, 'Multiannual Indicative Programme between the Republic of South Africa and the European Union for the period 2014–2020'.

[136] See http://ec.europa.eu/europeaid/countries/south-africa_en (accessed 9 December 2016).

[137] Gross National Income (GNI) is defined by the World Bank as 'the sum of value added by all resident producers plus any product taxes (minus subsidies)

Collating an accurate picture of aid flows in the SADC region is difficult because it tends to be highly fragmented in the individual countries. While Namibia has been classified as an upper-middle income country since 2009, the EU has made provision under the 11th EDF for up to €68 million to promote education and skills training in the country. In 2015, Namibia will receive up to €15 million through the Annual Action Programme[138] for assistance in these two core sectors. Angola, which has seen economic growth through its oil revenues, is also currently classified as an upper-middle income country. Under the 10th EDF, Angola received €214 million for governance, support to economic and social development, rural development, food security and demining.[139] Currently, there is no data available with regard to allocation under the 11th EDF as the programming is ongoing. It is unclear how the differentiation principle of the 11th EDF will affect the provision of financial assistance to the ACP, especially as alternative sources of funding are available through the Aid for Trade (AfT) initiative.

CONCLUDING REMARKS

Adopting a historically sensitive approach to the nature of exclusivity in the EU's external competence to conclude international agreements, this chapter has demonstrated how the EU has the qualities of both a market power and a normative power. The financial commitment of the EU Member States to the ACP countries under the 11th EDF, in spite of the principle of differentiation introduced in accordance with the *Agenda for Change*, arguably sends a reassuring message to the ACP States that the EU is keen to preserve its special relationship.

In requiring that Article 207 TFEU is read in light of Article 21(1) TFEU, the Lisbon Treaty enables the EU to export universal values through its trade agreement but, in doing so, appears to bring within the scope of the CCP broader objectives not typically associated with economic liberalisation. The precise nature of the legal relationship between Article 207 TFEU and Article 209 TFEU, in the context of

---

not included in the valuation of output plus net receipts of primary income (compensation of employees and property income) from abroad.'

[138] Commission Decision, 'Annual Action Programme 2015 in favour of the Republic of Namibia to be financed from the 11th European Development Fund' COM (2015) 5025 Final of 24 July 2015.

[139] DG International Cooperation and Development, 'Angola' accessed 9 December 2016 at http://ec.europa.eu/europeaid/countries/angola_en.

cooperation agreements, lacks sufficient clarity and this dimension of the Treaty demands greater attention. If the two provisions are indeed inextricably linked, this would mark yet another shift in the EU's external relations towards a development-friendly trade framework, in cooperation agreements at least. In the next chapter, the legal character of the principle of sustainable development will be examined from the view of interrogating the trade:development interface.

4. The normative legal character of sustainable development

This chapter shifts the focus away from the regional and commercial focus of the EPAs toward an understanding of how the principle of sustainable development might be conceived under the new legal regime. Defined as trade *and* development agreements, this chapter considers the new trade relationship between the EU and the ACP countries is one of partnership 'centred on the objective of reducing and eventually eradicating poverty consistent with the objectives of sustainable development and the gradual integration of ACP countries into the world economy'.[1] Embedding a 'stronger social dimension'[2] within the process of globalisation is an aim of the EPAs and this can be achieved through the promotion of 'development-friendly' trade.

Regionalism as a development strategy has been a stated goal of the WTO, as noted at the Singapore Ministerial Conference:

> ... trade relations of WTO Members are being increasingly influenced by regional trade agreements, which have expanded vastly in number, scope and coverage. Such initiatives can promote further liberalisation and may assist least-developed, developing and transition economies in integrating into the international trading system.[3]

In order that the EPAs are WTO compliant they have been negotiated as Article XXIV legal regimes. As outlined in Chapter 2, Article XXIV rests on the assumption that trade is reciprocal: countries each agree to open

---

[1] Article 1 of the 'Partnership Agreement between the members of the African, Caribbean, and Pacific Group of States of the one part, and the European Community of the other part, signed in Cotonou on 23 June 2000' [2000] OJ L317/3 as amended through Decision No. 3/2008 of the ACP-EC Council of Ministers of 15 December 2008, [2008] OJ L352/59 to adopt the revised provisions set out in [2010] OJ L287/3, hereinafter referred to as the 'Cotonou Partnership Agreement 2014'.

[2] Article 2 Cotonou Partnership Agreement 2014.

[3] WTO, Singapore Ministerial Declaration, adopted 13 December 1996 (WT/MIN(96)/DEC).

their markets to one another, on the basis that 'substantially all trade' is liberalised within that regional space. In trade terms, the word 'reciprocity' implies granting mutual concessions with equally beneficial gains to be made by all. The construction of this term assumes homogeneity of production potential and opportunity, overlooking the socio-economic reality of development among vastly heterogenous trading states. That said, it has historically been the practice in North-South cooperation for developed countries to offer preferential access to their markets for developing countries. The legal basis for non-reciprocal and preferential treatment was rooted in the idea that the 'rich' can help the 'poor' through some kind of 'welfare obligation' at the multilateral level.[4] This was the dominant ideology in the post-colonial GATT policy and has characterised North-South relations to the current day. Rather than helping developing countries integrate into the global economy, preferential trade deepened post-colonial dependencies and further isolated developing countries from the rest of the globalising world.

The EPA negotiations illustrate the complex nature of liberalisation under North-South RTAs, and because each member has a different status of social, economic and human development, each member is likely to feel the impacts of reciprocal trade differently. Securing special and differential treatment, while ensuring that the EPAs were WTO compatible, was a significant challenge for the negotiators, given that these two objectives are seemingly at odds with one another as Article XXIV does not contain a 'special and differential treatment' (SDT) element. Nevertheless, the promotion of sustainable development is a stated aim of the EPA legal regime and this chapter examines the extent to which the principle of sustainable development is characterised as a justiciable legal norm.

The first section of this chapter presents an overview of the emerging field of law and development. In the second section, the legal classification of the principle of sustainable development will be assessed. The third and fourth sections provide an examination of the jurisprudence from the WTO's Dispute Settlement Body (DSB) and the International Court of Justice (ICJ) where it will be shown that the multilateral and international legal frameworks have fastened onto a normative concept of development that serves as a hermeneutic, or interpretive, tool.

---

4 R. Hudec, *Developing Countries in the GATT Legal System*, 2nd edn (Cambridge: Cambridge University Press, 2011).

DEVELOPMENT THROUGH LAW

Development is generally understood to be both a process and a discourse, but has been conceptualised from many theoretical perspectives.[5] As a discourse, development comprises a set of 'knowledges, interventions and world views' although it is neither a 'benign nor innocent' vision.[6] The earliest evidence of development as a discourse is found in moral philosophy and ethics,[7] but the first significant paradigmatic shift in development theory came with the influential work of Adam Smith[8] and David Ricardo,[9] whose collective work focused on the economic value of development. While both Smith and Ricardo promoted the ideology of free trade, the concept of comparative advantage was introduced by Ricardo, and this remains a cornerstone of the multilateral system today. Development as economic growth has evolved over time, shifting from the state-centric vision of classical economics[10] to one of minimal state intervention advocated by liberalism.[11] Rejecting the ethical notions of development as freedom, economic models promote a shared vision of development rooted in production, efficiency and wealth maximisation through the functioning of markets.

A notable shift in economic development theory came in the 1970s, with the concept of market fundamentalism – a theory based on the assumption that free markets will encourage an efficient allocation of resources – becoming increasingly fashionable. In response to the

---

5 For a comprehensive analysis of theories of development, see: V. Desai and R.B. Potter (eds), *The Companion to Development Studies*, 3rd edn (Abingdon and New York: Routledge, 2014).

6 J.D. Sidaway, 'Post-Development' in Desai and Potter (eds) *The Companion to Development Studies* (n. 5), 227.

7 Early ethical inquiry associated development as achieving a state of 'happiness' and living 'the good life'. For example, a concept of development can be seen in Aristotelian virtue ethics in his concept of *eudaimonia.* See: C. Cordner, 'Aristotelian Virtue and Its Limitations' (1994) 69(269) *Philosophy* 291–316.

8 A. Smith, *Wealth of Nations* (London: Wordsworth Editions Ltd, 2012) first published 1776.

9 D. Ricardo, *On the Principles of Political Economy and Taxation* (Dover: Dover Publications, 2004), first published 1817.

10 For a comprehensive overview of classical theory, see: J. Ravenhill, *Global Political Economy*, 3rd edn, (Oxford: Oxford University Press, 2011).

11 For an account of liberalism and multilateralism, see: A. Moravcsik, 'Taking Preferences Seriously: A Liberal Theory of International Politics' (1997) 51(4) *International Organisation* 513–66.

increasingly differentiated nature of modern society, a range of institutions have emerged governing aspects of social behaviour that had previously been governed and regulated by the nation-state.[12] Institutions have assumed a central position in the global order and set 'the rules of the game of society'[13] providing a framework for efficient production, ensuring the maximisation of capital and investment flows. Market fundamentalism, as a development strategy, was crystallised through the Washington Consensus,[14] was a programme of economic reform focusing on macroeconomic stabilisation, free trade and market integration. Although 'neoliberalism' is itself a contested concept[15] it broadly refers to a set of economic policies and prescriptions that have become the dominant ideology over the past 25 years. Neoliberalism proposes that power and wealth are concentrated in multinational corporations and transnational networks.[16] The role of the state is minimal, with intervention in the global economy from government agencies considered to be most undesirable.[17] The pursuit of economic freedom is key, with institutional frameworks rooted in libertarian values which are 'characterised by strong private property rights, free markets, and free trade'.[18]

With the growing prominence of international institutions came a renewed interest in the relationship between law and development.

---

[12] Robert Keohane, a leading liberal institutionalist, defines an 'institution' as a 'general pattern or categorization of activity or to a particular human-constructed arrangement, formally or informally organised'. See R.O. Keohane, 'International Institutions: Two Approaches' (1988) 32 *International Studies Quarterly* 386.

[13] D.C. North 'The New Institutional Economics and Third World Development' in J. Harris, J. Hunter and C.M. Lewis (eds), *The New Institutional Economics and Third World Development* (London: Routledge, 1995), 23.

[14] The term was first coined by American economist, John Williamson, to describe these economic prescriptions. Over time, the term has become associated with the broader neoliberal trade agenda, in spite of Williamson's objections.

[15] There is no single definition of 'neoliberalism' and it is not a homogenous philosophy. For an excellent overview of the differing accounts of neoliberal thought, see A. Saad-Filho and D. Johnston, *Neoliberalism: A Critical Reader* (London: Pluto Press, 2005).

[16] A. Lang, *World Trade Law after Neoliberalism: Reimagining the Global Economic Order* (Oxford: OUP, 2011).

[17] R. Munck, 'Neoliberalism and Politics, and the Politics of Neoliberalism' in Saad-Filho and Johnston, *Neoliberalism: A Critical Reader* (n.15), 60–9. See also R. Nozick, *Anarchy, State and Utopia* (Oxford: Basil Blackwell, 1974).

[18] D. Harvey, *A Brief History of Neoliberalism* (Oxford: Oxford University Press, 2005), 2.

Scholars of law and development propose that the legal reforms can be used as a 'development strategy'.[19] That the WTO and other global institutions adopt a neoliberal ideology is self-evident and the rationalisation of the legal order can act as an external constraint to the realisation of a broader conception of development. Over time, the economic measure of development has become a central norm of international financial institutions and since the late 1940s, the global financial institutions, such as the World Bank and the International Monetary Fund (IMF), have used the measure of 'gross domestic product' (GDP) per capita to determine the development status of every country. The World Bank classifies countries as 'high-income', 'middle income', 'low-middle income' and 'low-income', depending on their measure of GDP per capita.[20] In the WTO, it is for each member to determine their own development status, although the World Bank framework remains influential.

Although the international legal framework has institutionalised the dominant economic ideology, competing theories of development have emerged which seek to reveal the multifaceted nature of development. It is widely acknowledged that the global economy is riddled with inequality – political, economic and social – and the polarity of wealth within a population, be it local or global, raises issues of distributive justice.[21]

---

[19] M. Trebilcock and M.M. Prado, *An Advanced Introduction to Law & Development* (Cheltenham, UK and Northampton, MA, USA: Edward Elgar, 2014), 47.

[20] Interestingly, the WTO does not provide a classificatory framework and instead allows each country to determine its own development status.

[21] Utilitarianism conceptualises development as a measure of maximising utility. Developed primarily through the works of Jeremy Bentham and John Stuart Mill classical utilitarianism is a theory of distributive justice where the state is warranted for maximising human 'well-being'. When the balance of pleasure over pain is as great as it can be this is maximising social utility. Utilitarianism deals with the sum total rather than the distribution at the micro-level and therefore arguably it does not respect rights of everyone, but just the majority. For Rawls, development is rooted in social contract and requires the redistribution of 'primary goods' in accordance with the 'difference principle' to ensure that the least advantaged in society are looked after. Under a Rawlsian framework, individual liberty is given lexical priority over equality but nevertheless, redistribution of assets is a key part of a functioning society. His theory is procedural in nature, concerned with the processes necessary to promote a more equitable distribution of wealth within society. But, much like the libertarian school, Rawls' theory of justice fails to address the consequences that flow from his procedural approach.

Challenging the rational construction of economic development, neo-Marxist dependency theory proposes that society is stratified according to an unequal distribution of wealth. As each group seeks to advance their own interest against rival groups, a social structure begins to emerge distinguishing a dominant class from the subordinate class. The dominant class seeks to protect its position and will use the law as ideology to ensure the social stratification remains intact.[22] Law, in this sense, becomes an instrumental tool for domination through its role as a medium of social integration.

It is argued that market fundamentalism has proven a successful project because, for the past 60 years, we, as a global community, have been led to believe that capitalism is the *only* way for countries to develop. Since Margaret Thatcher famously coined the term 'there is no alternative' the world has globalised in accordance with neoliberal capitalist principles. Whether knowingly or not, the concept of development as economic growth has become an accepted part of our vernacular, a taken-for granted truth in our uncritical philosophy. So far, the catastrophic nature of capitalism predicted by traditional Marxist thought has been avoided although, admittedly, there have been notable market failures including the most recent financial crises. Nevertheless, we remain under the capitalist spell and the EPAs continue to be framed as rational legal regimes through which the neoliberal concept of development is embedded.

Moving away from the consequentialist theories of justice, Amartya Sen argues that the focus of development should be on human capabilities to achieve a life that each individual values and, in order to do so, the means to realising substantive freedom must be established.[23] Contesting the instrumentalist view that places emphasis on contractual obligations and property rights, this approach proposes that the rule of law may be considered to be both a *means* to development but also a *justified end* of development. Bridging the schools of ethics and economics, Amartya Sen proposes a theory of development where freedom is both the principal means and the principal end of development.[24] Moving against the orthodox instrumentalist assumption that economic growth presupposes other substantive freedoms, Sen argues that these

---

[22] A. Hunt, 'Problems of the State: Law, State and Class Struggle' (1976) *Marxism Today* 178–87.

[23] M. Nussbaum, 'Capabilities as Fundamental Entitlements: Sen and Social Justice' (2003) 9 *Feminist Economics* 33.

[24] A. Sen, *Development as Freedom* (Oxford: Oxford University Press, 2001).

values should be seen as primary goals which will in turn stimulate growth. Development is conceptualised as 'a process of expanding the real freedoms that people enjoy'[25] economic growth perceived as a 'means' towards the realisation of those substantive freedoms. Agency plays a central role in Sen's concept of development, with his 'capability approach' offering an alternative to neoclassical economic thought. A theory of welfare economics, Sen's approach is rooted in the idea that each individual has the capability to achieve the type of life that they value.

Sen identifies five types of distinct, but interrelated, freedoms that advance the capabilities of a person: political freedom, economic facilities, social opportunities, transparency guarantees, and protective security.[26] Development as a process should, therefore, play an instrumental role in promoting these freedoms so that people can have lives that they value:

> Expanding the freedoms that we have reason to value not only makes our lives richer and more unfettered, but also allows us to be fuller social persons, exercising our own volitions and interacting with – and influencing – the world in which we live.[27]

Experience has shown that promoting economic freedom can, in fact, lead to substantive unfreedom(s). For example, Angola is classified as an 'upper-middle' income country by the World Bank because of its huge income generated by oil revenues each year. This implies significant economic freedom. However, the Multidimensional Poverty Index shows that approximately 77 per cent of the Angolan population live below the poverty line,[28] in other words, the majority of the population experience substantial unfreedoms on a daily basis. This illustrates the danger of conceptualising development through a monological theory because it leads to a skewed vision of the nature of development as a multi-dimensional concept.[29]

---

[25] *Ibid*, 3.

[26] *Ibid*, 10.

[27] *Ibid*, 16–17.

[28] Oxford Poverty and Human Development Initiative (OPHI), 'Country Briefing: Angola' (July 2010) accessed 9 December 2016 at www.ophi.org.uk/wp-content/uploads/Angola.pdf.

[29] Nevertheless, there are some success stories of how an emphasis on aggressive economic liberalisation can lift people out of poverty. For example, the East Asian 'Tigers' have experienced unprecedented growth through the adoption of unilateral liberalization policies.

This leads to the question of what role international economic law can play in promoting the realisation of not only economic freedom, but social, cultural and political freedom. Roberto Mangabeira Unger proposes that the role of the legal thinker is to develop a theory of law that does 'justice to social-democratic commitments'.[30] For Habermas, a just theory of global law is one in which each free and equal legal person is entitled to human rights. Far from advocating the creation of a world government, Habermas proposes that a world organisation should be established through which the protection of human rights and the maintenance of peace are institutionalised.[31] 'Just' legal regimes serve to protect these rights, institutionalising their normative content in other spheres of social life. Through a detailed examination of legal frameworks at the EU and WTO level, this chapter argues that the method of legal analysis is rationally constructed, and restricts the possibility for transformative discovery of alternative legal methods.

Acknowledging the constraints of historically situated legal analysis, and abandoning the assumptions of neoliberalism, enables alternative visions of development to be explored. The importance of economic growth as an integral part of any model of development is acknowledged, but it is argued that economic value is not the *sole* factor of development, nor should it necessarily take priority over other considerations. As outlined above in the case of Angola, the experience of many developing countries is one of struggle – a struggle to eradicate inequality and to overcome the crises created from a lack of resources. Exploring alternative perspectives emancipates us from our existing bounded rationalist understanding of law and development. Revealing the unfreedoms perpetuated by the multilateral trading system, and in particular exploring the implications of economic unfreedom for developing countries, enables the discourse of development *through* law to be transformed.

For a more inclusive vision of sustainable development to be accepted, one that shifts the focus away from development as a purely economic process to one that reveals the emancipatory potential of development as a process of freedom and equality for those participating in the multilateral trading system, the legal framework needs to be reinterpreted. However, revision of the GATT is simply not on the agenda. To overcome the inherent development deficit of Article XXIV, and against the backdrop of a formalist legal framework, alternative means through

---

[30] R.M. Unger, *What Should Legal Analysis Become?* (London: Verso, 1996), 35.

[31] J. Habermas, 'A Political Construction for the Pluralist World Society?' (2007) 34 *Chinese Journal of Philosophy* 331–43.

which development as freedom can be promoted are required. In the EPA framework, the trade elements are scaffolded by provisions relating to sustainable development, environmental protection, good governance, respect for human rights, and the protection of labour standards giving the impression of a 'just' legal regime. However, this assumption will be interrogated throughout the remaining chapters of this book. The starting point for this interrogation is to ascertain the nature of sustainable development in law, or in other words, to establish whether the principle of sustainable development constitutes a legal principle or merely a policy objective to be achieved by the parties.

SUSTAINABLE DEVELOPMENT AS A JUSTICIABLE LEGAL NORM

Creating trade and development cooperation agreements on a regional level abstracts the regime out of the international arena and may render the operation of its principles non-justiciable at the international level. Although both the EU and the ACP States can initiate a dispute at the WTO where it relates to the EPA, the mandate of this organisation is predominantly economic and the extent to which its dispute settlement system has examined non-economic values has been limited. In general, social norms and human rights are examined in alternative legal fora, and at the international level most notably at the International Court of Justice (ICJ). An important caveat must be stated from the outset of this analysis. As the EU is not a member of the ICJ, the court does not have jurisdiction to hear any dispute brought against the EU; therefore, should a dispute arise in relation to implementation of the EPA the ICJ will not serve as an appropriate legal forum. Nevertheless, the principles enunciated through international law are binding on each individual Member State albeit not against the EU as a regional actor. Furthermore, the WTO's Dispute Settlement Body (DSB) is bound to interpret WTO provisions in light of international law. It would appear, therefore, that the justiciability of the development dimensions of the EPA will rely on the extent to which sustainable development constitutes a justiciable legal norm.

The framing of the EPAs as trade *and* development cooperation agreements seemingly reinforces the notion that sustainability should underpin the trade regime. Development emerged as a concept or principle of international law in the mid-1980s through two notable expressions of the United Nations. In 1986, the Declaration on the Right to Development ('the Declaration') was adopted and affirmed some of the fundamental principles of the Charter of the United Nations and the Universal Declaration of Human Rights. In the recital to the Declaration it is recognised that development is 'a comprehensive economic, social, cultural, and political process, which aims at the improvement of the well-being of the entire population and of all individuals on the basis of their active, free, and meaningful participation in development and in the fair distribution of benefits resulting therefrom'.[32] Article 1 of the Declaration expresses development as an 'inalienable human right' while Article 2 identifies each individual as 'the central subject of development [who] should be the active participant and beneficiary of the right to development'. As a human right, the right to development is equal to other human rights and is both an individual and a collective right where the State bears the duty of respecting, protecting and fulfilling that right. The 'human-centred development' approach has been restated in the EPAs, which demonstrates that the parties are rhetorically mimicking the international legal framework.

While the Declaration, adopted through UN Resolution 41/128, is not legally binding its principles are anchored in other legally binding international instruments. The Office of the High Commissioner on Human Rights (OHCHR) identifies 17 international instruments which directly link with a dimension of the principle of development set out in the Declaration.[33] This highlights the complex matrix of interests to

---

[32] United Nations, *Declaration on the Right to Development* (4 December 1986), A/RES/41/128.

[33] Binding instruments in which aspects of the right to development are anchored include: Charter of the United Nations; Universal Declaration of Human Rights; International Covenant on Civil and Political Rights; International Covenant on Economic, Social, and Cultural Rights; Convention on the Elimination of All Forms of Discrimination against Women; Convention on the Rights of the Child; Convention on Rights of Persons with Disabilities; International Convention on the Protection of the Rights of All Migrant Workers and Members of their Families; ILO Indigenous and Tribal Peoples Convention; International Convention on the Elimination of All Forms of Racial Discrimination; Convention on Cluster Munitions; Convention on the Prohibition of the Use, Stockpiling, Production and Transfer of Anti-personnel Mines and on Their Destruction; Comprehensive Nuclear-Test-Ban Treaty; Convention on the Prohibitions or Restrictions on the Use of Certain Conventional Weapons which may be deemed to be Excessively Injurious or to have Indiscriminate Effects; Convention on the Prohibition of the Development, Production and Stockpiling of Bacteriological (Biological) and Toxin Weapons and on their Destruction; Treaty on the Non-proliferation of Nuclear Weapons; Arms Trade Treaty.

which legality may attach, while not recognising development as an international legal norm itself, *per se*.

Shortly after the adoption of the Declaration, the Rio Declaration followed suit. Sustainable development refers to development that 'meets the needs of the present without compromising the ability of future generations to meet their own needs'.[34] This implies that sustainable development represents the synthesis of two principles: *intergenerational equity* and *intragenerational equity*.[35] Intergenerational equity refers to the 'sustainable' part of the term relating to the need to ensure our future generations are able to enjoy the planet. Intragenerational equity refers to the 'development' aspect of the term and requires equity in the distribution of the development gains achieved internally and internationally. Through the integration of these two principles, the concept of sustainable development is realised. Most scholars accept that sustainable development is not a static concept but one that is evolutive in nature.[36] Some, however, propose that sustainable development is more concerned with intergenerational equity and offers only a 'faint suggestion' for intragenerational equity.[37] The Brundtland Report's oft-cited definition of sustainable development presupposes that the technical means for choosing the correct path to ensure that the needs of future generations currently exist. In doing so, it 'reflects a view that the environment is incredibly adaptive and resilient'.[38]

Article 27 of the Rio Declaration on Environment and Development provides:

> States and people shall cooperate in good faith and in a spirit of partnership in the fulfilment of the principles embodied in this Declaration and in the further development of international law in the field of sustainable development.

Herein, sustainable development is treated as a subcategory of international law rather than as a norm of international law *per se*. Sustainable development, as articulated in the Brundtland Report, raises a number of

---

[34] United Nations, 'Report of the World Commission on Environment and Development: *Our Common Future*' (Brundtland Report) of March 1987.

[35] V. Barral, 'Sustainable Development in International Law: Nature and Operation of an Evolutive Legal Norm' (2012) 23 *European Journal of International Law* 377–400, 380.

[36] *Ibid*, 382.

[37] M. Mcloskey, 'The Emperor Has No Clothes: The Conundrum of Sustainable Development' (1998) 9 *Duke Environmental Law and Policy Forum* 153–59, 154.

[38] *Ibid*, 155.

conceptual difficulties. It fails to distinguish between non-renewable and renewable resources, for example. Securing the needs of future generations does not provide any guidance on the distribution of non-renewable resources through the generations; neither does it prescribe the conditions for maintaining depleting resources. As the global population grows, the environment is placed under greater pressure to meet the material needs of the human population. The definition of sustainability set out in the Report rests on an assumption that human ingenuity will somehow overcome, that 'unforeseeable human discoveries in the future will rescue us'.[39] The converse is also true: the definition of sustainable development assumes that the environment will not flourish in the absence of economic development. Overall, this definition provides little in the way of clarification as to the legal nature of the concept of sustainable development. In general, sustainable development is conceived of as a multi-dimensional paradigm, drawing together human, social, economic, cultural and environmental dimensions of development. Each individual component or dimension comprises different social and ethical norms to which legality might attach. Depending on the specific nature of the issue, different standards might apply. The variability of standards is therefore merely a reflection of the variability of the concept itself.

Absent from Article 27 is detail of what constitutes 'international law in the field of sustainable development' and this led a number of scholars to interrogate the legal character of this area of law. In order to establish whether sustainable development is legal in character we must assess whether it has legal scope, that is whether it creates and produces legal effects, and whether it is recognised as a legal norm at an international level.[40] Sustainable development will be justiciable to the extent that its constituent elements form part of binding international law in accordance with Article 38(1) Statute of Rome. Under Article 38, the sources of international law are positive (enacted) law, customary law, and general principles of international law.

A number of arguments relating to the legal classification of sustainable development have been articulated ranging from the conceptualisation of sustainable development as a principle of customary international law to the idea that sustainable development is a new branch of international law. Others have suggested that the principle of sustainable development lacks legal character altogether and is nothing more than a

---

39 *Ibid*, 157.
40 Barral (n. 35), 383.

political objective. Philippe Sands has argued that international law in the field of sustainable development is:

> a broad umbrella accommodating the specialised fields of international law which aim to promote economic development, environmental protection and respect for civil and political rights. It is not independent and free-standing of principles and rules, and it is still emerging. As such, it is not coherent and comprehensive, nor it is free from ambiguity or inconsistency … Rather, it endorses on behalf of the whole of the international community (states, international institutions, non-governmental actors) an approach requiring existing principles, rules and institutional arrangements to be treated in an integrated manner.[41]

Sands rejects the notion of sustainable development as a norm of international law, as it lacks the character of international law. Nevertheless, its constituent parts 'coalesce' around a complex matrix of different legal principles. For Sands, it is the interconnection or integration of these different fields of law that promote economic development, environmental protection, and the protection of civil and political rights that gives sustainable development its character, albeit that character is rather evasive.

Virginie Barral proposes that the 'flexibility' of linguistic formulations does not *ab initio* circumscribe the normativity of sustainable development as a legal norm:

> … the softness of the obligations set out in a treaty provision should not be an obstacle to its validity and binding legal nature. For Weil, the '*caractère imprécis ou peu contraignant de certaines dispositions insérées dans des traités … n'a rien à voir avec celle de leur caractère juridique …*[42]

So, articulating sustainable development goals as aspirational with the parties 'striving toward' or 'promoting' does not proscribe their classification as 'perfect legal rules' and 'valid norms of international law'.[43] An argument can be made that the softness of these norms merely increases the *marge d'appréciation* in the execution of these particular norms:

> States are under an obligation to pursue sustainable development; they are bound by an obligation of means, and by implementing these countless

---

[41] P. Sands, 'International Law in the Field of Sustainable Development' (1994) LXV *BYIL* 303.

[42] Barral (n. 35), 384.

[43] *Ibid.*

treaties they contribute, day after day, to progressively making sustainable development requirements real.[44]

This leads Barral to assert that these norms are valid, but of a 'different object' that does not 'request a result to be achieved, but only means to be put in place to try to achieve that result'.[45] While this offers an attractive alternative conceptualisation of the normative legal character of sustainable development, it is undermined by the manner in which sustainable development is articulated in RTAs, for example. Sustainable development is projected as a diffuse principle, encompassing different dimensions which may interrelate and intersect, and while it certainly has a normative character, it is difficult to accept that the principle of sustainable development is a valid *legal* norm in and of itself. To this end, the most persuasive theory is that of Vaughan Lowe, who asserts that sustainable development is a modifying norm, or interstitial norm, and the 'concept's legal relevance is to be found in the pull it exerts on the judicial reasoning process.'[46] In other words, sustainable development is a normative principle that serves as an interpretive tool in the judicial process.

The following section will present an analysis of the cases that have drawn on the principle of sustainable development in both the WTO DSB and the ICJ adjudicative settings. It will be shown that the principle of sustainable development has been an important tool for the resolution of conflict of norms in a number of multilateral disputes and international law cases.

EMBEDDING SUSTAINABLE DEVELOPMENT IN INTERNATIONAL TRADE

Although the concept of sustainable development has not explicitly been interpreted through the jurisprudence of the DSB, elements of the concept have been used as a prism through which the provisions of the GATT have been interpreted. That social norms and moral concerns can be presented to justify WTO incompatible measures has been accepted in a number of cases. The significance of sustainable development, as an umbrella concept embracing various dimensions, has been identified in a number of disputes namely, *Shrimp-Turtles*, *Brazil-Retreaded Tyres*, and

---

44 *Ibid*, 398.
45 *Ibid*, 385.
46 *Ibid*, 378.

EC-Seals. The significance of these cases should not be understated, bearing in mind that the original mandate of the GATT 1947 was to embed liberalism within a loose organisation of states for the regulation of international trade.[47] Nevertheless, Article XX was included at that time to accommodate for the regulation of trade in accordance with both material and nonmaterial considerations, albeit the test for justifying the restriction of trade on the basis of nonmaterial concerns is extremely narrow and the exceptions under Article XX are 'limited and conditional'.[48] Furthermore, the membership of the WTO is diverse and many countries do not subscribe to what are perceived to be predominantly 'Western' values. In light of this, the preservation of pluralism must be a fundamental matter for the organisation to prevent the onset of a legitimacy crisis.[49] That said, to date, the Appellate Body has refused to import legal norms from elsewhere in international law and considers these norms to fall outside the scope of the interpretive function of the DSB, unless such a norm relates explicitly to the way in which a trade measure is applied.[50]

Disputes had been brought before the GATT's DSB relating to the justification of trade restrictions on the basis of environmental concerns.[51] In the *Tuna/Dolphin II* dispute, the GATT panel recognised that the 'objective of sustainable development … includes the protection and preservation of the environment'.[52] This demonstrates that prior to the WTO, there was a notable shift toward the recognition of sustainable development but that this constituted an 'objective' and not a legal norm,

---

[47] J. Ruggie, 'Embedded Liberalism and the Postwar Economic Regimes' in *Constructing the World Polity: Essays on International Institutionalisation* (London: Routledge, 2002).

[48] *United States – Import Prohibitions of Certain Shrimp and Shrimp Products*, Report of the Appellate Body, WT/DS58/AB/R (12 October 1998), para. 157.

[49] R. Howse and J. Langille, 'Permitting Pluralism: The *Seal Products* Dispute and Why the WTO Should Accept Restrictions Justified by Noninstrumental Moral Values' (2012) 37 *Yale Journal of International Law* 367–432.

[50] Appellate Body Report, *Mexico – Tax Measures on Soft Drinks and Other Beverages* WT/DS308/AB/R (6 March 2006).

[51] *Canada – Measures Affecting Exports of Unprocessed Herring and Salmon* GATT B.I.S.D. L/6268-35 S/98 (22 March 1988); *Thailand – Restrictions on Importation of and Internal Taxes on Cigarettes* GATT B.I.S.D DS10/R-37S/200 (7 November 1990); *United States-Restrictions on Imports of Tuna* GATT B.I.S.D. 39S/155 (3 September 1991) (*Tuna/Dolphin I*); and, *United States – Restrictions on Imports of Tuna* 33 I.L.M 839 (1994) (*Tuna/Dolphin II*).

[52] *Tuna/Dolphin II*, para. 5.42.

per se. The panel noted that the issue in this particular case was whether the United States could impose trade embargoes on tuna 'in pursuit of its environmental objectives'.[53] This case marks the first instance in which the DSB appears to take a balancing approach to the principles of free trade on the one hand, and the objective of sustainable development, on the other. Concluding the Uruguay Round in 1994, the Marrakesh Agreement sets out the consensus of members at the time the WTO was created:

> ... *Considering* that there should not be, nor need be, any policy contradiction between upholding and safeguarding an open, non-discriminatory and equitable multilateral trading system on the one hand, and acting for the protection of the environment, and the promotion of sustainable development on the other ...[54]

Subsequent disputes brought before the WTO's DSB have shed further light on the interrelationship between trade and sustainable development.

Shrimp/Turtles

Perhaps the most significant statements made to date from the DSB in relation to sustainable development derive from the findings of the Appellate Body in the *Shrimp/Turtles* dispute, concerning a US ban on the importation of shrimp and shrimp products.[55] The United States invoked Article XX(g) which provides that a trade restrictive measure may be adopted where it is '*relating to* the conservation of *exhaustible* natural resources'. Under Section 609, the United States banned all shrimp and shrimp products that had been harvested using trawlers that were not fitted with turtle excluder devices (TEDs) comparable to those used on US trawlers. This ban was justified on environmental grounds, on the basis that sea turtles often migrate through waters with shrimp and subsequently get caught in the trawlers nets. Section 609 was, therefore, implemented on conservation grounds to reduce harm to sea turtles. In analysing the legality of the US trade restrictive measure, the Appellate Body asserted that the objective of sustainable development set out in the Marrakesh Agreement 'gives *colour, texture* and *shading* to the rights and

---

53 *Ibid.*

54 WTO, 'Decision on Trade and Environment' adopted in Marrakesh on 15 April 1994.

55 Report of the Appellate Body, *US-Shrimp* (n. 48).

obligations of Members under the WTO Agreement generally, and under the GATT 1994, in particular'.[56]

The question of what constituted 'exhaustible natural resources' became a focal point for the Appellate Body. Noting that the GATT had been drafted over 50 years ago, the Appellate Body stated that treaty provisions, such as Article XX(g), must be read 'in light of contemporary concerns of the community of nations about the protection and conservation of the environment'.[57] Finding that the term 'natural resources' was not 'static' but is 'by definition, evolutionary' the Appellate Body concluded that both living and non-living resources fell within the scope of Article XX(g). Furthermore, as all seven types of sea turtle were listed under the Endangered Species list[58] the Appellate Body concluded that sea turtles are an 'exhaustible natural resource' within the meaning of Article XX(g).[59]

For a trade restrictive measure to be justified under Article XX(g) it must be '*relating* to the conservation of exhaustible natural resources'. Drawing on the *US-Gasoline* dispute, this was taken to mean that there must exist a 'close and genuine relationship of ends and means'.[60] While the relationship between Section 609 and the conservation of sea turtles was found to satisfy this limb of Article XX(g), the measure had been applied in a discriminatory measure and was a restrictive measure of trade. What is of most interest to the discussion on the judicialisation of the concept of sustainable development is what the Appellate Body did *not* say:

> We have *not* decided that the protection and preservation of the environment is of no significance to the Members of the WTO. Clearly, it is. We have *not* decided that the sovereign nations that are Members of the WTO cannot adopt effective measures to protect endangered species, such as sea turtles. Clearly, they can and should. And we have *not* decided that sovereign states should not act together bilaterally, plurilaterally, or multilaterally, either within the WTO or in other international fora, to protect endangered species or to otherwise protect the environment. Clearly, they should and do.[61]

---

56 *Ibid,* para. 155 (emphasis added).

57 *Ibid*, para. 129.

58 Sea turtles are listed as endangered under Appendix 1 of the Convention on International Trade in Endangered Species of Wild Fauna and Flora (CITES).

59 Report of the Appellate Body, *US-Shrimp* (n. 48), para. 134.

60 *Ibid*, para. 136.

61 *Ibid*, para. 185.

It has been argued that the WTO should permit trade restrictive measures that are founded in non-instrumentally rational norms and that in such a case 'the use of outright prohibition may be essential to express the moral sentiment underlying the measure'.[62]

EC-Seals

It is generally accepted that animal welfare falls within the broad notion of sustainable development. If the WTO were to proscribe the justification of trade restrictive measures for non-instrumental considerations then the ban on importation of certain products on religious grounds would affect many of its members.[63] In *EC-Seals*, the EU sought to ban the entry of all products made from seals into its market on the ground that the methods used to kill seals caused unnecessary pain and suffering.[64] A number of exceptions to the ban were provided including for those seals harvested by indigenous communities and those seals hunted for the sustainable management of marine resources. It is well documented that a trade restrictive measure may be justified under Article XX of the GATT, which provides the exceptions to GATT rules, including the protection of morals under sub-paragraph (a). Both Canada and Norway, two of the world's largest producers of seal products, were affected by the EU ban and sought to challenge its legitimacy in the DSB.

Animal welfare standards constitute an element of sustainability in the agro-food production process[65] and it has long been a normative concern of the EU as manifested most recently in the Lisbon Treaty, wherein animals are conceived of as 'sentient beings'.[66] This contrasts with the

---

[62] Howse and Langille (n. 49), 429.

[63] India, for example, justifies the ban on beef imports on religious grounds. See D. Barak-Erez, 'Symbolic Constitutionalism: On Sacred Cows and Abominable Pigs' (2010) 6(3) *Language, Culture and Humanity* 420–35.

[64] Regulation (EC) 1007/2009 of the European Parliament and of the Council of 16 September 2009 on Trade in Seal Products, [2009] OJ L286/38.

[65] B. Ilbery, 'Food Supply Chains and Sustainability: Evidence from Specialist Food Producers in the Scottish/English Borders' (2005) 22 *Land Use Policy* 331–44.

[66] Article 13 of the Lisbon Treaty provides: 'In formulating and implementing the Union's agriculture, fisheries, transport, internal market, research and technological development and space policies, the Union and the Member States shall, since animals are sentient beings, pay full regard to the welfare requirements of animals, while respecting the legislative or administrative provisions and customs of the Member States relating in particular to religious rites, cultural traditions and regional heritage.'

Shrimp/Turtle dispute, in which the Appellate Body noted that the US had shown no real effort toward the promotion of sea turtle conservation prior to the enactment of its trade embargo under Section 609.[67]

In the *Tuna/Dolphin III* dispute, the Panel noted:

> The protection of dolphins may be understood as intended to protect animal life or health or the environment. In this respect, a measure that aims at the protection of animal life or health need not, in our view, be directed exclusively to endangered or depleted species or populations, to be legitimate.[68]

The meaning of the public morals exception under Article XX has been taken to mean concepts that 'vary in time and space, depending upon a range of factors, including prevailing social, cultural, ethical and religious values'.[69] The Panel's approach was one of deference, concluding that each member can determine what constitutes 'public morals' based on the prevailing or widespread belief of that particular society. Adopting this approach enables regulation to serve a 'dual purpose' that both enables a member to 'express intrinsic moral beliefs *and* to protect defined interests'.[70] The *EC-Seals* dispute represents an extension of the Appellate Body recommendations in the *Shrimp/Turtle* dispute: both cases relate to the conservation of marine life, albeit justified on different grounds. Enabling members to import their moral considerations into trade practices preserves the pluralism of the international community. Collectively, the *EC-Seals*, *Shrimp/Turtle*, and *Tuna/Dolphin III* disputes demonstrate that animal welfare is both distinct from and related to conservation and sustainability objectives.

From the analysis of these disputes it is clear that the WTO has evolved beyond the GATT to recognise the importance of sustainable development as an interpretive tool to add colour to the provisions of the GATT. However, sustainable development has not been articulated in the jurisprudence as a norm of international law. Rather, it is identified as an interstitial norm which modifies the character of legal norms. A more

---

[67] Report of the Appellate Body, *US-Shrimp* (n. 48), para. 167.

[68] *United States – Measures Concerning the Importation, Marketing and Sale of Tuna and Tuna Products* Panel Report WT DS381/R (15 September 2011), para. 7.347.

[69] *United States – Measures Affecting the Cross-Border Supply of Gambling and Betting Services* Panel Report WT/DS285/AB/R (10 November 2004), para. 6.461.

[70] Howse and Langille (n. 49), 414.

comprehensive analysis of the legal character of sustainable development has emerged through the jurisprudence of the ICJ.

SUSTAINABLE DEVELOPMENT: A PRINCIPLE OF CUSTOMARY INTERNATIONAL LAW?

Sustainable development has been recognised by the ICJ as requiring the reconciliation between economic development and the protection of the environment. In the contentious case of *Gabĉíkovo-Nagymaros*,[71] relating to the construction of dams over the river Danube at Gabĉíkovo (Czechoslovakia) and Nagymaros (Hungary), the nature of sustainable development was examined for the first time in this legal forum. This case related to a Treaty signed in 1977 between the two countries which stated that a 'single and indivisible operational system' of the two dams would strengthen the socialist integration of the two neighbouring countries.[72] For various reasons, the dam proved to be a source of tension among economists and environmentalists in the two countries and eventually Hungary sought to abandon work on the dam. In its reference to the ICJ the Court was asked to consider, in part, the legality of Hungary's position. Hungary asserted that it wanted to terminate construction on the basis of environmental concerns. In their analysis, the Court submitted that the Parties 'should look afresh at the effects on the environment of the operation of the Gabĉíkovo power plant' to find a solution to the volume of water to be released into the Danube river. While Hungary's attempt to terminate was not legal in the context of the Treaty, Czechoslovakia could not force Gabĉíkovo into operation as this would undermine the indivisible nature of the agreement. Although the court interpreted economic norms in light of sustainable development, the Court nevertheless acknowledged that the solution to the dispute must be agreed between the parties. In recognising sustainable development as a 'concept',[73] the Court nevertheless fell short of attaching legality to that concept.

The principle of sustainable development was given a more generous interpretation in the separate Opinion issued by Judge Weeramantry. Herein, he claimed that sustainable development was 'more than a mere

---

[71] Case concerning *Gabĉíkovo-Nagymaros (Czechoslovakia v Hungary), Judgment of 25 September 1997* I.C.J. Reports 1997.

[72] In subsequent changes to the Treaty, the concept of 'socialist integration' disappeared.

[73] Case concerning *Gabĉíkovo-Nagymaros* (n. 71), para. 140.

concept' and should be understood as 'a principle with normative value'[74] which 'is an integral part of international law'.[75] In the Opinion, Weeramantry proposes that the principle of sustainable development is a *reconciliatory* norm that mediates and balances the conflicting interests of different norms; in this case, between economic reproduction and protection of the environment. The status of sustainable development as a reconciliatory norm derives from its acceptance through numerous international law instruments, which Weeramantry claims gives it special status as a principle of international law:

> The principle of sustainable development is thus a part of modern international law by reason not only of its inescapable logical necessity, but also by reason of its wide and *general acceptance by the global community*.[76]

Sustainable development as a reconciliatory norm enables the corpus of international law to develop in Grotian terms, that is not simply as a set of principles *a priori* but also as the emergence of new principles *a posteriori*. While environmental law remains in its formative years, Weeramantry submitted that this does not proscribe its potential to contain principles of international law that have emerged *a posteriori*. For Weeramantry, the rich diversity of cultures, civilisations, and legal traditions should play an important role in the interpretation of modern international law and calls for the 'future of international law to be interdisciplinary'.[77] Furthermore, in attributing the normative validity of sustainable development as a legal principle to the consensus expressed by the global community this reinforces the discourse theory of law.

Weeramantry's separate Opinion is worthy of close analysis, as he seeks to highlight the moral ideational forces that have seen international law interpreted in light of environmental concerns for hundreds of years. Citing a Buddhist sermon to the Indian King in the 18th century, which saw the King convert to the Buddhist tradition, Weeramantry asserts that this represents the first principle of environmental law:

---

[74] Separate Opinion of Vice-President of the ICJ, Judge Weeramantry, on the Case concerning *Gabĉíkovo-Nagymaros (Czechoslovakia v Hungary), Judgment of 25 September 1997* I.C.J. Reports 1997, para. 85.

[75] *Ibid*, para. 86.

[76] *Ibid*, para. 95.

[77] *Ibid*, para. 97.

> O great King, the birds of the air and the beasts have as equal a right to live and move about in any part of the land as thou. The land belongs to the people and all living beings; thou art only the guardian of it.[78]

Implicit in this statement are the principles of intragenerational and intergenerational equity which embody the spirit of sustainable development today. Adopting a historically sensitive understanding of the principle or concept of sustainable development is important for constructing the modern international legal framework and it is 'the task of the law … to convert such wisdom into practical terms'.[79]

Rejecting Weeramantry's argument that the principle of sustainable development has the character of international customary law, Lowe proposes that the principle 'exemplifies another species of normativity which is of great potential value' for interpreting the concepts of environmental law.[80] For Lowe, the principle of sustainable development lacks a sufficiently precise and generally accepted definition to import normative qualities. Rather, sustainable development is 'a convenient, if imprecise, label for a general policy goal which may be adopted by states unilaterally, bilaterally, or multilaterally'.[81] However, while sustainable development may lack the normative character of a legal principle it is arguably not altogether devoid of normative quality:

> Sustainable development can properly claim a normative status as an element of the process of judicial reasoning. It is a meta-principle, acting upon other legal rules and principles – a legal concept exercising a kind of *interstitial normativity*, pushing and pulling the boundaries of true primary norms when they threaten to overlap or conflict with each other.[82]

Defining sustainable development as an *interstitial* or *modifying* norm appears to make a similar normative claim as Weeramantry's notion of sustainable development as a reconciliatory norm. The indeterminate nature of the law enables the existence of this type of normative quality

---

[78] Sermon recorded in *The Mahavamsa,* Chapter XIV cited in the Separate Opinion of Vice-President of the ICJ, Judge Weeramantry, in the case concerning *Gabĉíkovo-Nagymaros (Czechoslovakia v Hungary), Judgment of 25 September 1997* I.C.J. Reports 1997, para. 99.

[79] *Ibid*, para. 100.

[80] V. Lowe, 'Sustainable Development and Unsustainable Arguments' in A. Boyle and D. Freestone, *International Law and Sustainable Development: Past Achievements and Future Challenges* (Oxford: Oxford University Press, 1999), 21.

[81] *Ibid*, 30.

[82] *Ibid*, 31.

as the law cannot be mechanistically applied in every case. Modifying norms do not depend on *opinio juris* or state practice for their legitimacy because they are not *legal* norms. As such, sustainable development is best conceived as a 'kind of prism'[83] through which primary legal rules can be interpreted and interrogated.

What is evident, however, through the juxtaposition of the Judgment of the ICJ and the separate Opinion of Judge Weeramantry is the rationalisation of legal argumentation. The judgment fails to define any content or character of the principle of sustainable development and obscures the carefully articulated illumination of the ideological forces behind the concept presented in the separate Opinion. From a legal perspective, this is perhaps unsurprising, for often the dissenting judgments provide a more critical line of legal reasoning than the majority judgment which represents an aggregate view of the individual judges adjudicating on a particular legal matter. In Weeramantry's opinion, there is sufficient evidence from across the globe to argue that the principle of sustainable development has the nature of customary international law.[84] This position, however, was not adopted by the ICJ in this case or in any subsequent case that draws on the principle of sustainable development as a reconciliatory norm.

Subsequently, in 2010, the ICJ revisited the relationship between sustainable development and economic development in the contentious case of *Pulp Mills* between Argentina and Uruguay.[85] In this dispute Argentina challenged, on environmental grounds, the legality of Uruguay's authorisation and construction of two pulp mills and associated facilities on the River Uruguay, which constitutes an international boundary between the two countries. Argentina argued that these actions violated the procedural requirements of the 1975 Statute on the River Uruguay,[86] which had been signed by both countries, and which provided for the 'optimum and rational utilization of the River Uruguay'. Argentina proposed that the 1975 Statute should be read in light of the principles of sustainable development as the river is a shared resource

---

[83] *Ibid*, 34.

[84] Separate Opinion of Vice-President of the ICJ, Judge Weeramantry, in the case concerning *Gabĉíkovo-Nagymaros (Czechoslovakia v Hungary), Judgment of 25 September 1997* I.C.J. Reports 1997, para. 104.

[85] Case concerning *Pulp Mills on the River Uruguay (Argentina v Uruguay), Judgment of 20 April 2010* I.C.J. Reports 2010.

[86] *Statute of the River Uruguay* (Argentina and Uruguay) Signed at Salto on 26 February 1975. The Statute was ratified and came into force on 18 September 1976 in Buenos Aires.

and that the application of these principles would give the 1975 Statute a 'dynamic interpretation'.[87] It was noted that the Court had previously described the procedural regime set out in the 1975 Statute as 'comprehensive and progressive'[88] and by drawing insights from *Gabčíkovo-Nagymaros*, the ICJ was satisfied that sufficient procedural safeguards were in place to enable the parties to enter into consultations with one another and formulate a mutually agreeable solution to the dispute. Through cooperation the risks of damage to the environment could be 'jointly managed'.[89] The court carefully considered the scope of various procedural requirements set out in the Statute, including Article 27, which read:

> The right of each Party to use the waters of the river, within its jurisdiction, for domestic, sanitary, industrial and agricultural purposes, shall be exercised without prejudice to the application of the procedure laid down in articles 7 to 12 when the use is liable to effect the régime of the river or the quality of its waters.[90]

Giving a dynamic interpretation to this legal provision and using sustainable development as a hermeneutic judicial tool, the ICJ found that there was a 'need to strike a balance between the use of the waters and the protection of the river consistent with the objective of sustainable development'.[91] Furthermore, the Court found that Article 27 'embodies this interconnectedness between equitable and reasonable utilisation of a

---

[87] Case concerning *Pulp Mills on the River Uruguay* (n. 85).

[88] *Ibid*, 133, para. 81.

[89] *Ibid*, 49, para. 77.

[90] Articles 7 to 12 of the Statute lay down the procedural requirements of the two parties, which requires notification 'if one Party plans to construct new channels, substantially modify or alter existing ones or carry out any other works which are liable to affect navigation, the régime of the river or the quality of its waters …' (Article 7). The notification period lasts up to 180 days (Article 8) and if no objections to the proposed works are received, then the Party may commence works (Article 9). The notified Party has the right to inspect the authorised works (Article 10). If the notified party has concerns about the proposed project, it must notify the other Party of its concerns within the 180 day period (Article 11) and if no agreement can be reached between the two Parties then recourse to the dispute settlement mechanism under Chapter VX is available (Article 12).

[91] Case concerning *Pulp Mills on the River Uruguay* (n. 85), 74, para. 177.

shared resource and the balance between economic development and environmental protection that is the *essence* of sustainable development'.[92]

That sustainable development finds its expression in so many legally binding documents and in the judgments of the ICJ and recommendations of the WTO's Appellate Body and Panel reports may, at the very least, imply a common sense among the international community that sustainable development is *relevant* to the interpretation of international legal norms. Indeed, the ICJ has recognised sustainable development as a 'current principle of general international law' which requires 'the integration of appropriate environmental measures in the design and implementation of economic development activities'.[93] While sustainable development appears to have garnered its status as a powerful interpretive mechanism for judicial bodies its quantitative role in the implementation of international legal rules has been minimal.[94] Nevertheless, the interpretive function of sustainable development is, arguably, reconstituting traditional legal concepts, albeit in a very incremental fashion.

CONCLUDING REMARKS

Sustainable development has appeared in hundreds of non-legally binding instruments such as the Rio Declaration and the European Consensus on Development. These instruments are not, of themselves, recognised as sources of international law and therefore cannot confer legality on sustainable development. However, more recently sustainable development has found its expression in many hundreds of international treaties and conventions, among them, the North-South RTAs negotiated by the EU with Korea and the ACP, respectively. Historically, sustainable development was found in the recitals of the Preamble to such international instruments. The inclusion of so-called 'sustainable development chapters' in the EU's most recent RTAs might suggest a shift toward the recognition of sustainable development as a norm of legal character. Arguably, however, the inclusion of development chapters represents little more than the politico-ethical scaffolding on which the hegemonic neoliberal capitalist trade regime is reproduced. In the following chapters it will be shown that development concepts are framed in vague,

---

92 *Ibid.*

93 *Award in the Arbitration regarding the Iron Rhine ('Ijzeren Rijn') Railway between the Kingdom of Belgium and the Kingdom of the Netherlands*, 27 RIAA (2005) 35, at para. 59.

94 Barral (n. 35), 398.

imprecise, and ambiguous language which does not lend itself to a conception of legal normativity.

Deconstructing the concept of sustainable development shows that the broad scope of the concept can render it inoperable and impotent. Little progress has been made in terms of quantitatively measuring the sustainability of trade agreements, for example. To this author's knowledge, there exists no metric on which the principle of sustainable development can be effectively measured. Indeed, economic development can itself be counterproductive for sustainable development as greater quantities of natural resources are used and larger volumes of pollutants are produced. The relationship between economic development and the other dimensions of development is complex and varied. If sustainable development has no operational value then it loses its currency and becomes nothing more than 'a boon to publicists who will paste new labels on old bottles and claim that every project that makes their clients rich is sustainable'.[95]

The jurisprudences of the WTO's DSB and the ICJ have done little to clarify the character of sustainable development. While both have referred to sustainable development as a concept, there has been a reluctance to recognise this as a norm of international law. It is not explicitly recognised as having customary status nor is it laid out as a principle of international law by a Treaty. That said, the positions put forward by both Sands and Lowe, that sustainable development as a concept or principle might be used to inform other legal frameworks or as a hermeneutic judicial tool, are persuasive. While the principle of *sustainable development* has seemingly defied legal classification, this chapter has shown that it plays an important role as an interstitial norm in the trade:environment interface.

---

[95] Mcloskey (n. 37), 159.

5. Transforming the ACP-EU 'special' relationship

This chapter focuses on the trade and cooperation framework between the ACP and EU, taking note of the paradigmatic shifts that have occurred in this 'special relationship' over time.[1] For many decades, the ACP countries enjoyed non-reciprocal preferential access to the EU market under the Yaoundé and Lomé agreements. Following changes at the multilateral level, and in accordance with the recommendations of the Appellate Body in the *EC-Bananas III* dispute, the ACP countries are no longer eligible to receive non-reciprocal market access for their exports to the EU market.[2] Nevertheless, the EU has been keen to preserve its long-standing relationship with former colonies in the ACP and has done so by offering reciprocal, but asymmetric, preferential market access under the Cotonou Agreement and through the Economic Partnership Agreement (EPA) framework. Although the primary purpose of the EPAs is to eradicate poverty and facilitate the gradual integration of ACP countries into the global economy,[3] these agreements mark a transformative shift in ACP-EU cooperation as trade facilitation and reciprocal market access now form key parts of the agreements.

---

[1] The relationship between the EU and ACP countries has been described as 'special' because it symbolises a unique bond between the European metropoles and their former colonies. For an overview of the changing dynamics of EU-African cooperation, see M. Farrell, 'Bridging the Gap between EU, Mediterranean and African relations: Partnership, Governance and (Re)-evolving Relations' (2010) 2 *L'Europe en Formation* 169–91.

[2] The only exception to this rule is where the country concerned qualifies for special and differential treatment.

[3] Article 1 Partnership Agreement between the members of the African, Caribbean, and Pacific Group of States of the one part, and the European Community of the other part, signed in Cotonou on 23 June 2000, [2000] OJ L317/3 as amended through Decision No. 3/2008 of the ACP-EC Council of Ministers of 15 December 2008, [2008] OJ L352/59 to adopt the revised provisions set out in [2010] OJ L287/3, hereinafter referred to as the 'Cotonou Partnership Agreement 2014'.

This chapter is divided into four substantive sections with the aim of providing a rich historical background of ACP-EU cooperation. From a critical perspective, this chapter explores the ideas and beliefs that have constituted the ACP-EU relationship and seeks to challenge the basis on which the relationship will proceed in the future. The first section outlines the concessions granted under the Yaoundé framework, which marks the first trade and development cooperation agreement between countries in the two regions. The second section discusses the transition from Yaoundé to Lomé, analysing the geopolitical factors that resulted in the first notable shift in the post-colonial relationship. In the third section, the transformation of the relationship toward reciprocity is examined with reference to the EU's Green Paper (1996) to highlight the ideational forces that have been the main thrust behind the new trade and development legal regime. The fourth section examines the scope of the proposed EPAs and, in particular, questions their appropriateness for ensuring a 'development-friendly' trade relationship between the EU and ACP sub-regions. EPAs are non-reciprocal market access agreements with a development assistance pillar designed to integrate ACP countries into the global economy. As such, the EPAs should be cohesive and foster deeper integration among the sub-regional groupings. However, with a strong focus on economic development it is argued that the EPAs constitute hegemonic legal regimes rather than a partnership rooted in equality.[4]

A PREFERENTIAL PAST

As far back as the 1500s, Western European countries such as Portugal, Spain, France, Great Britain (formerly the Kingdom of England) and the Netherlands had sought to harness the resource-rich countries across the Americas, Africa, Asia and Oceania. Through the process of colonisation, the Western European countries became more dependent on commodity exports such as minerals, precious metals, agricultural goods, sugar and textiles originating in the colonial regions.[5] Gradually, the relationship between the European metropoles and their colonies began to change. In the mid-20th century there were three important global shifts which acted

---

[4] W. Braude, *Regional Integration in Africa: Lessons from the East African Community* (Johannesburg: South African Institute for International Affairs, 2008), 260.

[5] W. Rodney, *How Europe Underdeveloped Africa*, 2nd edn (Fahamu, Kenya: Pambazuka Press, 2012).

as a catalyst for the shifting dynamics of European relations with their former colonies, namely the end of the Second World War (1945), the creation of the multilateral trading system under GATT (1947), and the eventual process of decolonisation (1960s onwards). These global changes were also paralleled by a major regional change in the EU, which eventually saw the creation of the single market and a unified Europe in 1992.[6]

In the post-WWII era, Western European countries were keen to promote peace and security within the region. As a result, the European Economic Community (EEC) and European Coal and Steel Community (ECSC) were formed in 1958 among six European states.[7] Both the EEC and ECSC were believed to be the stepping stone towards a 'federation of Europe' as a response to the nationalism which had triggered WWII. The post-WWII global environment was one of uncertainty and the EU was keen to secure its position within the emerging global order. A key part of this political strategy was to strengthen external economic relationships which included forging stronger alliances with the EEC's former colonies during the process of decolonisation. In Robert Schuman's 1950 speech, entitled 'A United States of Europe', the strategic relationship between the EU and Africa was revealed:

> This production [of coal and steel] will be offered to the world as a whole without distinction or exception, with the aim of contributing to raising living standards and to promoting peaceful achievements. *Europe, with new means at her disposal, will be able to pursue the realisation of one of her essential tasks: the development of the African continent.* (Emphasis added)[8]

France was particularly keen to preserve its relationship with the newly independent francophone African countries and, therefore, made it a condition of its accession to the EEC that its former overseas territories

---

[6] For a comprehensive overview of the EU's changing development policy see A. Mold (ed.), *EU Development Policy in a Changing World: Challenges for the 21st Century* (Amsterdam: Amsterdam University Press, 2007).

[7] The founding members of the EEC were Belgium, France, Italy, Luxembourg, the Netherlands, and West Germany.

[8] Schuman, 'A United States of Europe', reprinted in *Selection of Texts Concerning Institutional Matters of the Community from 1950-1982* (1982) cited in L. Bartels, 'The Trade and Development Policy of the European Union' (2007) 18 *European Journal of International Law* 715–56. As noted by Bartels, the italicised sentence was omitted from the text of the speech reproduced on the EU website, accessed 12 December 2016 at http://Europa.eu/abc/symbols/9-may/decl_en.htm.

became 'associated states' of Europe.[9] The original legal basis for granting special dispensation to the former colonies is found in Article 131 of the Treaty of Rome which provided that former colonies of Belgium, France and Italy could be classified as African Associated States (AAS). Initially, a country would qualify as an AAS for a period of five years.[10] Article 131 Treaty of Rome set out the objective of association to be the promotion of 'the economic and social development of the countries and territories and to establish close economic relations between them and the Community as a whole'. This special relationship has been preserved throughout the transformation of the EU and is now constituted in Part IV of the Lisbon Treaty, which is dedicated to the legal framework between the EU and its overseas territories. Article 198 TFEU preserves the original mandate of Article 131 Treaty of Rome, but further adds:

> In accordance with the principles set out in the Preamble of this Treaty, association shall serve primarily to further the interests and prosperity of the inhabitants of these countries and territories in order to lead them to the economic, social and cultural development to which they aspire.

From a historical perspective, Article 131 Treaty of Rome provided the legal basis for the creation of an interregional space between the European Community, of the one part, and those countries classified as AAS, of the other part, albeit not in the form of an Article XXIV legal regime. Codifying the relationship into the Treaty was an important mechanism for protecting European interests in foreign markets and paved the way for the Yaoundé Conventions, which were in operation between 1964 and 1975. In 1963, the first Yaoundé Agreement was signed between the EEC and 18 African nations and entered into force on 1 June 1964.[11] Consisting of mostly francophone African countries, the group was collectively referred to as the Associated African and Malagasy States (AAMS).

---

[9] See A. Flint, 'The End of a "Special Relationship"? The New EU-ACP Economic Partnership Agreements' (2009) 36 *Review of African Political Economy*, 79–92, 80.

[10] Article 136 Treaty of Rome.

[11] Countries receiving preferences under the first Yaoundé Agreement included Benin (formerly the République du Dahomey), Burkina Faso (formerly the République du Haute-Volta), Burundi, Cameroon, Central African Republic, Chad, Republic of Congo (formerly Brazzaville), the Republic of Congo (formerly Léopoldville), Côte d'Ivoire, Gabon, Madagascar, Mali, Mauritania, Niger, Rwanda, Senegal, Somalia and Togo.

FROM YAOUNDÉ TO LOMÉ

Yaoundé

The Yaoundé framework was primarily driven towards the expansion of trade, with the intention of eventually creating a free trade area between the two regions through a process of progressive liberalisation.[12] This process was reciprocal with both sides gradually eliminating duties and tariffs on certain products. In the early days of Yaoundé, the EEC's North-South development policy was essentially a manifestation of French foreign policy providing assistance to its former African colonies.[13] As a trade regime, Yaoundé incorporated an element of conditionality since development assistance was only provided in exchange for reciprocal, non-discriminatory market access. The colonies were perceived to be important markets for the economic development of the EEC, given their seemingly never-ending supply of energy and raw materials.[14] As peripheral countries, their resources were key to the reproduction of the EU as an emerging hegemonic global actor and Yaoundé served to protect the EEC's access to precious commodities within this inter-regional space.

A considerable development assistance package was included as part of the Yaoundé trade framework.[15] The EEC provided development assistance in a bid to integrate the developing markets into the global economy, with the first European Development Fund (EDF) created to provide financial support to the AASM countries in 1958.[16] The EDFs were designed to provide technical and financial aid to the former colonies. Development assistance was provided for cooperation in the key areas of: economic development; social and human development; and

---

[12] Bartels (n. 8).

[13] M. Sissoki, L. Osuji and W. Cheng, 'Impacts on the Yaoundé and Lomé Conventions on EC-ACP Trade' (1998) 1 *The African Economic and Business Review* 6–24, 8.

[14] M. van Reisen, 'The Enlarged European Union and the Developing World: What Future?' in A. Mold (ed.), *EU Development Policy in a Changing World: Challenges for the 21st Century* (Amsterdam: Amsterdam University Press, 2007), 31.

[15] L. Hinkle, M. Hoppe and R. Newfarmer, 'Beyond Cotonou: Economic Partnerships in Africa' in R. Newfarmer, *Trade, Doha, and Development: A Window into the Issues* (Washington, D.C.: World Bank, 2006), 263–80.

[16] For a history of the EDF, and current developments, see the EU's website accessed 12 December 2016 at http://europa.eu/legislation_summaries/development/overseas_countries_territories/r12102_en.htm.

regional cooperation and agreement. With the expiry of the first Yaoundé framework agreement in 1969, a second Yaoundé Convention was signed in the same year with entry into force on 1 January 1971 but in reality, Yaoundé II represented little more than an extension of Yaoundé I.

European political influence in developing countries began to weaken as the process of decolonisation took hold, and in light of the growing global dominance of the United States it was considered an essential part of the EEC's political strategy to reassert its power. During this period, there was a notable change in European development cooperation as the EEC sought to broaden its horizons beyond Africa to include developing countries more generally.[17] With the first wave of European enlargement came a renegotiation of the cooperation arrangement between the EU and AASM.[18] The accession of Denmark, Ireland and the United Kingdom to the EU in 1973 marked a new phase of cooperation in the ACP-EU relationship. Of particular importance to the United Kingdom was the preservation of the close ties it had maintained with its former colonies. This is perhaps unsurprising, given that the UK's reliance on commodities exported from its colonial markets was much higher than that of its European counterparts.[19] As a result, the EC's preferential agreements were multilateralised to include the British Commonwealth states. Parallel to the European expansion, the ACP group of states also became a unified region. In 1975, the former colonies organised into a unified political and economic bloc, known as the ACP region, for the purpose of facilitating trade with the EEC. This group came together under the Georgetown Agreement[20] in order that they could coordinate a common stance vis-à-vis the EC. In effect, the Georgetown Agreement created a new regional space spanning across the ACP and in doing so, the ACP countries were able to reassert some balance in the asymmetric relationship with the EC. With the shifts in the political economy of the

---

[17] For an excellent account of the changing dynamics of ACP-EU cooperation, see S. Hurt, 'Cooperation and Coercion? The Cotonou Agreement between the European Union and ACP states and the end of the Lomé Convention' (2003) 24 *Third World Quarterly* 161–76.

[18] N. Hutton, 'Africa's Changing Relationship with the EEC' (1974) 30 *The World Today* 426–35.

[19] A. Harryvan, *In Pursuit of Influence: The Netherland's European Policy during the Formative Years of the European Union, 1952–1973* (New York: PIE Peter Lang, 2009), 243.

[20] The Georgetown Agreement on the Organisation of the African, Caribbean and Pacific Group of States (1975).

relationship, the Yaoundé framework was abandoned and replaced by the Lomé Conventions.

Lomé

The first Lomé Agreement (1975) negotiated between the EEC and 46 ACP countries became operational in 1976.[21] Under the Lomé framework, the agreements were renegotiated every five years, with the exception of Lomé IV and Lomé IVbis which together ran for a period of 10 years. To accommodate the growing size of the group, a larger and more comprehensive EDF was concluded, granting a more generous development assistance package to the ACP than that offered under Yaoundé. By the end of the Yaoundé framework, the ACP countries had received approximately €2.2 billion from the EDF.[22] Under the Lomé framework, the ACP were to receive €40 billion over the course of 25 years.[23]

Underpinning the Lomé framework were the principles of stability, contractuality and non-reciprocity.[24] Preferences were granted for long periods of time to promote stable growth in a predictable trading environment. Preferences were jointly agreed which meant that contractually, the EEC could not unilaterally modify the terms of trade. Furthermore, the preferences were granted on a non-reciprocal basis which meant that ACP countries were under no obligation to extend preferential terms of trade to the EEC. Lomé marks a significant shift in the cooperation arrangement between the EC and ACP countries. For the first time, trade liberalisation was *non-reciprocal* which meant that ACP commodities could be exported to the EEC market on a virtually duty-free-quota-free (DFQF) basis. In real terms, this meant that just over

---

[21] For a detailed discussion of the shift to Lomé see D. Matthews, 'Lomé IV and ACP/EEC Relations: Surviving the Lost Decade' (1991) 22 *California Western International Law Journal* 1–58.

[22] Harryvan (n. 19), 250.

[23] Ambassador/Special Envoy G.A. Hylton, 'The Challenge of Integrating ACP States into the International Trading Regime: Venturing Outside the Lomé Framework', Paper delivered at the CTA International Seminar Brussels (27–29 November 2002).

[24] European Commission, 'Green Paper on Relations between the European Union and the ACP countries on the eve of the 21st Century: Challenges and Options for a New Partnership' (1996) COM (96) 570 Final, 16.

99 per cent of total ACP exports including agricultural products, could access the EEC market DFQF.[25]

Lomé was fundamentally discriminatory, conferring preferences on ACP developing countries at the expense of non-ACP developing countries. Article 7 of the Lomé Convention provided the legal base for non-reciprocity:

> In the view of their present development needs, the ACP shall not be required, for the duration of this Convention, to assume, in respect of imports of products originating in the Community, obligations corresponding to the commitments entered into by the Community in respect of imports of the products originating in the ACP States.[26]

While the Lomé framework was in force, there were also significant geopolitical events which affected the dynamic of ACP-EU relations. It is therefore important to consider the exogenous factors that have shaped the EU's attitude toward the ACP countries.

In the period 1973–1975, the oil crisis had taken hold on a global scale. OPEC oil prices quadrupled which resulted in a corresponding rise in export prices for commodities such as coffee, sugar, tea and food grains.[27] Against this background of rising global commodity prices, the EEC was keen to protect its privileged relationship with the ACP. To this end, the Lomé framework not only offered non-reciprocal market access for ACP commodities to enter the EC market DFQF but furthermore it established the commodity trading regime consisting of the protocols for beef, sugar, bananas and rum. Special concessions were also granted for beef, sugar, bananas and rum under specific Protocols annexed to the framework agreement.[28] The beef and sugar protocols were particularly beneficial for South African Development Community (SADC) countries since these are two significant exports to the EU. While all ACP countries enjoyed DQFQ access under the sugar protocol, the beef protocol

---

[25] F. Matambalya, *The New EU-ACP Partnership: Consequences for Eastern and Southern Africa* (Dar es Salaam: Friedrich Ebert Stiftung, 2001), 29.

[26] This approach was subsequently applied to the other Lomé framework agreements.

[27] R. Gibb, 'The European Union and the South' (2000) 21 *Third World Quarterly* 461.

[28] Article 368 Lomé IV confirms that the four protocols 'form an integral part' of the trade and cooperation framework.

provided that no *ad valorem* was to be paid although beef products originating in the ACP were subject to a duty.[29]

Another key element of the Lomé framework was the inclusion of STABEX and SYSMIN,[30] which were export schemes designed at protecting the markets of raw materials (STABEX) and minerals (SYSMIN) from fluctuating prices.[31] However, while STABEX and SYSMIN were designed to offset global fluctuations in commodity prices for exporters in the ACP, as a system, STABEX has attracted criticisms for various reasons. Most notably it has been criticised for its limited product coverage, its effect on commodity production and its discriminatory nature.[32] The STABEX/SYSMIN programmes encouraged monocultural production which by implication discourages diversification of the production base in developing economies. Conceived of as important development tools, these schemes did little to integrate the ACP into the global economy and merely reinforced the inequality and asymmetry that had come to characterise EU-ACP relations.

RESTRUCTURING THE EU-ACP RELATIONSHIP

During the second phase of European enlargement, the importance of ACP markets was gradually diminishing.[33] With the accession of Greece, Spain and Portugal into the Community its external relations extended further to their overseas territories in Latin America. The latter part of the 1970s resulted in the conclusion of trade, finance and technical cooperation agreements with countries in the Mediterranean, Asia and Latin America.[34] European policy went through another significant period of transition in 1986 when the members signed and ratified the

---

[29] For further information on the Protocols see A. Dunlop, 'What Future for Lomé's Commodity Protocols?' (1999) ECDPM Paper accessed 12 December 2016 at http://ecdpm.org/publications/future-lomes-commodity-protocols/.

[30] The legal bases for these schemes are found in Articles 186–212 (STABEX) and Articles 214–219 (SYSMIN) of the Fourth Lomé Convention.

[31] W. Brown, 'Restructuring North-South Relations: ACP-EU Development and Cooperation in a Liberal International Order' (2000) 27 *Review of African Political Economy* 367–383, 378.

[32] P. Collier, P. Guillamont, S. Guillamont Jeanneney and J.W. Gunning, 'Reforming Stabex' (2002) 22 *The World Economy* 669–82.

[33] O. Barbarinde and G. Faber, 'From Lomé to Cotonou: Business as Usual?' in S. Bilal and R. Grynberg (eds), *Navigating New Waters: A Reader on ACP-EU Trade Relations* (London: Commonwealth Secretariat, 2007).

[34] European Commission Green Paper (n. 24), 9.

Single European Act (SEA), creating the single market.[35] The impetus behind the drafting of the SEA was the 1985 White Paper[36] which highlighted the need to remove physical, technical and fiscal barriers to trade in order to complete the internal market. Creating the single market was a process of internal deregulation leading to a unified Europe, as we know it today. This process was initiated in part as a response to the slow growth, high inflation and high unemployment that had marred Europe for most of the 1970s and 1980s.[37] Without a doubt, European enlargement had far-reaching effects beyond the members of the Community. While it was expected that deregulation of the internal market would lead to growth for the EC and third countries, it was also feared that it could have diversionary effects. Removing the internal physical, technical, and fiscal barriers to trade meant that developing countries were subject to a unified system of import rules rather than 15 separate rules and standards of the individual EC countries.

The end of the Cold War and the fall of the Berlin Wall also signalled a new phase of reconstruction for Europe. Following the collapse of the Soviet Union, Europe redefined its materialist strategic direction. With the barriers to Eastern Europe now eradicated, the EU sought to strengthen its ties with neighbouring countries. While Africa was no longer a pawn in the politics of East versus West, there was a growing fear that the special relationship between the EU and ACP was disintegrating.[38] In the early post-Cold war years, the EU provided financial assistance to the countries in Central and Eastern Europe as part of its external economic policy. However, the increase in financial assistance to these countries corresponded with a decline in aid to the ACP beneficiaries.[39]

Arguably, the combination of external changes at the global level and within the EU marked a paradigmatic shift away from a *partnership of equals* in the ACP-EU relationship. Lomé no longer fitted the (neo)liberal paradigm of the EU's trade strategy, which had itself undergone significant transformation in light of the ongoing negotiating stalemates at the

---

[35] The SEA was signed in February 1986 and ratified on 1 July 1987.

[36] European Commission, 'Completing the Internal Market' *White Paper* COM (85) 310 Final, Brussels (1985).

[37] C. Kwarteng, *Africa and the European Challenge: Survival in a Changing World* (Aldershot, UK and Brookfield, VT, USA: Avebury, 1998), 6.

[38] *Ibid,* 10.

[39] See Barbarinde and Faber (n. 33), 29 and I. Montana, 'The Lomé Conventions from Inception to the Dynamics of Post-Cold War, 1957–1990s' (2003) 2 *African and Asian Studies* 63–97.

multilateral level. Indeed, the reconstruction of the EU-ACP relationship reflects the growing need of the EU to secure benefits at a bilateral level that could not be achieved multilaterally. As such, the EU began to reformulate its external relations, particularly with developing countries, to secure its place as a leader in the global order. In doing so 'relics from the past, such as Lomé and ACP need[ed] to be sacrificed'.[40]

Some developing countries, particularly in Africa, became concerned that the reconstruction of a unified Europe would lead to higher levels of protectionism and these fears were not without foundation in light of their growing dependence on European aid and trade. Compounded by the failure of import substitution policies and structural adjustment programmes (SAPs) to deliver on the forecasted economic growth, African economies were increasingly vulnerable to exogenous shocks and global price fluctuations. As outlined in Chapter 3, EU development policy has long echoed that of the global financial institutions. Indeed, the EU has submitted that its development policy and common commercial policy should be complementary and seen as 'two facets of the Union's external identity'.[41] The SAPs that characterised international development assistance provided by the IMF and World Bank in the 1980s were indeed supported in part by the EDF.[42] When it became evident that the SAPs did not have the desired effect of bolstering economic growth among the developing nations notion of 'good governance' became the hallmark of the World Bank and IMF's financial assistance programmes.

This policy shift was also reflected in the Lomé framework, with the EU incorporating a 'good governance' aspect to its trade facilitation and development cooperation.[43] The successive Conventions allowed the EU and ACP to adapt objectives under the Lomé framework, without really questioning the substance of that framework. This meant that the Conventions could incorporate new instruments on export loss (STABEX/SYSMIN) and structural adjustment, which reflected the development thinking at the time. As it turns out, this was not necessarily

---

40 Flint (n. 9), 82.

41 European Commission Green Paper (n. 24), 3.

42 N. Udombana, 'Back to Basics: The ACP-EU Cotonou Trade Agreement and Challenges for the African Union' (2004) 40 *Texas International Law Journal* 59–108.

43 N. Slocum-Bradley and A. Bradley, 'Is the EU's Governance "Good"? An Assessment of EU Governance in its Partnership with ACP States' (2010) 31 *Third World Quarterly* 31–49; I. Minta, 'The Lomé Convention and the New International Economic Order' (1984) 27 *Howard Law Journal* 953–74.

the most beneficial course of action for developing countries in the ACP region.

From the outset, Lomé was perceived as a 'progressive agreement linking developed and developing countries in a spirit of partnership and equality'.[44] Lomé extended beyond trade in goods to include provisions on human rights, political dialogue and good governance. Lomé provided valuable concessions in certain sectors, especially agriculture and fisheries. Without the DFQF access offered under Lomé, many ACP agricultural exports would have been subject to an average tariff of 23 per cent.[45] It has been argued that the EU does not articulate its policy objectives effectively through its trade relationship with the ACP, and as such, it 'acts in such a way that its processes of governance and their outcomes fail to fulfil the criteria for good governance that it sets for others'.[46]

Indeed, European policy is framed in a manner that fails to achieve the primary objective of poverty eradication and instead places limitations on the developing country's ability to realise economic development and broader social development ideals.[47] The slow creep of neoliberal ideals over the years has become so deeply embedded within the ACP-EU relationship that the relationship is now one characterised by inequality, asymmetry and dependence. The Lomé partnership became symbolic of a 'donor relationship' with the connotation of a 'senior/junior' relationship rather than a 'partnership of equals'.[48] Such is the depth of the dependence on the EU, that 'each time the European economies sneeze, the African economies catch pneumonia'.[49]

However, the ACP-EU relationship was yet to undergo its most important change since its creation. At the multilateral level, the conclusion of the long-running bananas dispute would have unprecedented effects for the dynamic of ACP-EU cooperation. Together with the other various exogenous and endogenous forces that had contributed to the

---

[44] G. Crawford, 'Evaluating European Union Promotion of Human Rights, Democracy and Good Governance: Towards a Participatory Approach' (2002) 14 *Journal of International Development* 911–926.

[45] Gibb (n. 27), 466.

[46] Slocum-Bradley and Bradley (n. 43), 32.

[47] M. Farrell, 'A Triumph of Realism over Idealism? Cooperation between the European Union and Africa' (2005) 27 *European Integration* 263–83, 266.

[48] S. Hurt, 'The EU-SADC Economic Partnership Agreement Negotiations: "Locking" in the Neoliberal Development Model in Southern Africa?' (2012) 33 *Third World Quarterly* 495–510.

[49] A. Adedeji, cited in Kwarteng (n. 37), 52.

restructuring of this interregional relationship, the conclusion of the bananas dispute marks the turning point for ACP-EU cooperation with a shift towards reciprocity.

THE LONG ROAD TO RECIPROCITY

Although the *EC-Bananas* dispute was briefly discussed in Chapter 2, its transformative significance for ACP-EU cooperation cannot be overstated. This case marked a new chapter in the construction of the ACP-EU relationship as the imperialist flavour to the EU's external trade strategy began to manifest.[50] The EU's Green Paper was issued in 1996 and outlines the main reasons for reforming cooperation with 77 ACP countries. Shifting from policies rooted in contractual relations, the EU's proposed trade strategy for the ACP was an expression of neoliberal trade policy through which the EU's normative conception of development could be exported.

Although the relationship has been described as a *partnership*, the EU recognised the asymmetry in the relationship and attributed this to the ACP region's increasing dependency on aid and the limited institutional capacity to implement effective trade measures. These factors have made putting the 'partnership' into practice, and engaging in meaningful political dialogue, more difficult. In acknowledging that ACP is not a political, economic or social homogenous space the EU submitted that cooperation should be tailored in such a way as to accommodate for the diversity of the region. On this basis, the EU proposed dividing the ACP countries into groups according to the level of economic development. Differentiation according to geographical regions and levels of development is a distinguishing feature of the Cotonou Agreement and, more recently, of the EU's Development Cooperation policy. The Cotonou Agreement differentiates between least developed countries (LDCs) and non-LDC developing countries in the ACP region, affording different treatment to each group. Non-LDC developing countries are required to liberalise at a faster pace than LDCs. However, this distinction proves to be problematic in relation to regional integration as a development strategy.[51]

---

[50] D. Canterbury, 'European Bloc Imperialism' (2009) 35 *Critical Sociology* 801–23.

[51] L. Hinkle and M. Schiff, 'Economic Partnership Agreements Between Sub-Saharan Africa and the EU: A Development Perspective' (2004) 27 *World Economy* 1322.

Stability, contractuality and non-reciprocity were the underpinning principles of the Lomé regime. However, the value of preferences has declined over time and as a result of multilateral liberalisation, it is likely to decline yet further. Industrialisation did not materialise in the expected way during the Lomé period and the ACP countries did not witness significant growth nor did their production bases diversify.[52] The lack of supply-side factors was also an important element of the ACP's ultimate failure to benefit from the Lomé preferences. In light of the disappointing growth experienced by most ACP countries under the Lomé framework, the EU was keen to reform both the trade and development assistance pillars under the new framework agreement.

The EU placed emphasis on the need for financial and technical support for the ACP countries during the transitionary phase of the new WTO-compliant trade framework, which saw the marriage between economic liberalisation and the promotion of broader development objectives. Submitting that its relationship with the ACP had become 'increasingly dominated by the dependence on aid, the needs of the moment and crisis management'[53] the EU proposed that the political dimension of the relationship must be strengthened and reinforced. Implicit in strengthening the political dimension was the inclusion of non-economic values such as the respect for human rights and good governance, and the creation of a European conflict prevention and settlement policy. As outlined in Chapter 3, this parallels the values which have since been set out in Articles 207 TFEU and 209 TFEU read in light of Article 21(1) TFEU.

Perhaps one of the most significant proposals outlined in the Green Paper was the reconstruction of the ACP bloc into distinct sub-regional configurations.[54] Arguing that a 'one-size-fits-all' trade policy is inappropriate for a region that is so diverse economically and politically, the EU suggested that these countries would benefit from changing the form of cooperation to regional arrangements:

> The creation of political and economic areas which go beyond national boundaries has been recognised as a necessary step for Europe and is so for the ACP states as well. The path of regional cooperation and integration seems advisable not only because of the generally inadequate size of many

---

52 European Commission Green Paper (n. 24), 17.

53 *Ibid*, 12.

54 *Ibid*, 41.

ACP countries but also because such an option can encourage political leaders to adopt a more strategic approach to developing their economies.[55]

The proposal to divide the ACP regional space into separate sub-regional spaces attracted criticism from the ACP countries. In response to the EU's proposal, the ACP countries adopted the Libreville Declaration[56] in 1997 expressing their own concerns in relation to the proposed reciprocal trade arrangements. The ACP confirmed their desire to 'strengthen the unity and solidarity of the Group and retain it as a geographical entity' while enhancing 'the political identity of the ACP group to enable it to act and speak with a single voice in all international fora'.[57] In a letter dated 6 April 1998 from the Prime Minister of Jamaica to the President of the European Commission, the concerns of the ACP States were reiterated:

> We have repeatedly reaffirmed our determination to maintain ACP solidarity and the integrity of the ACP as a negotiating partner. This should be the fundamental basis for the future negotiations; but it will be jeopardised from the outset were we to agree to negotiating structures the EU is now contemplating. Indeed now the European Union should have nothing to gain by seeking to fragment relationships between ACP countries that have been nurtured into maturity over 25 years of Lomé experiences – at least if it is serious about furthering the development of ACP countries and assisting our integration into the world economy.[58]

It was the collective ACP view that only ACP solidarity could 'save what is best and improve what is not'.[59] However, the EU was committed to splitting the ACP bloc into seven distinct negotiating configurations that were to align with existing regional initiatives across Africa, the Caribbean and the Pacific. Given the express desire to remain as one economic and political negotiating bloc, it is important to consider whether the ACP countries were coerced into negotiation in this fashion and, if so, for what purpose? Richard Bernal, the former Chairman of the CARICOM

---

55 *Ibid*, 44.

56 ACP Secretariat, Libreville Declaration (1997), accessed 12 December 2016 at http://www.acp.int/content/libreville-declaration.

57 *Ibid*, Articles 8a and 8b, respectively.

58 Letter to the European Commission from the Prime Minister of Jamaica, P.J. Patterson of 6 April 1998 cited in R. Bernal, *Globalisation, Trade and Economic Development: The CARIFORUM-EU Partnership Agreement* (New York: Palgrave Macmillan, 2013), 23.

59 *Ibid*, 25.

Prime Ministerial Committee on External Negotiations and a lead participant in the negotiations of the Lomé Conventions argues that CARIFORUM was the only pre-existing regional group when the sub-division of the ACP into 'six artificially designed regional groupings' was decided.[60] As such, he proposes that the 'other five groupings were nothing more than imagined communities that the Europeans were arrogant enough to assume they could forge into functioning entities'.[61] Bernal concludes that these six groups were based on 'crude geographic proximity and therefore as arbitrary as the European imperialist partition of Africa in the late nineteenth and early twentieth centuries'.[62]

The Libreville Declaration acknowledges the political and economic changes which have transformed the trade relationship with the EU but urges developed countries, in particular the EU, to support the development process in the region. Article 3 of the Libreville Declaration recognises:

> ... the importance of regional integration, intra-ACP cooperation and cooperation among ACP and other developing countries as a means of promoting the socio-economic development of our countries and strengthening our solidarity.

Furthermore, the ACP countries requested that the future trade relationship builds upon the Lomé acquis ensuring equality between partners:

> We draw attention to the inequities of the international economic order and to the continued absence of a level playing field, and hence, the need for special and differential treatment of developing countries in the application of rules and regulations governing international economic transactions.[63]

In the Green Paper, the EU identified four potential options for future trading arrangements with the ACP countries. First, the ACP could opt to trade as one bloc maintaining the status quo with some changes. In accordance with the principle of differentiation, the common basis of the agreement would be the same for all countries but there would be some differences for trade, finance and technical cooperation which would be conditional on the level of each individual country's development status.

---

60 Since the beginning of the negotiations, there are now seven sub-regional ACP blocs as the Eastern and Southern Africa (ESA) EPA group split into two, retaining the ESA group and creating the East African Community (EAC) group.

61 Bernal (n. 58), 34.

62 *Ibid.*

63 ACP Secretariat (n. 56).

The second option presented to the ACP countries would be to negotiate one overarching agreement as a bloc which would then be supplemented with separate bilateral agreements. Negotiation of bilateral agreements could take place between the EU and individual countries or groups of countries with similar levels of development. Third, the EU proposed the creation of regional ACP configurations to replace the existing Lomé framework. This would involve regional trade agreements that were WTO compliant. This option reflects the general direction of EU external economic policy. Finally, the EU suggested the creation of a cooperation agreement for landlocked least developed countries (LLDCs) in the ACP bloc. However, this final option was considered by the EU to be an inappropriate solution to the existing trade problems.

Since 2002, the ACP countries have been negotiating new trade agreements, known as Economic Partnership Agreements (EPAs), with the EU in sub-regional groupings in line with the third option. The term 'partnership' is now prominent in EU rhetoric, replacing that of 'association' first used during Yaoundé. Of the seven negotiating blocs, only four have concluded the negotiations of full EPAs,[64] and the CARIFORUM EPA is the only comprehensive agreement currently being applied. The following section aims to show that the normative nature of *partnership* has been abstracted from the legal framework of the EPAs and through the strategic orientation of the EU's materialist capitalist rationality, the EPAs mark a further hegemonic shift in ACP-EU relations.

THE COTONOU AGREEMENT

The Cotonou Partnership Agreement (CPA) replaces the Lomé regime, is WTO compatible conferring reciprocal preferences, and is in place for 20 years. It has been revised twice, first in 2005 and most recently in 2010, with the ACP countries and the EU now in consultation with regard to how the partnership will change post-2020 when the Cotonou Agreement comes to an end.[65] Signed in Benin on 23 June 2000 between the EU and 77 ACP countries, the CPA bridges together trade and development

[64] The negotiations in the Central Africa, Eastern and Southern Africa, and Pacific groups are ongoing.

[65] European Commission and European External Action Service, 'Towards a New Partnership Between the European Union and the African, Caribbean, and Pacific Countries After 2020' Summary Report of 18 March 2016, Ref. Ares(2016)1372862.

cooperation comprising three pillars: the political dimension, development cooperation, and trade liberalisation. Preferences granted under the trade pillar expired in 2007 and have since been replaced by the regional EPAs, which have been conceptualised as 'drivers of development' for the ACP.

Although the defining characteristics of the Lomé regime were non-reciprocity and discrimination, cooperation under Lomé had disappointing results for ACP producers. Rather than bolstering economic growth in ACP, the Lomé preferences had the opposite effect with trade shares falling over the years. Between 1976 and 1994, the ACP countries' share of EU-bound exports fell from 6.7 per cent to 2.4 per cent.[66] In part, this was a result of the changing global political environment, the unification of Europe and the multilateral reduction of tariffs at the GATT level. However, in response to the general decline of ACP trade performance on the global market, the EU-ACP negotiations began to focus on reciprocal trade which would encourage competitive practices and promote the restructuring of these failing economies.[67]

For decades, ACP production has been predominantly monocultural with a focus on poor-performing agricultural commodities.[68] This, coupled with tariff reductions at a multilateral level, has stifled economic development at the ACP level. Without doubt, successive tariff reductions at the multilateral level have eroded the preferences traditionally enjoyed by ACP under the preferential agreements with the EU. In addition, the lowering of the EU's common external tariff from 10–12 per cent (early 1970s) to 3–4 percent (post-Uruguay) has further diminished the significance of the preferences enjoyed by the ACP in real terms.[69] It was therefore vital that the new trade regime would foster economic growth and integrate the developing markets of ACP countries into the global economy.

In terms of EU development cooperation, Article 208 TFEU outlines the primary objective of development cooperation to be the reduction and eradication of poverty. Article 209 TFEU provides the legal base from which the EU can negotiate trade agreements bilaterally and regionally to

---

[66] Hurt (n. 17), 165.

[67] M. McQueen, 'ACP-EU Trade Cooperation after 2000: An Assessment of Reciprocal Trade Preferences' (1998) 36 *Journal of Modern African Studies* 669–92.

[68] A. Abass, 'The Cotonou Trade Regime and WTO Law' (2004) 10 *European Law Journal* 439–62.

[69] P. Brenton, 'The Changing Nature and Determinants of EU Trade Policies' CEPS Working Document No. 150 (October 2000), 4.

achieve the objectives set out in Article 21(1) TFEU and, in particular, sub-paragraph (d) to 'foster the sustainable economic, social and environmental development of developing countries, with the primary aim of eradicating poverty'. This is reiterated in Article 1 of the CPA, which defines the overarching objectives of the EPAs:

> The partnership shall be centred on the objective of reducing and eventually eradicating poverty consistent with the objective of sustainable development and the gradual integration of the ACP countries into the world economy.

Development is given a broad understanding in the CPA, reflecting the many dimensions of development expressed in the evolving soft law at the international level. One of the fundamental objectives of the new regime is outlined in Article 34(1) Cotonou, which states that 'economic and trade cooperation shall aim at fostering the smooth and gradual integration of the ACP states into the world economy'. Linguistically, the conjugative verb 'shall aim' does not appear to confer an imperative legal obligation. While the flexibility of the linguistic formulation may not *ab initio* circumscribe the legal normativity of the obligation[70] it appears that the EPAs, as legal regimes, should *aspire* to achieve a 'development-friendly' trade regime that improves the competitiveness of ACP countries.

The CPA: A Participatory Space

In a similar spirit to the policies of the IMF and World Bank, the CPA reiterates the need for ACP countries to 'own' their development process and coordinate strategies to help eradicate poverty.[71] Political dialogue is an important element of the Cotonou Agreement with emphasis placed on the need to facilitate discussion on agreed priorities, shared agendas and issues of common interest. Traditionally, within the EU-ACP context, we tend to think of states as the only actors involved in the negotiation process. Critical constructivism goes beyond other political economy models of trade analysis in placing the focus on '*by whom, for whom* and *for what purpose*' regionalism is pursued.[72] In doing so, it seeks to

[70] V. Barral, 'Sustainable Development in International Law: Nature and Operation of an Evolutive Legal Norm' (2012) 23 *European Journal of International Law* 377–400, 384.

[71] Article 2 Cotonou Partnership Agreement 2014.

[72] F. Söderbaum, *The Political Economy of Regionalism: The Case of Southern Africa* (Basingstoke and New York: Palgrave MacMillan, 2004).

highlight the involvement of *all* actors that may influence the construction, deconstruction and reconstruction of a regional space.

An important innovation of the Cotonou framework was the increased role of non-state actors in the negotiation and consultative processes. Article 4 of the revised CPA, entitled 'The Actors of the Partnership' provides:

> … the parties recognise the complementary role of and potential for contributions by non-state actors, ACP national parliaments, and local decentralised authorities to the development process, particularly at the national and regional levels.

Expanding the discursive space in which deliberative and participative processes can take place increases the likelihood of a fairer bargaining environment, especially in the case of asymmetric relationships. Participation is a fundamental element of enabling a country to 'own' their development process.

EU development policy has long echoed that of the global financial institutions. Indeed, the EU has submitted that its development policy and multilateral trade should be complementary and seen as 'two facets of the Union's external identity'.[73] At the international level, financial assistance to developing countries has changed course since the 1990s. The concept of 'country ownership' has been the focal point of IMF and World Bank strategies since the introduction of Poverty Reduction Strategy Papers (PRSP), which replaced the SAPs. Country ownership involves each country determining its own economic and development strategies according to its individual needs using financial assistance from the multilateral institutions to support this process.[74] It connotes the forging of a relationship, based on partnership and equality, between a developed country and a developing country.

However, the former ambassador of Trinidad and Tobago, Ambassador Cumberbatch, warned of a decline in EU interest in the ACP states throughout the EPA negotiations.[75] While regular meetings between EU and ACP Heads of State which were common throughout the Lomé partnership had 'contributed significantly to the closeness of the relationship and the success of co-operation' Cumberbatch complained of a lack of attendance by EU Ministers at the ACP-EU Council during the EPA

---

[73] European Commission Green Paper (n. 24), 3.

[74] W.H. Buiter, 'Country Ownership: A Term Whose Time Has Gone' (2007) 17 *Development in Practice* 647–52, 647.

[75] Bernal (n. 58), 32.

negotiations. He attributed the EU's lack of interest in the EPAs in part because of the 'sterility of the agendas and procedures where important political issues do not feature'. Presence at other fora in which ACP matters are of interest, for example the African Union (AU), suggests that the EU still has an interest in Africa, at least. Economically, the ACP countries may not be as significant to the EU as previously thought, however, politically their cooperation and partnership remains important.[76]

An interesting aspect of country ownership programmes is the emphasis placed on stakeholder involvement. For many years, the restructuring of the EU-ACP relationship has been met with a great deal of scepticism. Stephen Hurt explores the degree of consent and coercion present in the EU-ACP relationship and argues that in promoting *dialogue* and *partnership* the EU is encouraging ACP countries to *own* their development process.[77] However, the fact that the EU presents EPAs as the only alternative to Lomé preferences implies a coercive force in the relationship:

> The use of the WTO as the major justification is understood not as a simple 'reason' in this case, but as a strategic attempt by the EU to externalise responsibility for its own policy. What has been shown to be an essentially coercive policy direction does not require domestic consensus if it can be shown that it is the only alternative.[78]

Country ownership necessitates the involvement of stakeholders to engage in the participatory process of creating the development strategy. This approach has been adopted in the CPA, which envisages a more enhanced role for non-state actors (NSAs) in the consultative EPA process. While this development under Cotonou is innovative, it is perhaps unsurprising given the neoliberal model of development pursued by the EU. In particular, the CPA provides a more significant role for private actors in the trade negotiation process. Article 21 outlines the importance of ensuring that 'cooperation' leads to a 'favourable environment for private investment and the development of a dynamic, viable, and competitive private sector'. Futhermore, cooperation should support

---

76 M. Broberg, 'The European Union-Caribbean Relation: On the Apparent Deterioration of the EU-Caribbean Relationship' (2016) 21 *European Foreign Affairs Review* 75–94.

77 Hurt (n. 17), 163.

78 *Ibid*, 74.

the implementation of 'structural policies designed to reinforce the role of the different actors, especially the private sector'.[79]

Charles Kwarteng acknowledges the importance of non-governmental forces in shaping regional processes:

> It will be important that African leaders encourage social groups, such as journalists, trade unions, marketing and industrial groups, students and non-governmental organisations, to play a role in Africa's regional integration ... Like Europe, private sector development should be the linchpin of the strategy to integrate African economies ... In an effective regional market, the private sector becomes the principal actor, while the public sector plays the role of formulator and regulator of policies.[80]

Through the project of interregionalism, the EU is able to carve out a space in which its norms can potentially be diffused. In this way, the EU is *Europeanising* regional processes in the ACP through the promotion of neoliberal economic policies which are reinforced through the normative actions of the international financial institutions.[81] It seems that the EPAs no longer embody the development spirit expressed in the CPA, and the role of NSAs has been important in highlighting the development deficit of these legal regimes.

While the increasing role of NSAs, such as civil society and private firms, is a welcome intervention into the ACP-EU trade regime, it could nevertheless weaken the process of democratisation in ACP countries.[82] Unlike governments these groups are not democratically elected and there is some concern about the legitimacy of their participation in predominantly inter-state trade relations. This book does not claim that every aspect of trade negotiation should be open for discursive participation; however, civil society and the private sector possess special knowledge about the interrelation between social, economic and cultural issues and could therefore positively contribute to the construction of 'development-friendly' trade regimes. NSAs and the media play an

---

79 Article 22 Cotonou Partnership Agreement 2014.

80 Kwarteng (n. 37), 43–4.

81 A. Storey, 'Normative Power Europe? Economic Partnership Agreements and Africa' (2006) *Journal of Contemporary African Studies* 331–46; O. Rutazibwa, 'The Problematics of the EU's Ethical (Self)Image in Africa: The EU as an "Ethical Intervener" and the 2007 Joint Africa-EU Strategy' (2010) 18 *Journal of Contemporary European Studies* 209–28; T. Haastrup, 'EU as Mentor? Promoting Regionalism as External Relations Practice in EU-Africa Relations' (2013) *Journal of European Integration* 1–16.

82 Hurt (n. 17), 172.

important part in raising awareness about important issues in the public sphere and can act to keep 'checks and balances' on the strategic orientations of the state. In the context of the EPA negotiations, non-state actors have played an important role in confronting the rationality of the new legal regimes. This will be discussed in Chapter 8 in relation to the SADC EPA.

ECONOMIC PARTNERSHIP AGREEMENTS: DRIVERS OF DEVELOPMENT

Underlying the EPAs are four core values and ideals, namely, partnership, regional integration, development and multilateral compliance.[83] Throughout the negotiation phase it was understood that through the EPA framework ACP countries would retain preferential access to the EU on the basis that ACP markets are progressively liberalised for EU commodities. Reciprocity in the EU-ACP relationship therefore benefits the EU significantly, as it will for the first time in their trading history enjoy DFQF access to the ACP region. This confers far greater access than offered under Lomé, which was generally most favoured nation (MFN) or better depending on the particular product. Requiring the liberalisation of 'substantially all trade' among an existing regional integration arrangement may cause friction between members as they negotiate which products should be included and excluded from the EPA. That said, the ACP markets are relatively insignificant in terms of volumes of trade for the EU. Although some Caribbean officials have informally expressed concern about the nature of the EPAs, claiming that they have 'been cut from a cloth that first of all suits the African ACP countries', each EPA has been tailored to the specific regional grouping.[84] For example, the CARIFORUM states wanted an EPA that liberalised services as this is their strongest industry, while the SADC states have opted for a goods-only EPA as their primary trade with the EU is that of commodities. Through the negotiation phase, each regional partner has detailed those products that shall be classified as 'sensitive' and excluded from the

---

[83] European Commission, 'Proposal for the Regulation of the European Parliament and of the Council amending Annex 1 to Council Regulation (EC) No 1528/2007 as regards the exclusion of a number of countries from the list of regions or states which have concluded negotiations' COM (2011) 598 Final.

[84] Broberg (n. 76), 80.

schedule of liberalisation.[85] That said, where countries within the regional grouping select the same products, each country could potentially select a different phasing plan. The EPA negotiations may even exacerbate existing political tensions as countries scramble to protect their sensitive industries from liberalisation. It was feared that EPAs could exacerbate political tensions between countries as they sought to protect their sensitive sectors. However, a critical reflection on the SADC and CARIFORUM EPAs in Chapters 8 and 9, respectively, will demonstrate that some of these fears have been unfounded.

It has been estimated that the adjustment costs for implementing the EPA will amount to at least €9 billion for the ACP.[86] Under the 9th EDF, when the initial negotiation phase started, the ACP received approximately €650 million for the provision of trade-related assistance, with just €40 million allocated for facilitating support for the EPA negotiations in southern Africa.[87] In spite of this notable shortfall, the EU Commission has insisted that there would be no separate financial envelope that is specifically designated for supporting the EPA implementation in ACP countries.[88] Under the 11th EDF, the EU has committed in principle €30.5 billion to the ACP and support will be provided through national indicative programmes (NIPs), regional indicative programmes (RIPs) and through the Africa-EU Strategic Partnership and Caribbean-EU Strategic partnerships. In addition, and as outlined in Chapter 3, further funding may be available through private institutions such as the European Investment Bank.

Throughout the protracted negotiation period, the European Commission remained unapologetic for the scope of liberalisation proposed under the EPAs. Conceptualising the EPAs as fundamental to the development process across the ACP, the Commission stated:

> EPAs are part of the overall effort to build up the economic governance framework, the stable transparent and predictable rules necessary to lower the costs of doing business, attract fresh domestic or foreign investment and make ACP producers more diversified and competitive. This is why the EPAs must be comprehensive, dealing with all the rules and issues that concern private

---

[85] C. Stevens, 'The EU, Africa and EPAs: Unintended Consequences of Policy Leverage' (2006) 44 *Journal of Modern African Studies* 441–58, 445.

[86] Flint (n. 9), 86.

[87] C. Milner, 'An Assessment of the Overall Implementation and Adjustment Costs for the ACP Countries of Economic Partnership Agreements with the EU', Commonwealth Secretariat Report (September 2005), 31–3.

[88] ECDPM, 'EPA Development Support: Possible Scenarios for EPA-related support mechanisms' ECDPM *In Brief* No. 16 (November 2006).

> investors and traders. As a result, issues such as competition policy and investment rules are no luxury but fundamental factors that affect the decisions of traders and investors.[89]

Herein, the Commission is defining governance through an economic lens reinforcing the prioritisation of economic value over social, cultural and political norms. Embedding neoliberal values into the concept of development, the normative content of the concept becomes increasingly obscured.

It is expected that the EPAs will create a more stable economic environment in the ACP countries which in turn will be more attractive to investors.[90] As confidence among investors grows and the financial environment stabilises, it is likely that private actors will pump yet more investment into the region. This investment cycle is one of the expected dynamic effects of the EPAs. Sufficient financial assistance and appropriate conditions of trade will need to be in place to initiate shifts in the patterns of investment and production in order to realise the dynamic effects of the EPA framework. To this end, the trade effects of EPAs are ambiguous. It is feared that the EPA will result in domestic ACP producers being crowded out by more efficient EU investors who will be keen to harness the potential economies of scale across ACP.[91]

The EPAs have courted controversy because they go beyond what is necessary for WTO compliance. Article XXIV does not contain a provision for SDT, so concluding the EPAs as Article XXIV legal regimes presents an analytical puzzle. Since the negotiations began in 2004, the EU has been pushing for the inclusion of so-called 'new generation' issues which include services, government procurement, competition policy and investment policy.[92] For some time, developing countries have refused to incorporate new generation issues into the Doha Development Round, claiming that to do so would adversely affect their levels of development.[93] The incorporation of new generation issues leaves developing ACP countries in a particularly precarious negotiating position because many have not yet established domestic or regional initiatives on services, investment or competition policies.

---

[89] European Commission cited in Storey (n. 81), 341.

[90] Matambalya (n. 25), 23.

[91] Storey (n. 81), 340.

[92] A. Young, 'Trade Politics Ain't What it Used to Be: The European Union in the Doha Round' (2007) 45 *Journal of Common Market Studies* 789–811.

[93] M.F. Jensen and P. Gibbon, 'Africa and the WTO Doha Round: An Overview' (2007) 25 *Development Policy Review* 5–24.

Noting the unsuccessful growth experienced under Lomé, it is perhaps undeniable that trade facilitation now needs to extend beyond simply the removal of tariffs. Peter Draper proposes that the liberalisation of core services sectors such as telecommunications, finance, energy and transport will result in 'unambiguous benefits' for African countries. He notes:

> … if manufacturing and agriculture are to thrive in a globally competitive market, then producers in these sectors must have access to low-cost, cutting edge service inputs. Yet in Sub-Saharan Africa these sectors are poorly serviced by local suppliers, let alone state enterprises, with little prospect of dynamic growth in the future.[94]

If African countries fail to liberalise the services sector at all, then the production base will remain undiversified. Within the EPA context, there is of course the risk that more competitive EU suppliers will be quick to capture the small and vulnerable markets of African countries. To avoid this scenario, African countries could opt to liberalise unilaterally. To this end, negotiating the liberalisation of the services sector intra-regionally should take precedence over negotiations at the inter-regional level.

However, alternative market access tools may also be used which will effectively restrict ACP products being imported into the EU. Among these are strict rule of origin regimes which incorporate the EU rules on geographical indications, technical barriers to trade (TBT), and sanitary and phytosanitary (SPS) measures.[95] TBT and SPS measures have become increasingly significant non-tariff barriers to trade and typically take the form of strict regulatory or certification requirements. Under Article 4 of the WTO SPS Agreement, an exporter must provide sufficient scientific evidence to demonstrate *equivalence*, or in other words, to show that production process meets the same standards of that in the importing state. Equivalence can be formally demonstrated through the negotiation of Mutual Recognition Agreements (MRAs).[96] Requiring reciprocity and equivalence could create a greater disparity between the

---

[94] P. Draper, 'EU-Africa Trade Relations: The Political Economy of Economic Partnership Agreements' (2007) *ECIPE Jan Tumlir Policy Essays*, No. 02/2007, 14–15.

[95] For a discussion on the impact of non-tariff barriers to trade for developing countries see A. Disdier, L. Fontagné and M. Mimouni, 'The Impact of Regulations on Agricultural Trade: Evidence from the SPS and TBT Agreements' (2008) 90 *American Journal of Agricultural Economics* 336–50.

[96] D. Prévost, 'Sanitary, Phytosanitary and Technical Barriers to Trade in the Economic Partnership Agreements between the European Union and the ACP countries' ICTSD Issue Paper No. 5 (August 2010).

EU and ACP in the EPA framework if the ACP countries cannot meet the prescribed standards of the EU or if the costs of doing so render their products uncompetitive. For example, food safety measures at the EU level have become increasingly onerous over the years and unless the ACP countries can provide adequate proof that the requisite standards have been met, the market access offered under the EPAs will be illusory. As such, the practical effects of complying with non-tariff barriers to trade have broader concerns for competitiveness not just interregionally, but internationally.[97] These problems are further compounded by the fact that the TBT and SPS provisions in the EPAs have been articulated in vague and ambiguous terms.

The process of technical harmonisation has also proven to be an obstacle for ACP exports entering the EC. These non-tariff barriers to trade affect ACP producers, particularly in Africa, where manufacturers lack the infrastructure to comply with the unduly high levels of standards imposed by the EU:

> Huge structural and supply incapacities in LDCs continue to ensure that they cannot meet rules of origin requirements for exports of importance to them, such as industrial and agricultural products. Consequently, they cannot fully utilise the EU's duty free quota free access offer.[98]

The strict labelling requirements and health and safety standards place heavy restrictions on the production base in developing countries.[99] The Taubira Report, commissioned by the French government during its EU Presidency, highlighted the deficiencies of the EPA and called for the European Commissioner to reconsider its position.[100] Taubira argued that the high food safety measures in operation in Europe 'constitute more effective obstacles than tariffs'. However, little has been done to simplify these onerous conditions.

Under the EPA framework, developing ACP countries are being asked to make greater concessions through regional arrangements than they have been required to make at the multilateral level. The EPAs are being

---

[97] M. Doherty, 'ACP-EU Agreements: Sanitary and Phytosanitary Measures' ECDPM Discussion Paper No. 68 (October 2005).

[98] A.I. Ukpe, 'Will EPAs Foster the Integration of Africa into World Trade?' 54(2) *Journal of African Law* 212–31, 215.

[99] P. Goodison and C. Stoneman, 'Europe: Partner or Exploiter? The G-90 and the ACP' (2004) 31 *Review of African Political Economy* 725–34, 730.

[100] For a discussion on the Taubira Report and its implications for the EPA negotiations see: J. Senona, 'EPAs and Doha Round: Development or Discontent' (2009) 8 *Journal of International Trade Policy* 60–83, 70–1.

negotiated in line with WTO policy and with the EU's controversial CAP protected. Paul Goodison argues that the EPAs are little more than a strategic instrument for the EU to penetrate and further exploit developing country markets:

> ... it is clearly in the EU's economic interests to persuade these developing countries to eliminate tariffs on trade with the EU, whilst maintaining tariffs on imports from the EU's competitors.[101]

Examining the relationship between the international regulatory framework and the development policies of the EU, Richard Gibb argues that pursuing the neo-liberal trade agenda has undermined international social and development programmes.[102] Indeed, the EU's reluctance to remove new generation issues from the EPA agenda seems to contradict its self-proclaimed recognition in the Green Paper of the vulnerable economic situation facing most ACP countries. Even today, the EU's technical barriers to trade are notoriously rigorous. While liberalisation on the proposed scale could, under certain conditions, prove to be beneficial for many African countries, this benefit will only be realised if the adequate governance structures, laws and institutions necessary to facilitate the programme of reform are created.

Concerned with the uncertainty surrounding the new legal regime, the negotiations failed to conclude by the 2007 deadline. It was feared that if the EPAs were not concluded in accordance with the scheduled deadline of 1 January 2008, then the ACP countries would be left in a precarious trading position vis-à-vis the EU. While the LDCs would continue to enjoy preferential access to the EU under the EBA, non-LDCs would lose their preferences and would have to apply for generalised system of preferences (GSP) or revert to MFN. In response to this, the Commission decided to divide the post-2007 negotiation process into two separate phases.[103] The first phase would consist of initialling an interim goods-only EPA between the ACP and EU countries. This would then be followed by the second phase, which would involve further negotiations towards a full EPA including trade and non-trade related issues. EU Regulation 1528/2007 governed the trade regime for the EU and ACP

---

[101] P. Goodison, 'EU Trade Policy and the Future of Africa's Trade Relationship with the EU' (2007) 34 *Review of African Political Economy* 247–66.

[102] Gibb (n. 27), 459.

[103] S. Woolfrey, 'State of Play in the SADC-EU EPA Negotiations' in A. Bösl, G. Erasmus, T. Hartzenberg and C. McCarthy, *Monitoring Regional Integration in Southern Africa Yearbook*, Vol. 9 (Stellenbosch: tralac, 2009), 113.

countries that had negotiated the EPAs prior to the expiry of the waiver. This included the SADC-EPA countries who had agreed to initial the interim EPA. It was intended that the countries would then be committed, or 'locked-in', to continuing negotiations towards a full EPA.

WITHDRAWAL OF REGULATION 1528/2007

With the 2008 deadline passing with only one comprehensive EPA concluded, the EU offered DFQF access to the ACP countries that were willing to sign an interim EPA before the expiry of the Cotonou waiver at the end of 2007. Transitional arrangements had also been made for rice and sugar under Regulation 1528/2007. The proposal received mixed reactions but the ACP countries continued with the negotiation process in order to secure DFQF access to the EU market. In the context of the SADC EPA region, Botswana, Lesotho, Mozambique and Swaziland in the SADC-EPA group initialled and signed the interim agreement, while Angola, South Africa and Namibia refused to do so. With the African and Pacific countries failing to sign and implement the agreements, the EU expressed increasing frustration with the slow pace of progress towards concluding full EPAs. Consequently, it threatened to withdraw DFQF access granted under Regulation 1528/2007 by 2014 if countries had not taken the appropriate steps towards ratification of EPAs.[104] This coincided with the restructuring of the EU's GSP which, like the EU's development assistance programme, had introduced a framework of differentiation.[105] With an exclusive focus on providing preferential access to those countries that needed it most, the restructuring of GSP left the ACP countries uncertain as to whether they would qualify under the new regime.

The European Commission submitted that four years of DFQF access has provided enough breathing space for the ACP countries to commit to ratification and further negotiation. In failing to progress further, the EU proposed that there were 18 ACP countries no longer meeting the requirements under the market access Regulation 1528/2007. Threatening the withdrawal of the Regulation left the ACP countries at an important crossroads with the EU in terms of trade policy and they were left with two choices. They could either commit to strengthening the partnership

[104] European Commission, 'Access to EU markets for exporters from African, Caribbean and Pacific Countries', EC Memo, accessed 12 December 2016 at http://trade.ec.europa.eu/doclib/docs/2011/september/tradoc_148215.pdf.

[105] Regulation (EU) No. 978/2012 of the European Parliament and of the Council.

with the EU through the conclusion of comprehensive EPAs or abandon the relationship altogether, reverting to either MFN access or access under GSP or EBA where the country concerned qualified for such preferences. In its proposal to remove the Regulation, the Commission reiterated the objectives of EPAs:

> ... they can create a sustainable long-term partnership with the EU in which free market access is maintained ... which also supports regional integration, strengthens economic governance, and helps attract investment.

Regulation 1528/2007 was enacted as a temporary measure to bridge the gap between negotiations and ratification of the EPAs. However, overall the negotiations have progressed at an excruciatingly slow pace. In some regions, such as southern Africa, the negotiations took over ten years to conclude. While the EU's proposal to withdraw market access under the Regulation undoubtedly placed greater pressure on the ACP countries to decide whether or not to continue with the EPA negotiations it must be remembered that the negotiations had been ongoing since 2002 and, therefore, perhaps the EU's desire to move past the negotiating impasse was not unreasonable.

JOINT AFRICA-EU STRATEGIC PARTNERSHIP

Alongside the EPAs, the African States and EU have forged a strategic partnership since 2006 to strengthen their special relationship and it is important to situate the EPA process within this partnership. The Joint Strategic Partnership sets out the context, shared vision, and principles of the relationship between the EU and African States. In Article 1, the Partnership states:

> Africa and Europe are bound together by history, culture, geography, a common future, as well as by a community of values: the respect for human rights, freedom, equality, solidarity, justice, the rule of law and democracy as enshrined in the relevant international agreements and in the constitutive texts of our respective Unions.

It speaks of a 'shared vision' through which the partnership will be based on equality[106] and 'a Euro-African consensus of values, common

---

[106] Article 9(a), Council of the European Union, 'The Africa-EU Joint Strategic Partnership: A Joint Africa-EU Strategy' of 9 December 2007 I6344/07 (Presse 291) hereinafter the 'Joint Africa-EU Strategy'.

interests and common strategic objectives'.[107] Aiming to bridge the development divide through 'the strengthening of economic cooperation and the promotion of sustainable development', the EU-Africa Strategy identifies four key objectives relating to peace and security, governance and human rights, trade and regional integration, and key development issues.[108] The first objective is to 'elevate' the EU-Africa political partnership through which 'both sides will *treat Africa as one*' with the EU and AU working side-by-side to forge a deeper partnership.[109] Promoting 'strong, representative and legitimate' multilateral institutions to address global concerns is the third objective.

Perhaps of most interest to this book are the second and fourth long-term objectives, which outline the development aims of the Partnership and should be read in conjunction with one another. The second objective provides that the Partnership shall:

> … strengthen and promote peace, security, democratic governance and human rights, fundamental freedoms, gender equality, sustainable economic development, including industrialisation, and regional and continental integration in Africa, and to ensure that all Millennium Development Goals are met in African countries by the year of 2015.[110]

This is further enhanced by the fourth objective which states that the Partnership aims:

> To facilitate and promote a broad-based and wide-ranging people-centred partnership, Africa and the EU will empower non-state actors and create conditions to enable them to play an active role in development, democracy building, conflict prevention and post-conflict reconstruction processes. Both sides will also promote *holistic approaches to development processes*, and make the Joint Strategy a permanent platform for information, participation and mobilisation of a broad spectrum of civil society actors in the EU, Africa and beyond. Ongoing dialogue with civil society, the private sector and local stakeholders on issues covered by this Joint Strategy will be a key component to its implementation.[111]

Differentiation in the Development Cooperation policy of the EU, outlined in Chapter 3, reinforces the objective of the Africa-EU Joint Strategy which envisages a shift away from continuous donor support

---

107 Article 4 Joint Africa-EU Strategy.
108 Article 10 Joint Africa-EU Strategy.
109 Article 8(i) Joint Africa-EU Strategy.
110 Article 8(ii) Joint Africa-EU Strategy.
111 Article 8(iv) Joint Africa-EU Strategy.

toward improvement of Africa's productive capacities.[112] Liberalisation of the private sector underpins the Joint Strategy's objective to improve trade cooperation through regional integration initiatives.[113] In relation to the EPAs, the Joint Strategy provides in Article 45:

> The EPA-agreements, as *instruments for development*, are to be implemented at the sub-regional level, however, the AU-EU dialogue is relevant to the overall process of regional integration and interface with the developing Regional Economic Communities. Both sides stress the need for the EPA process to be supportive of Africa's regional and continental integration agenda on the basis of the Abuja Treaty.

Rhetorically, at least, the Joint Strategy delivers a partnership based on equality and one which appears to recognise the unique aims of African regionalisms, as both regional and continental in their focus. The Joint Strategy recognises the many dimensions of development, and dedicates 13 provisions to promoting human and social development, gender equality, and environmental sustainability.[114] Interestingly, the Joint Strategy provides a statement on gender equality to 'mainstream gender equality in all strategies, policies, programmes, and actions'.[115] In the context of trade, the commitment toward eradicating the 'feminisation of poverty' has been recognised.[116]

Implementation of the Africa-EU Joint Strategic Partnership takes place through various state and non-state actors, with a meeting of Heads of State and Government every three years.[117] Throughout the interim period between Summits, the Africa-EU Troika meets on a biannual basis to review and monitor the implementation of the Strategic Partnership.[118] Dialogue is strengthened by regular contact between the EU institutions and the Commissions of the AU.[119] Although the Joint Partnership is based on equality between the partners, it is almost entirely funded by the EU and its Member States contributing to over 80 per cent of the AU's

---

112 Article 38 Joint Africa-EU Strategy.
113 Article 40 Joint Africa-EU Strategy.
114 Articles 55–68 Joint Africa-EU Strategy.
115 Article 63 Joint Africa-EU Strategy.
116 *Ibid.*
117 Article 95 Joint Africa-EU Strategy.
118 Under Article 100, the Troika consists of Senior Officials and Ministers of the AU and EU who are mandated to speak on behalf of Africa and the EU, respectively.
119 Article 103 Joint Africa-EU Strategy.

Commission programme budget.[120] Following the EU Commission's proposal to create a Pan-African Programme (Panaf),[121] which would cover other programmes that do not fall explicitly under other thematic funding programmes, a fund of €845 million has been allocated for the period of 2014–2020.[122]

CONCLUDING REMARKS

This chapter has provided a historical account of the ACP-EU relationship illustrating the significance of the transformative shifts through the Yaoundé, Lomé, and Cotonou legal frameworks. Noting the construction and subsequent deconstruction of the ACP as a regional bloc into seven 'imagined' constructions, it has been shown that the ACP-EU relationship has been constituted through law. As the ACP enter into a new phase of cooperation through the EPAs, this chapter has critically assessed the extent to which the legal regime genuinely fosters both commercial and social concerns. In other words, it has sought to identify the nature of the EPAs as having both economic and developmental potential. It has been argued that the EU's dominant discourse frames EPAs as instrumental tools to promote development and governance through predominantly neoliberal values, undermining the normative conception of development as freedom.

---

[120] The Africa-EU Partnership, 'Financing the Partnership' [undated] accessed 12 December 2016 at http://www.africa-eu-partnership.org/en/about-us/financing-partnership.

[121] Panaf is funded under the EU's Development Cooperation Instrument and, in accordance with the Roadmap 2014–2017, the budget covers five key aspects of cooperation: peace and security; democracy, good governance and human rights; human development; sustainable development and inclusive growth; and global and cross-cutting issues.

[122] The Africa-EU Partnership, 'Financing the Partnership' (n. 120).

6. African regionalisms as flexible legal regimes

The purpose of this chapter is to construct a theoretical framework that enables us to understand African regionalisms. Predominantly, the literature analysing the implications of the EPAs have an economic focus, and one which overlooks the complex effects of the new trading regime for regionalism on the African continent. Earlier in this book it was claimed that the rationalist approaches overlook important and historically situated ideational forces that may influence the construction of regionalism.[1] Rationalist theories lack an intersubjective dimension and fail to account for the symbolic interactionism between actors and the meanings certain objects may have towards them.[2] Constructivism is inherently intersubjective in nature, recognising that identities are the basis of interests and that we construct the meaning of our experiences. It allows us to explore a historically sensitive approach to nature of the EPAs and their effects for regionalisms in Africa as we search for the reasons behind, and explanations for, state and non-state actor behaviour in shaping the landscape of the global economy.

In part, this book aims to challenge traditional models of regionalism in order to establish why states and other actors behave as they do in regional processes. Abandoning the assumptions of conventional theories in order to understand the logic of regionalism in Africa, the frame of analysis must be reconceptualised. Classical models of regional integration are inadequate for the study of regionalisms in developing countries

[1] It was noted that classical realists, such as Morgenthau and Hobbes identify egoism and power politics as part of human nature whereas neorealists, such as Waltz, attribute power politics to anarchy. For an interesting discussion on power politics and anarchy see A. Wendt, 'Anarchy Is What States Make of It: The Social Construction of Power Politics' (1992) 46 *International Organisation* 391–425.

[2] Herbert Blumer coined the phrase 'symbolic interactionism' as a social theory and method. For further commentary see P. Manning and G. Smith, 'Symbolic Interactionism' in A. Elliott (ed.), *The Routledge Companion to Social Theory* (Routledge, 2010), ch 3.

since the conditions that encourage trade creation, such as strong internal infrastructure coupled with industrialisation, are often not present.[3] This is particularly so in relation to the EPAs, where it has already been identified that there has emerged a substantial financial deficit for development assistance under the EPA development envelope.

Fredrik Söderbaum highlights the problems associated with analysing African regionalism from a conventional theoretical standpoint, and submits that:

> … whereas mainstream theories are often based on highly normative assumptions about the state and how regionalism/regional integration should proceed, the reality of the post-colonial state in Africa is that it cannot be taken for granted; it needs to be problematised, and it is often a different animal than it pretends to be.[4]

Providing an extensive account of regionalisms across Africa is beyond the scope of this book, however, this chapter will touch upon some of the main challenges facing the project of African regionalism drawing on scholarship in legal philosophy and political economy.

The first section of this chapter will consider the intersection of culture, politics, ethnicity and economic policy in the post-colonial African state. Although there are vast political differences between African states, a fundamental tenet of this chapter is that most, but not all, African countries operate under a political framework of 'disorder' and share a common form of governance rooted in neopatrimonial strategies.[5] While practices of patronage and rent-seeking on the continent are rife, making the project of regionalism more difficult,[6] African governance nevertheless works to an extent. Therefore, it is perhaps more

---

[3] A. Aly, *Economic Cooperation in Africa: In Search of Direction* (Boulder: Lynne Rienner Publishers Inc, 1994), 37; G. Harrison, 'The World Bank, Governance and Theories of Political Action in Africa' (2005) 7(1) *British Journal of International Politics* 240–60.

[4] F. Söderbaum, 'African Regionalism and EU-African Interregionalism' in M. Telò (ed.), *European Union and New Regionalism: Regional Actors and Global Governance in a Post-Hegemonic Era*, 2nd edn (Aldershot: Ashgate, 2007), 186.

[5] P. Chabal and J-P. Daloz, *Africa Works: Disorder as Political Instrument* (London: James Currey, 1999).

[6] J. Herbst, *States and Power in Africa: Comparative Lessons in Authority and Control* (Princeton: Princeton University Press, 2000).

accurate to say that neopatrimonialism permeates the local and institutional levels in different ways, as the consequence of different developmental stages, and can have both beneficial and detrimental effects depending on the particular country setting.

In the second section, Africa's historical journey towards regional integration from the early days of independence to the current day will be traced. We will see that African regionalism has historically pursued a different approach than the neofunctional origins of the EU. African regionalism tends to pursue multi-policy objectives and has been used both as a development and governance strategy, albeit to differing degrees of success. This has led to their conceptualisation by James Gathii as 'flexible legal regimes'.[7] These objectives may include peace-building components as well as policies to strengthen infrastructure and promote trade. Admittedly, African regionalisms have not displayed the level of integration or coherence as that of the EU, but that should not preclude an assessment of the African project as its own form of legitimate authority. Rejecting a binary comparison of EU regionalism versus African regionalism, a fundamental claim of this book is that African regionalisms should be understood on their own terms and within their own historical, social and political context.

The third section of this chapter will examine the role of regionalism as a form of governance and assess the way in which African regionalisms are used as a means to boost the image of African nations to the wider world. It will be argued that, in doing so, regionalism as a mode of governance maintains and lends legitimacy to national States in which neopatrimonial relationships are deeply embedded. By problematising African governance and by showing how regionalism is used as an alternative mode of governance, this chapter aims to emphasise the vulnerable position of African countries in the global economy. In doing so, it reinforces the argumentative narrative of this book that developing countries need special provision when negotiating North-South RTAs. What this chapter will show is that African countries are already marginalised in the multilateral system and the neutral language of Article XXIV, coupled with the formalism of the EPAs, merely enables economically stronger countries to exploit African markets under the guise of 'WTO compliant' legal regimes.

---

[7] J.T. Gathii, *African Regional Trade Agreements as Legal Regimes* (Cambridge: Cambridge University Press, 2011).

TOWARDS DEMOCRACY OR A PSEUDO WESTERN FAÇADE?

In 1989, the World Bank published a report on African development and stated that 'underlying the litany of Africa's development problems is a crisis of governance'.[8] Although democratic reform over the past two decades has been described as the 'second independence' for African nations,[9] there have been internal and external constraints that have significantly hampered the transition to democracy across Africa.[10]

Since the days of independence, most of sub-Saharan Africa has made the transition from single party to multi-party political systems. While this may suggest that the principle of democracy has become embedded within many African countries, there are also signs that the process of democratisation is 'fraying at the edges'.[11] According to Richard Joseph, a political system is democratic 'to the extent that it facilitates citizen self-rule, permits the broadest deliberation in determining public policy, and constitutionally guarantees all the freedoms necessary for open political competition'.[12] However, the transition to democracy has been problematic in many African States and there seems to be no 'one size fits all' approach to the process, with many of Joseph's defining features of a democratic political system seemingly missing from the institutional framework.[13] For example, in Ghana and Senegal, there seems to have been a relatively successful transition to democracy, whereas countries like Sierra Leone and Liberia have experienced a more protracted process toward democratic governance.

The question of how African leaders establish legitimacy is a key part of understanding governance. This chapter proposes that African political

---

[8] World Bank, *Sub-Saharan Africa: From Crisis to Sustainable Growth: A Long Term Perspective Study* (Washington, D.C.: World Bank, 1989), 60.

[9] P. Ekeh, 'The Concept of Second Liberation and the Prospects of Democracy in Africa: A Nigerian Context', Paper given at the Conference on Dilemmas of Democracy in Nigeria, University of Wisconsin, November 10–12 1995, cited in L. Anderson, *Transitions to Democracy* (New York: Columbia University Press, 1999).

[10] Patrick Chabal provides an extensive account of the many interpretations of 'democracy'. See P. Chabal, 'A Few Considerations on Democracy in Africa' (2002) 74 *International Affairs* 289–303.

[11] *Ibid*, 290.

[12] R. Joseph, 'Democratization in Africa after 1989: Comparative and Theoretical Perspectives' (1997) 29 *Comparative Politics* 363–82, 365.

[13] M. Bratton and N. van de Walle, 'Neopatrimonial Regimes and Political Transitions in Africa' (1994) 46 *World Politics* 453–89, 454.

power is best understood in terms of neopatrimonial rule and rent-seeking.[14] Grounding the following analysis in a neopatrimonial frame requires a careful articulation of what this term actually means. In a Weberian sense, neopatrimonialism refers to a specific source of legitimacy and authority in which, through various ideal types, the dominance of those in power is understood.[15] Weberian analysis is of the hermeneutic tradition and is therefore complementary to the constructivist philosophy, but it is important to note that the origins of patrimonialism did not carry with it connotations of corruption, violence or a weak state.[16] Rather, Weber's concept of patrimonialism is founded on the impersonal nature of bureaucracy which is characterised by legal rationality. Moving beyond legal philosophy, scholars of political science use the term (neo)patrimonialism to define systems in which the political relationship between the ruler and the ruled is maintained through personal connections, patrons and clients, with the 'neo' suffix often used in reference to the post-colonial form of governance. Although this type of relationship may foster trust and cement social bonds on a small scale, as patrimonialism permeates larger social and institutional structure it is believed to 'distort power, corrupt authority, and fuel aggrandizement'.[17]

It is useful here to draw on the concept of neopatrimonialism, or 'big man rule' as it is also known, to problematise the African state. Big man rule is a patron-client relationship that is the principal mechanism through which political and economic life in African countries is

---

[14] The concepts of 'patrimonialism', derived from Max Weber's work, and 'neopatrimonialism' have been used in development studies and African studies for some time for understanding African politics. Distinguishing between the two concepts is not easy. 'Patrimonialism' refers to a form of governance through personal rule. 'Neopatrimonialism' or 'modern patrimonialism' is a hybrid concept dealing with the relationship between personal rule and legal-rational bureaucracy. These concepts are not useful for rational choice theorists or Marxist theorists, and as such they tend not to overlook them completely. Some criticise 'neopatrimonialism' as merely providing an account of governance rather than what policies a state might pursue. See T. Mkandawire, 'Aid, Accountability and Democracy in Africa' (2010) 77 *Social Research: An International Quarterly* 1149–82.

[15] M. Weber, *The Theory of Social and Economic Organisation*, A.M. Henderson and T. Parsons (trans) (New York: The Free Press, 1947).

[16] A. Pitcher, M. Moran and M. Johnston, 'Rethinking Patrimonialism and Neopatrimonialism in Africa' (2009) 52 *African Studies Review* 125–56, 126.

[17] *Ibid*, 129.

regulated.[18] Internally, governance structures in the early days of independence were weak and the ability to self-govern was often exacerbated by ethnic tensions among the populace.[19] That said, reciprocity in the relationships between the ruler and the ruled is an inherent aspect of neopatrimonialism in the Weberian sense. So, while the politics of a neopatrimonial state are typically constituted by the presence of corruption, nepotism, ethnicity and clientelism there must nevertheless exist an acceptance of sorts, or reciprocity, by those being governed.[20]

Economically, running African economies based on patronage had only lined the coffers of Africa's political elite to the detriment of their already fragile economies and further polarised the financial divide between the rich and poor:

> African leaders have sought to deter extraconstitutional challenges by recruiting more elites into their patronage coalitions. Leaders visibly expand their coalitions through government appointments to discourage potential rivals from coordinating other elites against them.[21]

Historically, political legitimacy was gained in many states through personal relationships of patronage. However, as economic means began to run out it became increasingly difficult to sustain this system. In general, African political regimes were perceived as 'corrupt, inept, predatory and unrepresentative'[22] and gradually citizens began to withdraw from the state. As political legitimacy weakened the legal legitimacy of rules was also eroded. It was the collapse of the neopatrimonial state that was in part responsible for the rise in the informal economy, as

---

[18] L.R. Arriola, 'Patronage and Political Stability in Africa' (2009) 42 *Comparative Political Studies* 1339–62, 1343.

[19] D. Bräutigam and S. Knack, 'Foreign Aid, Institutions and Governance in Sub-Saharan Africa' (2004) 52 *Economic Development and Cultural Change* 255–85.

[20] For a detailed discussion on neopatrimonialism and Weber's concept of legitimate authority, see Pitcher, Moran and Johnston (n. 16), 125–156. However, a problem with neopatrimonial discourse is the tendency to overemphasise all political power as personal power and all public affairs as privatised affairs. See generally: G. Erdmann and U. Engel, 'Neopatrimonialism Reconsidered: Critical Review and Elaboration of an Elusive Concept' (2007) 45 *Commonwealth and Comparative Politics* 95–119, 101.

[21] Arriola (n. 18), 1345.

[22] B. Riddell, 'Things Fall Apart Again: Structural Adjustment Programmes in Sub-Saharan Africa'(1992) *Journal of Modern African Studies* 53–68, 60.

a reaction against the demands of the state.[23] Over time, single-party political systems became increasingly repressive as they became unable to manage the economic and development needs of the state during crises. As reciprocity between the ruler and the ruled began to dissipate, foundations of neopatrimonialism began to splinter and the legitimacy of those in power became less potent.

However, the celebration of the 'second independence' was short-lived. While the number of elections increased in the early days of independence, so too did the number of coups:

> Many of the old dictators are still firmly entrenched, whilst some of the new leaders who have joined the 'club' have in recent years been devising ever more sophisticated ways to perpetuate their rule while using the democracy slogan as a convenient mask to disguise their despotic practices. It is these same rulers who must now implement or support the AU's democracy agenda.[24]

As the quality of democracy declined across African nations, many saw 'democracy' as little more than maintaining the status quo.[25] For Patrick Chabal and Jean-Pascal Daloz, the African state represents nothing more than a 'décor' or a 'pseudo-Western façade masking the realities of deeply personalised relations'.[26] It follows that the institutions and infrastructure of the state were also entirely built on personal networks. What has been interpreted as a process of democratisation across sub-Saharan Africa was also a façade, or 'surface phenomenon', for legitimating personal rule and domination.[27] As a result, 'good governance' in a neopatrimonial system is a concept devoid of substance because it is built solely on personal networks: if the personal networks are removed the state collapses and reveals itself to be nothing more than an empty shell.

---

23 C. Clapham, 'Degrees of Statehood' (1998) 24(2) *Review for International Studies* 143–57.

24 C.M. Fombad and Z. Kebonang, 'AU, NEPAD and the APRM: Democratization Efforts Explored', H. Melber (ed.) (Uppsala: Nordiska Afrikainstitutet, 2006), 10.

25 M. Bratton and D. Posner, 'A First Look at Second Elections in Africa' in R. Joseph (ed.), *State, Conflict and Democracy in Africa* (Boulder: Lynne Rienner, 1998), 377–408.

26 Chabal and Daloz (n. 5), 16.

27 Chabal (n. 10), 291.

Chabal and Daloz propose that political actors in Africa 'seek to maximise their returns on the state of confusion, uncertainty and sometimes even chaos' in what they describe as the process of 'political instrumentalization of disorder'.[28] In this paradigm, 'disorder' is understood to be a condition that can offer opportunities to those who possess the requisite knowledge to play the political game. This conceptualisation is antithetical to the Western projection of democracy, and in using this paradigm Chabal and Daloz are able to highlight the unique features of contemporary African states. They submit that Africa is heading in a distinctly non-Western direction and pursuing 'modernity without development'.[29] Most African States are 'modern', in the sense that some portion of their populations can access the latest technologies, for example. Yet emphasis on the 'traditional' remains, with practices such as witchcraft and polygamy commonplace across the African continent. The political, economic and social experiences of most contemporary African states are often not congruent with a typically Westernised model of politics or development. Pursuing development on their own terms is a unique feature of the African political experience and one that should be both celebrated and scrutinised.

Conceiving neopatrimonialism as an institutional regime, Michael Bratton and Nicolas van de Walle propose that political change is 'conditioned by the mechanisms of rule embedded in the ancien régime'.[30] Political leaders in power for long periods of time establish rules, codes and standards for political participation and regulate the extent to which political opposition can or will be tolerated. Formalising norms through legal, social and political institutions legitimises the authority of the leader and reinforces a sense of reciprocity because the rules are, in general, accepted by those being governed. Scholars from colonial studies go further and argue that Africa's current governance crisis is a direct result of the behaviour learned, or mimicked, from colonial leaders:

---

[28] Chabal and Daloz (n. 5), xviii.

[29] *Ibid*, 125.

[30] M. Bratton and N. van de Walle (n 13).

> The selfish and exploitative character of the master-colony relationship that reigned in the colonialism time continued in different forms even after colonialism was long gone, and continues to impact contemporary African politics.[31]

The dominant discourse in the literature asserts that colonialism disrupted the historically constructed patterns of authority among African societies and, by consequence, neopatrimonialism arises because the leader relies on neopatrimonial strategies to survive. In reality, it seems to matter little that the leader lacks legitimacy in a Weberian sense. While it has been argued that neopatrimonial rule is a consequence of certain stages of economic development,[32] so too has it been argued that neopatrimonialism hinders economic growth.[33] However, it cannot be said that *all* African states have failed to exhibit legitimate rule in the post-colonial era. Arguably, Botswana, for example, has been shown to exhibit legitimate rule in the early days of independence and did not resort to neopatrimonial strategies.[34] Neopatrimonialism of this type is conceptualised as an institutionalised form of governance, with personal relationships permeating the institutional political framework.

Anne Pitcher et al have contested the application of neopatrimonialism as a 'catch all' concept to define the political economy of Africa.[35] They argue that patrimonialism is 'a form of authority and belief, not a regime type – a kind of legitimacy, not a pathology.'[36] Rejecting neopatrimonialism as a 'catch all' phrase enables African political systems to be interrogated at a deeper analytical level. It is a fundamental claim of their work that the application of the Weberian concept of neopatrimonialism through various disciplines to analyse the African state is rooted in a misreading of Weber. A strict reading of Weber certainly gives a more nuanced understanding of legitimacy and authority, but it is from a generalised account of the African state in terms of institutional or

---

[31] J.A. Alemazung, 'Post-Colonial Colonialism: An Analysis of International Factors and Actors Marring African Socio-Economic and Political Development' (2010) 3 *Journal of Pan African Studies* 62–84, 65.

[32] R. Theobold, 'Patrimonialism' (1982) 34 *World Politics* 548–59.

[33] P. Englebert, 'Pre-Colonial Institutions, Post-Colonial States, and Economic Development in Tropical Africa' (2000) 53 *Political Research Quarterly* 7–36.

[34] This is contested by E. Budd, *Democratization, Development, and the Patrimonial State in the Age of Globalization* (New York: Lexington Books, 2004).

[35] Pitcher, Moran and Johnston (n. 16), 129–56.

[36] *Ibid*, 149.

regime neopatrimonialism that the more specific nature of regionalism in Southern Africa can be interrogated.

African countries face challenges when trading with Western countries through North-South RTAs because each arrangement operates under a different political paradigm and development is not homogenous either between the regions, or between each individual country party to the agreement. While African political leaders may sign-up to the predominantly Western values in regional trade agreements (RTAs), they may have little intention of adhering to them. In the latter part of this chapter it will be shown that regionalism may itself be a 'façade' giving a false impression of the political and economic stability of African states. While this may work for African RTAs, the story is very different for North-South RTAs where the dominant (and likely Western) member will be in a stronger position to enforce the terms of the RTA. It is for this reason that the conceptualisation of the EU as a 'norm exporter' lays itself open to accusations of economic imperialism and neocolonial practices.

External Constraints on African Democratisation

Having considered the internal constraints that have shaped the existing political regimes of many African states, it is important to consider the exogenous factors that have further affected the path towards democracy. Externally, there are four main factors that have influenced political transition in Africa: the conservative attitude of the West to North-South cooperation under the Reagan and Thatcher regimes; the shift from import substitution to structural adjustment programmes (SAPs); the collapse of communism and the end of the Cold War; and, more recently, the global financial crises. The implications of each factor shall be considered briefly below.

In the late 1960s, as decolonisation began to take hold, foreign assistance was offered to support the political regimes of newly independent African nations. British and EU aid have always been highly concessional with aid being tied to loans or specific programmes.[37] Formalising development assistance through particular legal frameworks has enabled EU countries to dictate the terms on which African countries

[37] There is a distinction between development aid and emergency aid. For the purposes of this discussion, we are referring to the former. For a detailed discussion on the problematic nature of tied aid see A. La Chimia and S. Arrowsmith, 'Addressing Tied Aid: Towards a More Development-Oriented WTO?' (2009) 12 *Journal of International Economic Law* 707–47.

can pursue development. However, under the Reagan and Thatcher regimes, foreign policy towards African leaders markedly changed:

> The West became more critical of the failures of African regimes and their repressive excesses ... In short, the West lost patience with the 'excuses' given by African rulers (or their supporters) to explain the ruin of their policies.[38]

Tired of offering 'hand-outs' there was a significant decline in aid during the Thatcher and Reagan administrations.[39] With the Conservative Party in power for almost two decades in the United Kingdom, there was a notable shift away from development assistance towards investment in private and commercial interests.[40] This shift in policy coincided with the implementation of the World Bank's SAPs. While SAPs are tailored to each individual country, J. Barry Riddell distinguishes four elements common to all SAPs namely, currency devaluation, the reduction of state interference in economic matters, elimination of subsidies, and trade liberalisation.[41] Each element of the SAP can have a substantial impact on the overall economic development of a country and the ability of each individual to realise their other substantive freedoms. Currency devaluation, for example, effectively reduces the value of local currency vis-à-vis imported items and makes exported goods less expensive. Often, as a result of currency devaluation, basic and essential items become more expensive with the unwanted consequence that the standard of living decreases. This is just one example of how economic development reform can adversely affect the realisation of the social and cultural dimensions of development or to use the language of capability theory, how economic freedom can lead to other unfreedoms

As part of the SAPs, the IMF promoted the removal of state interference so as to allow market forces to determine the economic development of each nation. African governments have always taken an active role in their economic policy, albeit this has often associated with corruption, particularly in relation to the public sector. This is unsurprising given that neopatrimonialism involves the management, and mismanagement, of the public authorities and public funds. A decline in

---

38 Chabal (n. 10), 293.

39 Margaret Thatcher famously dismissed aid as 'hand outs'. See generally T. Killick, 'Political Autonomy and the History of British Aid to Africa' (2005) 23 *Development Policy Review* 665–81.

40 D.H. Lumsdaine, *Moral Vision in International Politics: The Foreign Aid Regime 1949–1989* (Princeton: Princeton University Press, 1993), 43.

41 Riddell (n. 22).

infrastructure and services within the public sector, coupled with the forcible decline in government involvement, encourages African economies to adopt the liberal ideology and in doing so aims to reconstruct the political institutional framework of Africa. Thus this has a notable adverse effect on local people who work in the public sector.[42]

While subsidising sectors can assist the struggling population to afford goods, subsidies are fundamentally market distortions and cannot exist indefinitely. When a subsidy programme is eventually phased out goods become more expensive and the standards of living may decline. Encouraging trade liberalisation through the intensification of agricultural exports to developed countries in return for processed goods was thought to be an integral part of stimulating growth in the agricultural sector of African countries. It was assumed that this practice would boost economic growth generally and support social and cultural development, the assumption that economic freedom will inevitably lead to the realisation of other non-economic freedoms. Overall, the conditionalities attached to the SAPS were designed to integrate struggling developing countries into the global economy. Their failure to do so had significant implications for African economies, and the ghosts of the SAPs continue to haunt developing countries today.

Although African countries have generally followed the economic policies prescribed by the international financial institutions, they have not delivered the expected results.[43] A notable exception is Ghana where the SAPs have had mixed results leading to what some have described as a process of 'uneven development'.[44] Jay Oelbaum argues that the role of neopatrimonialism, in capturing the resources of the international financial institutions within a framework of personal relationships enabled then President, Jerry Rawlings, to implement neoliberal reforms in spite of there being very little public support for such programmes.[45] Rawlings' military government was praised for reducing government spending and for privatising state-owned enterprises. The commitment shown in

---

[42] *Ibid*, 57.

[43] J.K. Akokpari, 'The AU, NEPAD and the Promotion of Good Governance in Africa' (2004) 13 *Nordic Journal of African Studies* 243–63, 244.

[44] K. Konadu-Agyemang, 'The Best of Times and the Worst of Times: Structural Adjustment Programs and Uneven Development in Africa: The Case of Ghana' (2004) 52 *The Professional Geographer* 469–83.

[45] J. Oelbaum, 'Populist Reform Coalitions in Sub-Saharan Africa: Ghana's Triple Alliance' (2002) 36 *Canadian Journal of African Studies* 281–328.

implementing the SAPs reforms have led some to argue that this government regime was to an extent honest and free from corruption.[46]

The African continent remains marginalised within the global order, with its share of world trade accounting for just 3.2 per cent in 2012 marking a decline, particularly for trade among Sub-Saharan countries. However, it is worth noting that Africa has fared relatively well during the current global financial crisis with average growth of approximately 5 per cent.[47] This book argues that the abstract focus of these policies, with their state-centric vision embedded within a neoliberal frame, has led to the emergence of a World Bank theory of political change that makes for an uncomfortable bedfellow with the political reality of the post-colonial African state.[48]

The misguided economic policies of newly independent states meant that African countries had failed to establish a strong industrial base and they were unable to compete with the rest of the world. African countries have accumulated a staggering amount of external debt over the years in a bid to rectify these failed economic policies. Behind Africa's debt burden are many intersecting issues such as widespread political corruption, ecological disasters, humanitarian crises and pandemic health problems.[49] Southern Africa's debt burden was further heightened by the former Apartheid regime, which is believed to have cost the region approximately US$115 billion.[50] The level of external debt is becoming increasingly onerous for these countries, especially as the region fails to attract significant foreign direct investment, and as a result there is an even heavier reliance on international aid. Unfortunately, the failure of the SAPS coincided with the collapse of communism in the Soviet Union in 1989. For some African countries, such as Angola and Mozambique, which had grown accustomed to receiving aid from the Eastern bloc, the

---

[46] J. Ayelazuno, *Neo-Liberalism and Resistance in Ghana: Understanding the Political Agency of the Subalterns in Social-Historical Context* (Toronto: New York University Press, 2011), 410.

[47] World Bank, 'Despite Global Slowdown, African Economies Growing Strongly – New Oil, Gas and Mineral Wealth an Opportunity for Inclusive Development' *World Bank Press Release* (4 October 2012) accessed 12 December 2016 at http://www.worldbank.org/en/news/press-release/2012/10/04/despite-global-slowdown-african-economies-growing-strongly-world-bank-urges-countries-spend-new-oil-gas-mineral-wealth-wisely.

[48] Harrison (n. 3).

[49] G. Ayittey, *Africa Unchained: The Blueprint for Africa's Future* (Basingstoke: Palgrave Macmillan, 2005).

[50] C.B. Thompson, 'Regional Challenges to Globalisation: Perspectives from Southern Africa' (2010) 5 *New Political Economy* 42.

collapse of communism was acutely felt. As the bipolar world disappeared and the West reigned supreme, African leaders knew that they must implement, or at the very least be perceived to be implementing, democratic reforms in order to attract aid from Western donors.[51] Recognising that Africa's crisis was both political *and* economic, the international institutions shifted Africa's development programme from the fundamentally economic framework of SAPS to the model of 'good governance' in the World Bank's Poverty Reduction Strategy Papers.[52]

Towards 'Good Governance': Mimicking the West

For decades, donors have tried to stimulate growth through the so-called 'Governance Agenda' which is a framework designed by the international financial institutions to eradicate poverty through the implementation of neoliberal economic policies and by reinforcing principles of 'good governance'.[53] Good governance is defined by the World Bank as 'predictable, open and enlightened policy making; a bureaucracy imbued with a professional ethos; an executive arm of government accountable for its actions; and a strong civil society participating in public affairs; and all behaving under the rule of law'.[54] In other words, good governance is the Western ideal against which developing countries are now measured in order to qualify for concessions and assistance. From this definition, we can see that the Governance Agenda encouraged developing countries to 'mimic' the behaviour of developed countries, not only through economic policy but by replicating internal institutional frameworks and promoting public-private partnerships. Development is still market-led, but rests on the idea of having an organised and effective state infrastructure.

In its 2010 report,[55] the World Bank centred its analysis on the effect of weak governance and corruption for African development. Corruption

[51] U. Tar, 'The Challenges of Democracy and Democratisation in Africa and the Middle East' (2010) 3 *Information, Justice and Society* 81–94.

[52] P. Chabal, 'The State of Governance in Africa' (2010) SAIIA Occasional Paper 26 accessed 12 December 2016 at http://dspace.cigilibrary.org/jspui/bitstream/123456789/29713/1/SAIIA%20Occasional%20Paper%20no%2026.pdf?1.

[53] T. Kelsall, 'Going with the Grain in African Development?' (2008) 26(6) *Development Policy Review* 627–55.

[54] World Bank, *Governance: The World Bank's Experience* (World Bank Publications, 1994).

[55] World Bank, *African Development Indicators 2010*, (The World Bank, 2010). The World Bank herein defines 'corruption' as 'the abuse of public office for private gain'.

serves a political function for the ruling elites across African nations, acting as a source of patronage which strengthens the system of political power. Going beyond the 'big time corruption' associated with big man rule it argued that corruption is entrenched so deeply in African societies that it has penetrated frontline services at the bottom level.[56] As ruling elites seek to privatise state resources, they 'distribute favours and create a base of consensus for their privileged position'.[57] Expanding the definition of corruption to include less obvious forms broadens the frame of analysis and enables us to consider the role of non-state actors in perpetuating corrupt behaviour. This report, while still geared towards liberal policies, acknowledges the complex nature of governance and recognises that a multitude of actors may play a part in Africa's macroeconomic and development strategy. Identifying and preventing subversive forms of corruption at the micro-level may be difficult, but will need to be combatted if African countries are to thrive in terms of economic growth and development (broadly conceived).

Corruption is problematic, not least because it siphons off a country's resources away from the people, but because it makes investing in that country less attractive.[58] Most foreign direct investment flowing into Southern Africa is aimed at the mining (minerals and metals) sectors. Similarly, intraregional investment tends to be concentrated in the mining, quarrying and petroleum, finance, business services, transport and communication sectors. Over ten years ago, the UK's Department for International Development (DFID) conducted a series of studies to assess the relevance of the 'governance agenda' for African countries. In 2003, the 'Drivers of Change' programme was launched and the studies found that the realities of power and culture across African countries posed formidable obstacles to the implementation of the good governance agenda.[59] Programmes need to be sensitive to the political, economic and social peculiarities of each region and each nation if they are to deliver real benefits. That said, if we accept that the African state is a 'façade' then it seems that corruption is an inevitable consequence of that façade.

---

[56] *Ibid*, xi.

[57] *Ibid*, 3.

[58] J. Luiz, 'Challenges and Prospects for Economic and Business Development in Africa' in J. Luiz (ed.), *Managing Business in Africa* (Oxford: Oxford University Press, 2006).

[59] 'Drivers of Change' country studies are available online at http://www.gsdrc.org/topic-guides/political-economy-analysis/examples/drivers-of-change-country-studies/ (accessed 12 December 2016).

Implementing the neoliberal economic policies prescribed by the international financial institutions failed to address the underlying issues that have fragmented the African continent. In Africa 'the contemporary state system ... is not comparable to the "Western" state in terms of sovereignty and legitimacy, stability and capacity, to implement policies or control the distribution of resources'.[60] As such, these countries are not well-equipped to insulate themselves from external shocks. For primary commodity producers, like those in Africa, an international financial crisis can have disastrous consequences. Countries in sub-Saharan Africa are net-food importing countries and therefore heavily reliant on external markets, so it is unsurprising that the financial and food crises affected this region more than any other. While there has been an incremental decline in the number of people suffering from undernourishment across Sub-Saharan Africa, it is estimated that 220 million people, or just over 23 per cent of the population in this region, experience food insecurity.[61] The crash of the market in the 1980s has led some commentators to refer to this period as Africa's 'lost development decade'[62] and it seems that the most recent financial crises of 2008 could lead to even greater unfreedom(s).

FROM FRAGMENTATION TO UNIFICATION?

Contemporary Africa is an evolving construct of its pre- and post-colonial past, with its cartography carved out by the Europeans according to their material needs with little regard for the cultural, social and linguistic commonalities that had existed between African people for many centuries.[63] As a result, the continent is characterised by fragmented small markets, weak economies and a substantial number of landlocked countries. Pursuing a regional approach to integration was

---

[60] M. Farrell, 'A Triumph of Realism over Idealism? Cooperation Between the European Union and Africa' (2005) 27 *European Integration* 270.

[61] See FAO, IFAD and WFP, 'The State of Food Insecurity in the World: Meeting the 2015 International Hunger Targets: Taking Stock of Uneven Progress' (Rome: FAO, 2015).

[62] B. Tsie, 'States and Markets in the Southern African Development Community (SADC): Beyond the Neoliberal Paradigm (1996) 22(1) *Journal of Southern African Studies* 75–98, 77.

[63] M. Soko and J.P. Lehmann, 'The State of Development in Africa: Concepts, Challenges and Opportunities' (2011) 14 *Journal of International Studies* 97–108, 100 and C. Clapham, 'Democratisation in Africa: Obstacles and Prospects' (1993) 14(3) *Third World Quarterly* 423–38, 424.

therefore one way in which African countries could rationalise the fragmented continent they had inherited and create a larger space for economic development through legal regimes.[64] Regionalism therefore offered a politico-legal mechanism through which the artificial geographical demarcation bequeathed by colonialism might be corrected or, at the very least, a means through which the harmful effects of the imagined cartography of Africa could be minimised.

For some time, regionalism has been seen as a key part of Africa's development strategy.[65] Having implemented the fiscal policies prescribed by the international financial institutions, and having adopted neoliberal economic principles as a foundation for regional integration, we can see that African countries have 'mimicked' the strategies of developed countries:

> For too long, the impression has been created that African development strategies and life styles are an imitation – indeed, a poor imitation – of the strategies and lifestyles developed elsewhere for other societies with different historical, cultural, economic and political background … we, in Africa, have become the mimic people. Although we pretend to be real, to be original, to be learning and to be preparing ourselves and our countries for self-reliant development processes and for an authentically African life style, all we really have succeeded in doing is mimic other societies and their life styles.[66]

The African approach to economic integration is somewhat unique, as it has simultaneously pursued both continentalism and functionalism. Continentalism advocates the unification of all African states creating a borderless Pan-African continent and embodies the notion of strengthening cooperation among African nations as a response to colonialism. Functionalism, on the other hand, proposes that political unity will arise through the creation of sub-regional groupings rather than through the

---

[64] F.N. Ikome, *From the Lagos Plan of Action to the New Partnership for Africa's Development – The Political Economy of Regional Initiatives* (Midrand: Institute for Global Dialogue, 2007), 33.

[65] E. Aryeetey and A.O. Oduro, 'Regional Integration Efforts in Africa: An Overview' in J.J. Teunissen (ed.), *Regionalism and the Global Economy: The Case of Africa* (The Hague: FONDAD, 1996).

[66] A. Adedeji, 'Alternative Patterns of Development and Life Styles for the African Region' Workshop organised by UNECA and UNEP (March 1979) cited in A. Adedeji, 'The Evolution of the Monrovia Strategy and the Lagos Plan of Action: A Regional Approach to Economic Decolonisation' Lecture for Nigerian Institute for Social and Economic Research (24 March 1983) accessed 12 December 2016 at http://link.bu.edu/portal/The-evolution-of-the-Monrovia-strategy-and-the/a-ao3ku6ms4/.

creation of a global African community. Gradualists in Africa, such as political leaders Thabo Mbeki and Yoweri Museveni, have argued for an incremental approach to pan-Africanism through regionalisation.[67] Given the diverse ethnic, cultural and political makeup of Sub-Saharan Africa, adopting an incremental approach is perhaps more realistic than the creation of a Pan-African state. Unsurprisingly, these competing approaches have caused a great deal of tension and resulted in contradictory and conflicting integrative processes.

Speaking with One Voice: A Unified Africa

The project of regionalism in Africa was promoted in the immediate post-colonial era by pan-Africanists, most notably, President Kwame Nkrumah of Ghana. Known more familiarly among his people as the 'Osagyefo', or the 'redeemer', Nkrumah captured the hearts of many Africans with his impassioned speeches casting out colonialism and welcoming in a new dawn for Africa. Nkrumah's pan-Africanism embodied a holistic approach to rebuilding Africa centred on economic and social development, with the continent speaking with 'one African voice'.[68] Nkrumah believed neoliberalism to be the biggest threat to the pan-African project and inherent to Nkrumian ideology is the egalitarian provision of education. African pedagogy was seen as one means through which the neoliberal agenda could be rejected and it was expected that education for all would preclude the advancement of neocolonial values by African elites.[69]

In his speech announcing the creation of Ghana's external broadcasting company, Nkrumah called for Africa to be understood on its own terms:

> We stand for peace and friendship with the world. We are neither anti-West nor anti-East. We have our own way of life, a socialist way based on sound cultural foundation and an African background. Those who wish to understand our actions must first begin to study and appreciate this background. They should not judge us from ignorance and they should not expect us to

---

[67] A.F. Snyman, 'Regional Organisations and Their Members: The Question of Authority' (2009) XLII *Comparative and International Law Journal of Southern Africa* 189–209, 189.

[68] K. Nkrumah, 'The Voice of Africa' Speech by Osagyefo the President on the Opening of the Ghana External Broadcasting Service (27 October 1961) accessed 12 December 2016 at http://www.nkrumah.net/index.html.

[69] K. Nkrumah, 'Guide to Party Action: Address' (3 February 1961) accessed 12 December 2016 at http://www.nkrumah.net/index.html.

> become mere copy-types of their past or present, however good these may be to themselves.[70]

As Nkrumaism was gaining momentum, the tension between continentalism and functionalism became particularly pronounced.[71] As the continentalists sought to unite Africans and surge towards the creation of a supra-national Pan-African state, leaders in Nigeria were focusing on the merits of functional integration and the prospects of creating sub-regional groupings.[72] These competing ideologies resulted in the creation of two distinct regional groupings: the Casablanca Group (January 1961)[73] and the functionalist Monrovia Group (May 1961).[74] It was a goal of the Casablanca group to promote pan-Africanism through a series of phases. Within the Monrovia Group, the francophone countries formed a splinter group known as the Brazzaville Group[75] as they were apprehensive of cooperation with the Anglophone states and were wary of Nigeria, which was perceived to be an emerging regional hegemon. However, the incremental approach to pan-Africanism eventually prevailed with the creation of the Organisation of African Unity (OAU) in 1963. It was here that pan-Africanism, albeit a less radical form than that envisaged by Nkrumah, first found expression in the creation of the OAU institutional framework.

From the mid to late 1960s, and as more countries gained independence, there were further attempts to modify existing regional arrangements. However, these early attempts at regionalism were relatively unsuccessful. This is unsurprising given that newly independent states had only just been released from the yokes of colonialism:

---

70 Nkrumah (n. 68).

71 G.M. Khadiagala, 'Governing Regionalism in Africa: Themes and Debates', Policy Brief 51 (Centre for Policy Studies: Johannesburg, 2008).

72 African Development Bank Group 'Group Evolution' accessed 12 December 2016 at http://www.afdb.org/en/about-us/history/group-evolution/.

73 The Casablanca group consisted of: Algeria, Egypt, Ghana, Guinea, Libya, Mali and Morocco.

74 The Monrovia group was comprised of: Cameroon, Chad, Congo-Brazzaville, Congo (Kinshasa), Côte d'lvoire, Dahomey (Benin), Ethiopia, Gabon, Upper Volta (Burkina Faso), Liberia, Madagascar, Mauritania, Niger, the Central African Republic, Senegal, Sierra Leone, Somalia, Togo and Tunisia.

75 The 'Brazzaville Group' consisted of: Cameroon, Congo-Brazzaville, Côte d'lvoire, Dahomey (Benin), Gabon, Upper Volta (Burkina Faso), Madagascar, Mauritania, Niger, the Central African Republic, Senegal and Chad. Collectively, these countries had formed the African and Malagasy Union in 1960 at Brazzaville.

> States spawned by the process of colonialism were by no means nations; rather they represented shells of territorial independence in which the kernel of national identity had been planted by the independence movements.[76]

Political leaders were more concerned with rebuilding and preserving the state than pursuing regional projects. Countries bought into the notion of regionalism to the extent that it would enable them to secure domestic interests.[77] It is clear that the origins of African regionalisms are grounded in an entirely different premise to the peace and security objectives of the EU: they are 'flexible' legal regimes. African regionalisms are founded on the conceptualisation of regionalism as a vehicle to bolster state sovereignty and as a means to promote development broadly defined. Abandoning rationalist approaches to regionalism, countries began to embark on regional initiatives that incorporated cooperation in different policy areas and not simply trade. These RTAs were flexible and innovative legal regimes in their orientation, albeit they lacked the requisite political will to fully operationalise them in a meaningful way.

During the 1970s–80s, countries committed to creating larger regional integration arrangements and in 1980, the Lagos Plan of Action (LPA) was adopted. As part of the LPA strategy, three Regional Economic Communities (RECs) in Sub-Saharan Africa were constructed: West Africa; Central Africa; and, Southern and Eastern Africa. It was anticipated that these regional groups would then amalgamate into a single African market.[78] In an attempt to rationalise regional integration in Africa, the UN Economic Commission for Africa (UNECA) created five sub-regional economic groupings: North Africa; West Africa; Central Africa; East Africa; and, Southern Africa. These regional groupings are still in existence today and form the basis of analysis for African regional integration studies.

In Western Africa, the Economic Community of West Africa (CEAO) and the Economic Community of West African States (ECOWAS) were created in 1973 and 1975, respectively. Similar processes of regional integration took place in Central Africa with the formation of the Economic Community of Central African States (ECCAS) in 1983. In

---

[76] Ikome (n. 64), 33.

[77] Some examples of regional arrangements from this period include: the Customs and Economic Union of West Africa (UDEAO)86; The Customs and Economic Union of Central African States (UDEAC)86; and the East African Community (EAC) in 1967.

[78] C. McCarthy, 'The Southern African Customs Union in Transition' (2003) 102 *African Affairs* 605–30, 608.

Southern Africa, three new arrangements were organised including: the Preferential Trade Area, which was relaunched in 1993 as the Common Market for Eastern and Southern Africa (COMESA) and the Southern African Development Coordination Conference (SADCC), which was revised and renamed in 1992 as the Southern African Development Community (SADC). It was expected that the adoption of a sub-regional and incremental strategy would ultimately lead to a Pan-African economic community.

This represented the first major blueprint for Africa's development through regionalism, with the goal of creating a fully integrated market by the year 2000. As part of this strategy, the Abuja Treaty was adopted in 1991, which called for the creation of an African Economic Community (AEC) by 2028. Another milestone was reached in 2002, when the African Union was established replacing its predecessor, the Organisation of African Unity. Together, the LPA and the Final Act of Lagos played a major role in influencing regional integration strategies as legal regimes across the continent. In forging links between the fragmented economic markets of post-colonial Africa, regional cooperation agreements were perceived as the building blocks of a Pan-African organisation. From this analysis it is clear that a norm of regionalism as not only a development strategy but as a path toward pan-Africanism was emerging.

A 'New Partnership For African Development'?

More recently, African states committed to a programme for development under the auspice of the African Union known as the New Partnership for Africa's Development (NEPAD). This formed part of Thabo Mbeki's strategy for an 'African Renaissance'.[79] NEPAD was created in 2001 as the successor to the 1980 Lagos Plan of Action and focuses on the need to improve infrastructure in Africa to facilitate cross-country investment and foster regional integration.[80] The objectives of NEPAD are development focused, aiming to eradicate poverty and inequality in Africa, to promote empowerment and improve the economic status of women, and

---

[79] T. Mbeki, 'The African Renaissance' Speech delivered on 13 August 1998 accessed 12 December 2016 at http://www.dfa.gov.za/docs/speeches/1998/mbek0813.htm.

[80] For an interesting account of NEPAD see C. Landsberg, 'The African Union and the New Partnership for Africa's Development (NEPAD): Restoring a Relationship Challenged?' (2012) 12 *African Journal on Conflict Resolution* 49–71.

to integrate African states into the global economy through sustained economic growth.

Analysis of NEPAD's framework document shows that, rhetorically at least, African leaders recognise how the governance framework of neopatrimonialism has gravely affected African development.[81] In paragraph 22, it states:

> Postcolonial Africa inherited weak states and dysfunctional economies, which were further aggravated by poor leadership, corruption and bad governance in many countries.

In paragraph 42, it continues:

> The *New Partnership for Africa's Development* recognises that there have been attempts in the past to set out continent-wide development programmes. For a variety of reasons, both internal and external, including questionable leadership and ownership by Africans themselves, these have been less than successful. However, there is today a new set of circumstances, which lend themselves to integrated practical implementation.

With its focus on governance, sustainable development, and the eradication of poverty, NEPAD is perhaps best understood as an attempt to institutionalise Africa's development objectives through a formal legal regime. One of the more innovative features of NEPAD is the African Peer Review Mechanism (APRM), under which African states commit to periodic review on a voluntary basis, in line with the objective for enhanced cooperation between the EU and Africa on democratic governance in the Joint Africa-EU Strategy. This process of self-assessment requires States to report on their governance reforms in four thematic areas: democracy and political governance; corporate governance; economic governance and management; and socio-economic development.[82] As of 1 January 2014, 34 of the African Union's 54 Member Countries had signed up to join the APRM, and 17 members have been peer reviewed.[83] The remaining 17 members are in various phases of the peer-review process but have not yet submitted their self-assessment.

---

[81] Accessed 12 December 2016 at http://www.nepad.org/resource/nepad-framework-document.

[82] NEPAD, 'APRM Annual Report: Africa's Self-Assessment for Good Governance' (2014) accessed 12 December 2016 at http://aprm-au.org/viewNews?newsId=76.

[83] Peer-reviewed countries include: Algeria, Benin, Burkina Faso, Ethiopia, Ghana, Kenya, Lesotho, Mali, Mauritius, Mozambique, Nigeria, Rwanda, Sierra Leone, South Africa, Tanzania, Uganda, Zambia.

Underlying the APRM are the principles of transparency and participative democracy, through which many non-state actors can engage with the self-assessment process. Adopting a 'carrot and stick' approach, where a state shows compliance with these principles it will improve their chances of an enhanced partnership with the G8.[84] Formally, the APRM lends itself to a legitimate form of authority over the states that have voluntarily joined the programme and seeks to overcome claims of institutionalised neopatrimonialism. Nevertheless, almost 40 per cent of African states are still not party to the system and this is certainly a shortcoming of the institution. Patrick Bond describes the APRM as Africa's 'neocolonial governance mask' with the work of the APRM grounded in neoliberal gimmicks.[85] In reality, civil society recommendations in the peer-review process are ultimately often overlooked by the state actors marking not only 'a tragic waste of time' but also a 'delay in genuine breakthroughs against injustice'.[86]

In spite of NEPADs institutional failures, it has been critical of the trend for North-South RTAs, highlighting Africa's weak position in the global economy. In paragraph 33 of the framework document, it is submitted:

> … greater integration has also led to the further marginalisation of those countries that are unable to compete effectively. In the absence of fair and just global rules, globalisation has increased the ability of the strong to advance their interests to the detriment of the weak, especially in the areas of trade, finance and technology. It has limited the space for developing countries to own their own development, as the system makes no provision for compensating the weak. The conditions of those marginalised in this process have worsened in real terms. A fissure between inclusion and exclusion has emerged within and among nations.

Although NEPAD identifies the internal and external political and economic constraints on African development, the question of whether leaders are genuinely committed to democracy and good governance remains unresolved. The response to NEPAD has been mixed, although

84 J.C. Ebegbulem, J.A. Adams and A.A. Achu, 'The Challenges of Integrating Africa into the Globalised World through New Partnership for Africa's Development (NEPAD)' (2012) 2 *International Journal of Humanities and Social Science* – Special Issue, 270–8, 273.

85 P. Bond, 'Removing Neocolonialism's APRM Mask: A Critique of the African Peer Review Mechanism' (2009) 36 *African Political Economy* 595–603.

86 *Ibid*, 602.

most are pessimistic of its overall utility.[87] At best, NEPAD represents a concerted effort by the African Union to support sustainable development through good governance and human rights protection, although it seems to lack clear priorities.[88] While it certainly places high expectations on African nations to 'get their house in order', whether these expectations can be realised is another matter altogether. Some argue that NEPAD is little more than a ruse by the ruling African elites to ensure that African resources stay on the continent and thus maintain the *status quo*.[89] In this regard, NEPAD serves as a governance mask. Other critics of NEPAD go further, and argue that it is a weapon of control by international creditors to 'lock-in' policy reforms, much like that of the SAPs.[90] There was an overwhelming lack of consultation around the implementation of NEPAD, which also raises questions about the legal legitimacy of this policy framework.[91]

In 2002, the legitimacy of the organisation was challenged when African leaders were presented with a test-case following Zimbabwe's controversial re-election of ZANU-PF leader Robert Mugabe.[92] It was readily accepted that Zimbabwe continued to flout the core principles of NEPAD (for which sanctions under NEPAD could be taken) yet African elites lined up behind Mugabe to support his re-election. A second blow came in the same year, when Senegalese President Abdoulaye Wade, one of NEPAD's keenest promoters, failed to acknowledge allegations of

---

87 I. Taylor, 'Can NEPAD Succeed without Prior Political Reform?' (2005) Copenhagen: Danish Institute for International Studies, Working Paper No. 2005/23; Bond (n. 85); Fombad and Kebonang (n. 24).

88 R. Murray, *Human Rights in Africa: From the OAU to the African Union* (Cambridge: Cambridge University Press, 2004); see in particular ch 8, 'Development, NEPAD and Human Rights'.

89 P. Chabal, 'The Quest for Good Government and Development in Africa: Is NEPAD the Answer?' (2002) 78 *International Affairs* 447–62.

90 D. Aredo, 'The New Partnership for Africa's Development: Prospects and Challenges' (2003) 21 *Organisation for Social Research in Eastern and Southern Africa (OSSREA) Newsletter* 24–30.

91 See: J.K. Akokpari (n. 43), 249 and E. Kagaruki, 'NEPAD has failed to solve Africa's myriad problems' *The Chronicle* (16 July 2011) accessed 12 December 2016 at http://www.thecitizen.co.tz/oped/1840568-1800138-ig2hrj/index.html.

92 I. Taylor, 'Commentary: The New Partnership for Africa's Development and the Zimbabwe Elections: Implications and Prospects for the Future' (2002) 101 *African Affairs* 403–412. A report issued by the civil society group 'Crisis in Zimbabwe Coalition' discusses the key issues relating to the re-election and NEPAD standards available at http://crisiszim.devpreview.net/2013-05-27-12-00-01/crisis-report.html.

corruption against Senegal.[93] Gradually, the pillars of NEPAD were slowly eroded by evidence of 'bad' governance and corruption which undermined the spirit of NEPAD and ultimately stripped it of any meaning. Thus, for some it seems that NEPAD lacks the right equipment to overcome the 'disorder' of African politics as it has failed in its mandate to solve the myriad of problems facing African nations. For others, it is key to the institutional architecture for turning Africa from a 'hopeless' to 'hopeful' continent.

REGIONS AS 'FLEXIBLE LEGAL REGIMES'

Where national governance is lacking, regionalism may provide an alternative, and arguably more effective, mode of governance. Every African nation is party to at least one interregional or subregional group, so there is at least some evidence of political commitment to regionalism. But what purpose does signing up to regional arrangements serve for the nation state? While African regionalisms are understood to be dynamic and pluralistic, it is useful to draw on Fredrik Söderbaum's work in which he identifies three common modes of regional governance in Africa: neoliberal market integration, regime boosting regionalism and shadow regionalisation.[94]

Neoliberal Market Integration

The market integration approach is most evident in the continentalist projects of regionalism such as the African Union, Lagos Plan of Action, Abuja and NEPAD. Continentalism promotes inward-looking, protectionist policies and collective self-reliance. It is a state-led process promoting interventionist measures, such as import substitution industrialisation, as a strategy to strengthen individual African countries to integrate them into the global economy. North-South dialogue is an integral feature of NEPAD, which calls for an improvement in the political and economic

---

[93] Zambian Economist 'Voting Lessons from Mr NEPAD' (5 September 2011) accessed 12 December 2016 at http://www.zambian-economist.com/2011/09/voting-lessons-from-mr-nepad.html.

[94] F. Söderbaum, 'Modes of Regional Governance in Africa: Neoliberalism, Sovereignty-Boosting and Shadow Networks' (2005) 10(4) *Global Governance* 419–36; F. Söderbaum, 'African Regionalism and EU-African Interregionalism' in M. Telò (ed.), *European Union and New Regionalism*, 2nd edn (Aldershot: Ashgate, 2007).

leadership across Africa. In essence, NEPAD is an African expression of the Washington Consensus. This was a liberal economic programme which encouraged developing countries to implement conservative macroeconomic policies with an emphasis on privatisation to promote economic growth. In moving the economic decision-making away from state-led policies and focusing on market forces, the Washington Consensus suggests that Africa's underdevelopment is a result of macroeconomic mismanagement and weak governance structures.[95] However, a weakening state is not necessarily synonymous with weakening governance, for power can be held by non-state entities. Furthermore, governance may be weak at the national level but could nevertheless be stronger at the regional level.

In terms of economic factors, development in Africa has certainly been affected by a lack of domestic capital markets, regional integration and an ongoing dependence on the export of primary commodities. The price of primary commodities is often volatile and determined by the larger and more developed countries. As it stands today, Africa remains caught in the 'poverty trap', unable to harness real and significant economic growth. Public-private partnerships are on the rise in some African regions. Spatial Development Initiatives (SDIs) are public-private partnerships targeted on a particular project at the micro-level, for example constructing roads. SDIs reinforce neoliberal policies by promoting privatisation and cooperation between the public and private sectors. They are designed to attract private investment and as a result they avoid the need for bureaucratic institutional frameworks. This shows that state-private sector relations can strengthen governance structures. However, as SDIs become increasingly commercialised and privatised, the element of 'partnership' begins to dissipate with the role of the state being reduced to a 'gigantic investment promotion agency'.[96]

In South Africa, there is a strong link between government institutions and the private sector which has allowed its corporate sector to transcend other national boundaries. Although other countries may complain about South Africa's corporate expansion into their territory, this would not be possible without the support of the political elite in the host countries. Some have argued that this is a new form of imperialism, suggesting that

---

95 J.J. Teunissen (ed.), *Regionalism and the Global Economy: The Case of Africa* (The Hague: FONDAD, 1996).

96 Söderbaum (n. 4), 191.

'the market forces and South African capital are now creating economically what the old apartheid regime failed to do politically'.[97] It seems as if South Africa is trying to create a Constellation of Southern African Economies (CONSEA) which of course, resonates with the apartheid programme of the Constellation of Southern African States (CONSAS). The collapse of the early attempts at regional integration highlights the 'limits of ambitious projects driven by the desire to unify in ending colonial rule and apartheid that could not easily be translated into projects of economic cooperation in post-colonial Africa'.[98]

'Regime Boosting' Regionalism

Although most African nations are recognised as satisfying the legal requirements of 'statehood', this chapter has shown that they often lack legitimacy. In general, they are perceived to be 'weak' states as they tend to focus on formal and absolute sovereignty in their external relations. In Africa, there has been an obsession with protecting absolute sovereignty and promoting a particular vision of their formal government to the outside world. This is not surprising, given that the post-colonial African state is still very young in relative terms. What is interesting is the way that African nations have piggy-backed on regionalism to boost the image of their own national regime. African nations tend to commit to regional governance that is both 'exclusivist' and 'centralised' in an effort to portray a stable domestic and regional regime.[99]

'Regime-boosting' regionalism seeks to 'strengthen the status, legitimacy, and the general interests of the political regime (rather than the nation state, *per se*), both on the international arena and domestically'.[100] In this regard, regionalism becomes the cosmetic to mask the neo-patrimonial state. Regime boosting is most often pursued by politically weak states, which typically have authoritarian regimes, who wish to portray an image of strength and legitimacy to the outside world. Showing support and loyalty to regional agreements enables the regime to raise their profile and status without facing any real sanctions for failing to implement those obligations. Signing policy instruments and praising the collective objectives contained in regional arrangements is simply a discursive act, giving a representation of sovereignty to their

---

97 *Ibid.*
98 Gathii (n. 7), 4.
99 Söderbaum (n. 94), 426.
100 *Ibid.*

regional neighbours and the rest of the world. In this way, regionalism is itself used as source of legitimacy for the regime:

> It seems that African leaders, while eager to make legal commitments in numerous and increasing numbers of treaties, are not equally willing to take responsibility for non-compliance, or indeed to completely surrender certain competencies to the supranational organisations created by these treaties.[101]

An important aspect of 'regime boosting' is the physical manifestation of the practice through Ministerial meetings and Summits. These are often grandiose affairs, full of pomp-and-ceremony sending a visual message to the rest of the world that the regimes are stable, prosperous and promote good governance. Summits and conferences are a form of social practice which enables members to construct a regional fallacy. This is particularly true for SADC, which will be explored in the following chapter.

A consequence of regime-boosting regionalism has been the proliferation of regional arrangements, creating a 'spaghetti bowl' of overlapping commitments. As there is no real substance to the agreements, members commit to many overlapping, and often conflicting, agreements. The majority of modern-day regional projects across Africa are situated within a neo-liberal economic and political discourse. They have been founded on the basis of market liberalism designed to promote free trade and therefore imitate an 'open regionalism' model. As most regional arrangements are market driven, in theory there is no contradiction in coexisting regional arrangements if they are all underpinned by the same rules. However, in practice, the problems arise in relation to complex rules of origin regimes that result in contradictory and conflicting trade regimes. In Southern Africa alone, there are five overlapping regional arrangements and in this respect, overlapping membership is evidence of the strategy of regionalism as a mode of regime boosting governance. Recent talks to create a mega-RTA, the African Tri-partite Agreement which would bring together three of Africa's REC – the East African Community (EAC), the Common Market for Eastern and Southern Africa (COMESA), and the Southern African Development Community (SADC) – bear the hallmarks of both market integration regionalism and regime-boosting regionalism. Perhaps African countries are better placed building infrastructure in existing regional communities rather than attempting to create a mega-RTA.

---

[101] Gathii (n. 7), xxviii.

For Ian Taylor, the 'crisis of the African state' is inextricably linked with hegemony, or a lack thereof, among Africa's ruling elite.[102] Using hegemony in the Gramscian sense, he identifies the gap between rhetoric and practice as the ruling elite in Southern Africa pursue liberal regional objectives through SADC, but in practice, the region fails to realise these goals. This means that the African state lacks the authority, legitimacy and accountability necessary to operate with any degree of political clout and as such, makes it more vulnerable to exploitation and marginalisation vis-à-vis more powerful nations in 'North-South' RTAs.

Shadow Regionalisation

An alternative mode of regional governance is 'shadow regionalisation', which is at times closely connected with 'regime boosting'. Daniel Bach and Fredrik Söderbaum have both developed a theory of shadow regionalisation that emerges in rent seeking environments, in a space between states.[103] Emerging from below, this form of governance prospers where regimes are rent-seeking:

> Shadow regionalisation draws attention to the fact that public officials and various actors within the state bureaucracy may be entrenched in informal market activities with the purpose to promote either political goals or their own private interests.[104]

State-society relationships have been reshaped by the forces of regionalism, globalisation and post-colonialism.[105] Political power is often informalised in Africa, with regimes being less concerned with the socio-economic welfare of the people and focusing instead on entrenching power through patronage. Rent-seeking occurs where political leaders purchase support for their regime through the distribution of state resources.[106] Bach proposes that regional organisations can 'capture' resources and, in doing so, they reinforce the systems of patronage. The

---

[102] I. Taylor, 'South African "Imperialism" in a Region Lacking Regionalism: A Critique' (2011) 32 *Third World Quarterly* 1233–53.

[103] D. Bach, 'The Global Politics of Regionalism' in M. Farrell, B. Hettne and L. van Langenhove (eds), *Global Politics of Regionalism: Theory and Practice* (London: Pluto Press, 2005).

[104] Söderbaum (n. 4), 195.

[105] D. Bach, *Regionalisation in Africa. Integration and Disintegration* (London: James Currey, 1999).

[106] Arriola (n. 18).

political elite are often myopic in their distribution of resources which can lead to conflict and political instability.

Using regionalism as a strategy to boost the regime is closely connected to shadow regionalisation. Much like a 'shadow state' the effect of 'shadow regionalisation' is to protect the regime through the creation of informal markets and networks from the bottom-up. So, while African countries will give the impression that they 'buy into' the Western model of regionalism, in reality they will almost certainly adopt policies that will support the neo-patrimonial state system.[107]

CONCLUDING REMARKS

This chapter has sought to achieve three aims. The first was to problematise the African state in an effort to show the chaotic and disorderly nature of politics in Africa. Drawing on the constructivist conceptual framework, and using the concept of neopatrimonialism, we have discussed the internal and external constraints that have affected the experience of many African states' transition to democracy. It was argued that these African states represent little more than an empty shell and as such the state is unable to govern itself or to implement successful economic development policies. As a result, African countries continue to be marginalised in the multilateral trading system vis-à-vis the rest of the world.

The second aim was to provide some background on the African experience of regionalism and highlight how this process is markedly different from the EU's experience. Regionalism has taken two distinctly different paths in Africa, with the competing approaches of functionalism and continentalism enjoying prominence at different stages of the integration process. However, while regionalism across Africa has not been homogenous, what is common to most of these arrangements is the lack of clear priorities. As a result, integration has been slow and superficial. This links with the final aim of this chapter which sought to explain how regionalism has been used as a mode of governance for African countries. We have seen that regionalism can serve three different purposes for governance in Africa: to pursue market integration; to give the false impression of good governance through regime boosting; and to protect the regime through informal markets.

---

[107] R. Gibb, 'Regional Integration and Africa's Development Trajectory: Meta-theories, Expectations, and Reality' (2009) 30 *Third World Quarterly* 718.

Overall, the purpose of this discussion has been twofold. First, providing an account of African governance and regional experience is necessary to contextualise the Southern African experience which we will discuss in the next chapter. While the democratisation of the Southern African region since 1994 has resulted in positive changes to the 'flexible' regional legal regimes, the legacy of apartheid has had significant implications for regional integration and cooperation. The feeling of mistrust among African countries, coupled with the endemic fear of South African dominance, has effectively paralysed the region economically and politically. However, it is also important to appreciate the importance of South Africa as a stabilising force in the region.

Second, this chapter has argued that many African states are unable to govern themselves and, as a result, they are unable to achieve the goals of sustainable development and poverty eradication set out by the various regional frameworks such as Lomé, Cotonou and NEPAD. Economically, and indeed politically, these countries assume a weak position in the global order. This leads to the conclusion that African countries are by no means on the same footing as stronger members of the WTO, such as the EU and USA, and as such entering into North-South RTAs should be approached with caution. Their inherent political and economic weakness leaves their lucrative markets rich with natural resources open to exploitation by others seeking to legitimise their authority through legal regimes. Interregionalism between the EU and ACP countries has been predominantly driven by the EU and, as the remaining chapters will show, the ability of these developing countries to voice their concerns has, to a degree, lost its persuasive significance. That said, the use of 'mimetic challenge' by the ACP countries has resulted in some small victories in the context of the EPA negotiations. As new interregional spaces are constructed through formal law, so too are existing regional spaces in Southern Africa being reconstituted within a neoliberal frame.

7. Regionalism in Southern Africa

This chapter conceives of regional arrangements in Southern Africa as 'flexible' legal regimes that have historically constituted a key part of the region's development strategy. Understood as a vehicle to bolster economic growth and development, regionalism in Southern Africa has also been conceptualised as a method for overcoming structural difficulties, such as political fragmentation in the post-colonial and post-Apartheid era. Regionalism serves economic, development, and political functions in this region where there is significant asymmetry between the Southern African states. In this chapter, it will be demonstrated that the regional differences between the Southern African states has created internal antagonisms and tensions that exacerbate the extent to which these states are integrated into the global economy. There is a great deal of untapped potential in this region but the members must become better integrated if they are to achieve their development objectives and eradicate poverty.

In the previous chapter it was argued that many African countries are pursuing a different model of development that is not congruent with the Western ideal formalised in Article XXIV and, as such, this presents challenges to cooperation with developed countries in North-South RTAs. Shifting the focus of analysis, this chapter explores the political economy of regionalism in Southern Africa. While there are many overlapping regional arrangements in Southern Africa, this chapter is limited to an examination of the two RTAs which are most likely to be affected by the EU-SADC EPA, the Southern African Customs Union (SACU) and the Southern African Development Community (SADC).[1] Integration is governed through a formalist rules-based system, albeit compliance with those rules has been lacking for some time. One important trend evident in the region is the emphasis of regionalism as a development tool with three pillars for integration: market integration, industrial development,

[1] The Common Market for Eastern and Southern Africa (COMESA) is a large RTA that consists of 19 Eastern and Southern African countries. The only SADC EPA country that is party to COMESA is Swaziland and therefore COMESA is omitted from this book as it is not directly affected by the SADC EPA.

and capacity building.[2] However, it is submitted that the lack of participation from non-state actors has severely limited the extent to which these three pillars can be achieved. In the Asian model of regionalism, for example, development integration has been predominantly led by private actors. However, as noted in the previous chapter, governments continue to lead the integration project in African regionalisms much to the detriment of realising the comprehensive development agenda.

Economic growth among SADC members differs dramatically, which is perhaps unsurprising given the varying size of countries, although the region has significant economic potential. From 2003–2013, the SADC economy as a collective grew on average 4.7 per cent annually. As the regional hegemon, South Africa's share of GDP in the region is approximately 52 per cent.[3] Protecting domestic industries therefore remains a primary concern for Southern African States, and addressing supply-side constraints is of equal importance. Regional policies on supply-side constraints have not yet been agreed and recourse to the use of border measures such as import tariffs, ROO, export tariffs and regulatory restrictions that favour domestic production remain in place.[4]

This chapter is divided into four substantive sections, with the first and second sections providing an overview of the historical setting from which SACU and SADC have emerged. In this book, it has been submitted that countries may pursue regionalism for different reasons and to achieve different ends. This chapter situates SACU and SADC in their historical origins in order to better understand how the creation of a new interregional space between the EU and Southern African countries may result in a reconstruction of the region. SACU has been driven primarily by South Africa as a tool for market integration and regional cooperation with neighbouring countries,[5] while SADC, in its original manifestation as SADCC, rejected the market integration approach and instead focused

---

[2] T. Hartzenburg, 'Introduction' in A. du Pisani, G. Erasmus, T. Hartzenburg and C. McCarthy (eds), *Monitoring Regional Integration in Southern Africa Yearbook 2013/14* (Stellenbosch: tralac, 2014), available online at https://www.tralac.org/publications.

[3] Data on GDP for the SADC region has been taken from The World Bank, *World Development Indicators*, accessed 13 December 2016 at http://dataworldbank.org/data-catalog/.

[4] Hartzenburg (n. 2), 2.

[5] See J. Ravenhill, *Global Political Economy*, 3rd edn (Oxford: Oxford University Press, 2011); and R. Gibb, 'Regional Integration and Africa's Development Trajectory: Meta-theories, Expectations and Reality' (2009) 30 *Third World Quarterly* 701–21.

on regional cooperation and development integration.[6] Both SACU and SADC are notified as Article XXIV RTAs.[7]

This analysis will be followed by a critique of the existing regional framework in the third section, with reference to the modes of governance that have been used in the region. As outlined in Chapter 6, neoliberal economic policies have been at the forefront of Africa's economic restructuring. In this section, the impact of neoliberal economic policies for regionalism in Southern Africa will be considered. Acknowledging the effect of neoliberal policies and globalisation on the region is an integral part of understanding how the region has been (re)constructed. It will be argued that internal and external forces have shaped the direction of regionalisms in Southern Africa and resulted in a market-led model of regionalism with a focus on neoliberal values. If we accept the neopatrimonial perspective outlined in Chapter 6, it becomes apparent that the conventional approaches to regionalism simply do not 'fit' with the economic, political and social reality of most African countries, including those in Southern Africa.

It is submitted that Southern African countries have been subject to the hegemonic influence of two actors: South Africa and the EU. As such, processes of regionalism have been framed in accordance with their ideologies and the SADC EPA presents a discursive site in which these two hegemonic forces meet. However, through collective political-will formation, or 'norms of solidarity',[8] Southern African States have challenged the hegemonic ideologies and influenced the (re)construction of both SACU and SADC. The final section of this chapter considers the extent of South African political and economic influence on regional integration in Southern Africa. It will be argued that developing countries in the region have effectively been 'locked-in' to hegemonic legal regimes, such as SACU, and as such they are already in a more vulnerable position vis-à-vis Western trading partners, like the EU.

---

6 M.C. Lee, *The Political Economy of Regionalism in Southern Africa* (Boulder: Lynne Rienner, 2003), 19–27. See generally T. Østergaard, 'Classical Models of Regional Integration – What Relevance for Southern Africa?' in B. Odén (ed.), *Southern Africa After Apartheid: Regional Integration and External Resources* (Nordic Africa Institute, 1993).

7 The literature offers no explanation for why these RTAs are notified under Article XXIV and not under the Enabling Clause, although the presumption would be that as SACU is a customs union and SADC is a FTA, they go beyond the minimum threshold of para. 2(c) of the Enabling Clause.

8 L. Dirar, 'Norms of Solidarity and Regionalism: Theorising State Behaviour Among Southern African States' (2016) 24 *Michigan State International Law Review* 667–723.

THE SOUTHERN AFRICAN CUSTOMS UNION (SACU)

As the oldest customs union in the world, SACU is recognised internationally as one of the more stable regional arrangements in Sub-Saharan Africa.[9] This grouping includes the five Southern African countries of Bostwana, Lesotho, Namibia, Swaziland (BLNS) and South Africa.[10] The origins of SACU date back to 1889 with the Customs Union Convention which united the British colony of the Cape of Good Hope and the Orange Free State Boer Republic. Subsequent agreements in 1893 and 1903 extended the union to other territorial areas in Southern Africa and eventually led to the creation of the 1910 union of South Africa.

In 1910, South Africa and the High Commission Territories (HCTs) of Bechuanaland (Botswana), Basutoland (Lesotho) and Swaziland formed a customs union. As independence was perceived to be non-viable for these territories, the colonial strategy included the proposed transfer of the HCTs to South Africa.[11] In light of this, the 1910 Agreement was drafted as a temporary arrangement with the eventual goal of the HCTs becoming part of South Africa and in the meantime, being administered by South Africa.

By virtue of its role as the administrator of the territories, South Africa became the principal decision-maker of the union. This is reflected in the extremely modest legal text of the 1910 Agreement, consisting of only six provisions. Perhaps of greatest significance at the time were the legal provisions for the free flow of goods within the union (Article 2) and a common external tariff (Article 9). Although this legal regime predates Article XXIV its underlying principles, rooted in economic liberalism, resonate with that provision. As this process was intended to merely expand the territorial boundaries of South Africa, rather than create a 'region' *per se*, an institutional framework was absent from the 1910 agreement. The lack of a supranational body to oversee the governance of the union was unsurprising, given the authoritative role South Africa played in governing the other territories. In order to unify the HCTs and

---

[9] World Trade Organisation (WTO), *Trade Policy Review: Southern African Customs Union*, Report by the Secretariat WT/TPR/S/114 (Geneva, WTO, 2003).

[10] On 21 March 1990, having gained independence from the Republic of South Africa, Namibia became party to the 1969 SACU Agreement.

[11] J. Sidaway and R. Gibb, 'SADC, COMESA & SACU: Contradictory Formats for Regional Integration in Southern Africa?' in David Simon (ed.), *South Africa in Southern Africa: Reconfiguring the Region* (Oxford: James Currey Ltd, 1998), 172.

South Africa, Article 4 of the Agreement stipulated that the legal and regulatory regimes should be brought into line with that of South Africa. This represents the early manifestations of regional legal hegemony in Southern Africa although pragmatically it would be unnecessary to maintain independent tariff and customs regimes under the proposed incorporation of the HCTs into South African territory.[12] Harmonisation of policies is normally a necessary element of customs union formation but in the case of SACU this has been a very one-sided process overlooking the particular development and economic needs of the HCTs. Through the legalisation of Apartheid, HCTs were characterised in terms of vulnerability and political instability. Since the HCTs were in a weak bargaining position they had very little representation or participation in the negotiation process.[13]

The union existed in this form for decades until the process of decolonisation began to gather momentum. As other countries across the continent were being recognised as independent states, it was only a matter of time before Southern African countries followed suit. It soon became evident that the temporary construction of the union would need to evolve in response to the changing political climate. Since its creation in 1910, SACU has undergone two significant transformations in response to the changing economic and political landscape of the region.

Governance through Regionalism and Apartheid

Following the independence of Botswana,[14] Lesotho,[15] and Swaziland,[16] collectively known as the 'BLS' states, the SACU Agreement 1969 ('SACUA 1969') was signed on 11 December 1969. A slightly more sophisticated agreement than its predecessor, the 1969 SACUA was rooted in neofunctionalism and focused on the economic and fiscal integration of the region. This reflects the popular ideology of the time with talks of creating a New International Economic Order and the

---

[12] C. McCarthy, 'The Southern African Customs Union in Transition' (2003) 102 *African Affairs* 611.

[13] D. Bach, 'Integration through Hysteresis: SACU in Comparative and Contextual Perspective' in D. Hansohm, W. Breytenbach, T. Hartzenberg and C. McCarthy (eds), *Regional Integration in Southern Africa Yearbook* (Vol. 5, Namibian Economic Policy Research Unit, 2005), 137–49.

[14] Botswana became an independent State on 30 September 1966.

[15] The Kingdom of Lesotho gained independence on 4 October 1966.

[16] The Kingdom of Swaziland became an independent State on 6 September 1968.

liberal rhetoric of the international financial institutions.[17] Under the new agreement the special position of BLS, as developing countries, was to be formally recognised. This is enshrined in the recital of SACUA 1969, which appears to be more development oriented as it expresses commitment towards improving the position of the newly independent BLS:

> Recognizing that the Customs Agreement concluded on 29 June 1910 … requires modification … to ensure in particular that these arrangements encourage the development of the less advanced members of the customs union and the diversification of their economies, and afford to all parties equitable benefits arising from trade among themselves and with other countries …

In principle the 1969 SACUA provided for a more consultative role for BLS in terms of the customs tariff (Article 5), allowed for infant industry protection (Article 6), and for the protection of smaller economies (Article 7). In spite of this, South Africa could withhold permission to implement such provisions reinforcing South Africa as the region's *de facto* leader. Under Article 11 of SACUA 1969, the government of Pretoria could deny access of goods from BLS into the South African market for any 'economic, social, cultural or other reason' thereby ensuring that its own competitiveness was not undermined. In this way, we can see the rising influence of Pretoria on the other members of the Union had been formalised and legitimised through this regional legal regime.

At this time, the regional governance was relatively weak. Internally, the Union had failed to implement common policies or an adequate institutional framework. A regional institutional framework was also in its infancy at this stage as the Agreement provided for the establishment of a Customs Union Commission under Article 20.1 SACUA 1969. This institution was comprised of a representative from each member to discuss any aspect of the union. However this was the only institution of the SACU 1969 arrangement and it was relatively ineffective.[18] At the very most, the 1969 Agreement was an attempt at market integration with the underlying purpose of ensuring peace and stability in the region. However, in terms of fiscal policy SACU remained a fundamental source of revenue for BLS.

---

[17] On 1 May 1974, the UN adopted a Declaration on the creation of a New International Economic Order which set out proposals for integrating developing countries into the global economy. The Declaration can be found at http://www.un-documents.net/s6r3201.htm (accessed 13 December 2016).

[18] See WTO (n. 9).

The Common Revenue Pool (CRP), which is still in operation today, collected customs and excise revenues within the union for division among the members. Under the revised SACUA 1969, BLS saw their revenue shares increase by 42 per cent as a new formula was enacted.[19] South Africa had long been in control of the trade and fiscal decisions of the union. As the dominant member of the group, the common external tariff (CET) 'is adopted from South Africa's tariff book' and prioritises South Africa's trade and development policy over that of the BLNS (Botswana, Lesotho, Namibia and Swaziland) states.[20] In terms of revenue collected through the CET, all moneys were managed by the Consolidated Revenue Fund of South Africa.[21] A complex revenue sharing formula has been devised,[22] which has been the subject of much debate for many years. The revenue formula specifies the proportion of revenue that will be allocated to each member of SACU on an annual basis. Distribution of the revenue generated through the common external tariff among member countries has been an area of concern for commentators of SACU and this will be discussed in greater detail in the following section.

Through legal formalism South Africa sought to construct the region in its image, but the process of political destabilisation in the 1970s unsettled regional progress. Liberation movements were gaining political strength in Southern Africa, particularly in Zimbabwe and Mozambique, and amid the threat of sanctions and embargos against Apartheid South Africa in the 1960s and 1970s, SACU proved to be an important mechanism for South Africa to maintain exchange linkages with the other African nations. In response to the economic sanctions imposed, South African firms sought safety in the territories of Lesotho and Swaziland. It was during this period that the existence of SACU remained critical for South Africa's economic survival. In relocating to Lesotho and Swaziland, the firms could continue production beyond the spatial bounds of South Africa whilst continuing to distribute their goods within South Africa on a tariff and quota-free basis. This action was a positive step in terms of directing investment into the poorer SACU States. However, it

[19] Information and historical data on SACU can be found at its website, accessed 13 December 2016 at http://www.sacu.int/show.php?id=394.

[20] G. Erasmus, 'Does SACU Face a Crisis?' Tralac Trade Brief No. US16TB02/2016 (June 2016) accessed 13 December 2016 at https://www.tralac.org/publications.

[21] Article 13 SACU Agreement 1969.

[22] Article 14 SACU Agreement 1969.

was a short-lived strategy and shortly after the sanctions were lifted the firms relocated within South Africa.

While establishing their roots in one country, it was commonplace for liberation movements to spill across national boundaries and gain momentum in other Southern African countries. In this respect the liberation movements became an integral part of regionalisation across geographic boundaries. The prolonged and protracted violence in Africa had significant socio-economic effects for the population in the region. As a result of the ongoing conflicts the region saw the decline of physical productive capital and investment, the destruction of infrastructure and an overall decrease in the standard of living.[23] Following a 25-year period of political unrest, the political economy of the region was dramatically transformed as white minority rule was formally abolished. With the election of the African National Congress (ANC) in 1994, led by Nelson Mandela, came renewed hope for the democratisation of the region, and at the fore of the political and legal agendas was the renegotiation of the SACU Agreement.[24]

Towards Democracy: A Region United?

In relation to its predecessors, the 2002 Agreement was more comprehensive and was dedicated to the building of institutions and strengthening the governance framework, promoting trade liberalisation and improving regulation and revenue sharing. In a similar spirit to the 1969 SACUA, the preamble reiterates the Union's commitment to regional integration and the importance of adopting a regional approach in order to facilitate trade among partners of unequal economic development. The objectives outlined in the 2002 SACUA mirror those of NEPAD and recognised the need for good governance and political stability as prerequisites for sustainable development. Importantly, Article 4 of the 2002 SACUA gives SACU legal personality and allows the bloc to negotiate free trade agreements (FTAs) with third countries collectively as a regional group. This was in stark contrast to the 1969 SACUA under which the SACU members were entitled to enter into bilateral negotiations where the other members did not object to such arrangements.

Article 31 SACUA 2002 sets out the legal basis for interregional cooperation and provides that SACU members act collaboratively when

---

[23] J. Blumenfeld, *Economic Interdependence in Southern Africa: From Conflict to Cooperation?* (London: Pinter Publishers Ltd, 1991).

[24] Ministers met on 11 November 1994 to discuss renegotiating the SACU Agreement, a process that would take nearly 10 years to complete.

negotiating with third countries. Under this provision, a SACU Member State can enter into a separate bilateral trade agreement with a third party only where the terms of such an agreement do not conflict with the agreement of the Union. In principle, the Article 31 requirement implies that SACU will operate as a more cohesive group. However, the Trade, Development and Cooperation Agreement (TDCA) between South Africa and the EU was negotiated *without* the participation of the remaining members of SACU. Furthermore, and more importantly for this inquiry, the SADC-EPA had been signed by three members of SACU with two members refusing to sign until further issues were resolved. The third section of this chapter will discuss these 'contentious' issues in further detail.

The Union's 'rising regionness' is evident in the institutional framework established under the 2002 Agreement. A key objective driving the renegotiation of the SACUA 1969 following the democratisation of the region was to bring BLNS into the decision-making process of the union.[25] It was with this in mind that the SACUA 2002 provides a more sophisticated and transparent structural framework with supranational institutions to democratically govern the union.[26] In recognising the bias of the earlier customs union framework, the 2002 Agreement introduces an intergovernmental institutional structure that is independent from the influence of Pretoria. The institutional framework is hierarchical and comprises the supreme decision-making body (the Council),[27] the Commission,[28] the Secretariat,[29] technical liaison committees,[30] and a dispute

---

[25] WTO (n. 9), 7.

[26] McCarthy (n. 12), 605.

[27] As the supreme decision making authority, the council is comprised of at least one minister from each Member State and shall oversee the overall functioning of the union (Article 8 SACUA 2002).

[28] The commission is responsible for overseeing the implementation of the agreement and monitoring the revenue pool (Article 9 SACUA 2002). It must report to the council and must convene regularly to ensure the union is operating efficiently.

[29] The Secretariat is responsible for the daily administration of SACU and must report to the Commission (Article 10 SACUA 2002). Among other administrative tasks, negotiation of trade agreements with third parties falls within the mandate of the secretariat. Regulation of the tariff levels and non-tariff barriers to trade are monitored by the tariff board, which makes recommendations to the Council (Article 11 SACUA 2002).

[30] Technical liaison committees will advise the commission in relation to four key areas: agriculture; customs; trade and industry; and, transport (Article 12 SACUA 2002).

settlement system.[31] Overall, this comprehensive institutional framework reflected the renewed commitment to strengthening the domestic and regional institutional framework in order to build a more democratic union. It evidences the institutionalisation of governance structures and economic policies *through* law. Furthermore, it not only demonstrates SACU's increasing level of *actorship* but more importantly, it provides an example of how the policies adopted by developed countries in their RTAs have been mimicked by Southern African countries. Rhetorically, the emphasis creating a coherent institutional framework sent a message to the outside world that Southern Africa was democratising through a formalisation of its legal regime.

SACUA 2002 has gone some way in trying to remedy the development deficit that had come to characterise the Union. In what was a controversial move at the time, SACUA 2002 introduced decision-making on the basis of consensus which, in theory at least, gives all the States the same voting power and right to veto.[32] While this was implemented in a bid to overcome the democratic deficit of the previous SACU regime, it could weaken the arrangement as decision-making by consensus can be a long process. It was feared that this may result in delayed implementation of common policies and undermine the collective interests of the group.[33] However, many of the specialised institutions have not materialised and since 2004 *ad hoc* interim arrangements have been in place. The SACU Tribunal has not been established, which leaves the parties with no recourse to dispute settlement should a dispute arise, and this failure merely exacerbates the institutional deficit of the regional group.[34]

The SACUA 2002 also recognised the need for economic development in the more vulnerable States of BLNS and included a provision for infant industry protection.[35] Given South Africa's comparative advantage

---

[31] Any dispute arising in relation to any aspect of implementation or application of the Agreement will be presented to an *ad hoc* tribunal composed of three members (Article 13 SACUA 2002). The Council may refer an issue to the tribunal for settlement and the tribunal will provide recommendations to the Council (Article 13.4 SACUA 2002). In its administrative role, the Secretariat may also provide assistance to the tribunal where necessary (Article 13.7 SACUA 2002).

[32] R. Gibb, 'The New Southern African Customs Union Agreement: Dependence with Democracy' (2006) 32 *Journal of Southern African Studies* 583–603, 599.

[33] M. Meyn, 'Economic Partnership Agreements: A "Historic Step" Towards a "Partnership of Equals"?' (2008) 26 *Development Policy Review* 515–28.

[34] Erasmus (n. 20).

[35] Article 26 SACUA 2002.

in most areas of trade, it is unsurprising that the BLNS suffer a significant trade deficit vis-à-vis South Africa. However, in reality there has been a lack of protection for local industries in BLNS against the competitive South African industrial base. This has been reported as one of the most disadvantageous aspects of the Union for BLNS.[36] The policy space of BLNS in SACU is extremely limited and their place within the regional group is threatened further by the current political and economic crises facing South Africa. While the revenue sharing pool has proven to be beneficial to BLNS, South Africa has indicated that it wants to amend the formula.[37] The future of SACU is uncertain and this has certainly prevented the members of the region from forming a common voice in the EPA negotiations with the EU. This will be explored further in the following chapter. Having traced the roots of SACU's regional past it is important to consider the other Southern African legal regime that will be affected by the EU-SADC EPA, the Southern African Development Community.

FROM SADCC TO SADC

Apartheid marked a period of great uncertainty for the region and having grown weary of their increasing dependence on South Africa, Botswana, Lesotho and Swaziland decided to form a collective as the Frontline States (FLS).[38] The ever increasing dependence on South Africa was perceived to be an 'unnatural legacy' of the colonial era and, in particular, the Apartheid regime, with the blend of capitalism and colonialism characterising the region's economic policy.[39] To counter the perceived threat of Apartheid South Africa and its liberal economic values, the Frontline States (FLS) launched the creation of the Southern African Development Coordination Conference (SADCC). In 1980, on signing the Lusaka Declaration (Southern Africa: Towards Economic Liberation), SADCC was born.

SADC's history is markedly different from that of SACU, and in a sense the ideational thrust behind its creation can even be described as a

---

36 Meyn (n. 33), 77.

37 Erasmus (n. 20), 4.

38 T. Hartzenberg and G. Maasdorp, 'Regional Integration Arrangements in Southern Africa: SACU and SADC' in Z. Iqbar and M. Khan (eds), *Trade Reform and Regional Integration in Africa* (Washington, D.C.: IMF, 1997), 433.

39 R. Gibb, 'Southern Africa in Transition: Prospects and Problems Facing Regional Integration' (1998) 36 *The Journal of Modern African Studies* 290.

reaction to SACU. At its inception, the SADCC consisted of nine Southern African countries: Angola; Botswana; Lesotho; Malawi; Mozambique; Swaziland; Tanzania; Zambia; and Zimbabwe. It explicitly excluded (Apartheid) South Africa and Namibia, the latter still subject to South African rule. Adopting an alternative approach to cooperation, the SADCC was a unique, decentralised organisation of States that shied away from regional bureaucracy.[40] Nevertheless, the State was still at the epicentre of the regional agenda, focusing on political and security cooperation over economic integration, and as such SADCC was a representation of the 'old regionalism' approach.[41]

The Lusaka Declaration, while not a legally binding treaty, sets out SADCC's mode of operation:

> SADCC has no treaty, no central authority, no common currency, not even a common language ... If SADCC countries do not have a common ideology it is because that was never intended and would be impossible to achieve.[42]

What the Lusaka Declaration suggests is that there was not an absence of a collective ideology but, rather there was a 'common sense' or shared uncritical philosophy, albeit one that prioritised individualism and embraced the diversity of ideological perspectives in the regional group. Luwam Dirar describes this shared philosophy as 'norms of solidarity' which 'regulate solidarity as a logic of appropriateness' among the Southern African States.[43] These norms of solidarity 'based on unity and comradeship define "African-ness" as good and lack thereof as bad'[44] and are internalised throughout the regional legal regimes.

Under the initial SADCC Programme of Action, the common ideological perspective of the regional arrangement was sectoral *cooperation* rather than economic *integration.* This symbolises the development

---

[40] G. Oosthuizen, *The Southern African Development Community: The Organisation, its Policies and Prospects* (Midrand: Institute for Global Dialogue, 2006), 63.

[41] C. Mulaudzi, 'New Regionalism in Southern Africa? Between South African Hegemony and Globalisation' (2009) XVI *Lusotopie* 47–65.

[42] SADCC, 'Southern Africa: Towards Economic Liberation – A Declaration by the Governments of Independent States of Southern Africa' made at Lusaka 1 April 1980, x.

[43] Dirar (n. 8), 669.

[44] *Ibid*, 671.

integration approach to regionalism, which is concerned with rectifying the problems of the market-led approaches to integration. Jens Haarlov submits that development integration is 'born out of the problems and dysfunction of the pure market integration approach' and suggests that it attempts to address these problems in three ways by changing the agenda of 'the objective of the integration process … the timing and level of interstate binding commitments, and … the distribution of cost and benefits of cooperation'.[45] Under this model, there is a shift of focus away from economic integration towards social and economic development. Political cooperation is a central aspect for development integration regionalism,[46] as a key point of this approach is to ensure equitable distribution of the benefits gained through regionalism. To this end, the countries must commit to a well-planned framework for regional industrial development.

Collectively, the members of SADCC recognised that economic integration was contingent on political cooperation and therefore, under the SADCC framework, each member was given a sector to coordinate. Each State was treated in the same way and had to procure funding for their sector irrespective of whether this would eventually be implemented in the sector-coordinating state or elsewhere. Sectors were prioritised according to the regional need and not in response to a rubric prescribing economic growth generated by the international financial institutions. Some SADCC states were more efficient at coordinating their designated sectors than others and some projects were more attractive to donors than others. Donor preference is another medium through which coercive force can be precipitated and by effectively selecting the programmes for support, non-state actors have historically influenced the construction of the region. SADCC referred to this approach as the development integration model, as it was designed to not only promote economic development but to improve its population's human development.[47]

For some, SADCC was 'neither a great failure nor … a resounding success'.[48] While its innovative approach to regionalism at first seemed

---

[45] J. Haarlov, *Regional Cooperation and Integration within Industry and Trade in Southern Africa: General Approaches: SADCC and the World Bank* (Aldershot: Avebury, 1997).

[46] Lee (n. 6), 24.

[47] C.B. Thompson, 'Regional Challenges to Globalisation: Perspectives from Southern Africa' (2000) 5 *New Political Economy* 41–57, 47.

[48] Oosthuizen (n. 40) 69. Trudi Hartzenberg and Gavin Maasdorp, in their 1997 article, highlighted that only 3 members attended at an AGM meeting

promising, the combination of collective political contradictions in the region and the lack of a coordinated institutional framework was a recipe for disaster. Its loose organisational structure resulted in an inability to impose a collective will and express norms of solidarity with decentralisation proving to be a major factor in its ultimate demise.[49] In 1992, the Treaty of Windhoek marked the transition from the SADCC to the Southern African Development Community (SADC), and a shift from 'old' to 'new' regionalism. Unlike the SADCC which was driven primarily by political motivations to counter the threat of South Africa, the mandate of the SADC was focused on economic integration and political cooperation.

The original SADC Treaty, referred to as the Windhoek Declaration, was initially signed by 10 countries[50] but eventually another four joined the configuration.[51] South Africa joined SADC in 1994, following its transition to democracy. The shift from SADCC to SADC marked the transformation of this regional group from a loosely-organised coordinating body to a regional arrangement committed to economic integration and community building through law, symbolising the neoliberal turn in the Southern African regional political economy.

The Treaty sets out the institutional structure of the SADC region. An important aspect of regionalism is the presence of an effective supranational institutional framework to oversee the running of the region's integration and cooperation strategy.[52] Deliberately avoiding an overly-bureaucratic institutional framework, SADC adopted a relatively modest organisational structure with just seven organs: the Summit (comprised of

---

which reiterates the notion that the member states did not take the organisation seriously. See Hartzenberg and Maasdorp (n. 38).

[49] Blumenfeld (n. 23), 139.

[50] Angola, Botswana, Lesotho, Malawi, Mozambique, Namibia, Swaziland, Tanzania, Zambia and Zimbabwe.

[51] South Africa (August 1994); Mauritius (August 1995); DRC (June 1998); Madagascar (August 2005). Although the Seychelles became a member of SADC in February 1998 it subsequently withdrew from the group.

[52] A. Afadameh-Adeyemi and E. Kalula, 'SADC at 30: Re-examining the Legal and Institutional Anatomy of the Southern African Development Community' in A. Bösl, A. Pisani, G. Erasmus, T. Hartzenberg and R. Sandry (eds), *Monitoring Regional Integration in Southern Africa: Yearbook* (Stellenbosch: tralac, 2010), 30.

Heads of State),[53] the Troika,[54] the Council of Ministers,[55] the SADC Tribunal,[56] SADC National Committees,[57] the Standing Committee of Officials,[58] and the Secretariat.[59] Most of these had existed under SADCC, with the Tribunal being the only new institution added to the framework.[60] With the suspension of the SADC Tribunal in 2012 for its failure to uphold the fundamental human rights of people in the Southern African region, the legitimacy and survival of SADC has been drawn into question.[61] In spite of this, SADC continues to work toward the creation of the African Tri-partite FTA alongside the East African Community (EAC) and the Common Market for Eastern and Southern Africa (COMESA).

Regional integration in the SADC originally focused on economic integration and development.[62] In 2003, the SADC's objectives and goals were set out in the Regional Indicative Strategic Development Plan (RISDP). While not a legally binding instrument, the RISDP states that the key objective is 'to deepen the integration agenda of SADC with a

---

[53] The Summit is the 'supreme policy-making' body of the SADC and is 'responsible for the overall policy direction and control of the functions' of the region (Article 10 SADC Treaty 1992). It meets once a year and decisions are made by consensus with all decisions being legally binding. The Summit appoints the Executive Secretary, which has a more administrative role within the Secretariat (Article 15 SADC Treaty 1992).

[54] The Troika is an organ on Politics, Defence and Security.

[55] Overseeing the implementation of SADC is the Council, which is composed of one Minister from each member state (Article 11 SADC Treaty 1992). The Council reports to the Summit and meets at least once a year.

[56] Established under Article 9 SADC Treaty 1992.

[57] Committees have been created to 'guide and coordinate cooperation and integration' within the specified sectoral areas. As such, they are governed by the appropriate Protocol. Each Commission reports to the Council and works closely with the Secretariat (Article 12 SADC Treaty 1992).

[58] The Standing Committee of Officials is essentially a technical advisory committee that reports to the Council (Article 13 SADC Treaty 1992).

[59] The Secretariat is the principal executive institution of SADC and manages the overall planning of SADC programmes (Article 14 SADC Treaty 1992).

[60] A. Saurombe, 'The Role of SADC Institutions in Implementing SADC Treaty Provisions Dealing with Regional Integration' (2012) 15 *Potchefstroom Electronic Law Journal* 458.

[61] M. Hansungule, 'The Suspension of the SADC Tribunal' (2013) 35 *Strategic Review for Southern Africa* 135–45.

[62] M. Soko, 'The Political Economy of Regional Integration in Southern Africa', *Notre Europe* Paper 63 (December 2007) accessed 13 December 2016 at http://www.eng.notre-europe.eu/011-1481-The-Political-Economy-of-Regional-Integration-in-Southern-Africa.html.

view to accelerating poverty eradication and the attainment of other economic and non-economic goals'.[63] Although the RIDSP lacks legal legitimacy it appears to enjoy political legitimacy, with the SADC States embarking on a mid-term review of the programme in the period 2012–2014. The RIDSP has subsequently been updated in 2015 and sets out the region's vision for 2015–2063, detailing the policies, priorities and strategies to 'revitalise' what it refers to as 'development regionalism' among SADC States.[64]

Accelerating industrialisation through beneficiation and value addition is the region's major priority; however, a significant challenge to implementing regional strategies has been a lack of funding. In May 2016, it was confirmed that SADC will receive financial assistance for implementation of the Roadmap from the African Development Bank (AfDB) on a programmatic approach, although no figure has been given. Aligning the Roadmap with national, regional, continental, and international aspects of trade and development norms has been considered to be fundamental to its success. The Roadmap is anchored on three pillars: industrialisation, competitiveness and regional integration.[65] With a primary orientation on industrialisation in the energy, technology, transport and water markets, the strategic thrust behind the Roadmap is a 'shift from reliance on resources and low cost labour to increased investment and enhanced productivity on both labour and capital'.[66] Engendering a major economic and technological transformation through regional initiatives is identified as fundamental to the Roadmap's success:

> The Strategy is designed as a modernization scheme, and is predicated on maximum exploitation of comparative advantage and creating enduring conditions for competitive advantage at enterprise level. The latter thrust requires earnest efforts aimed at enhancing technological setups and readiness, changes in the way of doing business, scaling-up productive capacity and enhancing economic interlinkages to unlock regional potential in general. Sustainability of the process would thus require turning the economies into knowledge-based and competitive structures.[67]

---

[63] SADC Secretariat, *Regional Indicative Strategic Development Plan* (Gaborone, 2003), 7.

[64] SADC Secretariat, *SADC Industrialisation Strategy and Roadmap 2015-2063*, approved on 29 April 2015, 20.

[65] Statement from the Executive Secretary, Dr Stergomena L. Tax, SADC Secretariat, *SADC Industrialisation Strategy and Roadmap 2015-2063*, approved on 29 April 2015.

[66] SADC Secretariat, (n. 64), 11.

[67] *Ibid*, 12.

Setting out various quantitative and qualitative goals in macro- and micro-economic terms, the Roadmap is an ambitious project. It calls for greater involvement of the private sector and the deepening of capital markets to enhance opportunities between foreign-domestic partners:

> Given the multi-faceted challenges of industrialization in the 21st century, a strong alliance between governments, the private sector and civil society is essential. The engine of progress will be the productive sector driven by entrepreneurial dynamics within the context of a developmental state.[68]

Reiterating the importance of compliance with existing regional legal norms, the Roadmap highlights the need for coherence and convergence of regional norms. Diversification through regional and global value chains should be a priority for the region, since all SADC States, with the exception of South Africa, produce only basic goods.[69] Growth through agricultural value chains, the mining sector, and more effective participation in global value chains are all perceived as central elements of the growth strategy.

The Roadmap provides an intelligible assessment of the challenges that have faced the SADC region, and identifies pragmatic ways forward. It envisages the empowerment of women and youth to participate effectively in the industrialisation process, and the importance of sustainable trading practices. Together with the economic aspects of development, it is clear that the SADC region defines development as an inclusive and 'broad notion' highlighting the interconnections between economic freedom and non-economic freedoms. Reconstructing the SADC space through a development-oriented programme with an *Africapitalist* flavour,[70] demonstrates a blend of convention and pragmatism; the desire to retain the conventional model of African regionalism while recognising the perceived need to adopt predominantly neoliberal values to integrate into the global economy. As a result, the Roadmap marks a transformative shift in the regional history of Southern Africa.

Trade in goods is governed through the Protocol on Trade (1996) as amended in 2010, and trade in services is regulated by the Protocol on Trade in Services (2012). Through these legal frameworks, the SADC members are committed to the creation of a free trade area that would

---

[68] *Ibid*, 33.

[69] *Ibid*, 27.

[70] Africapitalism, while not entirely antithetical to capitalism, is a term coined by Nigerian banker, Tony Elumelu, and is centered on the role of African entrepreneurs in developing the production base in Africa.

enable goods and services to flow freely through the community. The region is economically diverse and by approaching regional integration through an incremental approach, it was thought that the region's infrastructure would gradually improve. Sectoral cooperation therefore remains a defining characteristic of the SADC agenda. Regional cooperation, economic growth and infrastructure are inextricably intertwined as evidenced by the attempt of the SADCC to coordinate regional programmes to lower transport costs in order to improve the socio-economic situation. Infrastructure is particularly important on a macro- and micro-economic level because it contributes to growth, reduces costs, and improves living conditions and overall welfare. Improving infrastructure will not only facilitate economic growth but will also improve the socio-economic situation at the grass-roots level.

Stabilising public and private financial matters, especially their debt, is an imperative of the overall project of globalisation. Debt burden poses a serious challenge to the development process of some African countries, with four SADC countries classified as Heavily Indebted Poor Countries (HIPCs): Democratic Republic of Congo; Mozambique; Tanzania; and, Zambia.[71] In 2000, Zambia's external debt stood at US$5.09 billion which is the equivalent of 174 per cent of its GDP for the same year.[72] In 2015, its external debt was US$3.36 billion which represents 163 percent of its GDP in that year.[73] Given that the Southern African region is rich in strategic minerals such as chromium, diamonds, gold and petroleum, it may come as a surprise to some that many of these countries are so heavily indebted.

External forces have certainly affected the political economy of regionalism in Southern Africa. In the preceding chapter, it was argued that conventional theories fail to take into account the unique political context of Africa and the regional regimes emerging on the continent. For many African countries, the 'integration approach is developmental, and it has cogent, development-related justifications, which lie outside the framework of the conventional state theoretical analysis for its regional

---

71 The IMF provides that these countries may have qualified for, are eligible or potentially eligible and may wish to receive HIPC Initiative Assistance as of March 2016. Further information is available at https://www.imf.org/external/np/exr/facts/hipc.htm (accessed 13 December 2016).

72 S. Buthelezi, *Regional Integration in Africa: Prospects and Challenges for the 21st Century* (East London: Ikhwezi Afrika, 2006), 164.

73 Data extracted from Trading Economics available online at http://www.tradingeconomics.com/.

integration'.[74] To date, SADC's vision of regional integration has very much embraced free market, neoliberal principles which has exacerbated the pre-existing asymmetries and inequalities among the region's countries.[75] Adopting a post-colonial perspective, Richard Gibb argues:

> … the West has been able successfully to assert and reimpose a cultural, economic, linguistic and political agenda for regional integration in the South. This has resulted in, and is partly the product of, the West being able to impose and sustain a discursive hegemony over regionalism.[76]

Extending this perspective, it is submitted that South Africa has also played an integral part in shaping the normative framework through which the legal regimes have emerged. Its historical hegemonic position vis-à-vis the BLNS has enabled South Africa to dominate the regional strategy and while the region has undergone transformation, arguably this transformation has been circumscribed by South African interests and values.

Externally, the international financial institutions have also played an influential role in shaping the regional framework in Southern Africa. In 1999, during a speech to Southern African leaders, the US Deputy Secretary of Commerce, Robert Mallet, boldly declared:

> The global economy is here … unlike Europe, you don't have 40 years to get your act together … Unless there is a realization that the region has to be integrated … you are not going to make it … investors are going to decide [that] Africa is just not ready … We cannot remain in this posture of standing in the morass saying it is difficult to move because this is Southern Africa.[77]

SADC's vision of regionalism certainly dovetails with that of the international financial institutions which have promoted a model of 'open regionalism' that envisages a stronger role for the private sector and civil society in shaping the regional architecture of Southern Africa. The external influence of international donors and the hegemonic role of South Africa have contributed to the 'neoliberal turn' in SACU and SADC. Jessica Evans argues that the neoliberal turn in SADC has created

---

74 UNECA, 'Economic Report on Africa 2012: Unleashing Africa's Potential as a Pole of Global Growth' (UNECA, 2012), 19–20, accessed 13 December 2016 at http://repository.uneca.org/bitstream/handle/10855/21725/Bib-69455.pdf?sequence=1, 31.

75 J. Evans, 'The Neoliberal Turn in the SADC' (2010) *Nokoko* 101–129.

76 Gibb (n. 5).

77 Cited in Lee (n. 6), 119.

'internal antagonisms through bottom-up regional pressures and a subsequent reassertion of the state at the border'.[78] This is evidenced by the high levels of intraregional tariff and non-tariff barriers still present at the border. Excessively high transport costs pose a significant challenge for African countries in entering the global economy. In its 2012 report, the UN Economic Commission for Africa highlighted the problem:

> ... on average it takes 35 days for cargo to be exported and 42 days to be imported. In addition, it costs an average of US$1,899 to export and US$2,410 to import a 20-foot container of non-sensitive goods, with an average of eight documents required for export and nine for import.[79]

This is particularly problematic for landlocked countries where productivity is less efficient than their coastal neighbours, with their export level being approximately 30 per cent lower.[80] Geographically, the Southern African region is comprised of eight LDCs and six landlocked countries. Of the eight LDCs in Southern Africa, three are landlocked.[81] Benno Ndulu et al estimate that while trade volumes in landlocked countries are approximately 60 per cent lower than in coastal countries, the costs of transport are 50 per cent higher.[82] This is significant in terms of attracting investment, productivity and overall economic growth. Lesotho is one of the world's poorest countries with a per capita GDP of just $980 per annum and as a landlocked country, it remains exclusively reliant on South Africa for the transit of imports and exports into and out of the country.[83] The situation is not quite so bleak for Swaziland which is located close to the port of Maputo and therefore has some trade linkages beyond the geographic bounds of South Africa.

Inadequate infrastructure is a major obstacle to economic growth facing African countries. For SACU countries, the lack of physical

---

78 Evans (n. 75), 118.

79 UNECA Report (n. 74), 104–5.

80 B. Ndulu, L. Kritzinger-van Niekerk and R. Reinikka, 'Infrastructure, Regional Integration and Growth in Sub-Saharan Africa' in FONDAD, *Africa in the World Economy – the National, Regional and International Challenges* (Hague, 2005), 112

81 See UN Office of the High Representative for the Least Developed Countries, Landlocked Developing Countries and Small Island Developing States website, accessed 13 December 2016 at http://www.unohrlls.org.

82 Ndulu et al (n. 80), 106.

83 D. Gantz, *Regional Trade Agreements: Law, Policy and Practice* (Durham, NC: Carolina Academic Press, 2009), 436.

infrastructure results in increasing dependency on South Africa.[84] Regional cooperation, economic growth, and infrastructure are inextricably intertwined as evidenced by the attempt of SADCC to coordinate regional programmes to lower transport costs in order to improve the region's socio-economic situation. Infrastructure is particularly important on both macro- and micro-economic levels because it contributes to growth, reduces costs, and improves living conditions and overall welfare. Improving infrastructure will not only facilitate economic growth (economic freedom) but will also improve the socio-economic situation at the micro-level as non-economic freedoms are realised.

By 2008, SADC had achieved its aims of liberalising 85 per cent of its trade internally and thereafter officially launched the FTA negotiations. In a bid to strengthen the coherence of the region, SACU members liberalised 99 per cent of their products.[85] However, implementation of the RISDP has been disappointing:

> The majority of member states failed to set aside resources for planning and implementation of RISDP Programmes at national level, and the SADC National Structures, where they were created, did not possess the requisite capacity to effectively coordinate their implementation. Consequently, commitments to implementing agreements were often not carried out, which resulted in missed deadlines in several cases, most notably, the failure to establish the SADC Customs Union by the target date of 2010.[86]

Overall, SADC's achievements have been hampered by a lack of coordination from members and the failure to establish an adequate institutional framework to manage its programmes. SADC, in promoting liberal policies, has failed to take into account the political and economic reality of the region. To date, the decentralised and sector-based approach of the SADC has proven to be unsuccessful and the failure to implement the SADC Trade Protocol may be an indication that there is 'limited trade potential' among the SADC countries.[87]

---

[84] *Ibid*, 435.

[85] UNECA Report (n. 74), 80.

[86] Tralac, 'The Regional Indicative Strategic Development Plan: SADC's trade-led Integration Agenda', tralac Trade Brief S12TB02/2012 (2012) accessed 13 December 2016 at https://www.tralac.org/publications/article/4612-the-regional-indicative-strategic-development-plan-sadc-s-trade-led-integration-agenda.html.

[87] African Development Bank, 'Southern Africa Regional Integration Strategy Paper 2011–2015', (2011) accessed 13 December 2016 at http://www.afdb.org/fileadmin/uploads/afdb/Documents/Project-and-Operations/2011-2015%20-%

REGIONALISM AS 'REGIME BOOSTING'

An escape from the legacy of colonialism and Apartheid has proven almost impossible, and in spite of their regional initiatives yielding little growth these countries remain committed to the programme of regionalism. Historically, it had been suggested that regionalism was a 'matter of survival' for African countries.[88] In the Opening Address of an IMF conference, the former Prime Minister (and now President) of Namibia, Hage Geingob, stated:

> ... the salvation of African countries lies in strengthening regional blocs and promoting 'South-South' cooperation, thus enlarging the size of our own regional market, and at the same time ensuring that we are able to take advantage of globalization and liberalisation ... the success of regional cooperation largely depends on countries in the region consciously pursuing collective action, or spontaneous linkages emerging from accelerating growth rates.[89]

This suggests that regionalism serves another purpose in Southern Africa, namely to legitimise their political regime both regionally and internationally. It is no secret that SADC has been the recipient of substantial amounts of financial assistance since its creation.[90] During the 1980s over 90 per cent of funding for SADCC activities came from overseas donors, and in particular, from the West. Bowen identified that funding was predominantly sourced from the US, EU and the Nordic countries.[91] USAID provided $110 million over a five-year period to SADCC; however, this was given on the basis that Mozambique and Angola were excluded from the allocation because of their support for anti-government rebel forces. The EU's aid was provided through the Lomé III framework, with €776 million directed to SADCC. Between 1980 and 1985, Nordic states contributed 30 per cent of SADCC's OECD bilateral assistance. This adds to the 'regime boosting' culture of today's SADC

20Southern%20Africa%20-%20Regional%20Integration%20Strategy%20Paper.pdf, 10.

[88] African Development Bank, *Economic Integration in Southern Africa* (Abidjan: ADB, 1993), 1.

[89] Rt Hon. Hage G. Geingob (Prime Minister of Namibia) in 'Opening Address' (IMF, 1998), 4.

[90] Approximately 86% of SADC's project funding comes from overseas donors and the international financial institutions.

[91] B. Bowen, 'The Southern African Development Coordination Conference (SADCC)' (1990) *Trocaire Development Review* 29–45.

members. The funding for implementing regional initiatives comes from foreign donors, so Southern African countries can commit to various overlapping arrangements as they will not feel the cost of doing so.[92]

Conventional theoretical approaches assume rational state interaction and overlook the way in which political elites may shape policy preferences at the state level. They fuse market-led integration with a Western model of development, and this simply does not 'fit' with the African reality. 'Regime boosting' is a sophisticated form of regionalism which, as a mode of governance, promotes the national political interest at the national and international level. While liberal theories suggest that nationalism may prove to be an obstacle to regional integration, New Regionalism suggests that political leaders can actually promote state sovereignty through committing to regional schemes. In doing so, regionalism is a vehicle through which the domestic interest can be protected.

Söderbaum's study of regionalism in Southern Africa reveals that politicians are often involved in 'regime boosting'.[93] It is commonplace for governments to sign regional agreements, appearing to promote regional values and ideals, but in reality their motivation for doing so lies in the goal of raising the status of their own domestic regime. Somewhat paradoxically, weak states can have strong regional regimes and can use regionalism to bolster, rather than reduce, their sovereignty and legitimacy. In Southern Africa, SADC is a good example of how regional arrangements can be used to boost the image of each constituent member. SADC's neoliberal policies are at odds with the neopatrimonial African state and it should come as no surprise that SADC has not achieved many of its objectives.[94]

While the decentralised structure was a way of providing a 'sense of ownership' to the member states,[95] the sectoral coordinating units lacked administrative capacity and yet were still considered to be important.[96] In a sense, it shifted the relationship from one of regional cooperation to

---

[92] F. Söderbaum, 'African Regionalism and EU-African Interregionalism' in M. Telò (ed.), *European Union and New Regionalism: Regional Actors and Global Governance in a Post-Hegemonic Era*, 2nd edn (Aldershot: Ashgate, 2007), 194.

[93] F. Söderbaum, *The Political Economy of Regionalism: The Case of Southern Africa* (Basingstoke: Palgrave MacMillan, 2004), 96.

[94] I. Taylor, 'South African "Imperialism" in a Region Lacking Regionalism: A Critique' (2011) 32 *Third World Quarterly* 1233–53, 1248.

[95] SADC Secretariat, *Regional Indicative Strategic Development Plan* (Gaborone, 2003), 63.

[96] F. Söderbaum (n. 93), 194.

one of national ownership over a particular sector.[97] Over time, the scope of objectives brought under the auspice of SADC has risen and now includes: trade, transport, communications. To the outside world the members of SADC are portraying an image of a coherent regional arrangement that is constantly developing in an innovative fashion. In doing so, the members are able to raise the profile of their own governments by promoting regionalism as a *development strategy*. Even authoritarian governments of effectively failed states (Zimbabwe) and the tiny nations (Lesotho and Swaziland) can *appear* to have relatively stable formal governments. The reality is rather different:

> The problem is that many postcolonial states in Africa are to an overwhelming extent ruled by personal leaders, who are often portrayed as embodying the idea of the state. The personal rules often use the coercive instruments of the state to monopolize power and to further their own interests, including to deny or restrict the political rights and opportunities of opposing groups.[98]

In light of this, some have gone so far as to say that SADC is little more than a 'façade' or a 'state-led spectacle'.[99] The legitimacy of SADC as a regional mode of governance has been called into question recently in two distinct cases. First, in relation to the suspension of the Tribunal in 2012 and more recently, in its poor management of the political struggles in Lesotho.

Regional cooperation can also be an effective legal, political and economic mechanism for strengthening weak governance. Through law, the political and economic norms can be institutionalised to integrate society in these regional groups. However, signing up to lots of different agreements with little intention of fulfilling the commitments contained therein has resulted in a spaghetti bowl of regional arrangements in the Southern African region. At the heart of the problem of overlapping regionalism is the reluctance of Southern African members to put regional interests over national interests. For example, all SACU members are party to the WTO (1995), SADC (1994), African Growth and Opportunity Act (AGOA, 2000), and the AU. South Africa has traded with the EU *outside* the SACU region under the Trade, Development and Cooperation Agreement (TDCA) although the BLNS have been *de facto*

---

97 C. Mulaudzi, 'The Politics of Regionalism in Southern Africa', Occasional Paper no. 51 (Johannesburg: Institute for Global Dialogue, 2006), 11.

98 F. Söderbaum, 'Modes of Regional Governance in Africa: Neoliberalism, Sovereignty-boosting And Shadow Networks' (2004) 10 *Global Governance* 419–36.

99 Taylor (n. 94), 1249.

members by virtue of their membership to SACU. BLNS have preferences under the Cotonou Agreement, which have been extended under the recently signed full SADC EPA, but Swaziland has also joined COMESA (1996). Lesotho is the only SACU member to have access to the EU market under the EBA (2001) because it is classified as a LDC. Finally, Swaziland and Namibia are also parties of the Regional Integration Facilitation Forum (RIFF). Of the 14 SADC members, five are members of SACU, six are members of COMESA, one is a member of the East African Community (EAC), and two are members of the Indian Ocean Council. The significance of overlapping membership should not be underestimated as it is likely to result in trade diversion for most of Southern Africa as they try to satisfy their commitments under each RTA.[100]

What this discussion tells us so far is that the troubled economies of Southern Africa have been trapped in a cycle of dependency since the colonial period. They are dependent both on the EU and on South Africa. With the democratisation of Southern Africa, it was believed that the region would experience political stability and economic prosperity. However, having a customs union at the centre of the arrangement has brought with it contradictions and problems. What is clear is that South Africa's regional priority always has been, and probably always will be, SACU. In the following section we will consider whether Southern Africa has become a 'South-Africa centric' region.

SOUTH AFRICA: THE REGIONAL HEGEMON

In the early days of independence, it seemed that 'economic dependence had in many ways made political independence meaningless'.[101] Since the 1960s, there has been a growing relationship of economic dependence between South Africa and other Southern African countries. Forging stronger trade links with South Africa was perceived as mutually beneficial because in this way economic linkages were extended throughout the region. In practical terms and given the proximity of BLNS to

---

[100] Buthelezi (n. 72), 181.

[101] Sir Seretse Khama in SADCC 'Southern Africa: Towards Economic Liberation – A Declaration by the Governments of Independent States of Southern Africa' made at Lusaka 1 April 1980, viii.

South Africa and their membership to SACU, it is unsurprising that their economies are viewed as a mere appendage of South Africa.[102]

Given the history of the region, South Africa's relationship with Southern Africa is a delicate one. Economically, it is the strongest country in the region, accounting for 71.5 per cent of the region's GDP[103] and as such, it has the power to 'make or break' the region.[104] For example, approximately 80 per cent of Swaziland's exports are bound for South Africa while 81 per cent of imports are sourced from South Africa.[105] Similarly, Lesotho sources 95 per cent of its products from South Africa and exports 83 per cent to South Africa.[106] Namibia is reliant on both South Africa and the United Kingdom, with 47 per cent of its exports bound for these markets. Over 75 per cent of Namibian imports are sourced from these markets.[107] These figures demonstrate the extent of interdependency, with South Africa 'able to participate in a democratically organized customs union in a way that will allow it to remain master of its own development policy'.[108]

Compensation mechanisms, in the form of fiscal measures and the transfer of payments, may be implemented in a customs union framework to support the weaker members and buffer them from the harsh effects of trade diversion. In Southern Africa, fiscal measures include limited import duties which generate revenue on goods imported from South Africa. Applying limited import duties on the importation of goods from other SACU members may assist a weaker state, such as Lesotho, in domestic industry protection. In a similar vein, transfers of payments from richer to poorer members may be applicable. Earlier in this chapter, the importance of the CRP for developing countries in SACU was flagged. The CRP has increasingly become an economic 'crutch' to some

---

[102] C. Chipeta and K. Schade (eds), *Deepening Integration in SADC: Macroeconomic Policies and Social Impact* (Gaborone: Freidrich Ebert Foundation, 2007), 74.

[103] African Development Bank Group, (n. 87).

[104] A. Saurombe, 'The Role of South Africa in SADC Regional Integration: The Making or Braking of the Organisation' (2010) 5(3) *Journal of International Commercial Law and Technology* 124–31.

[105] UN Department of Economics and Social Affairs, 'World Statistics Pocketbook 2011' Series V, No. 36 (United Nations, 2012) accessed 13 December 2016 at http://unstats.un.org/unsd/pocketbook/Pocketbook%202011.pdf.

[106] *Ibid*, 111.

[107] *Ibid*, 135.

[108] McCarthy (n. 12), 630.

of SACU's members, in particular Lesotho and Swaziland. Colin McCarthy notes the underlying rationale of the revenue pool as providing 'an explicit mechanism to compensate for economic asymmetry, with the dominant economic member willing to bear the cost of such an arrangement'.[109] Historically, South Africa has blocked renegotiation of the SACU Agreement and threatened to leave SACU as the arrangement should it become too costly.[110] An extensive evaluation of the customs revenue sharing formula is beyond the scope of this book but it is worth noting the importance of the CRP for the union's members.

South Africa has also taken measures to strengthen cohesion among SACU members by implementing common fiscal policies. The Rand Monetary Area (RMA), created in 1974, established financial linkages between South Africa, Lesotho and Swaziland. Creation of the Common Monetary Area (CMA) in 1986, (between South Africa, Lesotho and Swaziland) has further cemented the relationship of dependency as the currencies of BLNS are linked to the South African Rand. Although the CMA does not form part of SADC's economic integration strategy, the CMA has relevance to the region vis-à-vis SADC's members.[111] The fiscal harmonisation within SACU, through the inclusion of excise duties and sales tax into the revenue formula, exhibits signs of an economic union and goes beyond the framework of a customs union.[112]

However, the creation of the CMA can be perceived as a strategic measure to protect South Africa's hegemonic role within the region. Overall, membership to SACU has been beneficial for BLNS even though the terms of the agreement have been skewed in favour of South Africa from the beginning. In 2015, South Africa reportedly paid in 51.7 billion Rand to BLNS out of an estimated revenue pool of 80 billion Rand, or approximately 64 per cent of the pool.[113] This shows that through the phases of transition South Africa has adjusted its position vis-à-vis BLNS in an effort to support their integration into the global

---

[109] McCarthy (n. 12), 620.

[110] T. Bertelsmann-Scott, 'SACU-One Hundred Not Out: What Future for the Customs Union?' SAIIA Occasional Paper (September 2010) accessed 13 December 2016 at http://www.saiia.org.za/occasional-papers/77-sacu-one-hundred-not-out-what-future-for-the-customs-union/file.

[111] Oosthuizen (n. 40), 55.

[112] Hartzenberg and Maasdorp (n. 38), 445.

[113] L. Eshnor, 'SA "not getting a fair share" of regional customs revenue' *Business Day Live* news report (9 March 2015) accessed 13 December 2016 at http://www.bdlive.co.za/business/trade/2015/03/09/sa-not-getting-a-fair-share-of-regional-customs-revenue.

economy. The amount of money South Africa provides to the CRP compared with how much it withdraws reinforces the importance of SACU to South Africa. However, the dominant position of South Africa also shows that it has the potential to determine the future direction of integration and cooperation in the region.

Until recently, South Africa has had sole charge over the interest of SACU which has undoubtedly heightened the polarisation of development in the region. BLNS are producers of primary commodities, in particular precious metals/gem stones and agricultural products.[114] However, the region lacks a common industrialisation or agricultural policy. Much like the EU's CAP, South Africa is keen to protect its valuable agricultural sector. It would be desirable if SACU implemented a common industrial policy with a common agricultural policy within the bloc so as to accommodate the needs of the weaker BLNS States.[115]

South Africa relies on skilled and un-skilled workers from the region to form part of its workforce.[116] Labour markets in Southern Africa have been linked for centuries, even before colonization, and since the mines required vast numbers of workers cross-border migration became commonplace. As the oscillating migrant flows across countries in Southern Africa increased, other countries became reliant on this as a source of employment for their nationals. Consequently, the export of labour services to some extent determined the standard of living back home and the domestic industries remained relatively underdeveloped.

While macro-regionalism has proved relatively unsuccessful in terms of implementation, there have been interesting processes of regionalisation at the micro-level in the form of Spatial Development Initiatives (SDIs). These initiatives indicate commitment to working collaboratively beyond the textual limitations of the 2002 SACUA. SDIs are an example of micro-regionalism and have been utilised across Southern Africa. SADC has initiated a number of SDIs including the Southern African Power Pool (SAPP), the Maputo Development Corridor (MDC), and the Beira Corridor, to name but a few.

Integration in the energy sector has seen the creation of the SAPP, as a means to integrate the power grids of Southern African countries and

---

[114] M. Tsolo, I. Mogotsi and G. Motlaleng, 'The Impact of European Union-South Africa Trade Development and Cooperation Agreement on Botswana, Lesotho, Namibia and Swaziland' (2010) 3 *Review of Economic and Business Studies* 135.

[115] Meyn (n. 33), 95.

[116] Saurombe (n. 60), 126.

distribute the electricity to those living in rural areas.[117] This project also includes rehabilitating Mozambique's Cahora Bassa hydroelectric dam situated on the Zambezi River. The MDC is one of the most prominent and successfully implemented SDIs creating a transport corridor spanning from Gauteng and Mputhalanga in South Africa to Maputo in Mozambique. The SDIs are designed to promote economic activity in areas that have potential to grow which is yet to be realised. Underpinning the SDI framework are the principles of international competitiveness, regional cooperation and encouraging more diversified ownership. SDIs are designed to be 'short-term and targeted attempts to stimulate economic "growth" by creating globally competitive spatial entities through new investment, infrastructural development and job creation'.[118] They are a means of attracting private investment using public sector interventions to boost the national and regional economy. This demonstrates that while SADC has not yet issued a coherent regional plan on trans-border initiatives, it nevertheless sees their value for promoting regionalisation at the micro-level.[119]

Micro-regionalism and the activities of the private sector play an important part in 'new' regionalism. South Africa's business sector are key actors in executing the principles of Thabo Mbeki's 'African Renaissance'[120] in an attempt to build Africa's economies. For example, South African breweries have relocated to Tanzania, while its retailers such as Shoprite are now established in Zambia, Zimbabwe, Mozambique and most recently, Nigeria. Some of the more notable investments include 'US$1.1 billion in Pande and Temane gas fields in Mozambique by South Africa's fuel corporation (SASOL); $860 million in the expansion of the Mozal aluminium smelter project by BHP Billiton, the Independent Development Corporation (IDC) and Mitsubishi, and millions were spent by mobile communications company Vodacom in Tanzania'.[121]

South African investment in Southern Africa has been received with mixed opinion. On the one hand, it reinforces the dependence that has

---

117 Mulaudzi (n. 41), 52.

118 F. Söderbaum and I. Taylor, *Regionalism and Uneven Development in Southern Africa: The Case of the Maputo Development Corridor* (Aldershot: Ashgate, 2003), 2.

119 D. Tivera and A Chimovu, 'Situating the Maputo Development Corridor' in Söderbaum and Taylor (n. 118).

120 For a comprehensive account see F. Cheru, *African Renaissance: Roadmaps to the Challenge of Globalisation* (Cambridge: Cambridge University Press, 2002).

121 Mulaudzi (n. 41), 52.

characterised the region for so long while on the other hand, it appears to be a progressive step towards regional integration led by an African (rather than Western) State. It is generally accepted that South Africa has great influence over, and interest in, the direction of regionalism in Southern Africa. As a result of its subscription to the neoliberal agenda, the region's economic policies are outward-orientated. Ian Taylor identifies the 'disjuncture' between the liberal policies promoted through RTAs and the socio-economic reality on the ground:

> ... the problem in advancing a regionalism based on liberalism in Southern Africa, despite the hegemonic support it may enjoy at the global level and from the regional economic giant (South Africa), is the absence of hegemony at the national level across the region, with few exceptions. This reality militates against any triumphant application of a liberal project in the subcontinent and calls into question the very viability of most of SADC's policy prescriptions, expectations and, indeed, basic suppositions. What remains and is current is a 'virtual regionalism,' perhaps satisfactory to donors and maybe also to Pretoria's leadership, who seek to pass themselves off as the region's leaders.[122]

To say that Southern Africa has been shaped *entirely* in South Africa's vision would be exaggerating the power dynamic in the region. While power is certainly polarised in the region, to conceive South Africa as some sort of 'norm entrepreneur' implies a level of control and stability that this book argues is simply not present. Certainly, South Africa has been a major influence in the region, but to say the region is carved from South Africa's vision is perhaps a little fanciful. Rather, it is submitted that the region has been constructed through the culmination of internal and external forces that have influenced regional processes over many decades.

CONCLUSION

This chapter has traced the evolution of regions as legal regimes in the Southern African region and noted how the region has been collectively defined through 'norms of solidarity'. An expression of collective political will against colonisation and Apartheid led to the creation of SADC as a response to the coercive role of South Africa in the region. The legitimacy of SACU, as one of the oldest regional legal regimes in the

---

[122] Taylor (n. 94), 1242.

world, has also been challenged through collective expressions of discontent at the normative dominance of South Africa. However, over time, these regional arrangements have become increasingly disorganised and ineffective, suggesting that the capacity for collective political will formation among the Southern African States is diminishing. While it may seem as though the ideational force behind norms of solidarity has lost its emancipatory potential, collective political will formation in the discursive space of the EPA negotiations has reinstated the significance of norms of solidarity. The significance of Southern African actors in confronting the hegemonic nature of these new legal regimes will be explored in the next chapter.

8. The SADC EPA: a driver of development?

This chapter provides a critical reflection on the negotiation process that has resulted in the conclusion of the final text of the Southern African Development Community Economic Partnership Agreement (SADC EPA). On 10 June 2016, the SADC EPA was signed concluding negotiations that had spanned over ten years. Marking the first trade agreement of its kind between the EU and a regional community in Africa, the SADC EPA sends a signal to the rest of the world that EU-Africa cooperation is as strong as it has ever been. However, the journey toward the conclusion of this agreement has been laborious, and at various stages throughout the negotiations it was feared the conclusion of the EPA would not be realised. Of all the newly constructed regional groupings, the SADC EPA has been described as the 'most acrimonious and divisive'.[1] Its cartography cross-cuts three existing regional legal regimes in the Southern African space – Southern African Customs Union (SACU), SADC, and Common Market for Eastern and Southern Africa (COMESA) – adding another layer of complexity to the African space. It is too early to estimate the extent to which the EPA will foster sustainable development and deepen existing regional bonds in Southern Africa, but the purpose of this chapter is to provide insight into the ideological struggle that has made this particular EPA configuration a site of contestation.

The strategic motivation for creating a new interregional space in Southern Africa was rooted in the perceived need for WTO compatibility of the post-Lomé trade framework. In transforming the special relationship between the EU and the African, Caribbean and Pacific (ACP) countries, the EU sought to create a new legally integrated space through which its normative conception of development could be precipitated. From the outset, it was clear that the success of the EPA negotiations would hinge on the convergence between institutionalised legal norms at

[1] B. Vickers, 'Between a Rock and a Hard Place' (2011) 100 *The Round Table: The Commonwealth Journal of International Affairs* 186.

the WTO level (Article XXIV compatibility) and the EU's normative preferences expressed through its external trade policy in relation to trade *and* development.[2] Overall, the perceived desirability of the EPA would be elicited from a good discursive fit between the ideational preferences of the EU and the Southern African countries.

Initially conceived of as negotiations toward a full and comprehensive EPA, much like that concluded between the Caribbean Forum (CARIFORUM) states and the EU, the final text of the SADC EPA falls short of the EU's original ambitions. Rather than promoting deep liberalisation of trade in services, investment, procurement and competition, its focus remains solely on the liberalisation of trade in goods. Drawing on constructivist theory, this chapter illustrates how the African countries have expressed a growing opposition to the EU's market power and have formulated normative arguments, through a method of mimetic challenge, to reinstate the development focus of the EPAs.[3] Central to the small victory of the SADC EPA negotiating group to conclude a goods only agreement is the lack of congruence between the institutional requirement that the EPAs conform to WTO legal rules and the EU's normative conception of development as a neoliberal norm.[4] Initially, these institutional and ideational norms appeared to reinforce and presuppose one another, but it will be shown that throughout the negotiations, the necessity of WTO compliance has led to contradictions in the EU's strategy on trade and development, which has opened up a discursive space through which opposition groups have challenged the legitimacy of these legal regimes. It is the apparent disconnect between the logic of rational bureaucratised institutions, which determine 'action in an unambiguous fashion in line with rationalist expectations'[5] and the logic of ideas, through which actions of people can be explained 'as a result of people interpreting their world through certain ideational elements',[6] that has undermined the original ambitions of the EPA. It is through the

---

[2] T. Heron, 'Trading in Development: Norms and Institutions in the Making/Unmaking of European-African, Caribbean, Pacific Trade, Development and Cooperation' (2014) 20 *Contemporary Politics* 10-22, 11.

[3] S. Hurt, D. Lee and U. Lorenz-Carl, 'The Argumentative Dimension to the EU-Africa EPAs' (2013) 18 *International Negotiation* 67–87.

[4] Heron (n. 2).

[5] C. Parsons, *How to Map Arguments in Political Science* (Oxford: Oxford University Press, 2007), 66–7.

[6] *Ibid*, 96.

reflexive and deliberative engagement of actors that ideational forces can discursively challenge the materialist orientations of institutions, like the EU.

The first section of this chapter will provide a factual presentation of the construction of the new interregional EU-SADC EPA space with reference to the contentious issues that were raised throughout the negotiation process. The second section presents an analysis of the final EPA, setting out the scope of liberalisation codified under the agreement. In the final section, the EPA as a discursive site for participation and deliberation will be analysed.

CONSTRUCTING A NEW INTERREGIONAL SPACE

The SADC EPA region is comprised of Angola, Botswana, Lesotho, Mozambique, Namibia, South Africa and Swaziland. Its total population is approximately 89 million people, with 91 per cent of the population living in the two largest States, South Africa and Mozambique. Over the last decade, the regions real GDP grew by 3 per cent although there is significant variation among the SADC EPA States. As an interregional partner, the EU remains a key target market for the SADC EPA region exporting approximately €31.5 billion worth of goods in 2015, with the majority of goods originating in South Africa.[7] However, this accounts for just 1.8 per cent of the EU's total value of imported goods into the region and demonstrates that the SADC EPA States are relatively insignificant in commercial terms for the EU compared to its major trading partners such as China and the USA.

In 2004, the EU launched the EPA negotiations with Southern African countries in Windhoek, Namibia. From the outset of the negotiations, the EU expressed reluctance at the inclusion of South Africa within the group, as it already enjoyed preferential access to the EU market under the Trade, Development and Cooperation Agreement (TDCA). Another likely reason for its reluctance to welcome South Africa into the SADC EPA group stems from the informal classification of countries at the WTO through which preferential terms of trade may be offered. Unlike the institutional frameworks of the Bretton Woods institutions, and with the exception of least developed countries (LDCs) which are classified by

[7] European Commission, 'Trade in Goods with ACP – Southern African Development Community (SADC)' Trade Statistics (2015) accessed 13 December 2016 at http://ec.europa.eu/trade/policy/countries-and-regions/regions/sadc/index_en.htm.

the United Nations, the WTO permits the self-declaration of country status within its forum. South Africa has self-declared its status as a developing country, a position that the EU has long struggled to accept. In spite of these reservations, South Africa joined the SADC EPA group in 2004 with two strategic objectives in mind.[8] First, preserving SACU's functional coherence was a key concern for the SADC EPA countries and by joining the group the fragmentation of the existing regional arrangements, such as SACU, would be minimised. Second, the TDCA required greater liberalisation of agricultural exports from South Africa than that offered by the EU. In joining the negotiations, South Africa was able to gain more equitable access to the EU market for its agricultural products. This has enabled South Africa to achieve improved market access for 32 agricultural products and, in particular, wine, sugar and ethanol.

With the deadline for the EPA negotiations to conclude set for the end of 2007, it was the expectation that the full EPA would be finalised and implemented by the beginning of 2008. However, the 2007 deadline lapsed and not one ACP EPA had been signed or put into operation. To avoid losing their preferences altogether the EU offered duty free quota free (DFQF) access to those countries in the ACP who initialled an interim EPA (IEPA) with the view to concluding a full EPA by 2014, under EC Regulation 1528/2007. Keen to retain their preferential access to the EU market, the SADC-EPA countries agreed to sign an IEPA, limited to trade in goods only. By late 2012, the negotiations had reached a stalemate with only a handful of SADC states applying the IEPA. Botswana, Lesotho, Mozambique and Swaziland initialled the IEPA on 23 November 2007 and subsequently signed the agreement in June 2009. Namibia raised concerns relating to the content of the IEPA and reluctantly initialled the agreement on 3 December 2007 on the understanding that these issues would be comprehensively addressed during the negotiations toward the full agreement.[9] Namibia did not, however, sign the IEPA and it continued to 'free-ride' on the DFQF access offered by the EU. As Namibia was, and continues to be, classified as an upper-middle income country it did not qualify for the EU's GSP preferences. Failure to sign and apply the IEPA could have had significant economic implications for Namibia, had the EU followed through on its threat to

---

[8] R. Davies, 'The SADC EPA and Beyond' (October/November 2014) 3 *GREAT Insights Magazine* accessed 13 December 2016 at http://ecdpm.org/great-insights/economic-partnership-agreements-beyond/sadc-epa-beyond/.

[9] M. Julian, 'EPA Update' (2010) 9(3) *Trade Negotatiation Insights* (March) accessed 13 December 2016 at http://ictsd.org/i/news/tni/72888/.

withdraw preferential access under Regulation 1528/2007. For all non-LDCs across the ACP, the very prospect of losing preferential access to the EU was inconceivable. Arguably, the threat of withdrawal stipulated under Regulation 1528/2007 played a significant role in coercing the ACP to conclude the new legal regimes.

Angola did not present a market access offer to the EU and therefore did not initial the IEPA.[10] Classified as a LDC, Angola will continue to access the EU market preferentially under the Everything But Arms (EBA) Initiative and has remained an observer throughout the negotiations. South Africa chose not to initial the IEPA and continued to trade with the EU through the TDCA during the interim period. On 15 July 2014, the full EPA was initialled in Pretoria marking the end of the negotiation phase. This has been followed by a signing ceremony on 10 June 2016 and ratification processes in each individual state will now follow. The full EPA, while limited to trade in goods, offers more favourable terms than the TDCA in parts, and it is likely that South Africa will be keen to implement the new interregional agreement. Based on the Caribbean experience, it is probable that implementation of the EPA may take some time while the regional machinery is established.

As an Article XXIV compliant arrangement, the EPA contains 122 Articles, 4 protocols, and 11 annexes, creating a new interregional space through which liberalisation of trade in goods will be phased in asymmetrically and 'commensurate to the specific needs and capacity constraints of the SADC EPA States'.[11] Current trade forecasts project modest growth in regional GDP of just 0.01 per cent by 2035 once the EPA has been operationalised, compared to the counterfactual position of there being no EPA in place.[12] This figure is based on the benefit of tariff reduction alone and does not take into account the effects that rules of origin, trade facilitation and non-tariff barriers to trade may have on the region's economies. Given the variable geometry of the region, the EPA is likely to affect the countries in different ways but overall there is an expected increase of a meagre 0.91 per cent of exports from the SADC EPA region to the EU by 2035.[13] Of the primary commodities exported to the EU, red meat and sugar are likely to benefit the most from the EPA

---

[10] S. Woolfrey, 'State of Play in the SADC-EU EPA Negotiations' in A. Bösl, G. Erasmus, T. Hartzenberg and C. McCarthy, *Monitoring Regional Integration in Southern Africa Yearbook 2009* (Stellenbosch: tralac: 2009), 116.

[11] Article 20 EU-SADC EPA.

[12] EU Commission, 'The Economic Impact of the SADC EPA Group-EU Economic Partnership Agreement' of June 2016, 3.

[13] *Ibid*, 4.

and its implementation will be important for producers across the region. That said, it is not clear at this stage how the EU's non-tariff barriers to trade, such as food safety, labelling, and certification requirements, will affect market access.

The following section will explore the contestation of the new inter-regional space between the EU and Southern Africa. An examination of the dialogue that took place at the State level will be presented. Angola, Namibia and South Africa (collectively referred to as 'ANSA') have challenged the boundaries of this legal regime, suggesting the perceived lack of 'discursive fit' between the EU's ideology and the norms of Southern Africa. The EPA has also been met with fierce opposition by some non-state actors, which will also be discussed in the final section of this chapter. An examination of the dialogue that has taken place between State and non-state actors reveals how the region is being inter-subjectively constructed and contested across different spatial levels.

CONTENTIOUS ISSUES

In effect, the EPA is creating a new interregional space between the EU and seven southern African countries, which cuts across three existing regional initiatives (COMESA, SACU and SADC). ANSA had struggled to accept the normative terms of the EPA framework and sought to contest the construction of the interregional space. Since only 7 of the 15 SADC countries decided to negotiate in the SADC-EPA configuration, the first few years of the negotiation process were spent addressing issues of overlapping membership. In June 2008, ANSA submitted a full list of concerns relating to the trade regime to the EU. It was expected that these issues would be discussed in parallel sessions to the second phase of negotiations and that they would be addressed in the full EPA.[14]

It was feared that the existence of two different trade regimes, with their respective different tariff commitments, could effectively undermine the SACU common external tariff. Given the split in the group, it was essential to ensure SACU tariff coherence. As negotiations reached a stalemate in late 2008, the EU issued a 'non-paper' proposing that South Africa align its tariff levels with the commitments undertaken by BLNS in the IEPA. In 2009, ANSA submitted a joint démarche to the EU in response to the 'non-paper' and reiterated their concerns with the

---

[14] Woolfrey (n. 10), 116.

EPA process raised in 2008.[15] The démarche issued by ANSA to the EU raised four key concerns about the EPA process. First, ANSA argued that under the existing negotiating framework SADC countries will fall into four separate EPA configurations with the overarching effect of creating four separate trade arrangements with the EU. Each EPA will include different schedules of liberalisation and market access commitments. Since all SADC EPA countries are party to SADC, but not all are members of SACU, it will be necessary for the region to implement appropriate customs administrative measures to avoid trade deflection throughout both SADC and COMESA. This will be complex, costly and time-consuming.

Second, it was feared that the differing levels of commitment on new trade issues, such as investment and services, would result in unavoidable long-term policy divisions within the region. While EU rhetoric supports regional integration in Southern Africa and encourages the SADC EPA region to deepen its intra-regional commitments before engaging with the EU, this was simply not feasible under the existing timeframe, especially given the existing governance crisis of the region outlined in Chapter 7. ANSA asserted that the creation of four separate EPAs would only hamper efforts to build a stronger regional market. To this end, ANSA argued that 'this runs counter to the EU experience where regional rules, regional market opening and integration among EU Member States takes precedence over market openings to non-EU members'.[16] Given the complexity of the proposed trade regime and its uncertain implications for Southern African countries, it was unsurprising that many of them expressed frustration at the perceived pressure that the EU was placing on them to sign the IEPA.

Third, ANSA was particularly concerned about Angola's position within the EPA negotiating framework. As a LDC emerging from protracted crises it is critical that the EPA supports its integration into the global economy at a reasonable pace. Revenue loss associated with tariff liberalisation could have far-reaching socio-economic effects for Angola's vulnerable economy and it was, therefore, important that the EU adopted a sensitive approach to this vulnerability at all times

---

15 For information on the ANSA Joint Démarche submitted to the European Commission on 6 January 2007, see S. Woolfrey, 'State of Play in the SADC-EU EPA Negotiations', ch 6 in A. Bösl, G. Erasmus, T. Hartzenburg, C. McCarthy (eds), *Monitoring Regional Integration in Southern Africa Yearbook* (tralac, 2009) available 19 December 2016 at www.tralac.org.

16 *Ibid*, 2.

throughout the negotiations.[17] The dumping of cheaper EU imports onto the Southern African markets was also a primary concern of the ANSA group.

ANSA requested that the EPA process be a unified one, with just one phase of signature and ratification of a final EPA. In 2013, only four SADC EPA countries had signed the IEPA (Botswana, Lesotho, Mozambique and Swaziland) which merely intensified the already fractious nature of the negotiations. Having signed the IEPA, a new legal regime was in place between the EU and four of the seven SADC-EPA countries having the effect of reducing policy space in the negotiations towards a full EPA. The démarche argued that the IEPA was 'seriously flawed', foreseeing negative implications for regional integration and development in Southern Africa.

The EPA treats the region as economically homogenous, which is simply not the case. Liberalisation could have far greater implications for weaker countries, such as Angola, than for South Africa. It is highly questionable whether the EPA regime will be complementary to existing trade frameworks and ANSA feared that creating the legal framework at this stage will make it more difficult to make changes to the legal regime in the future. Since economies across the SADC EPA region are, with the exception of South Africa, vulnerable, the process of liberalisation on the proposed scale would need to be phased in at a rate that would not further exacerbate their economic fragility. The extent to which the concerns of ANSA have been reconciled with the strategic interests of the other SADC-EPA States in the final EPA is, in part, the subject of inquiry of this chapter.

Trying to reach a common negotiating position among the SADC-EPA countries had been a major stumbling block in the region's negotiations with the EU. There was not only dissonance with the EU's proposal for the interregional space, but there was no shared intra-regional consensus, no expression of 'norms of solidarity', to counter the regime. Over time, a clear division has developed between Botswana, Mozambique, Lesotho and Swaziland on the one hand, and ANSA on the other hand. With the divergent approach to negotiations among the SADC-EPA countries, the functioning of SACU has come under threat.[18] In addition to potentially destabilising SACU, the negotiations have fragmented the SADC-EPA regional space. It is submitted that the diverging views of the regional

---

17 *Ibid*, 3.

18 A. Walker 'The EU-SADC EPA: The Moment of Truth for Regional Integration' (2009) 8(6) *Trade Negotiation Insights* (August), accessed 13 December 2016 at http://ictsd.org/i/news/tni/52416/.

members led to an incoherent and uncoordinated approach to the negotiations, leaving the region in a state of disorder. In turn, this weakened the legitimacy of the SADC-EPA region as a newly created legal regime.

Across the ACP bloc, a matrix of 21 contentious issues had been identified in the negotiation phase toward the conclusion of comprehensive EPAs.[19] In relation to the 18 African countries that had signed or initialled an interim EPA before the conclusion of a full EPA, the African Union expressed its concern in relation to nine 'contentious' issues, including: the definition of 'substantially all trade'; transitional periods; export taxes; national treatment; free circulation of goods; bilateral safeguards; infant industry; the most favoured nation (MFN) clause; and, the 'non-execution' clause.[20] Of most concern to the SADC group were the clauses relating to export taxes, 'make or break' clauses, and the MFN clause.[21] Preferential rules of origin (ROO), which draw in EU rules on geographical indications, were also considered to present challenges to the coherence of regionalism for Southern Africa.

In 2009, and in light of the ongoing internal antagonisms between the SADC EPA countries, a meeting was held in Swakopmund in which the most contentious issues would be considered in detail. Namibia raised particular concerns in relation to the definition of 'substantially all trade', the MFN clause, tariffs and ROO, and the definition of the parties. These concerns were annexed to the IEPA with the intention that they would be fully resolved prior to the conclusion of the full EPA. A critical reflection of the translation of the contentious issues into the final EPA text will be provided in the third section of this chapter. At the State level, Namibia played a pivotal role in leading the opposition to the EU's proposed EPA

---

[19] South Centre, 'EPA Contentious Issues Matrix: Key Problems and Recommendations', *South Centre Analytical Note* (2010) SC/TDP/AN/EPA/26 accessed 13 December 2016 at http://southcentre.org/index.php?option=com_content&view=article&id=1347%3Aepa-contentious-issues-matrix-key-problems-and-some-recommendations&Itemid=67&lang=en.

[20] African Union, 'Addis Ababa Declaration on EPA Negotiations' AU Conference of Ministers of Trade and of Finance, 3 April 2008 available 19 December 2016 at https://www.au.int/en/sites/default/files/decisions/9558-assembly_en_30_june_1_july_2008_auc_eleventh_ordinary_session_decisions_declarations_tribute_resolution.pdf, 2.

[21] M. Julian, 'EPA Update' (2011) 10(1) *Trade Negotiation Insights* (February) accessed 13 December 2016 at http://ictsd.org/i/news/tni/100543/.

framework, and it is worthwhile exploring the contentious issues in order to better understand the context in which the full EPA has now been concluded.

Defining 'Substantially All Trade'

In the previous chapters, the paradigmatic shift from reverse preferences to reciprocity in EU-Africa cooperation has been analysed. Following the *EC-Bananas* disputes, all interregional agreements between the EU and ACP must be WTO compliant. As a result, the EPAs must meet the conditions set out in Article XXIV. It will be recalled that the legal definition of regionalism, under paragraph 8 of Article XXIV, requires the liberalisation of 'substantially all trade' within a 'reasonable period of time'. This requirement, in addition to the transitional periods during which tariff reduction must be progressively phased in, was identified as a contentious issue for the African countries.

Generally speaking, the EU has interpreted the substantially all trade requirement as an overall tariff reduction of 90 per cent between the parties. Liberalisation under the TDCA covers approximately 90 per cent of bilateral trade between South Africa and the EU on the basis that 95 per cent of EU imports from South Africa will be liberalised within 10 years and 85 per cent of South African imports from the EU will be liberalised over a period of 12 years.[22] In terms of phasing in tariff reductions to zero, the common position has been to implement liberalisation schedules within 10 years. However, through the course of the EPA negotiations the EU has shown some flexibility in relation to the transition period for the SADC configuration, allowing Mozambique, for example, a longer period in which to phase in tariff preferences. This is in line with the EPA model as a reciprocal but asymmetric legal regime accommodating the needs of LDCs within the negotiating group.

Liberalisation under the SADC IEPA was asymmetric with Botswana, Lesotho, Namibia and Swaziland liberalising 86 per cent of EU imports over four years, and Mozambique liberalising 81 per cent of EU imports

---

[22] Trade, Development and Cooperation Agreement, [2004] OJ L/127 as amended by Decision 2006/166/EC. See Europa Summary of EU Legislation 'Trade, Development and Cooperation Agreement' [undated] accessed 13 December 2016 at http://europa.eu/legislation_summaries/development/south_africa/r12201_en.htm.

by 2023.[23] Once the full EPA has been ratified and implemented, 98.7 per cent of South African exports will enter the EU market DFQF while customs duties will be eliminated on all products originating in the remaining five countries.[24] These countries have chosen to liberalise predominantly industrial and fisheries products, excluding some agricultural commodities as 'sensitive'. As highlighted above, the liberalisation schedule for BLNS corresponds with that of the TDCA between the EU and South Africa. With this in mind, it should be pointed out that BLNS already offer the EU *de facto* reciprocity on substantially all trade by virtue of their membership of SACU. To this end, SACU trade relations with the EU are, *stricto sensu*, WTO compliant.

Given that liberalisation will have higher adjustment costs for ACP countries as they implement the new trade regime, flexibility in the transition period is considered to be an essential part of the agreement.[25] Tariff reduction will not only result in revenue loss but it will also affect uncompetitive industries. Liberalisation will therefore affect different countries in various ways. ACP countries requested flexibility in the liberalisation schedules in order that they can protect 'sensitive' products as it was expected that goods with an applied tariff exceeding 20 per cent would be classified as 'sensitive'.[26] Governments were keen to exclude goods with an applied tariff higher than 20 per cent because those are usually a significant source of government revenue, particularly in developing countries.

Non-tariff Barriers to Trade

Non-tariff barriers to trade, such as ROO, technical barriers to trade (TBT) and sanitary and phytosanitary (SPS) measures were also among the contentious issues raise by the SADC EPA States throughout the

---

[23] European Commission, 'Fact Sheet on the interim Economic Partnership Agreements: SADC Group' *European Commission* (2009) accessed 13 December 2016 at http://trade.ec.europa.eu/doclib/docs/2009/january/tradoc_142189.pdf, 1.

[24] ICTSD, 'African countries and EU sign Economic Partnership Agreement' Bridges Africa Newsroom report (21 June 2016) accessed 13 December 2016 at http://www.ictsd.org/bridges-news/bridges-africa/news/newsroom-17.

[25] C. Ochieng, 'The EU-ACP Economic Partnership Agreements and the "development question": Constraints and Opportunities posed by Article XXIV and Special and Differential Treatment Provisions of the WTO' (2007) 10 *Journal of International Economic Law* 363–95.

[26] C. Stevens, 'The EU, Africa and EPAs: Unintended Consequences of Policy Leverage' (2006) 44(3) *Journal of Modern African Studies* 441–58.

negotiations. One of the main sticking points throughout the negotiations had been the proposed ROO regime under the EPA. Dissatisifed with the proposed system of cumulation which adopted a predominantly EU system of geographical indicators, and the fisheries ROO for Namibia and Mozambique, the SADC EPA states sought to contest the inclusion of these potentially harmful provisions.[27]

The purpose of ROO is to determine whether a particular product will qualify for preferential market access under the terms of a preferential trade agreement (PTA). ROO are therefore an important regulatory tool for PTAs. Given their overtly technical nature, ROO may be considered restrictive market access tools. In general, only goods that manufactured within a particular State will qualify for the preferential terms of trade offered under a PTA. It therefore remains the responsibility of exporting agencies to determine whether a product has complied with the terms of ROO set out under the RTA. Under the Cotonou framework, the ROO regime was very similar to that offered under Lomé. Recalling that Lomé was a non-reciprocal trade arrangement, the ROO codified therein reflect a unilateral offer of preferential market access extended to the ACP countries by the EU.[28] As is common for most RTAs to which the EU is party, different products are subject to different rules under Cotonou. Agricultural products generally need to comply with the requirements for 'wholly obtained' goods, meaning that the animal must be reared in the exporting country in order for origin to be conferred, for example. On the other hand, manufactured products were generally required to comply with the rules of substantial transformation under the technical test or change of tariff classification.

ROO under Cotonou were arguably most restrictive in relation to fisheries, textiles and clothing. Clothing, in particular, requires a two-stage transformation process in the exporting country in order to qualify for preferential access. Harmonisation of ROO would facilitate the free movement of goods on the international market. However, the ROO regimes under the EPAs seem to introduce another layer of complexity to the ever-increasing spaghetti bowl dynamic. Under the EPA, the ROO are set out in Protocol 1 and suggest that this regime is more relaxed in relation to clothing, textiles and sugar when compared with the EBA or generalised system of preferences (GSP).[29]

---

[27] Julian (n. 21).

[28] E. Naumann, 'Rules of Origin under EPAs: Key Issues and New Directions' in S. Bilal and R. Grynberg (eds), *Navigating New Waters: A Reader on ACP-EU Trade Relations* (London: Commonwealth Secretariat, 2007), 308.

[29] Walker (n. 18), 3.

Over time, ROO have become increasingly important market access tools. They are useful for implementation of anti-dumping and countervailing duties and safeguard measures, for example. However, Naumann argues that many ROO regimes have developed beyond their original purpose:

> ... many ROO regimes have evolved to become instruments and guardians of protectionism. Strict origin rules make compliance onerous, if not indeed impossible, especially for many developing countries with less developed infrastructure or domestic production capabilities ... it is no longer sufficient for a country to be able to merely produce a given input. These have to be produced within a given competitive framework, incorporating efficient and competitive lead times, prices, quantitative, qualitative and other characteristics ... ROO are often still used to protect 'sensitive sectors' and political economy elements remain present in most ROO regimes.[30]

While the EPAs offer preferences to their members, the ROO constrain participation of products within the preferential scheme on the international market.[31] Consequently, the SADC States could be left with preferences but without access.

Definition of the Parties

For the purposes of the EPA, the SADC-EPA states are deemed to act collectively. Definition of the parties was, therefore, a source of much concern for the negotiating parties in Southern Africa. There is no legal basis for the creation of this sub-group within the existing regional initiatives. Furthermore, it means that all SADC-EPA states could be jointly and severally liable in any dispute involving one of its members. As the EPA aligns with the TDCA, it is not clear where action will be deemed to have been taken by SACU or by a SACU Member State individually.

Export Taxes

While less common than ordinary import duties, export taxes may be applied to protect certain products. Export taxes are not prohibited by the

---

[30] Naumann (n. 28), 305–6.

[31] P. Collier and A. Venables, 'Rethinking Trade Preferences: How Africa Can Diversify Its Exports' (2007) 30(8) *World Economy* 1326–45, 1326.

WTO although Article XI:1 GATT does provide for the general elimination of quantitative restrictions which includes forms of export restriction such as licences. The EU has argued that the elimination of export taxes and restrictions is a necessary part of liberalising 'substantially all trade' within the meaning of Article XXIV GATT. Historically, the application of export taxes and licences has been associated with governments who are encouraging 'rent-seeking' behaviour. Like much of Africa, rent-seeking is rife in Southern Africa, especially in resource rich countries. Countries in Southern Africa that are resource rich include Angola (oil), Botswana (diamonds) and South Africa (diamonds and precious metals). It is in these types of economies that export taxes may have been used to protect particular industries. New export taxes have been abolished under the full EPA, and this will be discussed in the following section.

TOWARD THE NEW LEGAL REGIME

Overall, the primary aim of the EPA is to contribute to the 'reduction and eradication of poverty through the establishment of trade partnership *consistent* with the objective of sustainable development'.[32] Article 1 of the EPA sets out further objectives of the agreement as promoting regional integration, improving the capacity of SADC EPA states in trade policy and trade-related issues, increasing the competitiveness and attractiveness of the SADC EPA States for foreign investment, and strengthening the existing relationship between the EU and the Southern African region 'on the basis of solidarity and mutual interest'.[33] Article 1(b) sets out the formalisation of the interregional space as a legal regime, underpinning the rationalist conception of regionalism for the implementation of 'an effective, predictable, and transparent regional regulatory framework for trade and investment between the Parties and among the SADC EPA States'. Constructing the interregional space should reinforce

---

[32] Article 1 'Consolidated Text of the Economic Partnership Agreements Between the European Union and its Member States, of the one part, and the SADC EPA States, of the other part' adopted in accordance with the Communication from the European Commission 'Proposal for a Council Decision on the signing and provisional application of the Economic Partnership Agreement between the European Union Member States, of the one part, and the SADC EPA States, of the other part' COM (2016) 8 Final of 22 January 2016, hereinafter referred to as the 'SADC EPA'.

[33] Article 1 SADC EPA.

and complement existing regional strategies on the African continent 'taking into account the respective levels of development needs, geographical realities, and sustainable development strategies'.[34]

Part II of the EPA sets out liberalisation for trade in goods. Data from the European Commission's Report on the SADC EPA published in June 2016, provides details of the scope of liberalisation.[35] All products, with the exception of munitions, originating from the BLMNS States (Botswana, Lesotho, Mozambique, Namibia, Swaziland) shall enter the EU on a DFQF basis.[36] South Africa has excluded 1.3 per cent of tariff lines and has liberalised 98.7 per cent of its tariff lines through full and partial liberalisation. Trade provisions of the TDCA have been incorporated into the EPA. However, the EU will now gain access to the South African market through SACU with the intention that 'SACU imposes a single common external tariff, as customs unions are expected to do'.[37] Collectively, SACU has agreed to fully liberalise 71.4 per cent of tariff lines, partially liberalise 12.1 per cent, and has excluded a total of just under 14 per cent of tariff lines. As the first trade agreement of its kind with the EU, Mozambique has committed to fully liberalise 74 per cent of tariff lines with the EU, listing 26 per cent of tariff lines as 'sensitive' and excluded from liberalisation. In the period 2013–2015, the EU imported just over €22 billion worth of goods from the SADC EPA region, with 78 per cent of those goods originating in South Africa.[38] Similarly, approximately €26.5 billion worth of goods was exported from the EU to the SADC EPA region, with South Africa importing 92 per cent of those goods. Trade between the EU and SADC EPA region is, therefore, very much skewed toward South Africa.

In form, at least, the final EPA complies with Article XXIV albeit the extent to which liberalization will facilitate both economic freedom and non-economic freedom(s) will need to be monitored throughout the implementation period. While there is no specified time period for monitoring the implementation of the Agreement, the Parties have committed to a continual process of monitoring by the SADC EPA states regional institutions and the interregional institutions that will be set up under the EPA.[39] The primary institution overseeing the implementation is the Joint SADC EPA States-EU Council, which will be composed of

34 Article 3(3) SADC EPA.
35 European Commission (n. 12), 15–16.
36 Article 24 SADC EPA.
37 European Commission (n. 12), 17.
38 *Ibid.*
39 Article 4 SADC EPA.

ministerial officials from the EU and the SADC EPA States.[40] Regular meetings will be convened and decisions in the Joint Council will be taken by consensus and will be legally binding.[41] Assisting the Joint Council is the EPA Trade and Development Committee, which will be composed of senior officials from each individual EPA State.[42] The EPA Trade and Development Committee is responsible for monitoring implementation of the agreement, the recommendations of the Joint Council, and the development cooperation provisions. Its functions include making recommendations on trade and development cooperation matters, although it remains subordinate to the Joint Council. Successful monitoring hinges on the commitment of both sides to engage in regular constructive dialogue and the establishment of appropriate monitoring methodologies to truly capture the trade *and* development aspects of implementation.

Protecting SADC EPA State Industries and Economies

The proposed abolition of export taxes under the EPA was a contentious issue raised by the SADC EPA states, as export taxes are a significant source of revenue for their economies. Under the EPA, no *new* customs duties or export taxes shall be introduced beyond those currently applied at the time of signature of the agreement.[43] In exceptional circumstances, and where justified for specific revenue needs, environmental protection, infant industry protection and industrial development, and food security, the BLMNS States may impose temporary customs duties and export taxes.[44] If a temporary duty or tax is applied, the BLMNS state must notify the EU providing all information and the 'motivation' for the duty or tax, and shall enter into consultations with the EU if necessary. At any one time, the BLMNS can impose temporary duties and taxes on only eight products.[45] Imposing temporary customs duties and export taxes is not an unqualified right and the Parties must adhere to certain conditions for the duration of their implementation.[46] Any dispute relating to the use of customs duties or export taxes shall be reported to the EPA Trade and

---

40 Article 101 SADC EPA.
41 Article 102 SADC EPA.
42 Article 103 SADC EPA.
43 Article 26 SADC EPA.
44 Article 26(2) SADC EPA.
45 Article 26(3) SADC EPA.
46 Article 26(4) SADC EPA.

Development Committee, and the Parties shall enter into a process of consultation.[47]

Developing countries have vastly different development needs compared with developed countries. While infant industry strategies have attracted criticism in the past for their failure to generate growth, this does not mean that they are completely redundant. As regional integration across the ACP is still in its relatively early form, there is perhaps still potential for new *regional* industries to emerge. As such, infant industry protection is required through the EPA to insulate African industries from EU products deemed to be internationally competitive. In the spirit of promoting sustainable development in the EU-SADC EPA relationship, the agreement codifies the generous provision of safeguards, which the EU asserts is complementary to the 'flexibility' of market access granted by the EU. Three different types of bilateral safeguards are available to the BLMNS states relating to agriculture,[48] food security[49] and infant industry protection.[50] A further special 'transitional' safeguard is offered to the BLNS states to acknowledge the sensitive nature of their markets[51] in addition to a safeguard on payments and capital movements which is available to all Parties.[52]

As predominantly primary commodity agricultural producers, cooperation in agricultural trade is of particular significance to the SADC EPA states. Under Article 68, the EPA establishes an 'agricultural partnership' between the EU and SADC EPA States underscoring the importance of agriculture for 'food security, generating rural employment, increasing incomes of farm households, creating an inclusive rural economy, and as a basis for wider industrialisation and sustainable development'. While export subsidies on agricultural products have been abolished under the EPA framework, in keeping with the recent conclusion of the Nairobi Ministerial Conference of 2015 at the multilateral level, agricultural safeguards have been included within the legal framework. The agricultural safeguard provides that where the agricultural product falls within Annex IV, the SADC State concerned may apply a duty on the EU product of no more than 25 per cent of the current WTO bound tariff or 25 percentage points, whichever is higher, but it cannot

47 Article 26(6)–(10) SADC EPA.
48 Article 35 SADC EPA.
49 Article 36 SADC EPA.
50 Article 38 SADC EPA.
51 Article 37 SADC EPA.
52 Article 70 SADC EPA.

exceed the prevailing MFN applied rate.[53] Agricultural safeguards may only be applied for a maximum duration of five months[54] and the SADC states must notify the EU in writing within ten days of applying the measure in addition to notifying the Trade and Development Committee.[55] Review of the measure may be conducted by the Trade and Development Committee at the request of either Party.[56] There is a limitation period for the operation of the agricultural safeguard provision of 12 years from the entry into force of the EPA.[57] Importantly, and pursuant to the provisions of Article 34, the SADC EPA states may invoke the agricultural safeguard 'where essential for the prevention or relief of critical general or local shortages' of food or other products to ensure food security.[58] In light of the special development situation of the SADC EPA states, the food security safeguard may be in operation for an unspecified period of time but will be subject to annual review. Once the circumstances of crisis cease to exist, the safeguard must be removed.

Each safeguard is governed by a set of procedural rules although in each case, the safeguard mechanism may be triggered where an increase in quantity of EU products causes or 'threatens to cause serious injury' to the BLMNS economies. In Chapter 2, the link between safeguards and Article XXIV was discussed in relation to the *Argentina-Footwear* dispute.[59] Much like the interpretive uncertainty surrounding the 'substantially all trade' requirement in the full EPA, there is ambiguity surrounding the precise nature of invoking the safeguard provision.[60] For example, the agreement does not define the meaning of 'serious injury' or 'disturbance' and appears to limit the triggering of the mechanism to an increase in quantities of imports rather than price or volume triggers.[61]

---

[53] Article 35(2) EU-SADC EPA.

[54] Article 35(3) EU-SADC EPA.

[55] Article 35(5) EU-SADC EPA.

[56] Article 35(6) EU-SADC EPA.

[57] Article 35(7) EU-SADC EPA.

[58] Article 36 EU-SADC EPA.

[59] *Argentina – Safeguard Measures on Imports of Footwear*, Report of the Appellate Body, WT/DS121/AB/R, 14 December 1999.

[60] However, under the Safeguards Agreement, developing countries are protected under Article 9.1 which states: 'Safeguard measures shall not be applied against a product originating in a developing country Member as long as its share of imports of the product concerned in the importing Member does not exceed 3 percent, provided that developing country Members with less than 3 percent import share collectively account for not more than 9 percent of total imports of the product concerned'.

[61] Article 34 EU-SADC EPA.

In failing to define what constitutes 'serious injury' it seems likely that its interpretation will be influenced by the strict application at the WTO level. Certainly, if the EU adopts a textual and formalist interpretive approach to the provision as it has done in disputes concerning Article XXIV, it seems likely that a strict and narrow interpretation will prevail. While the EPA provides generous provisions on safeguards 'it is difficult to foresee whether the use of such safeguards will be warranted in the future'.[62]

MFN Clause

The MFN Clause is enshrined in Article 28 of the EPA and its scope is far-reaching. Indeed, this book submits that the MFN Clause is arguably one of the most troubling aspects of the EPAs in general. Although the scope and application of Article 28 is asymmetric, its coverage is broad relating to customs duties (Article 26), fees and other charges (Article 27), and regional arrangements concluded after the date of signature of the EPA. The EU has committed to extending to the SADC EPA States 'any more favourable treatment' with any third parties, while the provision setting out the commitments of the SADC EPA States provides:

> With respect to customs duties ... and fees and other charges ... the SADC EPA States shall, upon the request of the EU, extend to the EU any more favourable treatment applicable as result of the SADC EPA States, *individually or collectively* as the case may be, becoming party to a preferential trade agreement with *any major trading economy*.

Within this clause are two terms that give rise to notable interpretive difficulties. First, the definition of the SADC EPA States acting 'individually or collectively' and second, the concept of a 'major trading economy'. As BLNS are part of SACU, it would not be unreasonable to infer that 'collective' action refers to an agreement that might be negotiated between SACU with another *major trading economy*, or the SADC-EPA States as a new legal entity entering into a trade agreement with another *major trading economy*. If this is the case, then the only country that might act individually is Mozambique. As one of the stated goals of the EPA is to harmonise the SACU region, as evidenced by the EU now accessing the South African market vis-à-vis SACU, this seems a plausible conclusion to draw.

---

[62] EU Commission (n. 12), 9.

'Major trading economy' is defined in the EPA as meaning 'any developed country, or any country accounting for a share of world merchandise exports above 1 percent' *or* 'any group of countries acting individually, collectively or through an economic integration agreement accounting *collectively* for a share of world merchandise exports above 1.5 per cent'.[63] In effect, this provision circumscribes the SADC EPA State's bargaining potential with countries like, China, and regional groups such as NAFTA, MERCOSUR, and ASEAN, all of which represent a share of world merchandise exports that exceeds 1.5 per cent.[64] An exclusion to the MFN provision applies where the SADC EPA states enter into a preferential arrangement with other ACP countries.[65] This is hardly surprising as the ACP countries do not have a significant presence in the share of world merchandise exports and in addition, the EPAs are likely to be broadly similar in terms of their scope and coverage for trade in goods.

In light of this, it seems difficult to reconcile the MFN clause with the development goals of the EPA framework. In the lead up to the conclusion of the full EPA, the South Centre called for the removal of this provision arguing that:

> … the MFN Clause carves out Africa's resources and markets for the EU, in line with EU's Global Europe Strategy. Forcing EPA Parties to provide equal treatment to the EU as what they might in the future provide to India, China and Brazil, impedes 'South-South' trade and undermines (future) negotiation positions with these other developing countries (but also the US and other major economies). Furthermore, it makes it difficult for LDCs to get Duty Free Quota Free market access from other developing countries.[66]

Incorporating the MFN clause into the Agreement protects the EU's relationship with the SADC EPA States and maintains its hegemonic position within the interregional space. It is submitted that by circumscribing the negotiating space of the SADC EPA States to pursue more beneficial terms of trade with other major trading economies without extending the same preferences to the EU is an attempt to limit the bargaining potential of the SADC EPA States. Furthermore, such a position is antagonistic to the concept of 'owning' one's development

---

[63] Article 28(6) EU-SADC EPA.

[64] World Trade Organisation, 'International Trade Statistics 2015 – Special Focus: World Trade and the WTO: 1995–2014' (2015) accessed 13 December 2016 at www.wto.org/stats, 26.

[65] Article 28(3) SADC EPA.

[66] South Centre (n. 19), 5–6.

process. The MFN clause represents a clever manipulation of Article 1 GATT and Article XXIV which legally formalises the EU's dominant position within this hegemonic North-South legal regime. In sum, it seems as though applying the MFN clause could actually hamper, rather than promote, the integration of ACP developing countries into the global economy.

Technical Barriers to Trade

In relation to non-tariff barriers to trade, such as technical barriers to trade (TBT) and sanitary and phytosanitary (SPS) measures, the EPA foresees the mutual cooperation between the Parties on priority issues and sectors. Cooperation should involve 'developing common views and approaches on technical regulatory practices, including transparency, consultation, necessity and proportionality, the use of international standards, conformity assessment requirements, the use of impact and risk assessment, [and] enforcement and market surveillance, where appropriate'.[67] Article 60 provides that SPS measures should be adopted *'only* to the extent necessary to protect human, animal or plant health or life in accordance with the provisions of the WTO SPS Agreement'. As the interregional legal framework is herein multilateralised, it seems probably that the 'necessity test' relating to SPS measures raised in the Article XX disputes at the WTO Dispute Settlement Body (DSB) will be relevant in the interpretation of SPS measures in the EPA. The Parties have agreed to consider negotiating mutual recognition agreements (MRAs), which relate to certification and food safety standards, in 'sectors of mutual economic interest'.[68] Overseeing and monitoring the cooperation on non-tariff barriers, the EPA Trade and Development Committee will provide consultations on relevant issues and assist in the identification and monitoring of priority sectors.[69]

Dispute Settlement

Emphasis on resolving disputes through cooperation and political dialogue, without recourse to a dispute settlement mechanism, is at the heart of the EPA. However, a dispute settlement mechanism is established under Chapter III of the EPA and provides that the Parties may initiate

67 Article 56 SADC EPA.

68 Article 56(g) SADC EPA.

69 Article 57 SADC EPA in relation to TBT and Article 65 in relation to SPS.

arbitration proceedings where they have failed to resolve a dispute using a consultative process.[70] Once the request to initiate arbitration has been received by the EPA Trade and Development Committee a Panel will be composed consisting of three members in accordance with Article 94 of the EPA. An arbitral report will be issued no later than 150 days following the composition of the Panel and within 90 days, where possible, if the dispute relates to perishable and seasonal goods.[71] Compliance with the panel's findings is expected to be executed within a 'reasonable period of time', the definition of this term to be established by the Panel on a case-by-case basis.[72] The measure adopted by the Party complained against to implement the Panel's recommendations shall be notified to the Panel and the respondent and where any dispute arises as to the compatibility of that measure with the EPA, the original Panel may rule on the matter.[73] In cases of non-compliance, the Party complained against may be required to pay compensation to the respondent although there is no obligation to do so.[74] The injured party may implement retaliatory measures if non-compliance continues.[75] Although the EPA dispute settlement mechanism is structured in a very similar way to the WTO's dispute settlement system, there is option for appeal under the EPA's institutional framework. While the Parties are not precluded from initiating a dispute within the WTO system for any matter arising under the EPA, if the Parties *have* initiated a dispute within the EPA dispute settlement mechanism they must not initiate a dispute under Article 6 of the WTO's Dispute Settlement Understanding until the proceeding under the EPA framework has been finalised. In this way, an appeal is technically available, albeit through an alternative forum.

Sustainable Development

The development chapter of the EPA comprises just five provisions (Articles 6–11), with development cooperation set out in Article 12. Ensuring that trade liberalisation leads to sustainable development remains a priority for the Parties and Article 6(2) of the EPA provides:

---

[70] Article 79 SADC EPA.
[71] Article 81 SADC EPA.
[72] Article 84 SADC EPA.
[73] Article 85 SADC EPA.
[74] Article 86(1) SADC EPA.
[75] Article 86(2) SADC EPA.

> The Parties reaffirm their commitments to promote the development of international trade in such a way as to contribute to the objective of sustainable development, in its three pillars (economic development, social development, and environmental protection) for the welfare of present and future generations, *and will strive to ensure that this objective is integrated and reflected at every level of their trade relationship.* (emphasis added)

This is further reinforced in Article 7 wherein the Parties agree to 'work cooperatively *towards* the relationship of people-centred sustainable development'. Separate provisions dedicated to environmental protection and labour standards (Articles 8–9) say very little about the way in which the EPA relates to these aspects of sustainable development. Aside from the recognition that the 'value' of 'international economic governance' and 'decent work' are important elements of sustainable development, the provisions do little more than require Parties to comply with existing international obligations. There is a margin of appreciation afforded to individual EPA states to establish their own levels of environmental protection and labour standards, provided that any regulatory reform in accordance with the EPA does not fall below existing standards. As such, the international commitments on labour standards and the protection of the environment in force at the date of signature should represent *de minimis* standards from which the Parties shall not derogate.[76]

An interrogation of the language used in the articulation of the sustainable development provisions is important for an analysis of the EPA as a trade and development cooperation agreement. Use of the phrases 'will strive' (Article 6) and 'work cooperatively towards' (Article 7) imply that the principle of sustainable development is not mandatory but rather one to which the Parties should aspire to achieve. As such, in the context of the EPA, the principle of sustainable development is not recognised as a legal norm *per se*, but rather the articulation of Article 6 and Article 7 suggest that the principle may be used as a hermeneutic interpretive tool, similar to the approach adopted by the ICJ and WTO's DSB, examined in Chapter 4. The objective of sustainable development is understood as requiring that the Parties 'fully take into account the human, cultural, economic, social, health, and environmental best interests of their respective populations and of future generations' through decision-making processes that 'embrace the fundamental principles of ownership, participation, and dialogue'.[77] Therefore, promoting 'development-friendly' trade will require the interregional legal regime to

---

[76] Article 9(3) SADC EPA.
[77] Article 7(2) SADC EPA.

create a participative discursive space through which mutual understandings on trade and development issues can emerge. Only from a deliberative process, involving both State and non-state actors, can the EPA as a legal regime make a normative claim to legitimacy.

Development Cooperation

Development cooperation may come in various financial and non-financial forms[78] and may include: policy development, regulatory and legislative reforms; institutional development; capacity building and training; technical advisory services; administrative services; support in SPS and TBT, especially in the negotiation of MRAs; and operational support.[79] Additional funding may be channeled through the Regional EPA Fund, an interregional financing mechanism, if the Parties decide to establish one.[80] Currently, the total funding available under the 11th EDF for SADC EPA implementation is €400 million, with €170 million granted through the National Indicative Programmes (NIPs) and €230 million through the East Africa-Southern Africa-Indian Ocean Regional Indicative Programme (EA-SA-IO RIP).[81] Additional funding of €600 million from intra-ACP programmes to support private sector development and €17 million from the Pan-African DCI is expected.[82] The NIPs will be focused and targeted toward agricultural business as trade in agricultural goods forms the primary focus of the EPA.

Further delays in the SADC EPA negotiations arose in response to the market access request submitted to the EU in 2010 wherein the SADC EPA countries requested tariff concessions in relation to agricultural commodities originating in South Africa.[83] Throughout the negotiation phase, the SADC EPA countries confirmed that they were willing to discuss 'cooperative agreements' on investment, procurement and competition but only on the basis that these discussions did not lead to legally binding obligations or a commitment to negotiate in these sectors going forward.[84] Although the negotiations towards a full EPA foresaw the

---

[78] Article 12(1) SADC EPA.
[79] Article 15 SADC EPA.
[80] Article 10(6) SADC EPA.
[81] European Commission (n. 12), 22.
[82] *Ibid.*
[83] M. Julian and M. Dalleau, 'EPA Update' (2011), *Trade Negotiation Insights*, Volume 10 Number 7, October 2011 accessed 13 December 2016 at http://ictsd.org/i/news/tni/115340/.
[84] *Ibid.*

liberalisation of services and investment, it had been agreed that policies on competition and procurement would not be negotiated until adequate regional capacity had been built.[85]

In short, it seemed apparent that the schedules of the IEPA could lead to heightened incoherence in the trade regime of the SADC-EPA region. While the commitments of BLNS align to a large extent with South Africa's commitments under the TDCA, there appears to be little alignment between BLNS and Mozambique. Furthermore, it was anticipated that the different, and conflicting, ROO regimes under the IEPA and TDCA will be problematic for the region. However, under the full EPA the ROO regime is actually more favourable than the framework of the TDCA with the Protocol on Geographic Indications granting greater protection to South African products, such as roobois, honeybush, and karoo lamb.[86] The shift toward more favourable ROO under the EPA is certainly a small victory for the SADC-EPA States.

THE EPA: A DISCURSIVE SPACE FOR DELIBERATION

The epistemological claims of this book are rooted in Habermasian discourse theory, set out in Chapter 1, as the EPAs have been constructed as legal regimes constituted through deliberative and participative processes among different stakeholders. Legitimacy of the agreements, it has been argued, rests on the extent to which the final EPA reflects the process of democratic self-legislation achieved through that deliberative process. Admittedly, Habermasian discourse theory is a grand theory but it offers a useful analytical lens through which the legitimacy of the EPA can be interrogated. This section aims to uncover the discursive space that emerged in the SADC-EPA deliberative process to highlight the different ideational forces that have shaped the outcome of the negotiations.

The failure of the EU to translate its special relationship with the ACP into comprehensive trade and development cooperation agreements presents an analytical puzzle. With its perceived strength as an international actor, the conclusion of comprehensive EPAs was thought to be a foregone conclusion in 2004. Understanding why the comprehensive EPAs in Africa failed to materialise requires an analysis of the different ideational forces that have emerged within the SADC EPA space from an

---

85 European Commission (n. 23), 3.

86 *Ibid.*

institutional and civil society perspective. A dominant materialist narrative that features throughout the literature accounting for this failure is the variability and heterogeneity of the ACP countries which has made the shift toward reciprocity an uneasy one.[87] However, these positivist accounts fail to accommodate non-material ideational motivations that have proved to be a valuable policy tool for developing ACP countries.

A more nuanced approach is offered by Tony Heron, who identifies the disjuncture between institutional and ideological norms in the bargaining process. Heron proposes that the EU's insistence on creating WTO compatible legal regimes, in light of the *EC-Bananas III* dispute, created the most significant obstacle to the negotiations.[88] Constructing 'imagined' regions from the ACP bloc, regions that were economically diverse, in order to satisfy the requirements of Article XXIV merely exacerbated what was already going to be a difficult process. From the European Commission's perspective, requiring Article XXIV compatibility 'would mean that the EU's future trade arrangements were perfectly in line with WTO provisions and require no exceptions'.[89] While this requirement initially appeared to coalesce with the EU's normative neoliberal conception of development, an assumption that liberalisation leads to economic development, it soon became obvious that the two ideals were incompatible. It was this incompatibility between the Article XXIV concept of a region as a legal regime and the normative concept of development that created a discursive space through which opposition to the EPAs could be articulated. Somewhat ironically, it was the EU's discourse of 'development friendly' trade that became a 'weapon of the weak' throughout the EPA negotiations.[90]

Various State and non-state actors sought to challenge the negotiation of the EPAs, although their strategies lacked sufficient coherence. Hurt et al propose that the African ACP countries engaged in a form of rhetorical

---

[87] M. Manger and K. Schadlen, 'Political Trade Dependence and North-South Trade Agreements' (2014) 58 *International Studies Quarterly* 79–91.

[88] T. Heron, 'Trading in Development: Norms and Institutions in the Making/Unmaking of European-African, Caribbean, Pacific Trade and Development Cooperation' (2014) 20 *Contemporary Politics* 10–22.

[89] European Commission, 'Guidelines for the negotiation of new cooperation agreements with the African, Caribbean and Pacific (ACP) countries' COM (97) 537 Final of 29 October 1997.

[90] Hurt, Lee and Lorenz-Carl (n. 3).

action known as 'mimetic challenge', a process which involves 'mimicking the discourses and norms of your main protagonist in a negotiation'.[91] Through this form of rhetorical action, the African states have challenged the strategic orientation of the EPA negotiations through a process of normative argumentation. Shifting the focus back on to development concerns enabled African states to offer a counterfactual discourse that became a source of influence in the bargaining process. Mimicking the normative principles underpinning the EU's external action, and reminding the EU of its commitment to both trade liberalisation *and* development, became a powerful weapon in the fight for a more balanced trade agreement that reflected the needs of the African countries. Mimetic challenge has also been exhibited through the rhetorical action of non-state actors through networks of civil society actors and private sector actors.

At the State level, representations were made to the EU by ACP government officials troubled by the proposed scope of liberalisation under the EPAs. In the CARICOM configuration, the President of Guyana refused to sign the full EPA until certain revisions were made and the review clause was included into the Agreement. Similarly, the delaying tactics of Namibia during the negotiation process of the SADC EPA surprised many. The actions of these two small and relatively weak governments in contesting the dominant discourse of the EPA framework was both unexpected and unprecedented. Neither Namibia nor Guyana possess the international presence or strength in negotiating power comparative to the EU, and yet both countries effectively stalled the negotiations of their respective regional EPAs. Rob Davies, the South African Minister for Trade and Industry, outlined the concerns of the SADC region:

> … the major problems have arisen from the EU's ambition to move beyond WTO compatible free trade agreements covering trade in goods, to agreements also embracing trade in services and new generation issues, involving serious commitments in areas such as investment, government procurement, competition policy and the like … [These issues] are *linked to global strategies to promote the offensive interests of European companies across the world*.[92]

---

[91] *Ibid.*

[92] R. Davies, 'Bridging the divide: the SADC EPA' (2008) 7 *Trade Negotiation Insights* 1-2 cited in T. Heron and P. Murray-Evans, 'Limits to Market Power: Strategic Discourse and Institutional Path Dependence in the European Union – African, Caribbean, and Pacific Economic Partnership Agreements' (2016) *European Journal of International Relations* 16 (emphasis added).

When the 2007 deadline to complete the EPA passed without success, the EU offered DFQF access to its market to the SADC-EPA countries that agreed to *initial* a 'goods only' interim EPA, on the basis that negotiations towards a full EPA would be ongoing. Angola and South Africa were already trading with the EU under separate legal regimes[93] and, therefore, the decision to initial/sign an interim agreement fell to the BLNS and Mozambique. While Botswana, Lesotho, Mozambique and Swaziland signed the interim EPA, Namibia refused to do so until the contentious issues had been adequately dealt with by the EU.[94] The then Prime Minister, and now Namibian President, Hage Geingob, has been particularly outspoken about the negotiations, arguing that the EPAs are not based on 'equal' partnership and that 'equal partners do not give each other deadlines'.[95] However, he noted that Namibia's status as a middle-income country had placed it in a 'tough negotiating position'.[96] Namibia eventually initialed the interim agreement and enjoyed DFQF access to the EU and was free riding on the interim EPA. However, the EU is Namibia's largest export market with approximately 30 per cent of products bound for the EU. So while Namibia actively challenged the EU's external policy, ultimately it knew the EU's market was a valuable source of revenue for the country.

The role of power in securing policy preferences cannot be overstated in the trade negotiation process. Using the 'carrot and stick' approach to trade, the EU makes attractive offers to developing countries that are often too weak to resist.[97] Where asymmetry in the bargaining positions of the parties is pre-existing, the dominant State will be able to exploit

---

93 As a least-developed country, Angola accesses the EU's market duty-free-quota-free under the 'Everything But Arms' Initiative. Since 2000, South Africa has traded with the EU under the Trade, Development and Cooperation Agreement (TDCA).

94 Botswana, Lesotho, Mozambique and Swaziland initialled the interim EPA on 23 November 2007. Namibia raised concerns relating to the EPA but initialled the interim agreement on 5 December 2007 with the understanding that the contentious issues would be comprehensively dealt with during the negotiations towards a full EPA. There are various contentious issues but those most relevant to the SADC-EPA countries include the MFN clause, abolition of export taxes and the definition of the parties.

95 M. Thomas, 'EU's decision to stick to deadline irks Geingob' *The Namibian* 9 August 2012 accessed 13 December 2016 at http://www.namibian.com.na/index.php?id=98498&page=archive-read.

96 *Ibid.*

97 E. Hafner-Burton, *Forced to Be Good: Why Trade Agreements Boost Human Rights* (Ithaca: Cornell University Press, 2009).

the weaker party and pursue its own preferred objectives. This is the case in the ACP-EU relationship which has become one characterised in part by the coercive measures of the EU through its threat to withdraw preferences altogether under Regulation 1528/2007 and supports the conception of these agreements as hegemonic legal regimes. ACP dependence on the EU has deepened over time and this has paved the way for the Europeanisation of the trade relationship. Noting the market power of the EU, Mareike Meyn argued that 'the EU largely failed to sell its EPA development concept to the ACP, but managed to push through the idea of a comprehensive free trade agreement by benefiting from an asymmetry of power and negotiating abilities'.[98] Power, therefore, played a significant role in securing the conclusion of the EPA negotiations even though there existed divergence between institutional norms and ideational norms.

Throughout the EPA negotiations, the role of non-state actors was pivotal in contesting the legitimacy of the agreements. This was made possible through the discursive space that had emerged from the incongruence of the necessity to negotiate WTO compatible agreements and the EU's normative conception of sustainable development. While the EPA negotiations are conducted at the international level by the relevant ministry, usually the Department for Trade and Industry, the CPA also envisaged stakeholder participation as 'complementary' to the development process.[99] The CPA outlines that non-state actors should be informed and involved in the negotiation process, given financial assistance to support local development policies and to promote strategic alliances. Participation is reinforced in Article 21 of the CPA, which outlines the importance of ensuring that 'cooperation' leads to a 'favourable environment for private investment and the development of a dynamic, viable and competitive private sector'. Cooperation between the state level and non-state level, or in Habermasian terms, between the *system* and *lifeworld,* should support the implementation of 'structural policies designed to reinforce the role of difference actors, especially the private sector'.[100]

Non-state actors are often highly specialised and are able to offer critical insight into the potential effects of the EPA for certain sectors and groups in society. Civil society therefore has an important role in shaping their countries' approach to protecting social, cultural, religious and

---

[98] M. Meyn, 'Economic Partnership Agreements: A "Historic Step" Towards a "Partnership of Equals"?' (2008) 26 *Development Policy Review* 516.

[99] Article IV Cotonou Partnership Agreement 2014.

[100] Article 22 Cotonou Partnership Agreement 2014.

ethnic normative interests. Private sector organisations are likely to be influenced by predominantly material interests, while civil society organisations act as 'discourse entrepreneurs'[101] representing the 'conscience of mankind'.[102] For example, at the EU level, the dominant discourse emerging from the business sector was strategically oriented and rooted in economic instrumentalism. Organisations such as the Confederation of European Business (UNICE) had an influential role in the negotiation process declaring that it acted as the 'voice of business in Europe'.[103] UNICE expressed its 'strong support' for the EPA as a tool for increasing the competitiveness of the ACP economies and urged the EU and ACP to promote good governance within the development cooperation aspect of the agreements, noting:

> A stable economic, social and political system based on the rule of law is the fundamental basis for economic development in the ACP and the EU. The EPA process should contribute to good governance by strengthening legal regimes and by promoting best practice in the ACP countries. Special consideration should be given to eradicating corruption, which undermines development and makes doing business very difficult at all levels.[104]

UNICE reiterated that the EPA should be complementary to other ongoing development initiatives and that the broad liberalisation schedule beyond goods will stimulate economic growth. However, it also acknowledges the need for 'targeted' development assistance to improve the standard of education and healthcare across the ACP countries.[105]

Promoting social, cultural and political normative conceptions of the 'good' generally falls beyond the remit of the private sector and is instead assumed by civil society organisations. Historically, human rights NGOs have 'tended to cluster geographically in economically affluent Western states rather than in developing countries, and ideologically in support of

---

[101] A. Holzcheiter, 'Discourse as Capability: Non-state Actors' Capital in Global Governance' (2005) 33 *Millennium: Journal of International Studies* 723–46.

[102] C. Welch, 'Human Rights and Development: NGOs' in P. Zeleza and P. McConnaughay (eds), *Human Rights, The Rule of Law, and Development in Africa* (Philadelphia: University of Pennsylvania Press, 2004).

[103] UNICE, 'Economic Partnership Agreements with Africa, Caribbean and Pacific Countries: UNICE Position on the EPA Process' Executive Summary (9 May 2005) accessed 13 December 2016 at https://www.businesseurope.eu/publications/unice-position-epa-process-economic-partnership-agreements-africa-caribbean-and-pacific.

[104] *Ibid*, 5.

[105] *Ibid*, 6.

civil and political rights far more than in support of economic, social and cultural rights'.[106] Successful discursive practices can be developed in the transnational public sphere where non-state actors create networks, or 'modes of association', to disseminate a critical message to both policymakers and the general public about the potential negative implications of trade agreements. Engaging in a deliberative and intersubjective process through which mutual understandings on normative expectations can be established, transnational campaigning contributes to the evolution of international norms.[107] In the context of the EPA negotiations, non-state actors employed discursive tactics to challenge the legitimacy of the agreement by confronting EU policy makers on the more contentious aspects of the agreements.[108] Once confronted by a counterfactual argument, the EU became trapped in reconciling its rhetoric of requiring WTO compliance and its own normative conception of development. In Habermasian terms, the EU's rhetoric was caught between strategic and communicative action.

Participation in the transnational public sphere, at the formal and informal levels, enables non-state actors to 'draw from abstract but socially shared systems of ideas (ideologies), craft and re-signify ideas according to their aims in specific socio-cultural-political contexts, and transmit them to others through written and oral language, or other visual symbols'.[109] Trade negotiations take place at the abstracted level, far removed from the lived experience of society. However, trade agreements inevitably impact the conditions under which society must survive. A fundamental role for non-state actors remains the translation of material interests and institutional ideology perpetuated at the state level into everyday language cognisable by society.[110] Once the technocratic barrier has been broken down, meaningful discursive strategies can be established through the communicative deliberative process at the societal level through which mutual understandings on a normative response to the proposed trade agreements can be organised. Of course, the success of such a deliberative process rests on the ability of civil society

---

106 *Ibid*, 201.

107 M. Keck and K. Sikkink, *Activists Beyond Borders: Advocacy Networks in International Politics* (Ann Arbor, MI: Michigan University Press, 1998).

108 See Hurt, Lee and Lorenz-Carl (n. 3); C. Del Falice, 'Power in Discursive Practices: The Case of the "Stop the EPAs" Campaign' (2014) 20 *European Journal of International Relations* 145–67.

109 Del Falice (n. 108), 150.

110 Oxfam International, Action Aid, and Christian Aid produced easily accessible texts of the EPAs for dissemination in the public sphere.

organisations to organise collectively through 'modes of association' and the interest of society to engage with that discursive practice.

At the international level, civil society groups such as Oxfam and Traidcraft have been campaigning against the EPAs for some time under the 'Stop the EPAs' coalition campaign. In its first public statement, the campaign sought to debunk myths about the EPAs in order to raise support for opposing these legal regimes.[111] Drawing on the material explanations for the EPAs put forward by institutions and governments, the coalition sought to explain how the EPA framework was *not* about development and did *not* require the extent of WTO compliance demanded by the EU. This document lacks a clear message as to how the EPAs are of relevance to the organisations of the coalition but arguably this approach gave a greater degree of legitimacy to the campaign as the arguments were firmly grounded in rationalist accounts of trade and development rather than 'unreasonable claims from civil society'.[112]

Del Falice identifies two approaches to the discursive strategies of the civil society coalitions: reformist and isolationist.[113] Reformist strategies concurred that the EPAs would lead to sustainable development through trade albeit the EPAs needed to be reformulated to achieve their objectives. Isolationist strategies, on the other hand, were focused on opposing the EPAs altogether, conceiving of these as hegemonic legal regimes that would merely reinforce structural dependency of the ACP on the EU. At the international level, the 'Stop the EPAs' campaign was more reformist in its orientation, while the regional strategy appears to exhibit a stronger isolationist flavour.

At a regional level, Third World Network and the Africa Trade Network have provided regular updates of the negotiation process and sought to oppose the EPA regime. For example, in 2009 African Trade Network released a declaration following its 9th Meeting on the EPAs, reaffirming their opposition and rejecting the proposed trade regime:

> We re-state our position that as free-trade agreements between two unequal parties, the EPAs are fundamentally anti-developmental. This is especially so in the particular context of Africa's weak, fragmented economies, which have been ravaged and distorted by years of European and (other) external domination ... We also assert that any alternative to the EPAs can only be

---

[111] EPAs (Economic Partnership Agreements) Coalition, 'Position Statement: Six Reasons to Oppose EPAs in Their Current Form' (November 2004) accessed 13 December 2016 at www.stopepa.de/img/six-questions-on-epas.pdf.

[112] Del Falice (n. 108), 154.

[113] *Ibid*, 154–5.

> defined as the right of, and support for, African and other countries of the ACP to determine their own policies and agenda for development.[114]

Contesting the legitimacy of the EPAs enabled some of the taken-for granted truths to be challenged, most notably, that the EPAs *will* promote economic growth (economic freedom) which in turn *will* promote sustainable development (non-economic freedoms). In Southern Africa, non-state actors involved in the EPA campaign include both civil society organisations and the private sector but have not been as organised as the international groups. For regional integration across Africa, the role of non-state actors is not to be underestimated:

> It will be important that African leaders encourage social groups, such as journalists, trade unions, marketing and industrial groups, students and non-governmental organisations, to play a role in Africa's regional integration ... Like Europe, private sector development should be the linchpin of the strategy to integrate African economies ... In an effective regional market, the private sector becomes the principal actor, while the public sector plays the role of formulator and regulator of policies.[115]

In Southern Africa, civil society organisations have sought to highlight what they perceive to be the existing problems with the EPA and aimed to secure a 'fairer' deal. In this light, the Southern African position appeared to be one of *reformist* discursive practice. This is not altogether unsurprising as there is a discursive fit at the institutional level between the EU and ACP that economic growth is the most important element of sustainable development. For example, in the Joint Declaration of the African Union Heads of State of 2006, the consensus among African officials was that the EPAs should be 'tools for the economic development of Africa' but that liberal trade policies alone 'may not by itself deliver economic development'.[116]

On the back of Namibia's political and economic campaign to challenge the EPA, the country has also played a pivotal role in elevating the voice of non-state actors in their campaign against unfair provisions in the EPA. In an open letter to the former EU Trade Commissioner, Karel

[114] Africa Trade Network, '9th ATN Meeting Declaration Forward with the Struggle to STOP EPAS' cited in Del Falice (n. 108), 155.

[115] C.O. Kwarteng, *Africa and the European Challenge: Survival in a Changing World* (Aldershot: Avebury, 1997), 43–4.

[116] African Union, 'Nairobi Declaration on Economic Partnership Agreements' African Conference of Ministers of Trade, 4th Ordinary Session, 12–14 April 2006, Nairobi.

de Gucht, non-state actors raised their concerns about the EPA.[117] Urging the EU to 'engage positively' with the SADC EPA states on the then unresolved contentious issues, a collective of 31 civil society organisations, all of whom are based in the EU Member States, highlighted the failure of the EU to take the concerns of the SADC EPA States seriously. In his response, Karel de Gucht committed to engage with the SADC EPA States in a 'constructive spirit' and noted that the EU had already conceded on some aspects of the proposed agreement:

> … EPAs are intended to build on existing regional integration processes and strengthen them. In the case of the SADC EPA group, the Council of Ministers recently approved the alignment of interim EPA tariffs with those included in the EU-South Africa Trade, Development and Cooperation Agreement to support integration in Southern African Customs Union SACU that comprises South Africa, Namibia, Botswana, Lesotho and Swaziland.[118]

The way in which the negotiations have been conducted has attracted criticism. Non-state actors and civil society organisations are often consulted separately and, therefore, are prevented from raising their issues before the key policy-makers. Formal spheres of action that should be deliberative have instead been colonised by the strategic orientation of EU trade policy-makers. Non-state actors have complained that they have been marginalised throughout the consultative process and that this had resulted in greater participation beyond the invited forum, in the informal space of society and the media. The African Trade Policy Centre has highlighted the problems facing civil society and non-state actors in the trade negotiations.[119] In their 2007 Review Report, the Centre noted that it had been difficult for non-state actors to procure information relating to the ongoing negotiations. Since civil society and the private sector were often not adequately informed about the current state of play, it leaves them ill-equipped to create a formal coherent discursive strategy to constructively engage in the EPA negotiating process. Arguably, the secrecy surrounding the negotiations not only isolated non-state actors

---

[117] Namibian Civil Society letter to Trade Commissioner Karel de Gucht, 'Re: Open Letter on undue pressure on Namibia to sign an interim EPA' (18 June 2010). The full text of the letter is available online at https://epawatch.eu/ (accessed 13 December 2016).

[118] Karel de Gucht, Letter in response to 'Open Letter on undue pressure on Namibia to sign an interim EPA' dated 12 July 2010 accessed 13 December 2016 at https://epawatch.eu/.

[119] African Trade Policy Centre, 'EPA Negotiations: African Countries Continental Review' (19 February 2007) Review Report, 32–34.

but it bred suspicion and mistrust among them. In a 2007 Report on civil society involvement in the EPA process, Mambara argues:

> Non-state actors must be provided with the timetables for the processes early enough to make necessary preparations. Non-state actors on the other hand must become more strategic in their own programming to make the Cotonou Partnership part of their objectives, improve networking and coordination in order to become more effective. Unless these issues are systematically dealt with, non-state actor participation in the EPA negotiations will remain just rhetoric.[120]

The lack of information available in the public domain made it increasingly difficult to monitor the efforts of non-state actors in their campaign and to establish the extent to which they have successfully led to reform in the final EPA text. Although there is explicit provision for the involvement of non-state actors in the EPA negotiations, there appears to have been little in the way of a cohesive strategy among civil society in the Southern African region. Rather than reaching a mutual understanding of normative concerns through a deliberative transnational public space, there appeared to be a range of discursive struggles represented by a range of non-state actors, and their lack of coordination appears to have limited their scope for potential.

The presence of non-state actors, or lack thereof, perhaps speaks loudly of the power dynamics in the relationship not only between the EU and SADC-EPA countries but also of the relationship between the governments and civil society. While the international 'Stop the EPA' campaign has grown, visible non-state actor participation in southern Africa is lacking. The lack of transparency in the negotiations undermines the spirit of the Cotonou Agreement and erodes the consultative process. It has already been noted throughout this book that countries in Southern Africa suffer from severe economic constraints, so it is perhaps unsurprising that the networks of NGOs are less coordinated than those based in the affluent West. Interestingly, these organisations have not mobilised around the discourse of rights. Instead, the emerging discourse is rooted in economic instrumentalism and estimating the implications of the EPA for economic growth in the region.

Perhaps the importance of social, cultural and human aspects of development are overstated for a region that is economically vulnerable. While the South African constitutional system protects socio-economic

---

[120] J.L Mambara 'An Evaluation of Involvement of Southern Africa's Civil Society in EPA Negotiations to Date' Trades Centre Report, Zimbabwe (June 2007), 7.

rights, that protection is subject to the availability of government resources.[121] So for Southern Africa, economic development may take priority over the democratisation for human rights protection.[122] The region faces both internal and external obstacles to human rights protection. Internally, the political and economic make-up of the SADC-EPA countries results in relatively weak rule of law and poor governance structures. Externally, the ever-growing demand for multilateral liberalisation, albeit through regional trade agreements, places even greater pressure on struggling nations.

It is the breadth and depth of liberalisation under the proposed EPA which causes most concern for the SADC-EPA countries. The African Union has expressed its dissatisfaction with the scale of liberalisation proposed under the EPA framework in its Nairobi Declaration:

> We ... shall not make services commitments in the EPAs that go beyond our WTO commitments and we urge our EU partners not to push our countries to do so. We expect to call upon the European Community to open up its services sectors in favour of African countries to satisfy, at the barest minimum, the requirements under Article V of GATS of substantial coverage and elimination of substantially all discrimination.[123]

The EU did not impose sanctions on those countries that had signed but not implemented their agreements. By drawing out the negotiation process unnecessarily, African countries or regions were able to maintain the *status quo* without severing the relationship with the EU. Aligning the EPA with the TDCA will go some way in preventing disintegration of SACU. Determining the extent to which discursive practices shape the material outcomes of the negotiations is not an easy task. This is especially the case for Southern Africa, where a lack of coordination among civil society and the private sector has hampered any real effort to engage in a coherent discursive practice opposing the EPAs. One EU official has been cited as saying that the campaigns have kept the EU 'on its toes'[124] certainly, the successes shown in the SADC and CARIFORUM EPAs in tabling the contentious issues for discussion might not have happened in the absence of the campaign.

---

[121] *Soobramoney v Minister of Health, KwaZulu-Natal* 1998 (1) SA 765 (CC); 1997 (12) BCLR 1696 (CC).

[122] Welch (n. 102), 203.

[123] Article 10 'Nairobi Declaration on Economic Partnership Agreements' African Union TI//TMIN/Decl.2 (IV).

[124] Del Falice (n. 108), 160.

CONCLUSION

This chapter has provided a historical account of the negotiations toward the conclusion of the full SADC EPA. Noting the concerns of the Southern African states, the final EPA has been designed to align with the TDCA, which will bring greater coherence to the region's overlapping memberships and, it is hoped, limit the divisive impact of the EPA. Another aspect of the Agreement to be celebrated is the inclusion of a ROO framework that provides better terms than that offered under the TDCA, which should promote intra-regional trade among SADC EPA members. Although liberalisation is limited to trade in goods for the time being, the inclusion of rendezvous clauses[125] on government procurement, intellectual property, competition policy and investment policy in the final SADC EPA text is to be welcomed. In the next and final chapter, the experience of the CARIFORUM states will be critically assessed with a view to providing some insight into what the African ACP countries might expect as they embark on the implementation of the EPAs.

---

[125] See Articles 16–19 of the SADC EPA. Article 16(5) provides that 'The Parties consider traditional knowledge as an important area and *may* cooperate on it in the future.' The scope of liberalization in intellectual property rights is, therefore, minimal.

9. Lessons from the CARIFORUM EPA

This chapter offers a critical reflection on the CARIFORUM EPA (C-EPA) following the conclusion of its first five year review with the aim of highlighting the challenges that may face other EPA regions in the implementation of their agreements. The C-EPA marks the first comprehensive EPA concluded between the EU and ACP, and the Caribbean states began the provisional implementation of the agreement in December 2008.[1] The CARIFORUM region is comprised of 15 Caribbean countries including: Antigua and Barbuda, The Bahamas, Barbados, Belize, Cuba, Dominica, Dominican Republic, Grenada, Guyana, Haiti, Jamaica, St. Kitts and St. Nevis, Saint Lucia, St. Vincent and the Grenadines, Suriname, and Trinidad and Tobago.[2]

Signed in October 2008 by all CARIFORUM states[3] with the exception of Haiti, the EPA has now been in operation for almost eight years. As the only full EPA signed by the ACP, it marks a significant step in the reformulation of ACP-EU cooperation. With the completion of the first five year review of the agreement, evidence shows that it is only partially implemented and there have been many obstacles standing in the way of full implementation. That the EPA negotiations were a lengthy and complex exercise in trade diplomacy has been well documented throughout this book. It is not the aim of this chapter to restate the challenges facing the African ACP countries but rather to analyse the experience of the Caribbean States in light of the evolving relationship with the EU. Of

[1] The implementation was phased in provisionally as stipulated under Article 243 of the C-EPA with effect from 29 December 2008.

[2] While Cuba is a member of CARIFORUM it is not a party to the CPA or the EPA, and does not derive any financial assistance from the EU. The following analysis is therefore limited to the CARIFORUM EPA States. For the purposes of this chapter, the term 'CARIFORUM' and 'Caribbean States' will be used interchangeably in reference to the CARIFORUM EPA States.

[3] The Caribbean Forum of the African, Caribbean, and Pacific Group of States (CARIFORUM) refers to Coordination forum, rather than an institution *per se*, which comprises a number of the Caribbean signatories to the 1975 Georgetown Agreement. It is also known as the Forum of Caribbean States.

all the ACP regional groupings, the negotiation toward a full and comprehensive EPA was relatively straightforward for the CARIFORUM states. This may suggest a stronger sense of 'discursive fit' or 'resonance' between the ideologies of the Caribbean countries and the EU, but it will be shown that a number of contentious issues were raised throughout the negotiations at the ACP level and interregional level.

By its very nature as one of the first North-South trade agreements, the C-EPA marks a major milestone in the historic relationship between the EU and the Caribbean States. Negotiated under the auspice of the CPA, the EPA now replaces those provisions of the CPA which lapsed on 31 December 2007. Deeper and progressive liberalisation across sectors not typically associated with trade between the EU and ACP have become legally institutionalised through the EPA, with both sides agreeing to liberalise trade in goods, trade in services, investment, procurement and competition while including provisions on labour and environmental standards. It is the only EPA to include such extensive trade provisions, in part because the Caribbean countries wanted to create a partnership through which their services industries might grow. With the first five year review now complete, it is time to reflect on the Caribbean experience and analyse whether the implementation of the EPA has produced the adverse effects predicted in the initial phase of the negotiations in 2004.

A great deal of scholarship in IPE has been devoted towards the examination of the negotiation phases. However, providing the background of the negotiation phase in this region demonstrates that it too represented a discursive space for deliberation. From this process of argumentation, the preferences expressed in the C-EPA were decided. It is the purpose of this chapter to explore the process of implementation and situate the current challenges within their historical context. The analysis contained in this chapter is by no means an exhaustive account of the EPA. However, as the only EPA that has been signed and ratified, and with implementation gradually taking place, it presents an interesting example for the other EPA regions to study. It will give those regions a sense of what they can expect once their EPAs have been ratified and the implementation process begins.

In the first section, a brief but historically sensitive account of the construction of the CARIFORUM region is presented. The second section provides a critical analysis of the regional negotiation phase, led by Caribbean Regional Negotiating Machinery and Caribbean Export. Herein, the legitimacy of the participatory process underpinned by the Cotonou Partnership Agreement is challenged using Habermasian discourse theory. Reference to the various State and non-state actors is considered as the new interregional space between the EU and CARIFORUM states continues to develop. In the third section the scope of liberalisation under the C-EPA is presented and the extent to which these objectives have been realised to date are examined. The fourth section provides a critical reflection on the Report of the Five Year Review, commissioned by the EU. Drawing insights from this Report will enable the other ACP groups to prepare for the possible challenges that they may face on implementation of their respective EPAs.

THE C-EPA: A SITE OF ARGUMENTATION

The CARIFORUM EPA comprises the EU and its Member States on one part and the CARICOM States and Dominican Republic (hereinafter 'CARIFORUM') on the other. Much like the other regional groupings, the C-EPA is intended to reinforce and strengthen existing regional integration initiatives.[4] However, the CARIFORUM EPA does not neatly map onto an existing Caribbean regional trade agreement (RTA), rather, it comprises the CARICOM States, some of whom are members of the Organisation of Eastern Caribbean States (OECS), plus the Dominican Republic. Similar to the SADC EPA, the CARIFORUM group constitutes the creation of a new regional integration initiative – an imagined space – or, at the very least, results in the expansion of an existing RTA.

An important starting point for this chapter is to acknowledge that the political economy of the CARIFORUM region is markedly different to that of the African regional groupings. The Caribbean States are wealthier, have a higher literacy rate, have a higher life expectancy, and have a more diverse ethnic composition than that of any African EPA group.[5] The dominant features of the CARICOM states are their small size and relative degree of economic openness. However, as is typical of smaller states, their production base remains undiversified and centres on the export of only a few key products. Trade taxes are an important source of revenue for these small Caribbean countries, and the liberalisation under the EPA could be financially significant. As their production

[4] Article 64 of the 'Economic Partnership Agreement between the CARIFORUM States, of the one part, and the European Community and its Member States, of the other part' [2008] OJ L289/I/4, hereinafter referred to as the 'C-EPA'.

[5] M. Broberg, 'The European Union-Caribbean Relations: On the Apparent Deterioration of the EU-Caribbean Relationship' (2016) 21 *European Foreign Affairs Review* 75–94, 87.

bases remain undiversified, this renders the Caribbean markets acutely vulnerable to exogenous shocks. While economic vulnerability can be a feature of larger and more developed countries, the CARICOM States are geographically located in a region that is also prone to more natural disasters than in other parts of the world. Their vulnerability is further compounded by their geographic nature as island nations. Consequently, it is imperative that small, economically vulnerable countries have adequate infrastructure and capacity to rebound from exogenous shocks, be they economic or non-economic in nature.[6]

The Caribbean States share a common history with the African and Pacific countries in relation to their trading relationship with the EU. ACP producers have been critically dependent on the EU market as a result of substantial development aid and the commodity protocols that had existed under Lomé. Prior to the Cotonou framework, export concentration was in some instances directly linked to former colonial ties. An example of structural dependence is evidenced through the banana trade. Destined for UK consumption, Dominica, St. Lucia, and St. Vincent and the Grenadines exported all of their bananas to this country.[7] Shifting toward a reciprocal, but asymmetric, trade regime under the EPA marked a departure from the preferential framework that had preceded it and the extent to which ACP countries will gain from the EPA will depend on the international competiveness of its products vis-à-vis not only in relation to other ACP countries but with the rest of the world.

Unlike the African ACP States, the Caribbean has developed a strong political profile through its participation in the ACP Secretariat and other international arenas. It boasts an organised regional arrangement, CARICOM, which spear-headed the negotiations on behalf of the Caribbean from the outset. This chapter will show that the technical know-how of the CARICOM staff coupled with its proactive engagement with the EPA negotiating process enabled it to secure significant benefits throughout the negotiations. As outlined throughout this book, the conclusion of the EPA was inevitable but the negative response to the proposed regime and the protracted nature of the negotiations threatened the EU's presence as a global actor on the international scene. Against the backdrop of the failing Doha Round and the unprecedented backlash toward the EPA

---

[6] A. Gonzales, 'Policy Implications of Smallness as a Factor in the Lomé, FTAA and WTO Negotiations' Caribbean RNM/IDB Regional Technical Cooperation Project (Bridgetown, September 2000).

[7] R. Bernal, *Globalization, Trade, and Economic Development: The CARIFORUM-EU Economic Partnership Agreement* (New York: Palgrave MacMillan, 2013), 93.

framework, the Caribbean region was able to 'capitalise on the anxiety of the EU to attain certain gains and concessions'.[8] Concluding the CARIFORUM EPA within the prescribed deadline proved to be beneficial for both the Caribbean negotiating group who secured better-than-expected trade concessions and for the EU as its profile as a normative global actor in the global economy was reinforced.

In the CARIFORUM region, the negotiations were led by the Caribbean Regional Negotiating Machinery (CRNM) which facilitated the participation of both state and non-state actors on various aspects of the proposed EPA, supported by Caribbean-Export (Carib-Export). A strong consultative process was important to ensure that those with the appropriate technical knowledge could air their views; it allowed the voices of civil society to be heard, and ensured transparency and ownership of the process.[9] Misconceptions about the EPA had been perpetuated by the media, citing commentators who had little experience of trade negotiations. One example of this misinformation was the belief that tax revenue would be adversely affected when, in reality, the EPA actually minimised the displacement of tax revenue.[10] The ideology that the Caribbean States would not be able to compete internally was becoming a 'taken-for granted truth' expressed through the common sense of society. However, from a trade practitioner's perspective, 'the EPA negotiations demonstrate that the region has the capacity to mediate the encounter with globalisation and can influence the terms of its integration in the global economy'.[11]

Carib-Export has been an important actor both in terms of improving intraregional trade and in negotiating the EPA framework for the Caribbean countries. Established in 1996 by an Inter-Governmental Agreement, it is the only regional trade and investment agency operating in the ACP. Carib-Export has received funding from the EU Commission under the 10th and 11th EDF for implementation of the EPA. It represents an example of Aid for Trade (AfT) and was selected to implement Phase II of the EU supported Caribbean Trade and Private Sector Development Programme (CTPSDP). The overall objective of Phase II is 'to contribute to the gradual repositioning and integration of the CARIFORUM countries into the world economy'.[12] Having recognised the information

---

[8] *Ibid*, 45.

[9] Broberg (n. 5), 87.

[10] *Ibid.*

[11] Bernal (n. 7), 52.

[12] OECD and WTO, 'Aid for Trade Case Study: Caribbean Trade and Private Sector Development Programme (CTPSDP)-Phase II' Report dated

deficit surrounding the EPA negotiations and the lack of private sector consultation through the process, Carib-Export was tasked with five objectives under Phase II of the CTPSDP: increase the competitiveness of the private sector through diversification of the production base; strengthen Business Support Organisations; foster better cooperation between the CARIFORUM business sector and the EU's Overseas Territories and French Caribbean Outermost Region; improve the regulatory environment in CARIFORUM States; and increase awareness of the EPA both in the public and private sectors.[13]

In the negotiation phase, Carib-Export identified priority areas for the Caribbean including the creative industries, the health and wellness sectors, professional services, agro-processing, light manufacturing, speciality foods, specialised tourism and alternative energy. Through a direct assistance programme that lasted 2.5 years ending in 2010, the EU provided support of €6.8 million, for firms and business support offices (BSOs) to improve their competitiveness and supply of related services, and to provide regional training.[14] This marked the first programme of assistance directly linked to the EPA. Among the challenges facing the implementing of the direct grant scheme was the limited participation of the CARIFORUM countries. While Jamaica, which has a well-established trade and investment organisation (Jamaica Trade & Invest) sought funding under the scheme, there was an overwhelming lack of interest expressed by Haiti, Suriname, Guyana and Dominica. In part, this may be a result of a lack of appropriate infrastructure in those countries and the lack of familiarity with the EU funding process. However, it speaks to a larger issue of heterogeneity in the region, both in terms of development and in terms of infrastructure to support development.

Implementing the EPA hinges on the financial assistance of the EU. For Phase II of the CTPSDP, the total cost of the programme was estimated at €11,879,069. Of this amount, the EU committed to provide a maximum of €7,900,000 with the remaining sums being sourced from CARIFORUM and the private sector.[15] In effect, two-thirds of the programme was financially supported by the European Commission.

---

23 February 2011 accessed 13 December 2016 at https://www.oecd.org/aidfortrade/47461989.pdf.

[13] *Ibid*, 2.

[14] *Ibid*, 3.

[15] Financing Agreement between the European Commission and the Caribbean Forum of ACP States (CARIFORUM) Agreement No. 9816/Reg RCA/003/04 under the 9th EDF.

Providing financial assistance through Carib-Export has highlighted the advantages of working with an established regional institution and reinforced the targeted approach of AfT. The EPAs do not explicitly set out financial commitments, although financial assistance is to be provided through the European Development Fund (EDF). Under the 10th EDF it is estimated that €580 million has been allocated toward implementation of the CARIFORUM EPA up to 2013.[16] Under the 11th EDF, funding for the implementation of the EPA will be provided through the Regional Indicative Programme (RIP) in the period 2014–2020. The 2014–2020 RIP outlines three focal areas for financial assistance including regional and economic integration, environmental concerns and sustainable energy, and crime and security. The EU Commission anticipates the provision of €346 million to be allocated over six years, although this figure may be subject to revision in accordance with the terms of the EDF. One of the key concerns regarding the EDF is the fact that *allocation is not an entitlement*.[17] The funds allocated are subject to review by the EU Commission and this could leave the Caribbean states uncertain as to what financial assistance they are entitled to receive.

It was the proactive role of the CARIFORUM states through their engagement with the negotiations that saw the region gain significant and unprecedented concessions in the final Agreement. For example, the phase of liberalisation was extended to 25 years, the EU agreed to a review clause to ensure the proper implementation and monitoring of the Agreement, and the original commitments on tax governance were scrapped. Furthermore, the EU had initially envisaged the creation of a CARIFORUM customs union, a goal which was subsequently abandoned. Bernal attributes the strength in bargaining on the basis of a 'historical friendship and contemporary links with EU member states' which enabled the CARIFORUM states to advance their interests in this interregional setting.[18]

Each EPA region will be affected by liberalisation in different ways and this is why stakeholders tried to impress upon the European Commission in the lead up to the 2008 deadline the need for carefully tailored free trade agreements (FTAs). The negotiations of the EPA

---

[16] European Parliament, 'The CARIFORUM-EU Economic Partnership Agreement (EPA): The Development Component' March 2009 EXPO/B/DEVE/2008/60, 7.

[17] EU Commission, 'Caribbean Regional Indicative Programme: 11th European Development Fund (EDF)', Ares(2015)3671530 of 7 September 2015.

[18] Bernal (n. 7), 45.

presented new and more complex technical issues to the CARIFORUM states, with the exception of the Dominican Republic which had already been exposed to comprehensive trade under CAFTA. There was a strong desire from the Caribbean States to include services liberalisation within the EPA although negotiating comprehensive liberalisation was not a view shared among African States, as outlined in Chapter 8.

The protracted nature of the EPA negotiations in the other ACP regional groupings has been documented throughout this book. However, the negotiations of the CARIFORUM EPA were, in comparison, less complex. In part, this is because the CARIFORUM region is markedly different from the other groupings which are comprised of predominantly least developed countries (LDCs)[19] and in part this is because the CARIFORUM states had different interests, and actively sought to liberalise trade in services. These two issues combined meant that the CARIFORUM Heads of State did not perceive delaying the negotiations as a sensible tactic. There was a real fear among ACP States that delaying the negotiations beyond the 2008 deadline would have an adverse impact on the ACP's access to the EU market, particularly in key commodities such as bananas, rice and sugar. Without the EPA, the ACP countries would be left exposed and reliant on the EU's Generalised System of Preference (GSP). It was unlikely that ACP producers would receive the same level of benefits under GSP as, in accordance with Article 1 of the GATT requiring most favoured nation status (MFN), preferences must be offered to all WTO Members. Furthermore, beef, bananas, sugar, citrus products, brown rice, aluminium oxide (alumina) and aluminium were all excluded from the GSP.[20] Concluding the EPA with the EU appeared to be the most sensible means through which better preferences could be secured.

Arguably, the ACP States could have delayed negotiations until another waiver had been requested and approved by the WTO, as was the experience of the African EPA negotiating groups. However, throughout the Doha Round the WTO implemented a new practice of requiring additional concessions to be granted to *other* WTO members in return for the approval of a waiver. When the Cotonou waiver was granted, for example, the EU was required to offer concessions to Thailand and the Philippines on loin tuna products as well as further reductions on banana liberalisation.[21] Following the *EC-Bananas III* dispute, it was a real

---

19 In the CARIFORUM region, only Haiti is classified as a LDC.

20 Bernal (n. 7), 43.

21 *Ibid.*

concern of the ACP countries that the Latin American countries would view the request for a new waiver as an opportunity to seek better concessions from the EU. This could have proven costly not only for the EU but also for the ACP countries where the banana trade could have become less competitive vis-à-vis Latin American bananas.

A Discursive Space for Deliberative Participation

In 2007, the EU commissioned Pricewaterhouse Coopers (PwC) to conduct Sustainability Impact Assessments (SIAs) on the EPA regions. Incorporating an empirical approach combining both quantitative and qualitative elements to the study of the proposed EPAs for certain sectors of key interest to the ACP regional groups, the SIA methodology was *prima facie* balanced and well-structured. Its methodology facilitated a participatory approach and enabled stakeholders to voice concerns over the EPAs. With participation at the heart of the EPA process, it is interesting to note that the earlier draft texts of the CARIFORUM EPA were not publicly available,[22] although it is likely that aspects of the proposed regime were disseminated by the CRNM in its consultative process. Furthermore, the report published by PwC outlines that non-expert stakeholders were excluded during the initial phase of consultations with most stakeholders representing the commercial private sector.[23] The under-representation of social groups and grassroots stakeholders throughout the formative stages of the negotiations at the ACP-EU level meeting is significant because it is through these 'modes of association' that the voices of citizens are most likely to be heard.[24] That is not to say that all aspects of the negotiations require the invitation of civil society. It goes without saying that there are many aspects of trade that require experts with technical knowledge in those areas. However, civil society representation is key for the promotion of dialogue regarding broader socio-economic implications of the trade regime. The private sector, political experts and civil society groups were represented

---

[22] Pricewaterhouse Coopers, 'European Commission Regional Workshop on Sustainable Development and Regional Trade Agreements – Caribbean Workshop on Building Sustainable Development Issues into Economic Partnership Agreements (EPAs)', Report of PwC (2006), 19.

[23] *Ibid*, 19.

[24] S. Benhabib, 'Toward a Deliberative Model of Democratic Legitimacy' in S. Benhabib (ed.), *Democracy and Difference: Contesting the Boundaries of the Political* (Princeton: Princeton University Press, 1996), 73–4.

by just 30 stakeholders in the PwC consultation process.[25] While the SIA methodology aligns with the Habermasian discourse paradigm of participative deliberation, as codified in the CPA, the failure to engage stakeholders undermines the concept of country ownership and the participatory process. Results from the workshop may indeed represent some consensus in the attitudinal trends of the Caribbean countries, but it cannot be said to have been a truly democratic or representative process.

Overcoming the shortcomings of the interregional workshops, the CRNM sought to disseminate information in a more meaningful and inclusive manner. Through the 'Public Education Outreach Program' civil society and the private sector were informed of the nature of the negotiations and potential implications of liberalising trade under the EPA.[26] Cabinets and Parliaments were briefed by the Senior-Director of CRNM, Ambassador Henry Gill, while CRNM engaged more broadly with the regional private sector and non-governmental actors including the Chamber of Commerce of the Bahamas, the Dominican Exporters Association, the Antigua Workers Union, the CARICOM Regional Organisation for Standards and Quality, and the 2008 Small States Forum. Supported by the Inter-American Development Bank under its Multilateral Investment Fund (MIF) project, CRNM targeted the public through an innovative month-long radio series called 'Caribbean Trade Beat Extra'.[27] A briefing document was also distributed outlining factual information relating to the EPA.[28] Interestingly, this document is no longer publicly available through the CRNM website, however, this author analysed the document in 2010 when it was available and noted its focus remained firmly on the positive implications of the EPA for the region.[29] This document emphasised the significance of the development assistance package of the EPA for supporting the implementation of the Agreement in a way that would support, and not harm, local producers. This is not to suggest that the CRNM wilfully misled the public, but

---

25 *Ibid.* In particular, see: 'Annex C: Participant List' which provides a full list of participants at the regional workshop.

26 Caribbean Negotiating Machinery, 'CRNM Continues its EPA Public Education Outreach Program' electronic Newsletter of the CRNM (16 October 2008) accessed 13 December 2016 at www.crnm.org.

27 *Ibid.*

28 Caribbean Regional Negotiating Forum, 'The Economic Partnership Agreement' CRNM Public Education Document (15 October 2008).

29 See C. Gammage, 'A "Sustainability Impact Assessment" of the Economic Partnership Agreements: Challenging the Participatory Process' (2010) 4 *Law and Development Review* 126–7.

rather demonstrates that development assistance was a significant motivation for the ACP when signing the EPA with the EU, since which date the EU has radically reformed its development cooperation programme.

CRNM as the regional negotiating machinery sought to present a united Caribbean front, although this was somewhat undermined by the President of Guyana, Bharrat Jagdeo, who openly criticised the EPA for breaking the tradition of ACP solidarity. He claimed that the proposal for a WTO-compatible EPA was 'contrary to the spirit of successive international agreements which argued that there should be special and differential treatment' of ACP countries. President Jagdeo highlighted the structural inequalities of the partners:

> If you combine the GDP of all the countries in our region, it would be less than the assets of a large bank in Europe, so you can imagine how unbalanced, how uneven the negotiations are because you're not negotiating as two equal partners. They got their way because they're essentially a bigger power and they can always threaten to cut off their markets ...[30]

Unsupportive of this view, the Prime-Minister of St. Vincent and the Grenadines, Ralph Gonsalves, argued that the Caribbean States would 'manage in the circumstances' and that it was 'better to sign than to not sign'.[31]

The extent to which civil society in the Caribbean was engaged in a participative process is not clear; however, one blog interface, 'Mutiny Onboard CARIFORUM' presents some of the responses of everyday people in the Caribbean to the EPA. One commentator notes that the CRNM has received substantial funding and technical training from the EU, leaving little choice but to present a positive image of the EPA:

> Can you imagine going to war (... although in this case it's more like Saul and the Israelites facing the Philistines at Socoh), and your opponents are bankrolling your campaign and training your army?[32]

Another commentator adds:

---

[30] Peter Ishyrion, 'Trade-Caribbean: EU Pact Hit by Last-Minute Revolt' Inter Press Service news report (August 2008) accessed 13 December 2016 at http://www.ipsnews.net/2008/08/trade-caribbean-eu-pact-hit-by-last-minute-revolt/.

[31] *Ibid.*

[32] Blog post by Micro Mock Engineer on 'Mutiny Onboard CARIFORUM' blog site [undated] accessed 13 December 2016 at https://barbadosunderground.wordpress.com/2008/08/25/cariforum-epa/.

> Would it be too much to ask for a 'detailed response' from individual leaders of Caribbean countries, as to why they are in favour of the EPA? Citizens of CARIFORUM can then evaluate their responses – those leaders in agreement – when comparing them to the position of President Bharrat Jagdeo of Guyana and other leaders who agree with him. The interval between pro-EPA and anti-EPA expositions can be used by citizens to study the relevant documentation, have an informed debate, and arrive at a decision. This would not necessarily produce total agreement, but at least citizens would be better informed of a decision taken on their behalf. They would also know the thinking that underpins their respective Government's analysis.[33]

One blogger attributes blame to both the EU and CARIFORUM for failing to take stock of the political and economic realities of Caribbean States:

> The European Commission is as culpable in forcing through an arrangement on a far from mature integration process as are Caribbean governments for agreeing to measures that did not match the regional economic or political reality.[34]

Admittedly, these views represent but a tiny snapshot of civil society and certainly cannot be said to be a representative account of the shared views of Caribbean societies, but they offer some insight into the want and need of the citizens of CARIFORUM for a genuinely engaged and participative process which would have given a greater sense of legitimacy to the EPA negotiations. These views are supported by the Caribbean Policy Development Centre, who in 2008 stated:

> When it comes to engaging our population and to taking on board dissenting voices, our leaders and technocrats are dismissive and insulting. We seemed to have forgotten the true nature of representative democracy. Debate fuels growth, new learning and change, and particularly about something so important, such debate should be encouraged and not stifled or ignored.[35]

Four phases of negotiation took place before the text of the comprehensive EPA was finalised. These phases were bi-regional in nature, between the CARIFORUM States on the one hand and the EU Member States on the other. As part of the negotiations, and concerned at the scope of

---

[33] Blog post by Yardbroom on 'Mutiny Onboard CARIFORUM' blog site (26 August 2008) accessed 13 December 2016 at http://bajan.wordpress.com.

[34] D. Jessop, 'Whatever Happened to the EPA?' Starbroek News, 21 February 2010 accessed 13 December 2016 at www.bilaterals.org.

[35] Statement by Caribbean Policy Department Centre Senior Programme Officer, Shantal Munro-Knight, cited in Ishyrion (n. 30).

liberalisation proposed under the EPA framework, the then President of Guyana withheld signature of the EPA until the EU agreed to the inclusion of a review clause to monitor the implementation of the Agreement. Article 5 of the EPA, the review clause, provides that the EU and CARIFORUM will:

> undertake to monitor continuously the operation of the Agreement through their respective participative processes and institutions, as well as those set up under this Agreement, in order to ensure that the objectives of this Agreement are realised, the Agreement is properly implemented and the benefits for men, women and children deriving from their Partnership is maximised.

Alongside the treaty obligations, the EPA provides a new institutional framework to oversee the monitoring and implementation of the Agreement. Four committees have been designated at the interregional level to oversee EPA implementation: CARIFORUM-EC Trade and Development Committee;[36] the CARIFORUM-EC Consultative Committee;[37] the Joint CARIFORUM-EC Council;[38] and the CARIFORUM-EC Parliamentary Committee.[39] In addition, a Special Committee on Customs Cooperation and Trade Facilitation (SCCCT) has been created to oversee the implementation of the customs cooperation and trade facilitation provisions of the C-EPA.[40] At a national level, the nature of the institutional framework varies from state to state. Article 243 of the EPA provides that each state 'shall designate a Coordinator' to oversee the provisional application of the Agreement. The language here is mandatory, requiring that each Member State does so. However, it does not clarify the form that the 'Coordinator' should take. It is likely that each state will delegate this role to a senior official. Within CARICOM a separate CARIFORUM Directorate has been established with an EPA Implementation Unit to oversee the regional implementation of the agreement.

It is important to remember throughout that while the negotiations are led, and trade agreements are concluded, by States it is the firms within a State that conduct international trade through export, import, investment and procurement. However, in the CARICOM States firms are typically much smaller than those operating in bigger, more developed countries. Referring to these firms as 'nanofirms', Bernal highlights some of the challenges that they will face entering the global economy:

---

[36] Article 230 C-EPA.
[37] Article 232 C-EPA.
[38] Article 227 C-EPA.
[39] Article 231 C-EPA.
[40] Articles 29-36 C-EPA.

> Firms in small developing countries are constrained by a business environment that is less conducive to attaining international competitiveness than that in large developing or developed countries. In these environments, economies of scale cannot be realised without involvement in export activity and firms can benefit from modern infrastructure, large markets, and enterprise clusters. Small firms in developed countries find it more difficult than large firms to overcome the difficulties of breaking into export markets and undertaking foreign investment.[41]

The largest CARICOM firm, the Grace Kennedy Group of Jamaica which specialises in food trading and financial services, has an international presence in the Caribbean, North and Central America, and the United Kingdom. Its annual revenue for 2015 is approximately US$624,000, although it has seen a fall in profits over the past two consecutive years.[42] By comparison, HSBC Holdings, which represents the largest EU firm by revenue, reported an annual revenue from global operations of US$70.27 billion and is ranked number 1 in the EU by Forbes.[43] Both pale in comparison to the largest US global conglomerate, Berkshire Hathaway, which has boasted an annual revenue of US$210.82 billion, making it the fourth biggest firm in the world.[44] Currently, the firm taking the number one spot on the Forbes Global 2000 list of the world's biggest public companies is a Chinese firm, ICBC, which specialises in the provision of financial services and banking.[45] That the firms operating in the CARICOM states are much smaller, employ fewer people, and have significantly less global reach is self-evident. In other words, the political economy of the region results in less competitive firms which makes the push toward the material core ever more difficult.

---

[41] Bernal (n. 7), 101.

[42] Grace Kennedy Limited, 'Annual Report 2015' accessed 13 December 2016 at http://www.gracekennedy.com/index.php/media-centre/gk-annual-reports/annual-reports. This report states that the annual revenue for 2015 was Jamaican $79,742,230 which equates to approximately US $624,000.

[43] Data obtained from Forbes online at http://www.forbes.com/companies/hsbc-holdings/. HSBC Holdings ranks 14th in the world according to the most recent Forbes data.

[44] Data obtained from Forbes online at http://www.forbes.com/companies/berkshire-hathaway/ (accessed 13 December 2016).

[45] Data obtained from Forbes online at http://www.forbes.com/companies/icbc/.

TOWARD COMPREHENSIVE LIBERALISATION

Signed in 2008, the C-EPA is an internally binding mixed agreement[46] requiring extensive regulatory and policy changes in the trade relationship between the EU and Caribbean States. It is a large document, consisting of 250 Articles, three Protocols, seven Annexes, and a number of joint and individual declarations and statements. Over 5,000 tariff lines are liberalised in the goods Schedules, bringing the document close to 1,000 pages in length. Liberalisation extends beyond trade in goods to include trade in services, competition, procurement and investment. In addition, the Agreement covers development cooperation with technical and financial assistance provided under the EDF. Therefore, the EU has exclusive competence to act in accordance with the common commercial policy (CCP) set out in Article 207 TFEU but the Member States have shared competence in those sectors that do not fall within the CCP.

Trade in Goods

Under the EPA, the CARIFORUM states have committed, as a regional bloc, to liberalisation of 61 per cent of the value of EU imports over a 10-year period, 82.7 per cent over 15 years, and 86.9 per cent over 25 years.[47] This brings the total liberalisation of imports from the EU to an impressive 90.2 per cent. Market access under the C-EPA has been unprecedented, with the EU granting similar market access arrangements to the CARIFORUM states as those offered under its EBA scheme.[48] The rationale for seeking to achieve greater coherence between the two trade regimes is to minimise differential treatment between LDC ACP countries and non-LDC ACP countries. In line with the reciprocal but asymmetric nature of the EPAs, the schedule of liberalisation will be phased in over a long period of time to minimise any potential shock to the CARIFORUM states as a result of implementation. However, the

---

[46] Article 233(1) EPA defines the parties and states the following: '… the European Community or its Member States or the European Community and its Member States within their respective areas of competence as derived from the Treaty establishing the European Community.'

[47] European Commission, 'Monitoring the Implementation and Results of the CARIFORUM-EU EPA Agreement' Final Report, EUROPEAID/129783/C/SER/multi Lot 1: Studies and Technical Assistance in All Sectors (September 2014), 71.

[48] Annex II of the C-EPA provides the market access commitments of the EU. See [2008] OJ L289/I/90-91.

implementation of the EPA assumes that the requisite infrastructure is in place to support the process. Failure to deliver the financial and technical assistance promised as part of the EPA has resulted in a slow pace of implementation of the EPA across the CARIFORUM Member States.[49] The loss of revenue that will be suffered through the removal of revenues, on the basis that substantially all trade is liberalised between the two regions, will require new taxation systems to be established in the CARIFORUM States. Revenue losses dovetails with a potential spike in EU imports as the CARIFORUM markets become more easily accessible. The CARIFORUM States will need to adopt measures that will enable their industries to remain competitive in order to reduce the adverse effects of liberalisation for domestic industries.

Shifting away from the preferential access granted under Lomé, the new regime for bananas, sugar and rice was of particular importance to the Caribbean commodity producers. Additional development assistance has been granted for ACP banana producers, as set out in the Joint Declaration of the Final Act of the Agreement,[50] to support the production of bananas in a changing global environment. In addition to the legal framework of the C-EPA, the EU has entered into the Geneva Agreement on Bananas with Latin American banana producers setting out its market access terms and bringing the longest-running WTO dispute to an end.

Transitional arrangements for sugar and rice have been included within Annex II of the C-EPA. Suriname and Guyana are two of the main ACP exporters of rice to the EU, and as LDCs, the transitional arrangements on rice are significant. The EPA offers better access to the EU market for rice producers and overcomes some of the problems that had affected both Suriname and Guyana under the Cotonou Agreement, the framework of which was not suited to their cycles of production and harvesting seasons.[51] Liberalisation of sugar was more complex as the phasing out of preferential access under the Lomé Sugar Protocol could have adversely affected the ACP sugar producers, and therefore required a more sensitive approach. The transitional mechanism consisted of two phases. In the first phase between the implementation of the Agreement in 2008 until 30 September 2009, additional tariff quotas at zero duty for

---

[49] South Centre, 'The EU-CARIFORUM EPA: Regulatory and Policy Changes and Lessons for other ACP Countries' Analytical Note SC/TDP/AN/EPA/32 (September 2013).

[50] [2008] OJ L289/II/1953.

[51] U. Hönich, 'Trade in Goods: Full Liberalisation in the EU' in A. Zampetti and J. Lodge, *The CARIFORUM-EU Economic Partnership Agreement: A Practitioner's Analysis* (The Netherlands: Kluwer Law International, 2011), 46.

sugar export were offered by the EU.[52] This was particularly significant for the Dominican Republic, as it was able to export sugar duty free for the first time in history.[53] From 1 October 2009 until 30 September 2015, a sugar safeguard mechanism was in force, marking the second phase of transition. Caribbean exports of sugar from non-LDCs can access the EU market duty free and are subject to a safeguard which the EU can trigger if the total sugar imports from all ACPs reaches 3.5 million tonnes or if the total imports from non-LDCs exceeds prescribed volumes within certain time frames.[54] If the EU triggers the safeguard mechanism, the ACP sugar imports revert back to MFN. The ACP Sugar Group agreed to a regionalisation of the sugar trade, meaning that each EPA region would have a set threshold that it could not exceed without reverting to MFN.[55] Volumes of trade were monitored through import licences[56] and statistical data shared between the two regions.

Trade beyond Goods

One of the more contentious aspects of the EPA framework is that liberalisation extends beyond the traditional format of tariff reduction for trade in goods. Liberalising trade in services and investment marks a new step not only in the ACP-EU relationship, but also more generally for North-South cooperation. For liberalisation of trade in services, Title II of the EPA sets out the general provisions on modes of supply, while Annex IV details sector and country specific commitments.[57] Included within the EPA is the liberalisation of modes of supply for trade in services including cross-border supply, consumption abroad (find modes in GATS), commercial presence (investment), and e-commerce, although there are some sectors excluded from liberalisation.[58]

---

[52] Council Regulation (EC) No. 1528/2007, [2007] OJ L348.

[53] The Dominican Republic was not a party to the Banana Protocol under the Lomé Conventions.

[54] For the period of 2008–2009, imports could not exceed 1.38 million tonnes; for the period 2009–2010, imports could not exceed 1.45 million tonnes; and, in the period 2010/11–2014/15, the total volume of imports could not exceed 1.6 million tonnes. See Hönich (n. 51), 49.

[55] The transitional safeguard measure was implemented under Commission Regulation (EC) No 828/2009, [2009] OJ L240.

[56] Article 3 Commission Regulation (EC) No 828/2009.

[57] Annex IV is also subject to horizontal commitments which affect all sectors.

[58] Article 65 C-EPA.

In theory, this means that Caribbean firms should be able to access the EU's market to expand their business and exports. Services represents the most significant sector for most of the CARIFORUM states and the EPA provides for the movement of natural persons. However, access may be restricted by Article 60(5) of the EPA, which states:

> Nothing in this Title shall prevent the Parties or the Signatory CARIFORUM States from applying measures to regulate the entry of natural persons into, or the temporary stay in, their territory, including those measures necessary to protect the integrity of, and to ensure the orderly movement of natural persons across their borders, provided that such measures are not applied in a manner as to nullify or impair the benefits accruing to any Party under the terms of a specific commitment.

So, where a specific commitment exists between the Parties, Article 60 cannot be invoked. It is difficult to ascertain whether the Caribbean States or the EU will utilise this provision as the terms of the EPA have been couched in ambiguous language.

Rules of origin are improved under the EPA for some Caribbean products compared with the former regime under the CPA. For example, Caribbean producers of apparel are now able to source fabric from anywhere in the world and export to the EU on a duty free quota free (DFQF) basis. In relation to the monitoring of rules of origin, the five year review has not yet taken place. In accordance with Article 10 of the EPA this should have occurred within the first five years of the Agreement entering into force.

At face value, the EU has liberalised its market extensively to foster stronger trade links with the CARIFORUM states. In practice, however, non-tariff barriers are presenting challenges in accessing the market.[59] Exporters of goods in CARIFORUM States must comply with sanitary and phytosanitary (SPS) measures imposed by the EU and this is hindering access to the market. Mutual Recognition Agreements (MRAs) have not yet been negotiated between the C-EPA partners and this means that the Caribbean States cannot prove equivalence to EU standards in some sectors. In the case of Barbados, for example, there is much work to be done before the country will be in a position to negotiate MRAs.[60]

---

[59] G. Greene, 'The CARIFORUM Economic Partnership Agreement: Lessons from Implementation' Report of The Commonwealth *Hot Trade Topics*, Issue 121 (2015).

[60] E. Humphrey and M. Cossy, 'Implementing the Economic Partnership Agreement: Challenges and Bottlenecks for the CARIFORUM Region' ECDPM Discussion Paper No. 117 of June 2011, 18.

Like many other CARIFORUM states, the certification and organisational structures simply do not exist yet and establishing the required infrastructure could prove costly. It will require both technical assistance and substantial financial assistance to establish these institutions before MRAs can be negotiated. This, in turn, creates a further delay in the implementation process. Overall, this creates the paradox of the C-EPA that it grants preferences to the Caribbean states without access to the EU market in some sectors because of non-tariff barriers to trade.

MFN Clause

The C-EPA incorporates an MFN Clause in Article 19 which provides that the Caribbean State must 'accord … any more favourable treatment applicable as a result of … becoming party to a free trade agreement with any *major trading economy*[61] after the signature of this Agreement'. An analysis of the interpretive difficulties of this provision has been outlined in Chapter 8 and shall not be restated here. However, while this particular provision courted much controversy in the lead up to the signature of the EPA, it is understood that to date neither party has sought to invoke the clause. It is not clear whether the Caribbean States are closely monitoring the EU's bilateral and regional negotiations with a view to using Article 19.[62] However, the CARICOM states continue to negotiate FTAs with Canada and the USA, so it is reasonable to assume that the EU may be monitoring these negotiations.

Sustainable Development, Environmental Protection and Labour Standards

Much like the EU's FTAs with other developing countries, the EPAs feature 'sustainable development' chapters and separate obligations that deal explicitly with environmental protection and labour standards. Throughout the agreement, reference is made to ensuring that trade

---

[61] The Agreement defines a 'major trading economy' as 'any developed country, or any country or territory accounting for a share of world merchandise exports above one (1) percent in the year before the entry into force of the free trade agreement referred to in paragraph 2, or any group of countries acting individually, collectively or through a free trade agreement accounting collectively for a share of world merchandise exports about one and a half (1.5) per cent in the year before the entry into force of the free trade agreement referred to in paragraph 2.'

[62] EUROPEAID Report (n. 47), 36.

liberalisation does not lead to the erosion of labour and environmental standards. Chapter 4 of the EPA is dedicated to the environment and sustainable development with the parties reaffirming 'the principles of sustainable management of natural resources and the environment are to be integrated at every level of their partnership, as part of their overriding commitment to sustainable development' set out in the Cotonou Partnership Agreement.[63] Recognising the environment and natural resources as 'thematic and cross-cutting issues' in trade liberalisation, the C-EPA aims to ensure that implementation is conducted in light of the principle of sustainable development.[64] Where matters of the environment and sustainable development are engaged, 'ownership, participation, dialogue and differentiation' are of particular importance.[65] In this way, the intersubjective quality of sustainable development is legally institutionalised within the EPA framework. Existing levels of environmental protection and public health laws and policies are conceived as *de minimis* standards, and the Parties commit to continuing to improve upon the existing legislative frameworks.[66] In keeping with the objective to strengthen regional initiatives, the C-EPA provides for the creation of a regional policy on international environmental standards to promote coherence within the interregional space.[67]

Part IV of the C-EPA sets out the 'General Exceptions' of the agreement which is essentially a restatement of Article XX GATT. The C-EPA also legally institutionalises core labour standards within the trade framework. Article 191 of C-EPA provides:

> The Parties reaffirm their commitment to the internationally recognised core labour standards, as defined by the relevant ILO Conventions, and in particular the freedom of association and the right to collective bargaining, the abolition of forced labour, the elimination of the worst forms of child labour and non-discrimination in respect to employment …

While the trade agreement is designed to boost employment and foster economic growth, it must do so in a manner that is conducive to '*decent* work for all, including men, women and young people'.[68] Again, a wide margin of appreciation is conferred on each nation-state to determine their regulatory frameworks in line with their social development policies

---

63 Article 183 C-EPA.
64 Article 183(2)-(4) C-EPA.
65 Article 183(2) C-EPA.
66 Article 184(1) C-EPA and Article 188 C-EPA.
67 Article 185 C-EPA.
68 Article 191(2) C-EPA.

provided that, in doing so, the Parties strive to improve upon those standards.[69] Much like the strategy for environmental protection, the C-EPA calls for a programme of 'social cohesion policies and measures to promote decent work at a regional level'.[70] Where implementation of the trade agreement raises concerns about the maintenance of core labour standards, the Parties may engage in a consultative process akin to that available for environmental matters.[71] As outlined in Chapter 8 the interpretive approach of the WTO Dispute Settlement Body is likely to be instructive where a dispute arises in relation to the provisions of the EPA relating to environmental standards and health policies.

Historically, the EU and CARICOM states have exhibited a high degree of discursive fit in relation to environmental protection. Both regions have cooperated in partnership on the negotiation of the Small Arms Treaty, international trade regulations, climate change, renewable energy, environmental protection, and the protection of children.[72] Based on this past practice of cooperation in other international fora, it is hoped that both sides will engage constructively in any consultations relating to the principle of sustainable development and core labour standards.

Dispute Settlement

Part III of the C-EPA sets out the provisions on Dispute Avoidance and Settlement. It is clear from the text of the agreement that the parties should *avoid* disputes wherever feasible through a process of consultations and mediation.[73] Only where a mutually agreed solution between the Parties cannot be met through the consultative process, can a Party initiate the arbitration procedure under Article 206 C-EPA. The dispute settlement mechanism of the EPA replicates that of the WTO. An arbitration panel will be composed of three arbiters following the submission of a request to the CARIFORUM-EC Trade and Development Committee.[74] The panel will issue recommendations once it has heard the dispute and the Parties will 'take any measure necessary to comply'[75] with the ruling within a reasonable period of time.[76] Failure to comply

---

[69] Article 192 C-EPA.
[70] Article 194 C-EPA.
[71] Article 195 C-EPA.
[72] Broberg (n. 5), 92.
[73] Articles 202-205 C-EPA.
[74] Article 207 C-EPA.
[75] Article 210 C-EPA.
[76] Article 211 C-EPA.

with the recommendation will result in further consultations or compensation to the injured party.[77] Unlike the framework of the DSB, there is no recourse to an appellate body. Where the Parties fail to reach an agreement on the way in which the measure should be brought into conformity with the recommendations of the panel, they can merely ask for further advice from the panel.

The panel is tasked with interpreting the provisions of the C-EPA in accordance with customary rules of interpretation of public international law, including the Vienna Convention on the Law of Treaties.[78] However, the ruling of the panel 'cannot add to or diminish the rights and obligations' set out in the EPA.[79] In its task of interpreting the agreement, the panel may seek the opinion of experts and interested parties may submit *amicus curiae* briefs.[80] This is a rather novel feature of the C-EPA Dispute Settlement procedure, as it could enable civil society organisations to voice their concerns to the panel when a dispute is initiated.

As the C-EPA is a trade *and* cooperation agreement, a dispute coming before the panel that relates to the compatibility of a trade measure with the principle of sustainable development is not unimaginable. Therefore, through the regional machinery of the EPAs, the interconnection between economic imperatives and the principle of sustainable development could be clarified further. If this is the case, the EPA dispute settlement mechanisms will represent one of the few, if not only, settings in which the EU's trade policies could be challenged on the grounds of sustainable development. It is likely that the principle of sustainable development will be used as a 'prism' to add 'colour, texture and shading' to the rights and obligations of the Parties under the EPA, in line with the approach of the DSB.

Protecting Regional Preference

A stated goal of the EPAs is not only to foster inter-regional trade in a 'development-friendly' manner but also to strengthen existing regional initiatives.[81] In the context of the CARIFORUM EPA, Article 4(2) states:

---

77 Article 212-213 C-EPA.

78 Article 219 C-EPA.

79 *Ibid.*

80 Article 217 C-EPA.

81 Article 4(1) of the CARIFORUM EPA states: 'The parties recognise that regional integration is an integral element of their partnership and a powerful instrument to achieve the objectives of this Agreement.'

> The Parties recognise and reaffirm the importance of regional integration among the CARIFORUM States as a mechanism for enabling these States to achieve greater economic opportunities, and enhanced political stability and to foster their effective integration into the world economy.

Furthermore, Article 4(4) provides:

> without prejudice to the commitments undertaken in this Agreement, the pace and content of regional integration are matters to be determined exclusively by the CARIFORUM States in the exercise of their sovereignty and in light of their current and future political ambitions.

Regional preference is protected under Article 238 of the EPA, which enables CARIFORUM States to deepen integration within the regional bloc without extending those preferences to the EU.[82] In addition to intra-regional integration of the CARIFORUM States, the text of the EPA identifies two further regional integration initiatives which it envisages should benefit from the agreement. Article 239 refers to the CARIFORUM States' relationship with the 'Outermost regions of the European Community', referring to France's Caribbean Outermost Regions (FCORs).[83] The potential for future cooperation with the EU Overseas Countries and Territories is referenced in Article 246 which would allow for the British and Dutch Overseas Countries and Territories[84] to accede to the agreement if all Parties agree.[85]

THE FIVE YEAR REVIEW

The Report on the 5 Year Review ('the Report'), commissioned by DG EuropeAid, presents the most comprehensive analysis of the EPA since its implementation in 2008. It is clear from the preceding analysis that the scope of liberalisation under the comprehensive CARIFORUM EPA

---

[82] This clause is reciprocal and the same rules apply to the EU.

[83] The FCORs comprise Martinique, Guadeloupe and French Guyana.

[84] The British and Dutch OTCs comprise Anguilla, Cayman Islands, Montserrat, Turks and Caicos Islands, Aruba, Curacao, and Saint Maarten.

[85] Article 246 (Revision Clause) provides: 'The Parties agree to consider extending this Agreement with the aim of broadening and supplementing its scope in accordance with their respective legislation, by amending it or concluding agreements on specific sectors or activities in the light of the experience gained during its implementation. The Parties may also consider revising this Agreement to bring Overseas Territories and Countries associated with the European Union within the scope of this Agreement.'

is far-reaching. The importance of realising the transformative potential, and the limitations, of the EPA cannot be understated: as the only full EPA that has been signed and applied *de facto* (if not *de jure*), the CARIFORUM EPA offers a glimpse into what life could look like after implementation in other EPA regions. Measuring the impact of the EPA for the Caribbean countries is a difficult task, but the Report seeks to identify and address some of the issues that have arisen during the implementation process.

The Report comprises three sections addressing: implementation, impact and key issues/conclusions. The Report makes for a disappointing, albeit not surprising, read. In conducting their research, the four person team were tasked with identifying 'economic (and social and institutional) results in key categories relevant to the Agreement'.[86] The structure of the Report, in pursuing this aim, identifies areas of implementation deficit with the purpose of addressing areas in which the implementation process has stalled or failed to meet expectations. Much like the SIAs conducted prior to the conclusion of the EPAs, this Report focuses on 'significant sectors' which are likely to change and, in particular, those areas of the Agreement 'that marked clear departures from the pre-2008 status quo'.[87]

The second part of the Report, which focuses on the impact of the EPA, is perhaps the most interesting from a trade and development perspective. As a FTA which is aimed at fostering trade, development and regional integration the C-EPA marks a shift away from traditional FTAs, which have focused on tariff liberalisation. As noted in the Report, the dynamic nature of the EPA has made quantitative economic modelling a less appropriate tool for measuring its impact.[88] Using both qualitative and quantitative indicators, the analysis aims to demonstrate the ways in which the EPA might have caused changes to the economy by measuring levels during the 2008–2013 period (the five year review period) and comparing this to the pre-2008 levels. In doing so, the analysis takes into account changes in the domestic regulatory, policy, legal and economic frameworks.[89] In assessing the 'EPA effect' on the CARIFORUM States, it is important to situate implementation within the broader political economy. A number of geopolitical exogenous shocks coincided with the EPA negotiation and implementation processes. In 2006–2008 the world experienced unprecedented hikes in the price of oil which had a

86 EUROPEAID Report (n. 47), 5.
87 *Ibid.*
88 *Ibid,* 61.
89 *Ibid.*

knock-on effect for the price of food. Shortly thereafter, the first financial crisis of 2008 sent shockwaves around the globe, affecting almost every economy.

Exogenous shocks have overshadowed the effectiveness of the EPA in terms of the benefits it could bring to the CARIFORUM region. The compilation of sudden rises in the cost of energy (oil) and food placed greater pressure on the governments of those countries to maintain stability. Of the CARIFORUM states, 13 are party to the PetroCaribe agreement under which oil is purchased at concessional rates.[90] To an extent, the membership of the PetroCaribe arrangement cushioned some Caribbean States from feeling the full effect of the oil crisis. Trinidad and Tobago was the only state to benefit from the oil crisis, experiencing a number of years of strong growth.[91] As an energy exporter of methanol, crude oil, ammonia, urea and liquefied natural gas, Trinidad and Tobago witnessed a boom in exports to the EU during the 2006–2008 period.[92] In the period 2010–2012, the export of liquefied natural gas rose by more than 250 per cent compared to trade values in 2008–2010.[93] Growth in the mining sectors of Guyana and Suriname also saw modest economic growth throughout the financial crisis.[94] However, the tourism industry in many CARIFORUM States has suffered badly as a result of the various global crises. In the immediate aftermath of the financial crisis, macroeconomic indicators demonstrate a significant fall in GDP across the Caribbean states. In the wake of the 'great recession', a number of large firms based in, and operating across, the Caribbean collapsed.[95] Following consultations with a number of stakeholders, the Report notes:

> … the recession had a negative impact on most discussions of (and efforts towards) implementation of the CF-EU EPA. Stakeholders in some countries indicated that even the relatively modest CF-EU EPA tariff cuts scheduled for 2011 and 2013 were delayed in part until the authorities could make an

---

[90] The CARIFORUM states that are party to PetroCaribe are: Antigua and Barbuda, The Bahamas, Belize, Dominica, Dominican Republic, Grenada, Guyana, Jamaica, St Lucia, St Kitts and Nevis, Saint Vincent and the Grenadines, and Suriname.

[91] EUROPEAID Report (n. 47), 65.

[92] *Ibid*, 79.

[93] *Ibid*, 80.

[94] *Ibid*, 65.

[95] The Report notes the closure of the Stanford Group (based in Antigua and Barbuda), the CLICO and BAICO insurance companies and the CL Financial Group (based in Trinidad and Tobago).

assessment of the potential revenue implications, given the significant pressure on Ministries of Finance to maintain (and increase) overall revenue. Other consultations indicated that the consideration and passage of new legislation related to CF-EU EPA implementation was delayed due to other pressing issues related to performance requirements under IMF arrangements or immediate legislation needed to address adverse economic developments.

It is clear that the complex processes required to apply the EPA, against a background of economic instability, has hampered the implementation of the Agreement. In the review period, the value of EU imports into CARIFORUM States has declined with the Report highlighting sharp falls in Trinidad and Tobago (37 per cent), Antigua and Barbuda (27 per cent), St Lucia (25 per cent), Barbados (25 per cent), the Bahamas and Jamaica (20 per cent in each), and the Dominican Republic (18 per cent).[96]

Three scenarios were modelled in the Report to assess the effect of implementation on the CARIFORUM states.[97] First, the 'EPA Review scenario' was measured in which the actual tariff reductions implemented by the EU and CARIFORUM States during the review period (2008–2013). Under this model, the prediction is that growth in CARIFORUM imports will increase modestly. By comparison, the situation regarding exports from CARIFORUM is likely to be maintained as the EPA continues the tariff scheme that had previously been in place under the CPA.[98] Second, the Report analysed the 'Full EPA scenario' which estimated the full impact of tariff liberalisation between the two countries over the full implementation period. Growth was expected to be much greater than that under the first model, but the volatility of trade in the review period does have a negative effect on the overall increase. Finally, the 'no-EPA counterfactual scenario' has been modelled which, in effect, hypothesises the state of trade in the CARIFORUM States had the EPA *not* been applied. This position assumes that the pre-2008 position remained unchanged and that the CARIFORUM States will benefit under the EU's GSP scheme.[99] Here, import values from the EU are predicted to remain the same as the pre-2008 position.[100] However, CARIFORUM export value to the EU would likely have fallen in dramatic fashion if the *status quo* had been maintained. This predicted negative impact is

---

[96] EUROPEAID Report (n. 47), 72.

[97] *Ibid*, 70.

[98] *Ibid*, 80.

[99] In light of the recent changes to the GSP, it is unlikely that all CARIFORUM countries would qualify to enjoy this preferential access.

[100] EUROPEAID Report (n. 47), 72.

attributed to the withdrawal of trade concessions under the CPA which would have meant all CARIFORUM States would be left seeking preferential access under the less favourable GSP scheme.[101]

Analysing actual liberalisation across a range of goods and sectors under the EPA reveals interesting trends with regard to the increase in import value. A number of reports prior to 2008 predicted a rise in agricultural imports to the CARICOM States. However, the actual trade data suggests that the CARICOM States are relying less on the EU for its agricultural imports and are instead sourcing these products from the neighbouring Latin American countries.[102] Suriname, on the other hand, has maintained close trading ties with the Netherlands and since the application of the EPA there has been an increase in import value of a wide range of products.[103] The somewhat muted effect of the EPA for liberalisation in agricultural goods is not surprising. Throughout the course of the negotiations, CARICOM was keen to ensure that the agricultural sector was protected and using the common external tariff excluded from the EPA almost half of its tariff lines in agriculture and fisheries.[104] With regard to the import of industrial products, there has been modest growth overall for EU products entering the Caribbean markets. However, it appears unlikely that this growth can be attributed to the EPA.[105]

With the exception of sugar, rice and munitions the EU has effectively maintained the *status quo* under the CPA and extended DFQF access to the CARIFORUM states under the EPA. As the EPA constitutes a binding legal instrument it was expected that the new trading framework, which is no longer granted under a WTO waiver, would bring greater certainty and predictability to the region for business and investors.[106] Mirroring the experience of EU products imported into the CARIFORUM states, analysis of the products exported from CARIFORUM states to the EU demonstrate similar levels of fluctuation.

In addition to tariff liberalisation there are four key aspects of trade in goods that might have had a positive effect on exports from the CARIFORUM states: changes in rules of origin, development cooperation projects, stronger enforcement of intellectual property rights

---

101 *Ibid*, 80.

102 *Ibid*, 75.

103 *Ibid*, 75.

104 *Ibid,* 76. Of a total of 1,122 tariff lines in these sectors the CARICOM States liberalised only 600.

105 *Ibid*, 78.

106 *Ibid*, 79.

and/or competition laws, and the removal of WTO-incompatible quantitative restrictions.[107] The Report notes that during the review period there was both a 'steep decline' in the value of CARIFORUM exports to the EU, and in the total value of exports to the rest of the world.[108]

Of all the CARIFORUM States, it appears that the Dominican Republic is the most advanced in terms of EPA implementation. In part, this is a result of a 'working consensus between the Government and the private sector' on EPA issues[109] and in part it is because the Dominican Republic offered tariff reductions to EU exporters on par with its schedule under the Dominican Republic-Central America FTA (DR-CAFTA). In doing so, the Dominican Republic offered more extensive liberalisation under the EPA compared with its other CARIFORUM counterparts.[110] For example, in relation to the liberalisation of tariff lines for industrial products a number of inputs, predominantly for construction and heavy industry, saw a significant increase in the value of imports from EU businesses. In the 2008–2012 period alone, there was a rise of 20 per cent in used tyres, glazed ceramic tiles, motor vehicles and building stone, to name but a few.[111] This rise in industrial products is in part due to the liberalisation of tariff lines but also in response to the construction boom in the Dominican Republic following the 2004 banking crisis. A similar increase in imports is seen for household and consumer products with imports in items such as leather handbags, washing machines and beauty products seeing a surge in the post-2008 climate. Adopting a deeper approach to liberalisation than the other CARIFORUM States through the EPA framework appears to have had a positive effect on trade for some sectors in the Dominican Republic.[112] However, in noting the special position of this Caribbean country, the Report identifies the 'Dominican paradox': a country which has experienced substantial growth but nevertheless suffers from 'stubbornly high' levels of poverty.[113] The development aspect of the C-EPA will, therefore, be of particular interest to the

---

[107] *Ibid.*

[108] *Ibid.*

[109] Humphrey and Cossy (n. 60), 25.

[110] EUROPEAID Report (n. 47), 74.

[111] *Ibid,* 77.

[112] It should be noted that some sectors that were *excluded* from the EPA have received even more favourable results with greater than USD1million in import value over the same period. Therefore, it is not entirely clear to what extent liberalisation can be attributed to the implementation of the EPA.

[113] EUROPEAID Report (n. 47), 103.

Dominican Republic in pursuit of the principle of sustainable development and eradicating poverty.

Throughout the analysis, the Report cautions against drawing strong causal links between the implementation of the EPA and changes in the value of EU imports into CARIFORUM states. This illustrates the overall difficulty of monitoring implementation of FTAs in general, as the nature of trade cannot be examined in isolation. External geopolitical factors may also have played a role in the fluctuating imports.

Lessons from the Five Year Review

Although the C-EPA goes far beyond what is required of WTO-compatibility under Article XXIV, liberalisation of services and investment is perceived to be a positive step forward by the Caribbean States.[114] As the most comprehensive trade agreement concluded by all of the CARIFORUM States, with the exception of the Dominican Republic, its success will depend on careful monitoring of the implementation process. The rate of progress across the region is uneven which has compounded the slow pace of EPA implementation. To date, the Dominican Republic has perhaps made the most progress in EPA implementation but this is to be expected given its experience in negotiating complex trade agreements and its proactive private sector.[115] On the other hand, the smaller OECS States have struggled to make meaningful progress toward utilising the benefits of the EPA.

In the first 'five year review' commissioned by the EU, the findings of the report suggest that the effect of the EPA has fallen short of original expectations. CARIFORUM states have not only been slow to ratify the EPA but implementation has been obstructed by a number of factors. Three 'deficits' are identified within the report, relating to awareness of the EPA, governance in the CARIFORUM region, and EU financial assistance. Collectively, these three deficits have slowed the pace at which the benefits of the EPA can be realised by the private sector.

Information Deficit

In 2011, Humphrey and Cossy highlighted the 'bottlenecks' in the implementation of the EPA which have created significant challenges for private sector actors.[116] Among the most significant of the 'political,

---

114 Humphrey and Cossy (n. 60), 3.

115 *Ibid,* 9.

116 *Ibid.*

communication-related, philosophical, cultural, institutional, financial, technical, [and] capacity-related' challenges was the information deficit that has adversely affected a smooth transition from Cotonou preferences to the EPA framework. Bridging the gap between the technical knowledge of the governmental bodies and the perceived lack of awareness among the general public and, in particular, the private sector has proven to be an especially difficult task:

> There is a saying that the 'greatest fear is the fear of the unknown'. This statement might accurately describe the relationship between most of the region's private sector and the EPA. They don't know much about it and they are unwilling to seek even readily available information. The private sector seems almost afraid of the Agreement, as though it represented some unknown and potentially destructive force, which they are reluctant to awaken.[117]

Failure by the lead negotiating organisations, including governments, to translate the benefits of the EPA into everyday language has enabled a narrative to gather pace in the region, that the EPA is harmful and exploitative. The Five Year Review supports and reinforces the findings of Humphrey and Cossy, concluding that there remains a notable information deficit in the region. Although CRNM and Carib-Export have sought to raise awareness of the benefits of the EPA throughout the CARIFORUM region, there remains a perception of an information deficit among the private sector.[118] Overcoming the fuelling of misunderstanding will require a more coordinated and participative approach from governments at the national and regional levels.

It was hoped that the EPA would act as a 'signal' to investors and businesses that the markets of the EU and CARIFORUM States are open. However, the Report shares concerns made in the pre-2008 environment that there is an overwhelming problem in terms of dissemination:

> despite a number of awareness-raising initiatives by both the EU and CARIFORUM, there is a surprising lack of knowledge of the opportunities afforded by the Agreement, and in some quarters, lingering concerns over its potential impact.[119]

---

117 *Ibid*, 5.
118 EUROPEAID Report (n. 47), 14.
119 *Ibid*, 115.

The noticeable lack of implementation of the EPA makes for worrisome reading, but is perhaps not surprising given the overwhelming lack of infrastructure in the CARIFORUM States in comparison to the EU:

> Many of the key elements that speak to private sector growth and investment decisions – the lack of availability of (and stringent conditions attached to) private sector financing for the cost and quality of electricity, basic utilities, transport and logistics – are not even covered in the CF-EU EPA, and are normally not covered in any FTA as they are part of a government's core regulatory space. Yet these issues were highlighted time and time again during the consultations held for this study as key barriers to competitiveness. This suggests that, while expectations for the CF-EU EPA were and should be high, there is a limit to what it can achieve.[120]

Overall, this suggests that dissemination of information through a space in which stakeholders can discursively engage in deliberative processes relating to EPA implementation is key to the success of this legal regime's future.

Implementation Deficit

Governance at the regional level has proven an obstacle in the effective implementation of the EPA. As outlined earlier in this chapter, the varying levels of development across the CARIFORUM region means that a variable geometry integration approach is likely to be the most suitable for engaging the Caribbean States in the EPA framework. Some countries, like Barbados and the Dominican Republic, have relatively well-established institutional and regulatory frameworks to support the changes to trade policy underpinning the EPA. On the other hand, Suriname and St. Vincent and the Grenadines lack sufficient capacity to facilitate effective implementation.[121] Concerns about the governance framework of the CARIFORUM Secretariat have also been raised, which have further hampered a coordinated implementation effort. The Dominican Republic made representations to the CARIFORUM Secretariat, on the basis that the EPA marked a shift toward *trade and development* and that the remit of the Secretariat was no longer solely relating to development assistance from the EU under the Caribbean Regional Indicative Programme (CRIP). Subsequently, in 2011, the CARIFORUM States committed to a reorganisation of the Secretariat. The CARIFORUM Directorate is now headed by a Director-General, who also

---

[120] *Ibid*, 117.

[121] Humphrey and Cossy (n. 60).

serves as the EPA Regional Coordinator, and it is hoped that the strengthened institutional approach will enable the CARIFORUM States to confront some of the challenges that they have faced so far. The failure of the CARIFORUM Secretariat to coordinate and organise itself at the interregional level raises questions about its governance at the regional level.

Another regional governance issue that challenges the implementation process is the 'regional preference' clause under Article 238 C-EPA. This clause provides that the CARIFORUM States must extend to one another 'any more favourable treatment and advantage' granted under the EPA. To date, only the Bahamas has implemented this provision and the remaining Caribbean countries appear reluctant to operationalise the regional preference clause. As a keen supporter of deepening and expanding the CARIFORUM-Dominican Republic FTA, the reluctance to engage with the regional preference clause has become a source of frustration among stakeholders in the Dominican Republic.[122] Such division over regional governance only exacerbates pre-existing tension in the region. To ensure coherence in the application of the EPA across the region, the CARICOM Heads of State requested that the Secretariat create an EPA Implementation Roadmap. It was hoped that this Roadmap would clarify issues such as the legislative and policy changes required to implement the Agreement as well as the funding available internally and externally to support capacity building.

At the interregional level, the operationalisation of the Joint CARIFORUM-EU institutions has not been forthcoming and in 2011 it was reported that only the Joint Council was functioning.[123] However, in the Joint Communiqué issued following the third meeting of the Joint Council in 2015, it was stated that all joint institutions are now operational.[124] The Five Year Review found that the monitoring mechanism, to be created in accordance with Article 5 C-EPA, had not yet been established as of May 2014. If the EPA is to lead to sustainable development in the CARIFORUM region, the creation of the joint monitoring mechanism must be prioritised. Monitoring is currently taking place through the Trade and Development Committee and through the national EPA Implementation Units.[125]

---

[122] EUROPEAID Report (n. 47), 16.

[123] Humphrey and Cossy (n. 60), 7.

[124] http://caricom.org/media-center/communications/communiques/joint-communique-third-meeting-of-the-joint-cariforum-eu-council (accessed 13 December 2016).

[125] EUROPEAID Report (n. 47), 16.

Financial Deficit

At the time the Report was issued, the EU was reformulating its programme of development cooperation and the 11th EDF had not been formally allocated. While the financial assistance provided under the EDF can, strictly speaking, be withdrawn, the EU has invested substantial amounts of funding into the EPA regions, as outlined in Chapter 3. This is a positive step forward in overcoming the financial constraints on the ACP countries. In theory, the ACP States will be eligible to receive a substantial amount of financing outside the EDF, through the AfT programmes. Humphrey and Cossy reported in 2011 that the only EU Member States to have committed financial assistance through AfT were the UK, under its CARTfund, and Germany. CARTfund committed €10 million for capacity building in the Caribbean region while Germany has funded the creation of the CARIFORUM EPA Implementation Network (CAFEIN) which is a platform for information sharing with all stakeholders. AfT is by its nature uncertain, and the total amount of funding that might be channelled through for EPA implementation is not known.

CONCLUSION

Although the SADC EPA States have signed a 'goods only' EPA, the experience of the Caribbean could serve as a cautionary tale. The Report of the Five Year Review found that the EPA 'signal', defined as the 'take-up of regulatory and market challenges and opportunities', has not been as far-reaching as initially hoped. While the Report identifies a number of deficits, what is most notable from the Report is that which is *not* really said: the effect of the EPA for sustainable development in the Caribbean. As trade and development agreements, these legal regimes should be promoting 'development-friendly' trade.

An effective monitoring mechanism is urgently needed in order to facilitate the next five year review. This mechanism should incorporate a more frequent, targeted and detailed approach to the implementation of the EPA by stakeholders and private businesses to adequately capture the reality of the trade agreement in each Caribbean country.[126] The evidence presented in this report suggests that better development indicators are needed to identify and measure the positive and adverse impacts of trade agreements for the development of people and regions. Overcoming the financial and capacity constraints must now be the focus moving forward

---

126 *Ibid*, 119–120.

if the EPA is to be implemented in a meaningful way. The EPA must not be seen as 'a laundry list of obligations' but 'a signal of a wider trade and development relationship'.[127]

---

[127] *Ibid*, 118.

Bibliography

Abass, A., 'The Cotonou Trade Regime and WTO Law' (2004) 10 *European Law Journal* 439–62.

Achebe, C., *Things Fall Apart* (London: Heinemann, 1976).

ACORD, 'Economic Partnership Agreements: A Threat to Food Sovereignty', ACORD Policy Briefing Paper no.1 (June 2007) available 19 December 2016 at http://www.acordinternational.org/silo/files/economic-partnership-agreements-a-threat-to- food-sovereignty.pdf.

Actionaid International 'Under the Influence: Exposing Undue Corporate Influence over Policy-Making at the World Trade Organisation', Report (January 2006) available 19 December 2016 at https://www.actionaid.org.uk/sites/default/files/doc_lib/174_6_under_the_influence_final.pdf.

ACTSA, 'Economic Partnership Agreements – An Update, ACTSA Briefing Paper' (2010) available 19 December 2016 at http://www.actsa.org/Pictures/UpImages/pdfs/EPAs%20Update%20-%20May%20 2010.pdf.

Adedeji, A., 'The Evolution of the Monrovia Strategy and the Lagos Plan of Action: A Regional Approach to Economic Decolonisation', Lecture for Nigerian Institute for Social and Economic Research (24 March 1983) available 12 December 2016 at http://repository.uneca.org/bitstream/handle/10855/5726/Bib-45065.pdf?sequence=1.

Adler, E. 'Seizing the Middle Ground: Constructivism in World Politics' (1997) 3 *European Journal of International Relations* 319–63.

Adriaensen, J. and M. González-Garibay, 'The Illusion of Choice: The European Union and The Trade-Labor Linkage' (2013) 9 *Journal of Contemporary European Research* 542–59.

Afadameh-Adeyemi, A. and E. Kalula 'SADC at 30: Re-examining the Legal and Institutional Anatomy of the Southern African Development Community' in A. Bösl, A. Pisani, G. Erasmus, T. Hartzenberg and R. Sandry (eds), *Monitoring Regional Integration in Southern Africa: Yearbook* (tralac, 2010).

African Trade Network, 'A Global Call for Action to Stop the EPAs' (Third World Network, 30 March 2006) available 19 December 2016 at http://twnafrica.org/indexx.html.

African Trade Policy Centre, 'EPA Negotiations: African Countries Continental Review' (19 February 2007) Review Report 32–4.

African Union, 'African Union and Regional Economic Communities Common Position Paper on EPAs', AU Conference of Ministers of Trade, 6th Ordinary Session (29 October–2 November 2010) Kigali.

African Union, 'Addis Ababa Declaration on EPA Negotiations' AU Conference of Ministers of Trade and of Finance, 3 April 2008 available 19 December 2016 at https://www.au.int/en/sites/default/files/decisions/9558-assembly_en_30_june_1_july_2008_auc_eleventh_ordinary_session_decisions_declarations_tribute_resolution.pdf.

African Union, 'Nairobi Declaration on Economic Partnership Agreements', AU Conference of Ministers of Trade, 4th Ordinary Session (12–14 April 2006).

Agnew, J., 'Mapping Political Power Beyond State Boundaries: Territory, Identity and Movement in World Politics' (1999) 28(3) *Millennium – Journal of International Studies* 499–521.

Agnew, J. and S. Corbidge, *Mastering Space: Hegemony, Territory and International Political Economy* (London: Routledge, 1995).

Ake, C., *Democracy and Development in Africa* (Washington, D.C.: Brookings Institute, 1996).

Akokpari, J.K., 'The AU, NEPAD and the Promotion of Good Governance in Africa' (2004) 13 *Nordic Journal of African Studies* 243–63, 244.

Alavi, S.J., 'Regional Trade Agreements among Developing Countries: Enabling Clause Revisited' [unpublished] accessed 9 December 2016 at http://papers.ssrn.com/sol3/papers.cfm?abstract_id=1737233.

Alemazung, J.A., 'Post-Colonial Colonialism: An Analysis of International Factors and Actors Marring African Socio-Economic and Political Development' (2010) 3 *Journal of Pan African Studies* 62–84.

Alessandrini, D., *Developing Countries and the Multilateral Trade Regime* (Oxford: Hart, 2010).

Aly, A., *Economic Cooperaiton in Africa: In Search of Direction* (Boulder: Lynne Rienner, 1994).

Anderson, K. and R. Blackhurst (eds), *Regional Integration in the Global Trading System* (New York: Harvester Wheatsheaf, 1993).

Andhikari, R. and P. Athukorala (eds), *Developing Countries in the World Trading System* (Cheltenham, UK and Northampton, MA, USA: Edward Elgar, 2002).

Aredo, D., 'The New Partnership for Africa's Development: Prospects and Challenges' (2003) 21 *Organisation for Social Research in Eastern and Southern Africa (OSSREA) Newsletter* 24–30.

Arriola, L., 'Patronage and Political Stability in Africa' (2009) 42 *Comparative Political Studies* 1339–62.

Arts, K. and A.K. Dickinson (eds), *EU Development Cooperation: From Model to Symbol* (Manchester University Press, 2004).

Aryeetey, E. and A.O. Oduro 'Regional Integration Efforts in Africa: An Overview' in J.J. Teunissen (ed.), *Regionalism and the Global Economy: The Case of Africa* (The Hague: FONDAD, 1996).

Ashiagbor, D., 'Embedding Trade Liberalization in Social Policy: Lessons from the European Union?' (2011) 32 *Comparative Labor Law and Policy Journal* 373–404.

Attri, V.N., 'Asian Economic Integration: An Emerging Sub-Paradigm in Regional Groupings' in A. Kumar Thakur and A. Sharma (eds), *Asian Economic Integration* (New Delhi: Deep & Deep Publications PVT Ltd, 2008).

Augier, P., M. Gasiorek and C. Lai-Tong, 'The Impact of Rules of Origin on Trade Flows' (2005) 20 *Economic Policy* 567–624.

Ayelazuno, J., *Neo-Liberalism and Resistance in Ghana: Understanding the Political Agency of the Subalterns in Social-Historical Context* (Toronto: New York University Press, 2011).

Ayittey, G., *Africa Unchained: The Blueprint for Africa's Future* (Basingstoke: Palgrave Macmillan, 2005).

Bach, D., 'The Global Politics of Regionalism in Africa' in M. Farrell, B. Hettne and L. van Langenhove (eds), *Global Politics of Regionalism: Theory and Practice* (London: Pluto Press, 2005).

Bach, D., 'Integration through Hysteresis: SACU in Comparative and Contextual Perspective' in D. Hansohm, W. Breytenbach, T. Hartzenberg and C. McCarthy (eds), *Regional Integration in Southern Africa Yearbook* (Vol. 5, Namibian Economic Policy Research Unit, 2005), 137–49.

Bach, D., 'Regionalism Versus Regional Integration: The Emergence of a New Paradigm in Africa' in J. Grugel and W. Hout (eds), *Regionalism Across the North-South Divide: State Strategies and Globalisation* (London: Routledge, 1999).

Bach, D., *Regionalization in Africa: Integration and Disintegration* (Oxford: James Currey, 1999).

Bagwell, K. and P. Mavroidis (eds), *Preferential Trade Agreements: A Law and Economics Analysis* (Cambridge: Cambridge University Press, 2011).

Bagwell, K. and R. Staiger, 'Will Preferential Agreements Undermine the Multilateral Trading System?' in J. Bhagwati, P. Krishna and A. Panagariya (eds), *Trading Blocs: Alternative Approaches to Analyzing Preferential Trade Agreements* (Cambridge, MA: MIT Press, 1999).

Bagwell, K. and R. Staiger, 'An Economic Theory of GATT' (1999) 89 *American Economic Review* 215–48.

Bagwell, K. and R. Staiger, 'Multilateral Tariff Cooperation During the Formation of Free Trade Areas' (1997) 38 *International Economic Review* 219–319.

Balassa, B., 'Trade Policies in Developing Countries' (1971) 61 *The American Economic Review* 178–87.

Baldwin, R., '21st Century Regionalism: Filling the Gap between 21st Century Trade and 20th Century Trade Rules' WTO Staff Working Paper ERSD-2011-08 (2011).

Baldwin, R., 'Multilateralising Regionalism: Spaghetti Bowls as Building Blocs on the Path to Global Free Trade' (2006) 29(11) *The World Economy* 1451–518.

Baldwin, R., 'A Domino Theory of Regionalism' in J. Bhagwati, P. Krishna and A. Panagariya (eds), *Trading Blocs: An Alternative Approach to Analyzing Preferential Trade Agreements* (Cambridge, MA: MIT Press, 1999).

Baracat, E. and J. Nogués, 'WTO Safeguards and Trade Liberalisation: Lessons from the Argentine Footwear Case', World Bank Policy Research Paper (Doc. WPS3614, May 2005).

Barak-Erez, D., 'Symbolic Constitutionalism: On Sacred Cows and Abominable Pigs' (2010) 6(3) *Language, Culture and the Humanities* 420–35.

Barbarinde, O. and G. Faber, 'From Lomé to Cotonou: Business as Usual?' in S. Bilal and R. Grynberg (eds), *Navigating New Waters: A Reader on ACP-EU Trade Relations* (London: Commonwealth Secretariat, 2007).

Barral, V., 'Sustainable Development in International Law: Nature and Operation of an Evolutive Legal Norm' (2012) 23 *European Journal of International Law* 377–400.

Bartels, L., 'Interim Agreements under Article XXIV GATT' (2009) 8 *World Trade Review* 339–50.

Bartels, L., 'The Legal Status of the Initialled EPAs and Legal Constraints on Renegotiation' (2008) available 19 December 2016 at http://www.ictsd.org/bridges-news/trade-negotiations-insights/news/the-legal-status-of-the-initialled-epas.

Bartels, L., 'The Trade and Development Policy of the European Union' (2007) 18 *European Journal of International Law* 715–56.

Bartels, L. and F. Ortino (eds), *Regional Trade Agreements and the WTO Legal System* (Oxford: Oxford University Press, 2006).

Beeson, M., *Regionalism and Globalisation in East Asia: Politics, Security and Economic Development* (Basingstoke: Palgrave Macmillan, 2007).

Benhabib, S., 'Toward a Deliberative Model of Democratic Legitimacy' in S. Benhabib (ed.), *Democracy and Difference: Contesting the Boundaries of the Political* (Princeton, NJ: Princeton University Press, 1996).

Bermann, G. and P. Mavroidis (eds), *WTO and Developing Countries* (Cambridge University Press, 2007).

Bernal, R., *Globalisation, Trade and Economic Development: The CARIFORUM-EU Partnership Agreement* (New York: Palgrave Macmillan, 2013).

Bertelsmann-Scott, T. 'SACU-One Hundred Not Out: What Future for the Customs Union?' SAIIA Occasional Paper (September 2010) available 19 December 2016 at http://www.saiia.org.za/occasional-papers/77-sacu-one-hundred-not-out-what-future-for-the-file.

Best, J., 'Legitimacy Dilemmas: The IMF's Pursuit of Country Ownership' (2007) 28 *Third World Quarterly* 469–88.

Bhagwati, J., 'The Broken Legs of Global Trade' Project Syndicate (2012) available 19 December 2016 at http://www.project-syndicate.org/commentary/the-broken-legs-of-global-trade.

Bhagwati, J., *Termites in the Trading System: How Preferential Agreements Undermine Free Trade* (Oxford: Oxford University Press, 2008).

Bhagwati, J., *The World Trading System at Risk* (Princeton, NJ: Princeton University Press, 1991).

Bhagwati, J., D. Greenaway and A. Panagariya, 'Trading Preferentially: Theory and Practice' (1998) 108 *The Economic Journal* 1128–48.

Bhagwati, J., P. Krishna and A. Panagariya, (eds), *Trading Blocs: Alternative Approaches to Analyzing Preferential Trade Agreements* (Cambridge, MA: MIT Press, 1999).

Bhagwati, J. and A. Panagariya, 'Preferential Trading Areas and Multilateralism – Strangers, Friends, or Foes?', in Bhagwati, J., P. Krishna and A. Panagariya, (eds), *Trading Blocs: Alternative Approaches to Analyzing Preferential Trade Agreements* (Cambridge, MA: MIT Press, 1999).

Bilal, S. and R. Grynberg (eds), *Navigating New Waters: A Reader on ACP-EU Trade Relations* (London: Commonwealth Secretariat, 2007).

Bilal, S. and F. Kratke, 'Blending Loans and Grants: To Blend or not to Blend?' ECDPM Report 2013 accessed 9 December 2016 at ecdpm.org/wp-content/uploads/2013/11/Blending-Loans-Grants-Blend-Not-Blend.pdf.

Bilal, S. and D. Liu, 'Contentious Issues in the interim EPAs: Potential Flexibility in the Negotiations' (2009) ECDPM Discussion Paper No. 89.

Bilal, S. and I. Ramdoo, 'Which Way Forward in the EPA Negotiations? Seeking Political Leadership to Address Bottlenecks' ECDPM Discussion Paper No. 100 (2010).

Bilal, S. and C. Stevens, 'The Interim Economic Partnership Agreements between the EU and African States: Contents, Challenges and Prospects' ECDPM Policy Management Report 17 (2009).

Blumenfeld, J., *Economic Interdependence in Southern Africa: From Conflict to Cooperation?* (London: Pinter Publishers Ltd, 1991).

Bohman, J., 'Critical Theory' in E. Zalta (ed.), The Stanford Encyclopaedia of Philosophy (Spring 2012 edition) available 19 December 2016 at http://plato.stanford.edu/entries/critical-theory/.

Bond, P., 'Removing Neocolonialism's APRM Mask: A Critique of the African Peer Review Mechanism' (2009) 36 *African Political Economy* 595–603.

Bormann, A. and M. Busse, 'The Institutional Challenge of the ACP/EU Economic Partnership Agreements' (2007) 25 *Development Policy Review* 403–16.

Bossche, P.v.d., *The Law and Policy of the World Trade Organisation: Text, Cases and Materials*, 2nd edn (Cambridge: Cambridge University Press, 2005).

Bowen, B., 'The Southern African Development Coordination Conference (SADCC)' [1990] *Trocaire Development Review* 29–45.

Bown, C.P. and B.M. Hoekman, 'WTO Dispute Settlement and the Missing Developing Country Cases: Engaging the Private Sector' (2005) 8(4) *Journal of International Economic Law* 861–90.

Boyle, A. and D. Freestone, *International Law and Sustainable Development: Past Achievements and Future Challenges* (Oxford: Oxford University Press, 1999).

Bratton, M. and D. Posner, 'A First Look at Second Elections in Africa' in R. Joseph (ed.), *State, Conflict and Democracy in Africa* (Boulder: Lynne Rienner, 1998).

Bratton, M. and N. van de Walle, 'Neopatrimonial Regimes and Political Transitions in Africa' (1994) 46 *World Politics* 453–89.

Braude, W., *Regional Integration in Africa: Lessons from the East African Community* (Johannesburg: South African Institute for International Affairs, 2008).

Bräutigam, D. and S. Knack, 'Foreign Aid, Institutions and Governance in Sub-Saharan Africa' (2004) 52 *Economic Development and Cultural Change* 255–85.

Brenton, P., 'Integrating the Least Developed Countries into the World Trading System: The Current Impact of EU Preferences under Everything But Arms', (2003) World Bank Policy Research Working Paper No 3018.

Brenton, P., 'The Changing Nature and Determinants of EU Trade Policies', CEPS Working Document No.150 (October 2000).

Brenton, P. and M. Minchin, 'Making EU Trade Agreements Work: The Role of Rules of Origin' (2003) 26 *The World Economy*, 755–69.

Bretherton, C. and J. Vogler, *The European Union as a Global Actor*, 2nd edn (London: Routledge 2006).

Broberg, M., 'The European Union-Caribbean Relations: On the Apparent Deterioration of the EU-Caribbean Relationship' (2016) 21 *European Foreign Affairs Review* 75–94.

Brown, W., 'Restructuring North-South Relations: ACP-EU Development and Cooperation in a Liberal International Order' (2000) 27 *Review of African Political Economy* 367–83.

Bruton, H.J., 'A Reconsideration of Import Substitution' (1998) *Journal of Economic Literature* 903–36.

Buckel, S. and A. Fischer-Lescano, 'Gramsci Reconsidered: Hegemony in Global Law' (2009) 22 *Leiden Journal of International Law* 437–54.

Budd, E., *Democratization, Development, and the Patrimonial State in the Age of Globalization* (New York: Lexington Books, 2004).

Buiter, W.H., 'Country Ownership: A Term Whose Time Has Gone' (2007) 17 *Development in Practice* 647–52.

Bull, H., 'The Twenty Years' Crisis Thirty Years On' (1969) 24 *International Journal* 625–38.

Busch, M. and E. Reinhardt, 'Developing Countries and General Agreement on Tariffs and Trade/World Trade Organisation Dispute Settlement' (2003) 37 *Journal of World Trade* 719–35.

Buthelezi, S., *Regional Integration in Africa Vol 1: Prospects and Challenges for the 21st Century* (East London, South Africa: Ikhwezi Afrika Publishing, 2006).

Cadot, O., A. Estevadeordal, A. Suwa-Eisenmann and T. Verdier (eds), *The Origin of Goods: Rules of Origin in Regional Trade Agreements* (Oxford: Oxford University Press, 2006).

Canterbury, D., 'European Bloc Imperialism' (2009) 35 *Critical Sociology* 801–23.

Caporaso, J., 'International Relations Theory and Multilateralism: The Search for Foundations' in J.G. Ruggie (ed.), *Multilateralism Matters: The Theory and Praxis of an Institutional Form* (New York: Columbia University Press, 1993).

Caribbean Negotiating Machinery, 'CRNM Continues its EPA Public Education Outreach Program' electronic Newsletter of the CRNM (16 October 2008) available 19 December 2016 at www.crnm.org.

Caribbean Regional Negotiating Forum, 'The Economic Partnership Agreement' CRNM Public Education Document (15 October 2008).

Carpenter, T., 'A Historical Perspective on Regionalism' in R. Baldwin and P. Low (eds), *Multilateralizing Regionalism: Challenges for the Global Trading System* (Cambridge: Cambridge University Press, 2009).
Carr, E.H., *The Twenty Years' Crisis: 1919–1939* (Basingstoke: Palgrave MacMillan, 2001).
Chabal, P., 'The State of Governance in Africa' (2010) SAIIA Occasional Paper 26 accessed 12 December 2016 at http://dspace.cigilibrary.org/jspui/bitstream/123456789/29713/1/SAIIA%20Occasional%20Paper%20no%2026.pdf?1.
Chabal, P., 'A Few Considerations on Democracy in Africa' (2002) 74 *International Affairs* 289–303.
Chabal P., 'The Quest for Good Government and Development in Africa: Is NEPAD the Answer?' (2002) 78 *International Affairs* 447–62.
Chabal, P. and J.P. Daloz, *Africa Works: Disorder as Political Instrument* (Oxford: James Currey, 1999).
Chaisse, J., 'Promises and Pitfalls of the European Union Policy on Foreign Investment – How will the New EU Competence on FDI Affect the Emerging Global Regime?' (2012) 15(1) *Journal of International Economic Law* 8.
Chan, A. and R. Ross, 'Racing to the Bottom: International Trade Without a Social Clause' (2003) 24(6) *Third World Quarterly* 1011–28.
Chase, K., 'Multilateralism Compromised: The Mysterious Origins of Article XXIV' (2006) 5 *World Trade Review* 1–30.
Cheru, F., *African Renaissance: Roadmaps to the Challenge of Globalisation* (Cambridge: Cambridge University Press, 2002).
Chikeka, C., *Africa and The European Economic Community 1957–1992* (Lewiston, NY: Edwin Mellen Press Ltd, 1993).
Chipeta, C. and K. Schade (eds), *Deepening Integration in SADC: Macroeconomic Policies and Social Impact* (Gaborone: Freidrich Ebert Foundation: 2007).
Christopher, A., 'Performance-Based Conditionality: A European Perspective' (2004) 32 *World Development* 1059–70.
Clapham, C., 'Boundaries and States in the New African Order' in D. Bach, *Regionalization in Africa: Integration and Disintegration* (Oxford: James Currey, 1999).
Clapham, C., 'Degrees of Statehood' (1998) 24 *Review for International Studies* 143–57.
Clapham, C., 'Discerning the New Africa' (1998) 74 *International Affairs* 263–70.
Clapham, C., 'Democratisation in Africa: Obstacles and Prospects' (1993) 14(3) *Third World Quarterly* 423–38.

Clough, M. 'The WTO Dispute Settlement System – A Practitioner Perspective' (2000) 24 *Fordham International Law Journal* 252–74.

Collier, P., *The Bottom Billion: Why the Poorest Countries are Failing and What Can Be Done About It* (Oxford: Oxford University Press, 2008).

Collier, P., P. Guillamont, S. Guillamont Jeanneney and J.W. Gunning 'Reforming Stabex' (2002) 22 *The World Economy* 669–82.

Collier, P. and A. Venables, 'Rethinking Trade Preferences: How Africa Can Diversify Its Exports' (2007) 30(8) *World Economy* 1326–45.

Cooper, S. and B. Taylor, 'Power and Regionalism: Explaining Regional Cooperation in the Persian Gulf' in F. Laursen (ed.), *Comparative Regional Integration: Theoretical Perspectives* (Aldershot: Ashgate Publishing Ltd, 2003).

Cordner, C., 'Aristotelian Virtue and Its Limitations' (1994) 69(269) *Philosophy* 291–316.

COSATU, 'Statement by the Congress of South African Trade Unions against the break-up of the Southern African Customs Union', (Polity, 01 July 2009) available 19 December 2016 at http://www.polity.org.za/article/cosatu-statement-by-the-congress-of-south-african-trade-unions-against-the-break-up-of-the-southern-african-customs-union-01072009-2009-07-01.

Crawford, G., 'Evaluating European Union Promotion of Human Rights, Democracy and Good Governance: Towards a Participatory Approach' (2002) 14 *Journal of International Development* 911–26.

Cremona, M., 'Balancing Union and Member State Interests: Opinion 1/2008, Choice of Legal Base and the Common Commercial Policy under the Treaty of Lisbon' (2010) 35 *European Law Review* 692.

Cronin, D., 'French Report Condemns EPAs', (tralac, 08 July 2009) available at: http://www.tralac.org/cgibin/giga.cgi?cmd=cause_dir_news_item&news_id=48448&cause_id=1694 accessed on 13 June 2011.

Curran, L., L. Nilsson & D. Brew, 'The Economic Partnership Agreements: Rationale, Misconceptions and Non-Trade Aspects' (2008) 26 *Development Policy Review* 529-553.

Dam, K., 'Regional Economic Arrangements and the GATT: The Legacy of a Misconception' (1963) 30 *The University of Chicago Law Review* 615-665.

Damro, C., 'Market Power Europe: Exploring a Dynamic Conceptual Framework' (2015) 22 *Journal of European Public Policy* 1336–54.

Das, D., *Regionalism in Global Trade* (Cheltenham, UK and Northampton, MA, USA: Edward Elgar, 2004).

Davenport, M. and S. Page, *Europe: 1992 and the Developing World* (Overseas Development Insitute, 1991).

Davey, W., 'A Model Article XXIV: Are There Realistic Possibilities to Improve It?' in Bagwell, K. and P. Mavroidis (eds), *Preferential Trade Agreements: A Law and Economics Analysis* (Cambridge: Cambridge University Press, 2011).

Davies, R., 'The SADC EPA and Beyond' (October/November 2014) 3 *GREAT Insights Magazine* available 19 December 2016 at http://ecdpm.org/great-insights/economic-partnership-agreements-beyond/sadc-epa-beyond/.

Davies, R. and J. Thurlow, 'Formal-Informal Economy Linkages and Unemployment in South Africa' (2010) 78 *South African Journal of Economics* 437–59.

Davis, C. and S. Bermeo, 'Who Files? Developing Country Participation in GATT/WTO Adjudication' (2009) 71 *The Journal of Politics* 1033–49.

Del Falice, C., 'Power in Discursive Practices: The Case of the "Stop the EPAs" Campaign' (2014) 20 *European Journal of International Relations* 145–67.

Dennis, P. and L. Brown, 'The ECOWAS: From Regional Economic Organisation to Regional Peacekeeper' in F. Laursen (ed.), *Comparative Regional Integration: Theoretical Perspectives* (Aldershot: Ashgate Publishing Ltd, 2003).

Desai, V. and R.B. Potter (eds), *The Companion to Development Studies*, 3rd edn (Abingdon and New York: Routledge, 2014).

Desta, M.G., *The Law of International Trade in Agricultural Products: From GATT 1947 to the WTO Agreement on Agriculture* (The Hague: Kluwer Law International, 2002).

Dimopoulos, A., 'The Effects of the Lisbon Treaty on the Principles and Objectives of the Common Commercial Policy' (2010) 15 *European Foreign Affairs Review* 153.

Dirar, L., 'Norms of Solidarity and Regionalism: Theorising State Behaviour Among Southern African States' (2016) 24 *Michigan State International Law Review* 667–723.

Disdier, A., L. Fontagné and M. Mimouni, 'The Impact of Regulations on Agricultural Trade: Evidence from the SPS and TBT Agreements' (2008) 90 *American Journal of Agricultural Economics* 336–50.

Do, V. and W. Watson, 'Economic Analysis of Regional Trade Agreements', in L. Bartels and F. Ortino (eds), *Regional Trade Agreements & the WTO Legal System* (Oxford: Oxford University Press, 2006).

Doidge, M., 'Joined at the Hip: Regionalism and Interregionalism' (2007) 29 *Journal of European Integration* 229–48.

Donnelly, J., *Realism and International Relations* (Cambridge: Cambridge University Press, 2000).

Draper, P., 'EU-Africa Trade Relations: The Political Economy of Economic Partnership Agreements' (2007) ECIPE Jan Tumlir Policy Essays, No. 02/2007.

Duddy, J.M., 'Geingob lays into EU' (The Namibian, 2009), available 19 December 2016 at http://allafrica.com/stories/200906010608.html.

Dunlop, A., 'What Future for Lomé's Commodity Protocols?' (1999) ECDPM Paper accessed 12 December 2016 at http://ecdpm.org/publications/future-lomes-commodity-protocols/.

Durkheim, E., *Suicide: A Study in Sociology* (Abingdon: Routledge, 2002).

Durkheim, E., *The Division of Labour in Society*, W.D. Halls (trans.) (New York: The Free Press, 1984).

Ebegbulem, J.C., J.A. Adams and A.A. Achu, 'The Challenges of Integrating Africa into the Globalised World through New Partnership for Africa's Development (NEPAD)' (2012) 2 *International Journal of Humanities and Social Science* – Special Issue 270–8.

Eccles, R. and N. Nitin (eds), *Networks and Organisations: Structure, Form and Action* (Boston, MA: Harvard Business School Press, 1992).

ECDPM, 'EPA Development Support: Possible Scenarios for EPA-related support mechanisms' ECDPM In Brief No. 16 (November 2006).

Economic Justice Network, 'Impacts of EPAs on Agriculture and Rural Livelihoods in the SADC Region', EJN of FOCCISA Report (undated), available 19 December 2016 at http://ejn.org.za/index.php/learning-centre/epa-issues/21-trade-ejn-research/91-impacts-of-epas-on-agriculture-and-rural-livelihoods-in-the-sadc-region.

Economic Justice Network, 'Trade and Development Cooperation Agreement, Southern African Development Community Configuration and European Trade Negotiations: In the context of the European Partnership Agreements', EJN of FOCCISA Report (undated), available 19 December 2016 at http://www.ejn.org.za/images/stories/Learning%20Centre/EPA%20Issues/1%20EJN%20ReResear/TDCA_SADC_EPAs_Web.pdf.

Edwards, S. and M. Savastano, 'Latin America's Intra-Regional Trade: Evolution and Future Prospects' in D. Greenaway, T. Hyclack and R. Thornton (eds), *Economic Aspects of Regional Trading Arrangements* (London: Harvester Wheatsheaf, 1989).

Ekeh, P., 'The Concept of Second Liberation and the Prospects of Democracy in Africa: A Nigerian Context', Paper given at the Conference on Dilemmas of Democracy in Nigeria, University of Wisconsin, November 10–12 1995, cited in L. Anderson, *Transitions to Democracy* (New York: Columbia University Press, 1999).

El-Ojeili, C. and P. Hayden, *Critical Theories of Globalisation* (Basingstoke: Palgrave McMillan, 2006).
Eldar, O., 'Reform of IMF Conditionality', (2005) 8 *Journal of International Economic Law* 509–49.
Elliott, A. (ed.), *The Routledge Companion to Social Theory* (London: Routledge, 2010).
Englebert, P., 'Pre-Colonial Institutions, Post-Colonial States, and Economic Development in Tropical Africa' (2000) 53 *Political Research Quarterly* 7–36.
EPA Watch, Namibian Civil Society letter to Trade Commissioner Karel de Gucht, 'Re: Open letter on undue pressure on Namibia to sign an interim EPA' (18 June 2010) available 19 December 2016 at http://epawatch.files.wordpress.com/2010/06/namibia-ngo-letter-100618.pdf.
Erasmus, G., 'Deeper Regional Integration in SADC: Do the EPAs undermine the Process', tralac Trade Brief SIITB03/2011 (March 2011).
Erasmus, G., 'Regional Trade Agreements: Developments and Implications for Southern African states' (2009) 1 *Namibia Law Journal* 29–35.
Erasmus, G., F. Flatters and R. Kirk, 'Rules of Origin as Tools of Development? Some Lessons from SADC' in O. Cadot, A. Estevadeordal, A. Suwa-Eisenmann and T. Verdier (eds), *The Origin of Goods: Rules of Origin in Regional Trade Agreements* (Oxford: Oxford University Press, 2006).
Erdmann, G. and U. Engel, 'Neopatrimonialism Reconsidered: Critical Review and Elaboration of an Elusive Concept' (2007) 45 *Commonwealth and Comparative Politics* 95–119.
Eriksen, E.O. and J. Weigård, *Understanding Habermas: Communicative Action and Deliberative Democracy* (London: Continuum, 2003).
Estevadeordal, A., J. Harris and K. Suominen, 'Harmonising Preferential Rules of Origin Regimes Around the World' in R. Baldwin and P. Low (eds), *Multilateralising Regionalism: Challenges for the Global Trading System* (Cambridge: Cambridge University Press, 2009).
Estevadeordal, A. and K. Suominen, 'Mapping and Measuring Rules of Origin Around the World', in O. Cadot, A. Estevadeordal, A. Suwa-Eisenmann and T. Verdier (eds), *The Origin of Goods: Rules of Origin in Regional Trade Agreements* (Oxford: Oxford University Press, 2006).
Ethier, W.J., 'The New Regionalism' (1999) 108 *The Economic Journal* 1149–61.
EU Commission, 'The Economic Impact of the SADC EPA Group-EU Economic Partnership Agreement' of June 2016.

European Commission and European External Action Service, 'Towards a New Partnership Between the European Union and the African, Caribbean, and Pacific Countries After 2020' Summary Report of 18 March 2016, Ref. Ares(2016)1372862.

European Commission, *Trade for All: Towards a More Responsible Trade and Investment Policy*, Trade Policy Strategy Report (15 October 2015).

EU Commission, 'Caribbean Regional Indicative Programme: 11th European Development Fund (EDF)', Ares(2015)3671530 of 7 September 2015.

European Commission, 'Monitoring the Implementation and Results of the CARIFORUM-EU EPA Agreement', Final Report, EUROPEAID/129783/C/SER/multi Lot 1: Studies and Technical Assistance in All Sectors (September 2014).

EU Commission, 'Access to EU markets for exporters from African, Caribbean and Pacific Countries', EC Memo (2011) available at http://trade.ec.europa.eu/doclib/docs/2011/september/tradoc_148215.pdf.

European Commission, *Europe 2020: A European Strategy for Smart, Sustainable and Inclusive Growth* (3.3.2010) COM (2010) 2020.

European Commission, 'Fact Sheet on the Interim Economic Partnership Agreements: SADC Group' *European Commission* (2009) available 19 December 2016 at http://trade.ec.europa.eu/doclib/docs/2009/january/tradoc_142189.pdf.

European Commission, 'Regional Strategy Paper and Regional Indicative Programme 2008–2013', (European Commission, 2008).

European Commission, European Commission DG Trade, 'Commissioner Mandelson's Open Letter to Namibian Civil Society, 2 September 2008', EPA Flash News (5 September 2008) available 19 December at http://trade.ec.europa.eu/doclib/docs/2008/september/tradoc_140482.pdf.

European Commission, 'Applying the arrangements for products originating in certain states which are part of the African, Caribbean and Pacific (ACP) Group of States provided for in agreements establishing, or leading to the establishment of, Economic Partnership Agreements' Council Regulation 1528/2007, [2007] OJ L348/2.

EU Commission, 'Proposal for the Regulation of the European Parliament and of the Council amending Annex 1 to Council Regulation (EC) No 1528/2007 as regards the exclusion of a number of countries from the list of regions or states which have concluded negotiations' COM (2011) 598 Final.

EU Commission, 'Civil Society Dialogue: Economic Partnership Agreements', Minutes of Meeting (25 September 2007) available 19 December 2016 at http://trade.ec.europa.eu/doclib/docs/2007/november/tradoc_136928.pdf.

EU Commission, 'Communication from the Commission to the Council: Communication to modify the directives for the negotiations of Economic Partnership Agreements with ACP countries and regions' COM (2006) 673 Final.

EU Commission, 'Trade for Development: EU-SADC Economic Partnership Agreement', DG Trade Report, (September 2005) available 19 December 2016 at http://trade.ec.europa.eu/doclib/docs/2006/february/tradoc_127350.pdf.

EU Commission, Financing Agreement between the European Commission and the Caribbean Forum of ACP States (CARIFORUM) Agreement No. 9816/Reg RCA/003/04 under the 9th EDF (2004).

EU Commission, Guidelines for the negotiation of new cooperation agreements with the African, Caribbean and Pacific (ACP) countries COM (97) 537 Final of 29 October 1997.

EU Commission, Green Paper on Relations between the European Union and the ACP countries on the eve of the 21st Century: Challenges and options for a new partnership, COM (96) 570 Final (1996).

EU Commission, Completing the Internal Market White Paper COM (85) 310 Final, Brussels (1985).

European Parliament, 'The CARIFORUM-EU Economic Partnership Agreement (EPA): The Development Component' March 2009 EXPO/B/DEVE/2008/60.

Evans, J., 'The Neoliberal Turn in the SADC' (2010) *Nokoko* 101–129.

Ewelukwa, U., 'Special and Differential Treatment in International Trade Law: A Concept in Search of Content' (2003) 79 *North Dakota Law Review* 831–78.

Farrell, M., 'From Lomé to Economic Partnerships in Africa' in F. Söderbaum and P Stålgren (eds), *The European Union and the Global South* (Boulder: Lynne Rienner, 2010).

Farrell, M., 'Bridging the Gap Between EU, Mediterranean and Africa Relations: Partnership, Governance and (Re)-Evolving Relations' (2010) 2 *L'Europe en Formation* 169–91.

Farrell, M., 'EU Policy Towards Other Regions: Policy Learning in the External Promotion of Regional Integration' (2009) 16 *European Public Policy* 1165–84.

Farrell, M., 'A Triumph of Realism over Idealism? Cooperation Between the European Union and Africa' (2005) 27 *European Integration* 263–83.

Farrell, M., B. Hettne and L. van Langenhove (eds), *Global Politics of Regionalism: Theory and Practice* (London: Pluto Press, 2005).

Fasan, O., 'Global Trade Law: Challenges and Options for Africa' (2003) 47 *Journal of African Law* 143–73.

Fatton, R., 'Bringing the Ruling Class Back In: Class, State and Hegemony in Africa' (1988) 20(3) *Comparative Politics* 53.

Fawcett, L., 'Regionalism from an Historical Perspective' in Farrell, M., B. Hettne and L.V. Langenhove (eds), *Global Politics of Regionalism: Theory and Practice* (London: Pluto Press, 2005).

Ferrer, J.N. and A. Behrens, 'Innovative Approaches to EU Blending Mechanisms for Development Finance' CEPS Special Report (18 May 2011) available 19 December 2016 at http://www.cps.eu.

Fierro, E., *The EU's Approach to Human Rights Conditionality in Practice* (The Hague: Kluwer Law International, 2003).

Findlay, R. and A. Panagariya, 'A Political-Economy Analysis of Free Trade Areas and Customs Unions' in J. Bhagwati, P. Krishna and A. Panagariya (eds), *Trading Blocs: Alternative Approaches to Analyzing Preferential Trade Agreements* (Cambridge, MA: MIT Press, 1999).

Finnemore, M. and K. Sikkink, 'International Norm Dynamics and Political Change' (1998) 52 *International Organisation* 887–917.

Fioramonti, L., 'The European Union Development Strategy in Africa: The Economic Partnership Agreements as a case of Aggressive Multilateralism' MERCURY e-paper No. 10 (August 2011) available 19 December 2016 at https://papers.ssrn.com/sol3/papers.cfm?abstract_id=2100538.

Fiorentino, R., J. Crawford and C. Toqueboeuf, 'The Landscape of Regional Trade Agreements and WTO Surveillance' in R. Baldwin and P. Low (eds), *Multilateralizing Regionalism: Challenges for the Global Trading System* (Cambridge: Cambridge University Press, 2009).

Flint, A., 'The End of a "Special Relationship"? The New EU-ACP Economic Partnership Agreements' (2010) 36 *Review of African Political Economy* 79–92.

Fombad, C.M. and Z. Kebonang, 'AU, NEPAD and the APRM: Democratization Efforts Explored', edited by H. Melber (ed.) (Uppsala: Nordiska Afrikainstitutet, 2006).

Freund, C. (ed.), *The WTO and Reciprocal Preferential Trade Agreements* (Cheltenham, UK and Northampton, MA, USA: Edward Elgar, 2007).

Friedman, D., 'On Economic Applications of Evolutionary Game Theory' (1998) 8 *Journal of Evolutionary Economics* 15–43.

Gammage, C., 'A "Sustainability Impact Assessment" of the Economic Partnership Agreements: Challenging the Participatory Process' (2010) 3 *The Law and Development Review* 108–135.

Gantz, D., *Regional Trade Agreements: Law, Policy and Practice* (Durham, NC: Carolina Academic Press, 2009).

Garcia, M. and A. Masselot, 'EU-Asia Free Trade Agreements as Tools for Social Norm/Legislation Transfer' (2015) 3 *Asia Europe Journal* 241–52.

Gathii, J.T., *African Regional Trade Agreements as Legal Regimes* (Cambridge: Cambridge University Press, 2011).

Gathii, J.T., 'The Neoliberal Turn in Regional Trade Agreements' (2011) 86 *Washington Law Review* 421–474.

Gavas, M., 'Reviewing the Evidence: How Well does the European Development Fund Perform?' *ODI Report* of 31 January 2012 accessed 9 December 2016 at https://www.odi.org/sites/odi.org.uk/files/odi-assets/publications-opinion-files/8218.pdf.

Gavin, B. and P. de Lombaerde, 'Economic Theories of Regional Integration' in M. Farrell, B. Hettne and L. van Langenhove (eds), *Global Politics of Regionalism: Theory and Practice* (London: Pluto Press, 2005).

Georgakopoulos, N., *Principles and Methods of Law and Economics: Basic Tools for Normative Reasoning* (Cambridge: Cambridge University Press, 2005).

Gerth, H.H. and C. Wright Mills, *From Max Weber: Essays in Sociology* (London: Routledge, 1991).

Gibb, R., 'Regional Integration and Africa's Development Trajectory: Meta-theories, Expectations and Reality' (2009) 30 *Third World Quarterly* 701–21.

Gibb, R., 'The New Southern African Customs Union Agreement: Dependence with Democracy' (2006) 32 *Journal of Southern African Studies* 583–603.

Gibb, R., 'The European Union and the South' (2000) 21 *Third World Quarterly* 457–81.

Gibb, R., 'Southern Africa in Transition: Prospects and Problems Facing Regional Integration' (1998) 36 *The Journal of Modern African Studies* 287–306.

Gibson, C., 'Of Waves and Ripples: Democracy and Political Change in Africa in the 1990s' (2002) 5 *Annual Review of Political Science* 201–21.

Gilpin, R., *The Political Economy of International Relations* (Princeton, NJ: Princeton University Press, 1987).

Ginsberg, R., 'Conceptualizing the European Union as an International Actor: Narrowing the Theoretical Capability-Expectations Gap' (1999) 37 *Journal of Common Market Studies* 429–54.
Goldstein, J. and J. Gowa, 'US National Power and the Postwar Trading Regime' (2002) 1 *World Trade Review* 153–70.
Gonzales, A., 'Policy Implications of Smallness as a Factor in the Lomé, FTAA and WTO Negotiations', Caribbean RNM/IDB Regional Technical Cooperation Project (Bridgetown, September 2000).
Goodison, P., 'EU Trade Policy and the Future of Africa's Trade Relationship with the EU' (2007) 34 *Review of African Political Economy* 247–66.
Goodison, P. and C. Stoneman, 'Europe: Partner or Exploiter? The G-90 and the ACP' (2004) 31 *Review of African Political Economy* 725–34.
Goto, J. and K. Hamada, 'Regional Economic Integration and Article XXIV of the GATT' (1999) 7 *Review of International Economics* 555–70.
Grace Kennedy Limited, 'Annual Report 2015' available 19 December 2016 at http://www.gracekennedy.com/index.php/media-centre/gk-annual-reports/annual-reports.
Gramsci, A., *Prison Notebooks*, J. Buttigieg (ed.) (New York: Columbia University Press, 1992).
Granovetter, M., 'The Impact of Social Structure on Economic Outcomes' (2005) 19 *Journal of Economic Perspectives* 33–50.
Granovetter, M., 'Problems of Explanation in Economic Sociology' in Eccles, R. and N. Nitin (eds), *Networks and Organisations: Structure, Form and Action* (Boston, MA: Harvard Business School Press, 1992).
Granovetter, M., 'Economic Action and Social Structure: The Problem of Embeddedness' (1985) 91(3) *American Journal of Sociology* 481–510.
Grant, A. and F. Söderbaum (eds), *The New Regionalism in Africa* (Aldershot: Ashgate Publishing Ltd, 2003).
Grant, C. and G. Chapman, 'Southern African Customs Union: Myths and Reality' SAIIA online article (23 March 2011) available 19 December 2016 at http://www.saiia.org.za/opinion-analysis/southern-african-customs-union-myths-and-reality.
Greenaway, D., T. Hyclack and R. Thornton (eds), *Economic Aspects of Regional Trading Arrangements* (New York: Harvester Wheatsheaf, 1989).
Greene, G., 'The CARIFORUM Economic Partnership Agreement: Lessons from Implementation', Report of The Commonwealth *Hot Trade Topics*, Issue 121 (2015).
Grieco, J.M., 'Anarchy and the Limits of Cooperation: A Realist Critique of the Newest Liberal Institutionalism' (1988) 42 *International Organisations* 485–507.

Grimm, S., 'EU Policies toward the Global South' in F. Söderbaum and P. Stålgren (eds), *The European Union and the Global South* (Boulder: Lynne Rienner, 2010).

Grossman, G.M. and E. Helpman, 'The Politics of Free-Trade Agreements' in J. Bhagwati, P. Krishna and A. Panagariya (eds), *Trading Blocs: Alternative Approaches to Analyzing Preferential Trade Agreements* (Cambridge, MA: MIT Press, 1999).

Grugel, J. and W. Hout (eds), *Regionalism Across the North-South Divide: State Strategies and Globalisation* (London & New York: Routledge, 1999).

Haarlov, J., *Regional Cooperation and Integration within Industry and Trade in Southern Africa: General Approaches: SADCC and the World Bank* (Aldershot: Avebury, 1997).

Haastrup, T., 'EU as Mentor? Promoting Regionalism as External Relations Practice in EU-Africa relations' (2013) *Journal of European Integration* 1–16.

Habermas, J., 'The Crisis of the European Union in Light of a Constitutionalization of International Law' (2012) 23 *European Journal of International Law* 335–48.

Habermas, J., *The Postnational Constellation: Political Essays* translated by M. Pensky (Cambridge: Polity Press, 2007).

Habermas, J., 'A Political Construction for the Pluralist World Society?' (2007) 34 *Chinese Journal of Philosophy* 331–43.

Habermas, J., *Between Facts & Norms*, translated by W. Rehg (Cambridge: Polity Press, 1996).

Habermas, J., *The Theory of Communicative Action: Reason and the Rationalisation of Society* Vol. 1, T. McCarthy (trans.) (London: Beacon Press, 1984).

Hafner-Burton, E., *Forced to Be Good: Why Trade Agreements Boost Human Rights* (Cornell University Press, 2009).

Haight, F.A., 'Customs Unions and Free Trade Areas under GATT: A Reappraisal' (1972) 6 *Journal of World Trade Law* 391–404.

Hall, K. and M. Sang, *Caribbean Community: The Struggle for Survival* (Trafford, 2008).

Hansungule, M., 'The Suspension of the SADC Tribunal' (2013) 35 *Strategic Review for Southern Africa* 135–45.

Harrison, G., 'The World Bank, Governance and Theories of Political Action in Africa' (2005) 7(1) *British Journal of International Politics* 240–60.

Harrison, G. and E. Ruström, 'Trade Wars, Trade Negotiations and Applied Game Theory' (1991) 101 *The Economic Journal* 420–35.

Harryvan, A., *In Pursuit of Influence: The Netherland's European Policy during the Formative Years of the European Union, 1952-1973* (New York: PIE Peter Lang, 2009).
Hartley, T., *Constitutional Problems of the European Union* (Oxford: Hart Publishing, 1999).
Hartzenburg, T., 'Introduction' in A. du Pisani, G. Erasmus, T. Hartzenburg and C. McCarthy (eds), *Monitoring Regional Integration in Southern Africa Yearbook 2013/14* (Stellenbosch: tralac, 2014).
Hartzenberg, T. and G. Maasdorp, 'Regional Integration Arrangements in Southern Africa: SACU and SADC' in Z. Iqbar and M. Khan (eds), *Trade Reform and Regional Integration in Africa* (Washington, D.C.: IMF, 1997).
Harvey, D., *A Brief History of Neoliberalism* (Oxford: Oxford University Press, 2005).
Harvey, D., *The Condition of Postmodernity* (Oxford: Blackwell, 1998).
Hawkins, T., 'Regionalism in Southern Africa' in G. Mills and C. Mutschler (eds), *Exploring South-South Dialogue: MERCOSUR in Latin America and SADC in Southern Africa* (Johannesburg: SAIIA, 1999).
Heita, D., 'Namibia Inspires NGOs' anti-EPA campaigns' (New Era, 26 March 2010).
Held, D., A. McGrew, D. Goldblatt and J. Perraton, *Global Transformations: Politics, Economics and Culture* (Stanford, CA: Stanford University Press, 1999).
Herbst, J., *States and Power in Africa: Comparative Lessons in Authority and Control* (Princeton, NJ: Princeton University Press, 2000).
Heron, T., 'Trading in Development: Norms and Institutions in the Making/Unmaking of European-African, Caribbean, Pacific trade and development cooperation' (2014) 20 *Contemporary Politics* 10–22.
Heron, T., 'Asymmetric Bargaining and Development Trade-Offs in the CARIFORUM-European Union Economic Partnership Agreement' (2011) 18 *Review of International Political Economy* 328–57.
Heron, T. and P. Murray-Evans, 'Limits to Market Power: Strategic Discourse and Institutional Path Dependence in the European Union – African, Caribbean, and Pacific Economic Partnership Agreements' (2016) *European Journal of International Relations* 1–25.
Hettne, B., 'EU Foreign Policy: The Interregional Model' in F. Söderbaum, and P. Stålgren (eds), *The European Union and the Global South* (Boulder: Lynne Rienner, 2010).
Hettne, B., 'Regionalism and World Order' in M. Farrell, B. Hettne and L. van Langenhove (eds), *Global Politics of Regionalism: Theory and Practice* (London: Pluto Press, 2005).

Hettne, B., 'Beyond the "New" Regionalism' (2005) 10 *New Political Economy* 543–71.

Hettne, B. and F. Söderbaum, 'Theorising the Rise of Regionness' (2000) 5 *New Political Economy* 457–73.

Hilf, M., 'The ECJ's Opinion 1/94 on the WTO – No Surprise, but Wise?' (1995) 6 *European Journal of International Law* 245–59.

Hinkle, L., M. Hoppe and R. Newfarmer, 'Beyond Cotonou: Economic Partnerships in Africa' in R. Newfarmer, *Trade, Doha, and Development: A Window into the Issues* (Washington, D.C.: World Bank, 2006), 263–80

Hinkle, L. and M. Schiff, 'Economic Partnership Agreements Between Sub-Saharan Africa and the EU: A Development Perspective' (2004) 27 *World Economy* 1321–33.

Hipold, P., 'Regional Integration According to Article XXIV GATT – Between Law and Politics' in A. von Bogdandy and R. Wolfrum (eds), *Max Planck Yearbook of United Nations Law* Vol. 7 (Koninklijke Brill NV, 2003).

Hirsch, M., 'The Sociology of International Economic Law: Sociological Analysis of the Regulation of Regional Trade Agreements in the World Trading System' (2008) 19 *European Journal of International Law* 277–99.

Hirsch, M., 'Rules of Origin as Trade or Foreign Policy Instruments? The European Union Policy on Products Manufactured in the Settlements in the West Bank and the Gaza Strip' (2002) 26 *Fordham International Law Journal* 572–94.

Hobbes, T., *Leviathan*, J.C.A. Gaskin (ed.) (New York: Oxford University Press, 1998).

Hoekman, B., 'Operationalizing the Concept of Policy Space in the WTO: Beyond Special and Differential Treatment' (2005) 8 *Journal of International Economic Law* 405–24.

Holdgaard, R., *External Relations of the European Community: Legal Reasoning and Legal Discourses* (Aalphen ann den Rijn: Kluwer Law International, 2008).

Holland, M., *The European Union and the Third World* (Basingstoke: Palgrave MacMillan, 2002).

Hollis, M. and S. Smith, *Explaining and Understanding International Relations* (Oxford: Clarendon Press, 1980).

Holzcheiter, A., 'Discourse as Capability: Non-state Actors' Capital in Global Governance' (2005) 33 *Millennium: Journal of International Studies* 723–46.

Hönich, U., 'Trade in Goods: Full Liberalisation in the EU' in A. Zampetti and J. Lodge, *The CARIFORUM-EU Economic Partnership Agreement: A Practitioner's Analysis* (Alphen aan den Rijn: Kluwer Law International, 2011).
Hooghe, L. 'Images of Europe: How Commission Officials Conceive Their Institution's Role' (2012) 50 *Journal of Common Market Studies* 87–111.
Hopf, T., 'Common-Sense Constructivism and Hegemony in World Politics' (2013) 67 *International Organisation* 317–54.
Horkheimer, M., *Critical Theory* (New York: Seabury Press, 1982).
Horlick, G., 'Straightening the Spaghetti Bowl' in K. Bagwell and P. Mavroidis (eds), *Preferential Trade Agreements: A Law and Economics Analysis* (Cambridge: Cambridge University Press, 2011).
Hormeku, T., 'Fall-Out from EPA Negotiations: Africa on the Brink of Disintegration', TWN Africa: African Trade Agenda, 3:1 (TWN, May 2009) available 19 December 2016 at http://twnafrica.org/ATA3_1-en-june2009.pdf.
Horwitz, M., 'The Rise of Legal Formalism' (1975) *The American Journal of Legal History* 251–64.
Howe, P., 'The Utopian Realism of E.H. Carr' (1994) 20 *Review of International Studies* 277–97.
Howse, R. and J. Langille, 'Permitting Pluralism: The *Seal Products* Dispute and Why the WTO Should Accept Restrictions Justified by Noninstrumental Moral Values' (2012) 37 *Yale Journal of International Law* 367–432.
Hsu, L., 'Applicability of WTO law in Regional Trade Agreements: Identifying the Links' in L. Bartels and F. Ortino (eds), *Regional Trade Agreements & The WTO Legal System* (Oxford University Press, 2006).
Huber, J., 'The Past, Present and Future ACP-EC Trade Regime and the WTO' (2000) 11 *European Journal of International Law* 427–38.
Hudec, R., *Developing Countries in the GATT Legal System*, 2nd edn (Cambridge: Cambridge University Press, 2011).
Hudec, R., 'The New WTO Dispute Settlement Procedure: An Overview of the First Three Years' (1999) 8 *Minnesota Journal of Global Trade* 1–49.
Humphrey, E. and M. Cossy, 'Implementing the Economic Partnership Agreement: Challenges and Bottlenecks for the CARIFORUM Region' ECDPM Discussion Paper No. 117 of June 2011.
Hunt, A., 'Problems of the State: Law, State and Class Struggle' (1976) *Marxism Today* 178–87.
Hunter, J. and C.M. Lewis (eds), *The New Institutional Economics and Third World Development* (London: Routledge, 1995).

Hurrell, A., 'One World? Many Worlds? The Place of Regions in the Study of International Society' (2007) 83 *International Affairs* 127–46.

Hurt, S.R., 'The EU-SADC Economic Partnership Agreement Negotiations: "Locking" in the Neoliberal Development Model in Southern Africa?' (2012) 33 *Third World Quarterly* 495–510.

Hurt, S.R., 'Cooperation and Coercion? The Cotonou Agreement between the EU and ACP States and the end of the Lomé Convention' (2003) 24 *Third World Quarterly* 161–76.

Hurt, S., D. Lee and U. Lorenz-Carl, 'The Argumentative Dimension to the EU-Africa EPAs' (2013) 18 *International Negotiation* 67–87.

Hutton, N., 'Africa's Changing Relationship with the EEC' (1974) 30 *The World Today* 426–35.

Hylton, G.A., 'The Challenge of Integrating ACP States into the International Trading Regime: Venturing Outside the Lome Framework', Paper delivered at the CTA International Seminar Brussels (27–29 November 2002).

ICTSD, 'African countries and EU sign Economic Partnership Agreement' Bridges Africa Newsroom report (21 June 2016) available 19 December 2016 at http://www.ictsd.org/bridges-news/bridges-africa/news/newsroom-17.

Ikome, F.N., *From the Lagos Plan of Action to the New Partnership for Africa's Development – The Political Economy of African Regional Initiatives* (Midrand: Institute for Global Dialogue, 2007).

Ilbery, B., 'Food Supply Chains and Sustainability: Evidence from Specialist Food Producers in the Scottish/English Borders' (2005) 22 *Land Use Policy* 331–44.

IMF, *Regional Economic Integration and the Globalisation Process: Report on the Proceedings of a Southern African Conference*, Windhoek 10–13 June 1998 (Dar es Salaam: Friedrich-Ebert-Stiftung, 1998).

Ingram, J.S., P. Ericken and D. Liverman, *Food Security and Global Environmental Change* (London: Taylor & Francis, 2010).

Irwin, D., *Free Trade Under Fire* (Princeton, NJ: Princeton University Press: 2009).

Ishyrion, P., 'Trade-Caribbean: EU Pact Hit by Last-Minute Revolt' Inter Press Service news report (August 2008) available 19 December 2016 at http://www.ipsnews.net/2008/08/trade-caribbean-eu-pact-hit-by-last-minute-revolt/.

Jackson, R. and G. Sørensen (eds), *Introduction to International Relations: Theories and Approaches* (Oxford: Oxford University Press, 2010).

Jakobeit, C., T. Hartzenberg and N. Charalambides, 'Overlapping Membership in COMESA, EAC, SACU and SADC: Trade Policy Options for the Region and for EPA Negotiations' GTZ Trade Programme Report (Eschborn 2005) available 19 December 2016 at http://hubrural.org/Overlapping-membership-in-COMESA.html?lang=en.

Jara, A., 'The WTO and International Trade Law After Doha: Where Do We Go From Here?' (2007) 25 *Berkeley Journal of International Law* 384–94.

Jensen, M.F. and P. Gibbon, 'Africa and the WTO Doha Round: An Overview' (2007) 25 *Development Policy Review* 5–24.

Jervis, R., 'Realism, Game Theory and Cooperation' (1988) 40 *World Politics* 317–49.

Jessop, D., 'CARICOM and the Dominican Republic: The Case for Reconciliation' (28 August 2015) *Argument and Insight* available 19 December 2016 at http://www.antillean.org/caricom-and-the-dominican-republic-reconcile-142/.

Jones, K., *The Doha Blues* (New York and Oxford: Oxford University Press, 2010).

Jones, P., 'The Caribbean Community (CARICOM): Origins, Achievements, The Future: Volume II' Economic Development Institute, *Information Booklet Series II* available 19 December 2016 at https://ideas.repec.org/p/wpa/wuwpdc/0411006.html.

Joseph, R., 'Democratization in Africa after 1989: Comparative and Theoretical Perspectives' (1997) 29 *Comparative Politics* 363–82.

Julian, M., 'EPA Update' *Trade Negotatiation Insights*, 9:3 (March 2010) available 19 December 2016 at http://ictsd.org/i/news/tni/72888/.

Julian, M. and M. Dalleau, 'EPA Update' (2011) *Trade Negotiation Insights*, Volume 10 Number 7, October 2011 available 19 December 2016 at http://ictsd.org/i/news/tni/115340/.

Kagaruki, E., 'NEPAD has failed to solve Africa's myriad problems' *The Chronicle* (16 July 2011) accessed 12 December 2016 at http://www.thecitizen.co.tz/oped/1840568-1800138-ig2hrj/index.html.

Kamidza, R., 'SADC EPA Information Seminar Failed Civil Society' SEATINI Bulletin, 10:7 (16 July 2007) available 19 December 2016 at http://www.sarpn.org/documents/d0002683/SEATINI_Bulletin_10-07_Jul2007.pdf.

Keck, A. and P. Low, 'Special and Differential Treatment in the WTO: Why, When and How?' (2004) WTO, Washington DC, Staff Working Paper ERSD-2004-03.

Keck, M. and K. Sikkink, *Activists Beyond Borders: Advocacy Networks in International Politics* (Ann Arbor, MI: Michigan University Press, 1998).

Kelsall, T., 'Going with the Grain in African Development?' (2008) 26(6) *Development Policy Review* 627–55.

Kelsey, J., 'Going Nowhere in a Hurry? The Pacific's EPA Negotiations with the European Union' (2007) *Victoria University of Wellington Law Review* 81–103.

Kemp, M.C. and H.Y. Wan Jr., 'An Elementary Proposition Concerning the Formation of Customs Unions' (1976) in Caroline Freund (ed.), *The WTO and Reciprocal Preferential Trade Agreements* (Cheltenham, UK and Northampton, MA, USA: Edward Elgar, 2007).

Keohane, R.O., *Power and Governance in a Partially Globalised World* (London: Routledge, 2002).

Keohane, R.O., 'International Institutions: Two Approaches' (1988) 32 *International Studies Quarterly* 379–96.

Kessie, E., 'The Legal Status of Special and Differential Treatment Provisions under the WTO Agreements' in G. Bermann and P. Mavroidis (eds), *WTO and Developing Countries* (Cambridge: Cambridge University Press, 2007).

Khadiagala, G.M., 'Governing Regionalism in Africa: Themes and Debates', Policy Brief 51, (Johannesburg: Centre for Policy Studies, 2008).

Killick, T., 'Political Autonomy and the History of British Aid to Africa' (2005) 23 *Development Policy Review* 665–81.

Konadu-Agyemang, K. 'The Best of Times and the Worst of Times: Structural Adjustment Programs and Uneven Development in Africa: The Case of Ghana' (2004) 52 *The Professional Geographer* 469–83.

Konstadinides, T., 'EU Foreign Policy under the Doctrine of Implied Powers: Codification Drawbacks and Constitutional Limitations' (2014) *European Law Review* 511–30.

Kornegay, F. and G. Olivier, 'The European Union and Africa's Regional Economic Communities: Asymmetrical versus Developmental Multilateralism' MERCURY Working Paper (April 2011).

Kösler, A. and M. Zimmek, *Elements of Regional Integration: A Multidimensional Approach* (Baden-Baden: Nomos, 2008).

Koutrakos, P., *EU International Relations Law*, 2nd edn (Oxford: Hart Publishing, 2015).

Krishna, P., 'Understanding Rules of Origin' in O. Cadot, A. Estevadeordal, A. Suwa-Eisenmann and T. Verdier (eds.), *The Origin of Goods: Rules of Origin in Regional Trade Agreements* (Oxford: Oxford University Press, 2006).

Krueger, A., 'Are Preferential Trade Agreements Trade Liberalising or Protectionist?' (1999) 13(4) *The Journal of Economic Perspectives*, 105–24.

Krueger, A., 'Why Trade Liberalisation is Good for Growth' (1998) 108 *The Economic Journal* 1513–22.

Krueger, A., 'Trade Policy and Development: How We Learn' (1997) 87 *The American Economic Review* 1–22.

Krueger, A., 'The Political Economy of the Rent-Seeking Society' (1974) 64 *The American Economic Review* 291–303.

Krugman, P., 'Regionalism versus Multilateralism: Analytical Notes' in C. Freund (ed.), *The WTO and Reciprocal Preferential Trade Agreements* (Cheltenham, UK and Northampton, MA, USA: Edward Elgar, 2007).

Krugman, P., 'The Move Towards Free Trade Zones, Implications of Trade and Currency Zones. A symposium sponsored by the Federal Reserve Bank of Kansas City' (1991).

Krugman, P., 'Is Free Trade Passe?' (1987) *Journal of Economic Perspectives* 131–44.

Kwarteng, C., *Africa and the European Challenge: Survival in a Changing World* (Aldershot, UK and Brookfield, VT, USA: Avebury, 1997).

Lacarte-Muró, J. and P. Gappah, 'Developing Countries and the WTO Legal and Dispute Settlement System: A View from the Bench' (2000) 3 *Journal of International Economic Law* 395–401.

La Chimia, A. and S. Arrowsmith, 'Addressing Tied Aid: Towards a More Development-Oriented WTO?' (2009) 12 *Journal of International Economic Law* 707–47.

Lamy, P., 'Stepping Stones or Stumbling Blocks? The EU's Approach Towards the Problem of Multilateralism vs Regionalism in Trade Policy' (2002) 25 *The World Economy* 1399–413.

Landsberg, C., 'The African Union and the New Partnership for Africa's Development (NEPAD): Restoring a Relationship Challenged?' (2012) 12 *African Journal on Conflict Resolution* 49–71.

Lang, A., *World Trade Law after Neoliberalism: Reimagining the Global Economic Order* (Oxford: Oxford University Press, 2011).

Langenhove, L.V., *Building Regions: The Regionalisation of the World Order* (Aldershot: Ashgate, 2011).

Laursen, F., 'Theoretical Perspectives on Comparative Regional Integration' in Finn Laursen (ed.), *Comparative Regional Integration: Theoretical Perspectives* (Aldershot: Ashgate Publishing Ltd, 2003).

Laursen, F., *Comparative Regional Integration: Theoretical Perspectives* (Aldershot: Ashgate Publishing Ltd, 2003).

Lawrence, R., 'Regional and the WTO – Should the Rules be Changed?' in C. Freund (ed.), *The WTO and Reciprocal Preferential Trading Agreements* (Cheltenham, UK and Northampton, MA, USA: Edward Elgar, 2007).

Lee, M., *The Political Economy of Regionalism in Southern Africa* (Boulder: Lynne Rienner, 2003).

Leutweiler, F. et al, *Trade Policies for a Better Future* (Geneva: GATT, 1981) cited in J. McMillan, 'Does Regional Integration Foster Open Trade? Economic Theory and GATT's Article XXIV' in K. Anderson and R. Blackhurst (eds), *Regional Integration in the Global Trading System* (New York: Harvester Wheatsheaf, 1993).

Libman, A. and E. Vinokurov, 'Regional Integration and Economic Convergence in the Post-Soviet Space: Experience of the Decade of Growth' (2012) 50 *Journal of Common Market Studies* 112–28.

Limão, N. and M. Olarreaga, 'Trade Preference to Small Developing Countries and the Welfare Costs of Lost Multilateral Liberalisation' in G. Bermann and P. Mavroidis (eds), *WTO and Developing Countries* (Cambridge: Cambridge University Press, 2007).

Lombarde, P. de., F. Söderbaum and F. Baert, 'The Problem of Comparison in Comparative Regionalism' (2010) 36 *Review of International Studies* 731–53.

Low, P., 'Is the WTO Doing Enough for Developing Countries?' in G. Bermann and P. Mavroidis (eds), *WTO and Developing Countries* (Cambridge: Cambridge University Press, 2007).

Lowe, V., 'Sustainable Development and Unsustainable Arguments' in A. Boyle and D. Freestone, *International Law and Sustainable Development: Past Achievements and Future Challenges* (Oxford: Oxford University Press, 1999).

Luhmann, N., *Social Systems* translated by D. Baecker and J. Bednarz (Stanford, CA: Stanford University Press, 1996).

Lumsdaine, D.H., *Moral Vision in International Politics: The Foreign Aid Regime 1949–1989* (Princeton, NJ: Princeton University Press, 1993).

Luiz, J., 'Challenges and Prospects for Economic and Business Development in Africa' in J. Luiz (ed.), *Managing Business in Africa* (Oxford: Oxford University Press, 2006).

Luiz-Fabri, H., 'Is There a Case – Legally and Politically – For Direct Effect of WTO Obligations?' (2014) 25 *European Journal of International Law* 151–73.

Lyakurwa, W. and O. Ajakaiye, 'Policy Advice and African Studies' in H. Melber (ed.), *On Africa: Scholars and African Studies – Contributions in Honour of Lennart Wohlgemuth* (Uppsala: Nordic Africa Institute), 207.

MacLeod, G., 'New Regionalism Reconsidered: Globalization and the Remaking of Political Economic Space' (2001) 25 *International Journal of Urban and Regional Research* 804–29.

Madava, T., 'Zimbabwe: SADC Troika Meeting in Limbo' Financial Gazette (Harare) 3 October 2012, available 19 December 2016 at http://allafrica.com/stories/201210041266.html.

Malmström, C., 'Values in EU Trade Policy – Targeting Corruption', Speech of 19 April 2016, 4th OECD Integrity Forum, Paris accessed 9 December 2016 at http://trade.ec.europa.eu/doclib/docs/2016/april/tradoc_154461.pdf.

Mambara, J., 'An Evaluation of Involvement of Southern Africa's Civil Society in EPA Negotiations to Date', Trades Centre Report: Zimbabwe (2007).

Manger, M. and K. Schadlen, 'Political Trade Dependence and North-South Trade Agreements' (2014) 58 *International Studies Quarterly* 79–91.

Manners, I., 'The Normative Ethics of the European Union' (2008) 84 *International Affairs* 45–60.

Manning, P. and G. Smith, 'Symbolic Interactionism' in A. Elliott (ed.), *The Routledge Companion to Social Theory* (New York: Routledge, 2010).

Mansfield, E.D. and H.V. Milner, 'The New Wave of Regionalism' (1999) 53 *International Organization* 589–627.

Mansfield, E.D. and E. Reinhardt, 'Multilateral Determinants of Regionalism: The Effects of GATT/WTO on the Formation of Preferential Trade Agreements' (2003) 57 *International Organisation* 829–62.

Marceau, G. and J. Wyatt, 'Dispute Settlement Regimes Intermingled: Regional Trade Agreements and the WTO' (2010) 1 *Journal of International Dispute Settlement* 67–95.

Martin, L., 'Interests, Power and Multilateralism' (1992) 46 *International Organization* 765–92.

Mashayekhi, M. and T. Ito (eds), 'Multilateralism and Regionalism: The New Interface' UNCTAD Report (2004) UNCTAD/DITC/TNCD/2004/7, 43 available 19 December 2016 at http://unctad.org/en/Docs/ditctncd20047_en.pdf.

Matambalya, F., *The New EU-ACP Partnership: Consequences for Eastern and Southern Africa* (Dar es Salaam: Friedrich Ebert Stiftung, 2000).

Matambalya, F. and S. Wolf, 'The Cotonou Agreement and the Challenges of Making the New EU-ACP Trade Regime WTO Compatible' (2001) 35 *Journal of World Trade* 123–44.

Matsushita, M., 'Legal Aspects of Free Trade Agreements: In the Context of Article XXIV of the GATT 1994' in M. Matsushita and D. Ahn (eds), *WTO and East Asia: New Perspectives* (London: CMP Publishing, 2004).

Matsushita, M. and D. Ahn (eds), *WTO and East Asia: New Perspectives* (London: CMP Publishing, 2004).

Matsushita, M., T. Schoenbaum and P. Mavroidis (eds), *The World Trade Organisation: Law, Practice and Policy*, 2nd edn (Oxford: Oxford University Press, 2006).

Mathis, J., 'The "Legalization" of GATT Article XXIV – Can Foes Become Friends?' in Bagwell, K. and P. Mavroidis (eds), *Preferential Trade Agreements: A Law and Economics Analysis* (Cambridge: Cambridge University Press, 2011).

Mathis, J., *Regional Trade Agreements in the GATT/WTO: Article XXIV and the Internal Trade Requirement* (The Hague: TMC Asser Press, 2002).

Matthews, D., 'Lomé IV and ACP/EEC Relations: Surviving the Lost Decade' (1991) 22 *California Western International Law Journal* 1–58.

Mattli, W., *The Logic of Regional Integration: Europe and Beyond* (Cambridge: Cambridge University Press, 1999).

Mavroidis, P., 'Remedies in the WTO: Between a Rock and a Hard Place' (2000) 11 *Journal of International Economic Law* 763–813.

Mbeki, T., 'The African Renaissance', Speech delivered on 13 August 1998 available 19 December 2016 at http://www.dfa.gov.za/docs/speeches/1998/mbek0813.htm.

McCarthy, C., 'The Southern African Customs Union in Transition' (2003) 102 *African Affairs* 605–30.

McCarthy, T., 'Kantian Constructivism and Reconstructivism: Rawls and Habermas in Dialogue' (1994) 105 *Ethics* 44–63.

McKinsey Global Institute, 'Lions on the Move: The progress and potential of African Economies' (June 2010) Report of McKinsey & Company accessed 8 December 2016 at http://www.mckinsey.com/global-themes/middle-east-and-africa/lions-on-the-move.

Mcloskey, M., 'The Emperor Has No Clothes: The Conundrum of Sustainable Development' (1998) 9 *Duke Environmental Law and Policy Forum* 153–9.

McMillan, J., 'Does Regional Integration Foster Open Trade? Economic Theory and GATT's Article XXIV' in K. Anderson and R. Blackhurst (eds), *Regional Integration in the Global Trading System* (New York: Harvester Wheatsheaf, 1993).

McQueen, M., 'ACP-EU Trade Cooperation after 2000: An Assessment of Reciprocal Trade Preferences' (1998) 36 *Journal of Modern African Studies* 669–92.

Meunier, S. and K. Nicolaïdis, 'The European Union as a Conflicted Trade Power' (2006) 13 *Journal of European Public Policy* 906–25.

Meyn, M., 'Economic Partnership Agreements: A "Historic Step" Towards a "Partnership of Equals"?' (2008) 26 *Development Policy Review* 515–28.

Meyn, M., 'The End of Botswana Beef Exports to the European Union?', ODI Policy Briefing (September 2007) available 19 December 2016 at http://www.odi.org.uk/resources/download/392.pdf.

Meyn, M. and J. Kennan, 'Economic Partnership Agreements: Comparative Analysis of the Agricultural Provisions', UNCTAD Report (2010) available 19 December 2016 at http://www.unctad.org/en/docs/ditctncd20093_en.pdf.

Mills, G. and C. Mutschler, *Exploring South-South Dialogue: MERCOSUR in Latin America and SADC in Southern Africa* (Johannesburg: SAIIA, 1999).

Milner, C., 'An Assessment of the Overall Implementation and Adjustment Costs for the ACP Countries of Economic Partnership Agreements with the EU' Commonwealth Secretariat Report (September 2005).

Minta, I., 'The Lomé Convention and the New International Economic Order' (1984) 27 *Howard Law Journal* 953–74.

Mkandawire, T., 'Aid, Accountability and Democracy in Africa' (2010) 77 *Social Research: An International Quarterly* 1149–82.

Mold, A. (ed.), *EU Development Policy in a Changing World: Challenges for the 21st Century* (Amsterdam: Amsterdam University Press, 2007).

Montana, I., 'The Lomé Conventions from Inception to the Dynamics of Post-Cold War, 1957–1990s' (2003) 2 *African and Asian Studies* 63–97.

Moore, M. (ed.), *Doha and Beyond: The Future of the Multicultural Trading System*, (Cambridge: Cambridge University Press, 2004).

Moravcsik, A., 'Taking Preferences Seriously: A Liberal Theory of International Politics' (1997) 51(4) *International Organisation* 513–66.

Morgenthau, H., *Politics Among Nations: The Struggle for Power and Peace* (New York: McGraw-Hill, 1948).

Mosoti, V., 'Africa in the First Decade of WTO Dispute Settlement' (2006) 9 *Journal of International Economic Law* 427–53.

Mourik, A.V., 'The Economic Theory of Customs Unions and Free Trade Areas' in Tacis & EIPA (ed.), *Free Trade Agreements and Customs Unions: Challenges and Constraints* (Brussels: EIPA, 1997).

Moyo, D., *Dead Aid: Why Aid is Not Working and How There is Another Way for Africa* (London: Penguin, 2010).

Mukherji, I., 'Asian Economic Integration' in Anil Kumar Thakur and Adesh Sharma (eds), *Asian Economic Integration* (New Delhi: Deep & Deep Publications PVT Ltd: 2008).

Mulaudzi, C., 'New Regionalism in Southern Africa? Between South African Hegemony and Globalisation' (2009) XVI *Lusotopie* 47–65.

Munck, R., 'Neoliberalism and Politics, and the Politics of Neoliberalism' in A. Saad-Filho and D. Johnston, *Neoliberalism: A Critical Reader* (London: Pluto Press, 2005).
Murray, R., *Human Rights in Africa: From the OAU to the African Union* (Cambridge University Press, 2004).
Naumann, E., 'Rules of Origin under EPAs: Key Issues and New Directions' in S. Bilal and R. Grynberg (eds), *Navigating New Waters: A Reader on ACP-EU Trade Relations* (London: Commonwealth Secretariat, 2007).
Ndayi, Z., 'Contextualising NEPAD: Regionalism, Plurilateralism and Multilateralism' (2009) 16 *South African Journal of International Affairs* 371–87.
Ndulu, B., L. Kritzinger-van Niekerk and R. Reinikka, 'Infrastructure, Regional Integration and Growth in Sub-Saharan Africa' in FONDAD, *Africa in the World Economy – the National, Regional and International Challenges* (The Hague: FONDAD, 2005).
Niekerk, J.P.V. and W.G Schulze, *The South African Law of International Trade: Selected Topics* (SAGA Legal Publications, 2000).
Nkrumah, K., 'The Voice of Africa' Speech by Osagyefo the President on the Opening of the Ghana External Broadcasting Service (27 October 1961) available 12 December 2016 at http://www.nkrumah.net/index.html.
Nkrumah, K., 'Guide to Party Action: Address by Osagyefo Dr Kwame Nkrumah at the First Seminar at the Winneba Ideological School' (3 February 1961) available 12 December 2016 at http://www.nkrumah.net/index.html.
North, D.C., 'The New Institutional Economics and Third World Development' in J. Harris, J. Hunter and C.M. Lewis (eds), *The New Institutional Economics and Third World Development* (London: Routledge, 1995).
Nozick, R., *Anarchy, State, and Utopia* (Oxford: Basic Books Ltd, 1974).
Nussbaum, M., 'Capabilities as Fundamental Entitlements: Sen and Social Justice' (2003) 9 *Feminist Economics* 33–59.
Nwobike, J.C., 'The Emerging Trade Regime Under the Cotonou Partnership Agreement: Its Human Rights Implications' (2006) 40 *Journal of World Trade* 291–314.
Ochieng, C., 'The EU-ACP Economic Partnership Agreements and the "Development Question": Constraints and Opportunities posed by Article XXIV and Special and Differential Treatment Provisions of the WTO' (2007) 10 *Journal of International Economic Law* 363–95.

OECD, 'Agricultural Policies in OECD Countries: Monitoring and Evaluation' OECD Report (2009) available 19 December 2016 at http://www.oecd.org/agriculture/agriculturalpoliciesandsupport/43239979.pdf.

OECD, *Handbook on Economic Globalisation Indicators* (OECD, 2005).

OECD and WTO, 'Aid for Trade Case Study: Caribbean Trade and Private Sector Development Programme (CTPSDP)-Phase II' Report dated 23 February 2011 available 19 December 2016 at https://www.oecd.org/aidfortrade/47461989.pdf.

Oelbaum, J., 'Populist Reform Coalitions in Sub-Saharan Africa: Ghana's Triple Alliance' (2002) 36 *Canadian Journal of African Studies* 281–328.

Ohmae, K., *The End of the Nation State: The Rise of Regional Economics* (London: Harper Collins, 1995).

Ojo, O. (ed.), *Africa and Europe: The Changing Economic Relationship* (London: Zed Books, 1996).

Omotola, J.S., 'Globalisation, New Regionalism and the Challenge of Development in Africa' (2010) *Africana* 103–35.

Onguglo, B. and T. Ito, 'In Defence of the ACP Submission on Special and Differential Treatment in GATT Article XXIV, ECDPM Discussion Paper 67 (2005).

Oosthuizen, G., *The Southern African Development Community: The Organisation, its Policies and Prospects* (Midrand: Institute for Global Dialogue, 2006).

Osaghae, E.E., 'The Character of the State, Legitimacy Crisis and Social Mobilisation in Africa: An Exploration of Form and Character' (1989) 14(2) *Journal of African Development* 27–47.

Osborne, M., *An Introduction to Game Theory* (New York: Oxford University Press, 2004).

Oshikoya, T., 'The Uruguay Round of Trade Negotiations: Implications for Africa' in O. Ojo (ed.), *Africa and Europe: The Changing Economic Relationship* (London: Zed Books Ltd, 1996).

Østergaard, T., 'Classical Models of Regional Integration – What Relevance for Southern Africa?' in B. Odén (ed.), Southern Africa After Apartheid: Regional Integration and External Resources (Nordic Africa Institute, 1993).

Østergaard, T., *SADCC: A Political and Economic Survey* (Copenhagen: Danida, 1990).

Outhwaite, W., *The Habermas Reader* (Cambridge: Polity Press, 1996).

Oyejide, A., 'Development Dimensions in Multilateral Trade Negotiations' in M. Moore (ed.), *Doha and Beyond: The Future of the Multicultural Trading System* (Cambridge: Cambridge University Press, 2004).

Panagariya, A., 'EU Preferential Trade Arrangements and Developing Countries' (2002) 25 *The World Economy* 1415–32.

Panagariya, A., 'Preferential Trade Liberalisation: The Traditional Theory and New Developments' (2002) 38 *Journal of Economic Literature* 287–331.

Panagariya, A. and R. Findlay, 'A Political-Economy Analysis of Free-Trade Areas and Customs Unions' in J. Bhagwati, P. Krishna and A. Panagariya (eds.), *Trading Blocs: Alternative Approaches to Analyzing Preferential Trade Agreements* (Cambridge, MA: MIT Press, 1999).

Panke, D., 'Lobbying Institutional Key Players: How States Seek to Influence the European Commission, the Council Presidency and the European Parliament' (2012) 50 *Journal of Common Market Studies* 129–50.

Parsons, C., *How to Map Arguments in Political Science* (Oxford: Oxford University Press, 2007).

Pauwelyn, J., 'Legal Avenues to Multilateralising Regionalism: Beyond Article XXIV' in R. Baldwin and P. Low (eds), *Multilateralising Regionalism: Challenges for the Global Trading System* (Cambridge: Cambridge University Press, 2009).

Pauwelyn, J., 'Enforcement and Countermeasures in the WTO: Rules are Rules – Toward a More Collective Approach' (2000) 94 *The American Journal of International Law* 335–47.

Payne, R.A., 'Persuasion, Frames and Norm Construction' (2001) 7 *European Journal of International Relations* 37–61.

Peel, J., 'A GMO By Any Other Name … Might be an SPS risk! Implications of Expanding the Scope of the WTO Sanitary and Phytosanitary Measures Agreement' (2000) 17 *European Journal of International Law* 1009–31.

Perry-Kessaris, A., 'Reading the Story of Law and Embeddedness through a Community Lens: A Polanyi-meets-Cotterrell Economic Sociology of Law?' (2011) 62 *Northern Ireland Legal Quarterly* 401–13.

Pitcher, A., M. Moran and M. Johnston, 'Rethinking Patrimonialism and Neopatrimonialism in Africa' (2009) 52 *African Studies Review* 125–56.

Prévost, D., 'Sanitary, Phytosanitary and Technical Barriers to Trade in the Economic Partnership Agreements between the European Union and the ACP countries' ICTSD Issue Paper No. 5 (August 2010).

Pricewaterhouse Coopers, 'European Commission Regional Workshop on Sustainable Development and Regional Trade Agreements – Caribbean Workshop on Building Sustainable Development Issues into Economic Partnership Agreements (EPAs), Report of PwC (2006).

Putte, L. van den and J. Orbie, 'EU Bilateral Trade Agreements and the Surprising Rise of Labour Provisions' (2015) 31 *International Journal of Comparative Labour Law and Industrial Relations* 263–83.

Qobo, M., 'The Challenges of Regional Integration in Africa in the Context of Globalisation and the Prospects for a United States of America' (2007) Institute for Security Studies Paper 145.

Ramdoo, I., 'ECOWAS and SADC Economic Partnership Agreements: A Comparative Analysis', ECDPM Discussion Paper No. 165 (September 2014) available 19 December 2016 at www.ecdpm.org/publications.

Ramsamy, P., 'SADC: Evolution and Perspectives' in G. Mills and C. Mutschler (eds), *Exploring South-South Dialogue: MERCOSUR in Latin America and SADC in Southern Africa* (Johannesburg: SAIIA, 1998).

Ramsamy, P., 'Challenges and Prospects for Regional Integration Strategies in Southern Africa' in IMF (ed.), *Regional Economic Integration and the Globalisation Process: Report on the Proceedings of a Southern African Conference*, Windhoek 10–13 June 1998 (Dar-es-Salaam: Friedrich-Ebert-Stiftung, 1998).

Ravenhill, J., *Global Political Economy*, 3rd edn (Oxford: Oxford University Press, 2011).

Ravenhill, J., *APEC and the Construction of Pacific Rim Regionalism* (Cambridge: Cambridge University Press, 2001).

Reisen, M.V., 'The Enlarged European Union and the Developing World: What Future' in A. Mold (ed.), *EU Development Policy in a Changing World: Challenges for the 21st Century* (Amsterdam: Amsterdam University Press, 2007).

Ricardo, D., *On the Principles of Political Economy and Taxation* (Dover: Dover Publications, 2004), first published 1817.

Richardson, M., 'Endogenous Protection and Trade Diversion' in C. Freund (ed.), *The WTO and Reciprocal Preferential Trade Agreements* (Cheltenham, UK and Northampton, MA, USA: Edward Elgar, 2007).

Riddell, J.B., 'Things Fall Apart Again: Structural Adjustment Programmes in Sub-Saharan Africa' (1992) *Journal of Modern African Studies* 53–68.

Rodney, W., *How Europe Underdeveloped Africa*, 2nd edn (Fahamu, Kenya: Pambazuka Press, 2012).

Rogerson, C., 'The Turn to "New Regionalism": South African Reflections' (2009) 20 *Urban Forum* 111–40.

Rosendorff, B.P., 'Stability and Rigidity: Politics and Design of the WTO's Dispute Settlement Procedure' (2005) 99(3) *American Political Science Review* 389–400.

Roux, W., 'The Interim EPA: Why Namibia Shouldn't Sign', Pambazuka News Article, Issue 444 (30 July 2009) available 19 December 2016 at http://www.pambazuka.org/en/category/features/58067.
Ruggie, J.G., 'Embedded Liberalism and the Postwar Economic Regimes' in *Constructing the World Polity: Essays on International Institutionalisation* (London: Routledge, 2002).
Ruggie, J.G., *Constructing the World Polity: Essays on International Institutionalisation* (London: Routledge, 2002).
Ruggie, J.G. (ed.), *Multilateralism Matters: The Theory and Praxis of an Institutional Form* (New York: Columbia University Press, 1993).
Rutazibwa, O., 'The Problematics of the EU's Ethical (Self)Image in Africa: The EU as an "Ethical Intervener" and the 2007 Joint Africa-EU Strategy' (2010) *Journal of Contemporary European Studies* 209–228.
Saad-Filho, A. and D. Johnston, *Neoliberalism: A Critical Reader* (London: Pluto Press, 2005).
Sachs, J.D. and A.M. Werner, 'Sources of Slow Growth in African Economies' (1997) 6 *Journal of African Economies* 335–76.
SADCC, 'Southern Africa: Towards Economic Liberation – A Declaration by the Governments of Independent States of Southern Africa' made at Lusaka 1 April 1980.
SADC Secretariat, 'Regional Indicative Strategic Development Plan' (Gaborone, 2003).
Sandberg, H.M., J.L. Seale Jr. and T.G. Taylor, 'History, Regionalism and CARICOM Trade: A Gravity Model Analysis' (2006) 42 *The Journal of Development Studies* 795–811.
Sands, P., 'International Law in the Field of Sustainable Development' (1994) LXV *BYIL* 303.
Saner, R. and L. Paez, 'Technical Assistance to Least-Developed Countries in the Context of the Doha Development Round: High Risk of Failure' (2006) 40 *Journal of World Trade* 467–94.
SANGOCO, 'South Africa Civil Society Speaks Out. Our Goals and Visions: Fighting Poverty and Inequality', SANGOCO Report, (September 2005).
Samatar, A.I., 'Structural Adjustment as a Development Strategy? Bananas, Boom and Poverty in Somalia' (1993) 69 *African Development* 25–43.
Saurombe, A., 'The Role of SADC Institutions in Implementing SADC Treaty Provisions Dealing with Regional Integration' (2012) 15 *Potchefstroom Electronic Law Journal* 454–85
Scheiper, S. and D. Sicurelli, 'Empowering Africa. Normative Power in EU-Africa Relations' (2008) 15 *Journal of European Public Policy* 607–23.

Schlemmer, E.C., 'South Africa and the WTO: Ten Years into Democracy' (2004) 29 *South African Yearbook of International Law* 125.

Schraeder, P.J., *African Politics and Society: A Mosaic in Transformation*, 2nd edn (Belmont, CA: Thomson-Wadsworth 2003).

Sen, A., *Development as Freedom* (Oxford: Oxford University Press, 2001).

Senona, J., 'EPAs and Doha Round: Development or Discontent' (2009) 8 *Journal of International Trade Policy* 60–83.

Sidaway, J.D., 'Post-Development' in V. Desai and R.B. Potter (eds), *The Companion to Development Studies*, 3rd edn (Abingdon and New York: Routledge, 2014).

Sidaway, J. and R. Gibb, 'SADC, COMESA & SACU: Contradictory Formats for Regional Integration in Southern Africa?' in D. Simon (ed.), *South Africa in Southern Africa: Reconfiguring the Region* (Oxford: James Curry Ltd, 1998).

Simon, D., *South Africa in Southern Africa: Reconfiguring the Region* (Oxford: James Curry Ltd, 1998).

Simon, H.A., 'Human Nature in Politics: The Dialogue of Psychology with Political Science' (1985) 79(2) *American Political Science Review* 293–304.

Sissoki, M., L. Osuji and W. Cheng, 'Impacts on the Yaoundé and Lomé Conventions on EC-ACP Trade' (1998) 1 *The African Economic and Business Review* 6–24.

Skogstad, G., 'Ideas, Paradigms and Institutions: Agricultural Exceptionalism in the European Union and the United States' (2002) 11 *Governance* 463–90.

Slocum-Bradley, N. and A. Bradley, 'Is the EU's Governance "Good"? An Assessment of EU Governance in its Partnership with ACP States' (2010) 31 *Third World Quarterly* 31–49.

Smith, A., *Wealth of Nations* (London: Wordsworth Editions Ltd, 2012) first published 1776.

Smith, K., 'The ACP in the European Union's Network of Regional Relationships: Still Unique or Just One in the Crowd?' in K. Arts and A.K. Dickinson (eds), *EU Development Cooperation: From Model to Symbol* (Manchester: Manchester University Press, 2004).

Snape, R., 'History and Economics of GATT's Article XXIV' in C. Freund (ed.), *The WTO and Reciprocal Preferential Trade Agreements* (Cheltenham, UK and Northampton, MA, USA: Edward Elgar, 2007).

Snidal, D., 'The Game Theory of International Politics' (1985) 38 *World Politics* 25–57.

Snyman, A.F., 'Regional Organisations and Their Members: The Question of Authority' (2009) XLII *Comparative and International Law Journal of Southern Africa* 189–209.

Söderbaum, F., 'African Regionalism and EU-African Interregionalism' in M. Telò (ed.), *European Union and New Regionalism: Regional Actors and Global Governance in a Post-Hegemonic Era*, 2nd edn (Aldershot: Ashgate, 2007).

Söderbaum, F., 'Exploring the Links between Micro-Regionalism and Macro-Regionalism' in M. Farrell, B. Hettne and L. van Langenhove (eds), *Global Politics of Regionalism: Theory and Practice* (London: Pluto Press, 2005).

Söderbaum, F., *The Political Economy of Regionalism: The Case of Southern Africa* (Basingstoke and New York: Palgrave MacMillan, 2004).

Söderbaum, F., 'Modes of Regional Governance in Africa: Neoliberalism, Sovereignty-Boosting and Shadow Networks' (2004) 10(4) *Global Governance* 419–36.

Söderbaum, F. and A. Sbragia, 'EU Studies and the "New Regionalism": What can be Gained from Dialogue?' (2010) 32 *European Integration* 563–82.

Söderbaum, F. and P Stålgren (eds), *The European Union and the Global South* (Boulder: Lynne Rienner, 2010).

Söderbaum, F. and I. Taylor, *Regionalism and Uneven Development in Southern Africa: The Case of the Maputo Development Corridor* (Aldershot: Ashgate, 2003).

Söderbaum, F. and L. van Hangenhove, 'The EU as a Global Actor and the Role of Interregionalism' (2005) 27 *Journal of European Integration* 249–62.

Soko, M., 'The Political Economy of Regional Integration in Southern Africa', Notre Europe Paper 63 (December 2007) accessed 13 December 2016 at http://www.eng.notre-europe.eu/011-1481-The-Political-Economy-of-Regional-Integration-in-Southern-Africa.html.

Soko, M. and J.P. Lehmann, 'The State of Development in Africa: Concepts, Challenges and Opportunities' (2011) 14 *Journal of International Studies* 97–108.

Sørensen, G., 'IR Theory after the Cold War' (1998) 24 *Review of International Studies* 83–100.

South Centre, 'The EU-CARIFORUM EPA: Regulatory and Policy Changes and Lessons for other ACP Countries' Analytical Note SC/TDP/AN/EPA/32 (September 2013).

South Centre, 'EPA Contentious Issues Matrix: Key Problems and Recommendations' Report (June 2010) Analytical Note, SC/TDP/AN/EPA/26.

South Centre, 'Article XXIV and RTAs: How Much Wriggle Room for Developing Countries?' Analytical Note (December 2008) SC/AN/TDP/RTA.

Spaak, T., 'Legal Positivism, Law's Normativity, and the Normative Force of Legal Justification' (2003) 16 *Ratio Juris* 469–85.

Srinivasan, T.N., 'Nondiscrimination in the GATT/WTO: Was There Anything There to Begin With and is There Anything Left?' (2005) 4 *World Trade Review* 69–95.

Stein, A., 'The Hegemon's Dilemma: Great Britain, the United States and the International Economic Order' (1984) 38 *International Organization* 355–86.

Stevens, C., 'The EU, Africa and EPAs: Unintended Consequences of Policy Leverage' (2006) 44 *Journal of Modern African Studies* 441–58.

Stevens, C., 'The Single European Market: Opportunities and Challenges in Trade' in O. Ojo (ed.), *Africa and Europe: The Changing Economic Relationship* (London: Zed Books Ltd, 1996).

Stoneman, C. and C. Thompson, 'Trade Partners or Trading Deals: The EU and US in Southern Africa' (2007) 34 *Review of African Political Economy* 227–45.

Storey, A., 'Normative Power Europe? Economic Partnership Agreements and Africa' (2006) 24 *Journal of Contemporary African Studies* 331–46.

Summers, L.H., 'Regionalism and the World Trading System' in C. Freund (ed.), *The WTO and Preferential Trading Agreements* (Cheltenham, UK and Northampton, MA, USA: Edward Elgar, 2007).

Sunstein, C., 'On Analogical Reasoning' (1993) 106 *Harvard Law Review* 741–91.

Sykes, A.O., 'Regulatory Protectionism and the Law of International Trade' (1999) 66 *The University of Chicago Law Review* 1–46.

Tannenwald, N., 'Ideas and Explanation: Advancing the Theoretical Agenda' (2005) 7 *Journal of Cold War Studies* 13–42.

Tar, U., 'The Challenges of Democracy and Democratisation in Africa and the Middle East' (2010) 3 *Information, Justice and Society* 81–94.

Taylor, I., 'South African "Imperialism" in a Region Lacking Regionalism: A Critique' (2011) 32 *Third World Quarterly* 1233–53.

Taylor, I., 'Can NEPAD Succeed without Prior Political Reform?' (2005) Copenhagen: Danish Institute for International Studies, Working Paper No. 2005/23.

Taylor, I., 'Commentary: The New Partnership for Africa's Development: Prospects and Challenges' (2002) 101 *African Affairs* 403–12.

Telò, M., *Europe: A Civilian Power?* (Basingstoke: Palgrave Macmillan, 2006).

Teunissen, J.J. (ed.), *Regionalism and the Global Economy: The Case of Africa* (The Hague: FONDAD, 1996).
Tharakan, P.K.M., 'European Union and Preferential Arrangements' (2002) 25 *The World Economy* 1387–98.
Theobold, R., 'Patrimonialism' (1982) 34 *World Politics* 548–59.
Thomson, A., *An Introduction to African Politics,* 2nd edn (London: Routledge, 2010).
Thompson, C.B., 'Regional Challenges to Globalisation: Perspectives from Southern Africa' (2000) 5 *New Political Economy* 41–57.
Torvik, R., 'Natural Resources, Rent Seeking and Welfare' (2002) 67 *Journal of Development Economics* 455–70.
Traidcraft, 'Economic Partnership Agreements: Building or shattering African regional integration?' Traidcraft Report (May 2007) available 9 December 2016 at http://www.traidcraft.co.uk.
Traidcraft, 'The Low Down on EPAs', Traidcraft Trade Update, Issue 6 (October –December 2006) available 9 December 2016 at http://www.traidcraft.co.uk.
Tralac 'The Regional Indicative Strategic Development Plan: SADC's trade-led Integration Agenda' tralac Trade Brief S12TB02/2012 (2012) available 12 December 2016 at: https://www.tralac.org/publications/article/4612-the-regional-indicative-strategic-development-plan-sadc-s-trade-led-integration-agenda.html.
Trebilcock, M. and M.M. Prado, *An Advanced Introduction to Law & Development* (Cheltenham, UK and Northampton, MA, USA: Edward Elgar, 2014).
Tsie, B., 'States and Markets in the Southern African Development Community (SADC): Beyond the Neoliberal Paradigm' (1996) 22(1) *Journal of Southern African Studies* 75–98.
Tsolo, M., I. Mogotsi and G. Motlaleng, 'The Impact of European Union-South Africa Trade Development and Cooperation Agreement on Botswana, Lesotho, Namibia and Swaziland' (2010) 3 *Review of Economic and Business Studies* 135.
Udombana, N., 'Back to Basics: The ACP-EU Cotonou Trade Agreement and Challenges for the African Union' (2004) 40 *Texas International Law Journal* 59–108.
Ukpe, A.I., 'Will EPAs Foster the Integration of Africa into World Trade?' (2010) 54(2) *Journal of African Law* 212–31.
Ulmer, K., 'Trade Embedded Development Models' (2015) 31 *International Journal of Comparative Labour Law and Industrial Relations* 305–29.
Ulrich-Petersmann, E., 'The WTO Constitution and Human Rights' (2000) *Journal of International Economic Law* 19–25.

UNECA, 'Economic Report on Africa 2012: Unleashing Africa's Potential as a Pole of Global Growth' (UNECA, 2012), 19–20, accessed 13 December 2016 at http://repository.uneca.org/bitstream/handle/10855/21725/Bib-69455.pdf?sequence=1.

UNECA, 'Economic Report on Africa 2011' (UNECA, 2011), 34 available 19 December 2016 at http://www.uneca.org/publications/economic-report-africa-2011.

Unger, R.M., *What Should Legal Analysis Become?* (London: Verso, 1996).

UNICE, 'Economic Partnership Agreements with Africa, Caribbean and Pacific Countries: UNICE Position on the EPA Process' Executive Summary (9 May 2005) available 19 December 2016 at http://www.businesseurope.eu.

United Nations, 'The Millennium Development Goals Report 2012', United Nations Report (2 July 2012) available 19 December 2016 at http://mdgs.un.org/unsd/mdg/Default.aspx.

United Nations, 'Report of the World Commission on Environment and Development: *Our Common Future*' (Brundtland Report) of March 1987.

Vandenberghe, J., 'On Carrots and Sticks: The Social Dimension of EU Trade Policy' (2008) 13 *European Foreign Affairs Review* 561–81.

van Reisen, M., 'The Enlarged European Union and the Developing World: What Future?' in A. Mold (ed.), *EU Development Policy in a Changing World: Challenges for the 21st Century* (Amsterdam: Amsterdam University Press, 2007).

Vickers, B., 'Between a Rock and a Hard Place: Small States in the EU-SADC EPA Negotiations' (2011) 100 *The Round Table: The Commonwealth Journal of International Affairs* 183–97.

Viner, J., *The Customs Union Issue* (Carnegie Endowment for International Peace, 1950).

Walker, A., 'The EU-SADC EPA: The Moment of Truth for Regional Integration', Trade Negotiation Insights 8(6), August 2009, available 19 December 2016 at http://ictsd.org/i/news/tni/52416/.

Waltz, K., *The Theory of International Politics* (Lake Zurich, IL: Waveland Press, 1979).

Wang, J, I. Masha, K. Shirono and L. Harris, 'The Common Monetary Area in Southern Africa: Shocks, Adjustment, and Policy Challenges', IMF Working Paper, WP/07/158 (2007).

Warleigh-Lack, A., 'Towards a Conceptual Framework for Regionalisation: Bridging "New Regionalism" and "Integration Theory"' (2006) 13 *Review of International Political Economy* 750–71.

Warleigh-Lack, A. and B. Rosamund, 'Across the EU Studies – New Regionalism Frontier: Invitation to a Dialogue' (2010) 48 *Journal of Common Market Studies* 993–1013.

Watson, M., 'The Historical Roots of Theoretical Traditions in Global Political Economy' in J. Ravenhill, *Global Political Economy*, 3rd edn (Oxford: Oxford University Press, 2011).

Weber, M., *Economy and Society: An Outline of Interpretive Sociology* Vol. 1, G. Roth and C. Wittich (eds) (Berkeley, CA: University of California Press, 1978).

Weber, M., *The Theory of Social and Economic Organisation*, A.M. Henderson and T. Parsons (trans.) (New York: The Free Press, 1947).

Welch, C., 'Human Rights and Development: NGOs' in P. Zeleza and P. McConnaughay (eds), *Human Rights, The Rule of Law, and Development in Africa* (Philadelphia, PA: University of Pennsylvania Press, 2004).

Wendt, A., *Social Theory of International Politics* (Cambridge: Cambridge University Press, 1999).

Wendt, A., 'Anarchy Is What States Make of It: The Social Construction of Power Politics' (1992) 46 *International Organisation* 391–425.

Winters, A., 'Preferential Trading Agreements: Friend or Foe?' in K. Bagwell and P. Mavroidis (eds), *Preferential Trade Agreements: A Law and Economics Analysis* (Cambridge University Press, 2011).

Wonnacott, P. and R. Wonnacott, 'Is Unilateral Tariff Reduction Preferable to a Customs Union? The Curious Case of Missing Tariffs' in C. Freund (ed.), *The WTO and Reciprocal Preferential Trade Agreements* (Cheltenham, UK and Northampton, MA, USA: Edward Elgar, 2007).

Woolfrey, S., 'State of Play in SADC-EU EPA Negotiations' in A. Bösl, G. Erasmus, T. Hartzenberg and C. McCarthy, *Monitoring Regional Integration in Southern Africa Yearbook 2009* (tralac, 2009).

World Bank, 'Global Development Finance: External Debt of Developing Countries' (2012) available 19 December 2016 at http://siteresources.worldbank.org/NEWS/Resources/gdf2010.pdf.

World Bank, *African Development Indicators 2010* (Washington, D.C.: World Bank, 2010).

World Bank, *Trade Blocs: A World Bank Policy Research Report* (Oxford: Oxford University Press, 2000).

World Bank, *Governance, The World Bank's Experience* (Washington, D.C.: World Bank, 1994).

World Bank, *Sub-Saharan Africa: From Crisis to Sustainable Growth: A Long Term Perspective Study* (Washington, D.C.: World Bank, 1989).

World Trade Organisation, 'Report (2012) of the Committee on Regional Trade Agreements to the General Council' 26 November 2012 WT/REG/22.

World Trade Organisation, 'Note on the Meeting of 20 March 2012' Sixty-fourth Session of the CRTA, WT/REG/M/64 (16 April 2012).

World Trade Organisation, 'The WTO and preferential trade agreements: From co-existence to coherence' WTO Report (2011).

World Trade Organisation, *WTO Annual Report 2009* (Geneva: WTO, 2009).

World Trade Organisation, 'Submission on Regional Trade Agreements: Japan Comments on the ACP Paper TN/RL/W/155', WTO Negotiating Group on Rules, TN/RL/W/165 of 8 October 2004.

World Trade Organisation, 'Development aspects of regional trade agreements and special and differential treatment in WTO rules: GATT 1994 Article XXIV and the Enabling Clause' Submission by the ACP to the WTO Negotiating Group on Rules, TN/RL/W/155 of 28 April 2004.

World Trade Organisation, 'Trade Policy Review: Southern African Customs Union', Report by the Secretariat WT/TPR/S/114 (Geneva: WTO, 2003).

World Trade Organisation, Singapore Ministerial Declaration, adopted 13 December 1996 (WT/MIN(96)/DEC).

Young, A., 'Trade Politics Ain't What it Used to Be: The European Union in the Doha Round' (2007) 45 *Journal of Common Market Studies* 789–811.

Zacarias, A., 'From Closed to Open Regionalism' in G. Mills and C. Mutschler (eds), *Exploring South-South Dialogue: MERCOSUR in Latin America and SADC in Southern Africa* (Johannesburg: SAIIA, 1999).

Zahrni, V., 'How Regionalization can be a Pillar of a More Effective World Trade Organisation' (2005) 39 *Journal of World Trade* 671–99.

Zeleza, P. and P. McConnaughay (eds), *Human Rights, The Rule of Law, and Development in Africa* (Philadelphia, PA: University of Pennsylvania Press, 2004).

Index